FRANK LLOYD WRIGHT

ARCHITECT

FRANK LLOYD WRIGHT
ARCHITECT

EDITED BY

TERENCE RILEY

WITH

PETER REED

ESSAYS BY

ANTHONY ALOFSIN

WILLIAM CRONON

KENNETH FRAMPTON

TERENCE RILEY

GWENDOLYN WRIGHT

The Museum of Modern Art, New York

The vision and vigor of Frank Lloyd Wright has had a profound effect on modern architecture. With a deep reverence for nature, Wright brilliantly utilized natural light, new materials, and a variety of forms to create environments that inspire their inhabitants.

In the spirit of this unique architectural achievement, Andersen Windows is pleased to support The Museum of Modern Art's exhibition *Frank Lloyd Wright: Architect*. Its models and newly restored drawings, many never before publicly shown, numerous photographs, and full-scale reconstructions provide a rare glimpse of the genius and enduring quality of Frank Lloyd Wright's lifework. This retrospective offers an understanding of architecture's power for creating environments that can enhance the quality and enjoyment of life.

Jerold W. Wulf
President & Chief Executive Officer
Andersen Windows, Inc.

Published on the occasion of the exhibition *Frank Lloyd Wright: Architect*, organized by Terence Riley, Chief Curator, with Peter Reed, Assistant Curator, Department of Architecture and Design, The Museum of Modern Art, New York, in cooperation with The Frank Lloyd Wright Foundation, Scottsdale, Arizona, February 20–May 10, 1994.

This exhibition is made possible by Andersen Windows, Inc., and by generous grants from the David H. Cogan Foundation and the National Endowment for the Humanities.

Additional support is provided by Lily Auchincloss, the National Endowment for the Arts, the Bertha and Isaac Liberman Foundation, Inc., Joel Silver, and the New York State Council on the Arts.

The publication accompanying the exhibition is made possible by The Henry Luce Foundation, Inc.

Library of Congress Catalogue Card Number: 93-081161
ISBN 0-87070-642-X (MoMA, T&H, clothbound)
ISBN 0-87070-643-8 (MoMA, paperbound)
ISBN 0-8109-6122-9 (Abrams, clothbound)

Published by The Museum of Modern Art
11 West 53 Street, New York, New York 10019

Clothbound edition distributed in the United States and Canada by Harry N. Abrams, Inc., A Times Mirror Company

Clothbound edition distributed outside the United States and Canada by Thames and Hudson, Ltd., London

Printed in the United States of America

Produced by the Department of Publications
The Museum of Modern Art, New York
Osa Brown, Director of Publications
Edited by Harriet Schoenholz Bee
Designed by Jody Hanson with Emily Waters
Production by Vicki Drake
Composition by U. S. Lithograph, typographers, New York
Printed by Litho Specialties, Inc., St. Paul
Bound by Midwest Editions, Inc., Minneapolis

Front cover: Frank Lloyd Wright and Aaron G. Green, Associate. Marin County Civic Center, San Rafael, California. 1957–62. Entrance. (Photo: © 1962 by Lucile Fessenden Dandelet, Marin County, California)

Back cover: Frank Lloyd Wright. Engineering Drawing. 1885. Surface parabola Pencil and ink on paper, 13 x 10⅝″. The Frank Lloyd Wright Foundation. (Photo: courtesy The Frank Lloyd Wright Foundation)

Frontispiece: Frank Lloyd Wright working on a drawing for The Mile High Illinois skyscraper in the Hillside Drafting Room, Taliesin, Spring Green, 1956. (Photo: OBMA, courtesy The Frank Lloyd Wright Foundation)

CONTENTS

FOREWORD

This book is published in conjunction with the exhibition *Frank Lloyd Wright: Architect*, a comprehensive retrospective of the achievement of this genius of American architecture. Coming thirty-five years after his death, this exhibition presents a new generational view of Wright and his architecture, as the Museum's first retrospective of his work, presented in 1940, reflected that of an earlier generation.

Developed from a broad cultural perspective, *Frank Lloyd Wright: Architect* addresses critical contemporary issues: the architect and society, the nature and character of domestic space and expression, the relationship of architecture and the environment, particularly in the design of communities.

The exhibition has benefited enormously from the unprecedented access to its archives granted to the Museum by The Frank Lloyd Wright Foundation. This cooperation was critical to the exhibition's inception, and it was provided graciously and most professionally by the Foundation. We are also very grateful to the other lenders, public and private, whose generosity helped to make this exhibition possible.

Crucial support for the exhibition was given early in its planning by Marshall S. Cogan and Lily Auchincloss, Trustees of this Museum with a special dedication to architecture. A major grant from Andersen Windows, Inc., underscores this company's history of commitment to architectural quality, and we are deeply grateful for Andersen's interest and encouragement. A major grant from the National Endowment for the Humanities and support from the National Endowment for the Arts were essential in guaranteeing that the exhibition could be developed and presented with appropriate scope. A grant from The Henry Luce Foundation, Inc., provided underwriting for this volume, for which we are most appreciative. We also thank the Bertha and Isaac Liberman Foundation, Inc., and Joel Silver for additional assistance.

Terence Riley, the director of the exhibition and contributor to this volume, ably assisted by Peter Reed, deserves our warm gratitude and admiration for the energy and insight he has brought to bear on *Frank Lloyd Wright: Architect* over the past two and a half years. Building on the initiatives of his predecessor as head of the Museum's Department of Architecture and Design, Stuart Wrede, he has ensured that this unusually ambitious project is stimulating both aesthetically and intellectually and will have lasting value and importance.

Richard E. Oldenburg
Director
The Museum of Modern Art

WILLIAM CRONON

INCONSTANT UNITY: THE PASSION OF FRANK LLOYD WRIGHT

"A foolish consistency," runs one of Ralph Waldo Emerson's most famous and misquoted aphorisms, "is the hobgoblin of little minds, adored by little statesmen and philosophers and divines. With consistency a great soul has simply nothing to do."[1] Rarely has anyone pursued this Emersonian injunction with greater single-mindedness than Frank Lloyd Wright. Intent on proving the greatness of his soul from a very early age, Wright cherished his inconsistencies as if they were among his most beloved creations. The extraordinary talent that enabled him to produce such an astonishing array of architectural forms was matched by an equally extraordinary ability to revel in the polarities of his own soul no matter how incompatible they seemed. Remembering Louis Henri Sullivan's quest for "the rule so broad as to admit of no exception," Wright declared that "for the life of me I could not help . . . being most interested in the exception proving the rule useful or useless."[2] Rebel, iconoclast, trickster: one might almost say that exception and inconsistency were the unifying passions of Wright's life, the ultimate proofs of an independence he cherished above all other things.

In his personal conduct, for instance, Wright's inconsistencies are as notorious today as they were during his lifetime. Here was a man of great charm and charisma, able, as his son John said, to "win over anyone when he really wanted something," who sooner or later offended, alienated, or infuriated almost everyone who crossed his path.[3] The jumble of adjectives that still swirls around his name—arrogant, generous, grandiose, whimsical, bullying, tender, manipulative, playful, and many others no less accurate—suggests how successful he was at leaving his audience perennially off-balance, half-outraged at his bombast and his violation of social norms, half-amused at his unpredictability and his unabashed enthusiasm for his own performance. Here was a man whose self-love seemed limitless, whose ego apparently knew no bounds, who nonetheless hungered for the validation he could only receive from admirers, disciples, and lovers. An extreme proponent of individualism and personal independence, he did his best work only when buttressed by soul mates who believed in his talent even more unshakably than he did. Wright said of himself that "he couldn't live, move and have his being, so it seemed, without a heart-to-heart comrade."[4] And yet his mistrust for his own dependence on such soul mates helped produce the lurches in his domestic life for which he eventually became infamous. The consummate designer of domestic space, who invariably made the hearth and its fire a metaphor for the sacred family circle, fled that circle when he feared that it threatened his own freedom. For ordinary people who watched Wright's behavior from afar, inconsistencies such as these often looked like irresponsibility—or worse, dishonor. Even today, when one inquires about Wright's reputation in his home state of Wisconsin, one usually hears, first, that he abandoned his family and, second, that he was not a man of his word—not a man whose honor could be consistently trusted. "You know," people say with considerable feeling almost half a century after the fact, "the man didn't pay his bills."

It would be easy to regard such personal inconsistencies as mere peccadilloes that fade into irrelevancy when set against Wright's undeniably brilliant artistic achievements. Certainly there is much to be learned by moving beyond the distractions of his formidable personality to confront his buildings directly. The trouble, unfortunately, is that Wright himself clearly believed his architecture to be an organic expression of the very personality that, in many ways, seems so problematic. Indeed, his affection for the inconsistent hobgoblins that strike terror in little minds was everywhere apparent in his professional practice. Proclaiming the need for a new "organic" architecture, he argued that buildings should respond to the natural conditions of their sites—and yet one of the most important innovations of his so-called Prairie style was to introduce shallow-pitched roofs into northern climates where winter snow accumulations threatened the integrity of any roof not steep enough to shed its load by force of gravity. The leakiness of Wright's roofs is nothing short of legendary, even to this day. Wright espoused a deep devotion to the "nature of materials," arguing that each should be employed only in ways that were consistent with its innermost qualities, and yet he repeatedly pushed those materials to the extreme limits of their tolerance, to the verge of failure and beyond.

He treated people in much the same way. Although he claimed that an architect should design each house to reflect the individuality of its owner, in fact, he behaved as if the owner's individuality mattered far less than the architect's.[5] In his view clients simply did not understand their own needs, and so the architect should reeducate their tastes to bring them in line with his own.[6] "It's their duty," he declared, "to understand, to appreciate, and conform insofar as possible to the idea of the house."[7] And so we have famous stories of houses with ceilings so low that anyone much taller than Wright—who stretched truth and height alike when he claimed to be five feet, eight inches tall—would regularly bump his head, and of homeowners who, after inviting Wright to spend the night, awoke to discover their living-room furniture completely rearranged, or even discarded, to match his own vision of the room.[8] (To be fair, many clients were quick to admit that Wright's taste was superior to their own, and expressed real gratitude for the new aesthetic values he taught them.[9]) His peremptory attitude toward anyone else's individual expression extended beyond his clients to the students who came to learn architecture at his feet. Although he constantly lectured them about the need for artistic independence and the paramount goal of developing their own individuality, in practice he demanded conformity, consistently refusing them the space to articulate any artistic vision at odds with the master's.[10] Indeed, one cannot imagine Frank Lloyd Wright as a student in his own Taliesin Fellowship.

"With consistency a great soul has simply nothing to do." If Emerson's preaching is true, then Wright's paradoxes surely seem to confirm the greatness that is everywhere evident in his buildings. And yet our dilemma in this is that Wright's inconsistencies are so endlessly fascinating and seductive (just as he intended them to be) that they get in the way of deeper questions about the sources of his inspiration (just as he intended they should do). The legend of Frank Lloyd Wright is no less masterful a creation than his architecture, and the two buttress each other. No artist has ever worked so hard to claim total originality for himself; none has sought more assiduously to deny the obvious influences that contributed to his special vision. To be inconsistent even in one's own behavior was another way of asserting that ordinary rules could not possibly apply to a genius so unprecedented that it claimed to violate virtually every tradition of Western architecture. Nothing would have pleased Wright more, surely, than for us to draw this lesson from the many paradoxes that he left scattered like red herrings across his path.

And so the historian faces several riddles when confronting Wright's life and work. One is the obvious question about his intellectual roots, the architectural traditions and broader cultural movements that, despite his many denials, did in fact lay the foundations for his own great achievements. In Wright's case, we are also faced with his amazingly prolific output not just of buildings but of *words*, for the man was an indefatigable talker and writer. Rarely has an architect said so much in defense of his own vision or tried harder to articulate a philosophy that would make aesthetic and moral sense of his creations. In reading his many books, lectures, letters, and polemics, one quickly becomes aware of Wright's obsession with certain ideas that he believed underlay all of his work. Over and over again he tells us that a truly great work of architecture must express harmony, simplicity, order, organic beauty, natural integrity, unity—indeed, even "consistency."[11] Here the mystery deepens, for this seemingly most inconsistent of men was among the most consistent defenders of consistency as a cardinal virtue in life and art. The challenge he has left us is thus to discover the unifying principles—what Emerson might have called the *un*foolish consistencies—that can resolve his many apparent contradictions.

In trying to discover the abstract principles that gave order to this disorderly life, one can begin by posing a very concrete riddle: Why did so many of Frank Lloyd Wright's roofs leak? Surely the ability of a roof to keep out water is just about the most basic proof of any building's integrity, and yet sooner or later a remarkable number of Wright's

roofs have failed this simple task. They have not kept organic nature—rain and snow—at bay. Some of the leaks are by now so famous that they have virtually become clichés. The angry phone call that Herbert F. Johnson, the president of S. C. Johnson & Son, Inc., made to Wright in the midst of a dinner party at his new house, Wingspread (see plates 275–277), because that party had been interrupted by a steady drip onto Johnson's bald head, and Wright's suggestion that the irate owner solve the problem by moving his chair, is so familiar that anyone acquainted with Wright will probably have encountered it many times, sometimes even told about completely different houses and owners.[12] The Johnson story may now be too familiar, but only because the experience it describes is so typical. When I recently visited the Unitarian Church in Madison, Wisconsin, of 1945–51 (plates 368–370), I gradually became aware during the sermon of a rather pleasant rhythmic sound from the back of the auditorium. When I turned to discover its source I saw amid the parishioners two garbage cans collecting the steady streams of water dripping from the ceiling.[13] The Madison Unitarians have learned to take such events in stride, though perhaps with not quite the good humor of Mrs. Richard Lloyd Jones, the wife of Wright's cousin, who responded to an inquiry about her own leaky roof by saying: "This is what happens when you leave a work of art out in the rain."[14]

In fact, the leakiness of Wright's roofs is only one item in a long list of structural failings—some of them much more serious—that have plagued his buildings. For this reason, trivial as they may seem, anecdotes about the drip on Johnson's head or about garbage cans catching water amid church pews carry the burden of a much larger question about Wright's work. For his critics, such stories stand as an implicit indictment, suggesting that for all his supposed brilliance he failed to meet some of the most basic obligations of sound architectural practice. His supporters respond defensively by blaming such problems on builders who, through perfidy or incompetence, failed to follow Wright's instructions; alternatively, they argue that *all* roofs eventually leak, no matter how competent the architect. For Wright's defenders his leaky roofs are a persistent embarrassment; for his critics they offer a perennial opportunity to prick his inflated reputation. But the riddle they pose becomes much more interesting if we take them seriously: they are, after all, a perfect symbol of the many other paradoxes in which Wright took such obvious and mischievous delight. If we acknowledge at the outset that Wright was unquestionably among the most brilliant and creative architects in all of human history—and there is no reason to deny him this claim—what then should we make of his leaky roofs? What clues can they give us about the unifying principles that defined order, integrity, and beauty for this strangely inconsistent but consistently visionary man?

THE LLOYD JONES LEGACY

Any investigation of Wright's unifying principles and the sources from which they sprang must begin with one of the more curious paradoxes of his long career: this man who more than any other symbolizes modern architecture in twentieth-century America was in fact profoundly a child of the nineteenth century in his aesthetic vision and moral philosophy. The architect Philip Johnson was perhaps unfair but not entirely wrong when he described Wright as America's greatest nineteenth-century architect.[15] Born in 1867, Wright was already approaching middle age at the turn of the new century and had long since imbibed the core values that would sustain him for the rest of his career. His longevity and his protean ability even very late in life to keep reinventing new architectural vocabularies should not obscure the fact that his moral compass never wavered from the beliefs he acquired as a young man. To the core of his being, Wright was a nineteenth-century romantic, steeped in idealist traditions that reached back through Louis Sullivan and Walt Whitman to the New England Transcendentalists and beyond.

To say this about him is neither to deny the originality of his genius nor to label him as somehow old-fashioned. Even a genius must speak in the language of his own day, respond to its obsessions, and work with the artistic and cultural resources it makes available to him. Indeed, one might say that the task of genius is to take ideas that are very much "in the air," profoundly a part of their time and place, and demonstrate their possibilities for the future in such strikingly original ways that they suddenly seem innovative and obvious at the same time.[16] This is surely what Wright did with such brilliance. One of the clearest proofs of his ability to speak to the twentieth century in the language of the nineteenth is the very vocabulary in which he did so, as much in his words as in his buildings. When Wright used terms like *organic, individualism, democracy,* and *nature* he was expressing nineteenth-century values that are subtly but crucially different from our own. All were infused with the values of romantic idealism. Wright shared with his nineteenth-century contemporaries a deep conviction that the chief task of science and art was to discover underlying principles of order—present not just in architecture but in literature, philosophy, music, mathematics, and, indeed, in the entire organic and inorganic universe—which would reveal the hidden unity of humanity and nature. To know these principles was to come as close as humanly possible to a direct encounter with God. Herein lay the meaning of the lines Wright so often quoted from Alfred Lord Tennyson:

Flower in the crannied wall,
I pluck you out of the crannies,
I hold you here, root and all, in my hand,
Little flower—but if I could understand
What you are, root and all, and all in all,
I should know what God and man is.[17]

The nineteenth-century figures to whom Wright turned for inspiration all shared with Tennyson this central conviction, which was far more literal for most of them than it would be for their twentieth-century counterparts: the flower in the crannied wall was as much an ideal as a physical object, and the principle it disclosed was nothing less than the face of God.

Wright learned to embrace this romantic vision of a divinely ordered and principled universe at a very early age. Of this we can be sure, even though his childhood is so shrouded in self-conscious myth-making that it is difficult to extract reliable information from his later accounts of it. His favorite fable—that his mother knew even as she carried him in her womb that he was predestined to be a great architect—has all the earmarks of hagiography, and there is little reason to worry much about its truth or falsehood.[18] Whatever Anna Wright's role in directing him toward architecture, she and her family were unquestionably the most important early source of his romantic idealism. There also can be no doubt about her high ambitions for her son, on whom she lavished far more love and devotion than on her husband William. Wright's father emerges from the record as a rather pathetic figure, a charming, personable, footloose spendthrift, talented but unfulfilled, who could never satisfy his demanding wife. William Wright finally walked out on his family, much as his son would do a quarter of a century later—though William's wife was eager for his departure and Frank's was not. Frank Lloyd Wright seems to have remembered his father chiefly for giving him an enduring love of classical music, especially Bach and Beethoven, and a belief that music was a near perfect metaphor for the principles that informed great architecture. "The composer," Wright later said, "is a builder. My father taught me to listen to a symphony as an edifice of sound. . . . Building is the same thing. It's taking a motif, a theme and constructing from it an edifice that is all consistent and organic—an organism as a whole."[19]

William Wright was a popular but discontented preacher, a competent linguist, a fine musician, and a frustrated composer. In his son's eyes—and his wife's—he too often fell short of the very ideals he preached.[20] And so he helped set the stage for a classic oedipal drama in which a brilliant son struggled without much difficulty to win his mother from his father's affections. The egotism and arrogance that would so typify Wright in later life were obvious legacies of that early family contest. In the words of his sister Maginel, Anna Wright "gathered all the strands of her yearning, wove them together, and fastened them once and for all to her son. He was more than her child. He was her protégé, her legacy. He would accomplish what she and her husband could not. From the start, her devotion to Frank was overwhelming."[21] Wright put it more succinctly: "The lad was his mother's adoration. She lived much in him."[22] Although her love for him was absolute, so were the standards by which she measured his performance. She served as his teacher, his taskmaster, and his most demanding but adoring audience, becoming his personal archetype of the devoted female companion who would unquestioningly subordinate her life, passion, and sense of mission to his own. Perhaps for this very reason, as his sister also reported, "she was not always easy with him, and she made the mistake of failing to mask her disapproval of the women to whom he was attracted, though sometimes they were strikingly like her in looks and in spirit."[23] From her, surely, he acquired the lifelong habit of regarding himself as a golden boy, an enfant terrible, a man-child so used to being forgiven no matter how grievous his

Figure 1: The Lloyd Jones family, 1883. Frank Lloyd Wright's grandfather Richard Lloyd Jones is seated to the left of the empty chair. His parents, Anna and William Carey Wright, are in the back row, third and fourth from the right; in front of them is his sister Jane. He is seated to the right of the empty chair, with sister Maginel on his lap. At the far right, second row, is the Reverend Jenkin Lloyd Jones.

faults—but also so needing to confirm that he still deserved the love his father had so pathetically lost—that he could not resist repeatedly testing the limits of those around him as a way of proving his own worthiness. As Wright's own son would say, Anna helped him become what he would never cease to be, an "overgrown, undisciplined boy with a genius for architecture."[24]

Anna's contributions to Wright's genius were by no means limited to his basic character and emotional needs. She came from a brilliant, clannish Welsh family, the Lloyd Joneses, and from them much more than from his father's kin Wright acquired his sense of family identity, his religious and philosophical outlook, and his first sustained encounter with what would become for him an ideal human landscape (figure 1). Christened Frank Lincoln Wright at birth, the would-be architect changed his middle name as a teenager to signal his commitment to his mother's family traditions.[25] The Lloyd Joneses had migrated to Wisconsin in 1845, eventually settling at a place called Hillside near where the Helena Valley met the Wisconsin River opposite the small town of Spring Green. Anna and her siblings had grown up there, and as a boy her son Frank spent his summers working on his uncles' farms. Despite being farmers, the Lloyd Joneses read widely from the leading thinkers of their day and were deeply committed to education and self-improvement: two of Anna's sisters eventually opened a progressive school near the family homestead, and one of her brothers went on to become a leading liberal theologian in Chicago. Family members were infused with the feeling that to be a Lloyd Jones was to be a person of special talent and conviction, whatever the line of work he or she might follow.

Perhaps most important, the family had a tradition of religious dissent, its members espousing a version of Unitarianism that mingled passionate, Welsh nonconformist beliefs with the more rarefied intellectualism of the New England Transcendentalists. Theirs was an extreme form of liberal Protestantism, suspicious of any institutional religion that got in the way of an individual's search for spiritual truth. "Truth Against the World" was their family motto, implying their belief—so basic to Wright's later sense of his own mission—that anyone who sought the truth and found it would surely have to defend it against the falsehoods of others whose motives and vision were much less pure. "The Unitarianism of the Lloyd-Joneses," Wright wrote, "was an attempt to amplify in the confusion of the creeds of their day, the idea of life as a gift from the Divine Source, one GOD omnipotent, all things at one with HIM. UNITY was their watchword, the sign and symbol that thrilled them, the UNITY of all things!"[26] When the family built its own small church in 1886—giving young Frank his first practical building experience as an assistant to the Chicago architect who designed it—they predictably named it Unity Chapel (figure 2).

Wright's own commitment to Unitarianism and to the principles of spiritual unity it espoused continued for the rest of his life.[27] One of his first large public buildings was Unity Temple, built in 1905–08 for the Unitarian congregation in Oak Park, Illinois (plates 74–82). In the 1930s he formally joined the First Unitarian Society in Madison, Wisconsin, and a decade later designed its famous meetinghouse (true to his family traditions, it was only with some difficulty that the congregation persuaded him not to carve the word *Unity* on the stone that still serves as its pulpit).[28] Wright would later say of it: "There, you see

Figure 2: Joseph Lyman Silsbee. Unity Chapel, Helena. 1886. Perspective. Whereabouts unknown. Earliest known published drawing by Frank Lloyd Wright

the Unitarianism of my forefathers found expression in a building by one of the offspring—the idea of unity—Unitarian. Unitarians believed in the unity of all things. Well, I tried to build a building here that expressed that sense of unity."[29] When he died a few years later, his funeral service was conducted by the minister of the Madison congregation, and he was buried in the cemetery of Unity Chapel near the Lloyd Jones farmsteads. Unitarianism's impatience with traditional Christianity, its refusal to impose any formal doctrinal tests on its adherents (not even the divinity of Christ or the existence of God), its eagerness to ransack all the world's great religions in its search for sacred meaning, its tolerance of iconoclasm and individual eccentricity, its embrace of science as a necessary part of any modern search for enlightened knowledge, its humanism, and above all its faith in the unity of spiritual truth—all of these values were made to order for the likes of Frank Lloyd Wright.

The faith of the Lloyd Joneses was more than just a religion for Wright; it also schooled him in the moral rhetoric that would forever shape his speech and writing. Wright might have been a great architect even if he had never been exposed to his family's Unitarianism, but it is hard to imagine his words and ideas without its influence. Reading his essays today, one repeatedly has the sense of listening to a sermon. Here, too, there was a powerful family example close at hand to serve as Wright's model for the intellectual as preacher, the preacher as intellectual. Wright's uncle Jenkin Lloyd Jones was one of Chicago's most popular ministers, a religious liberal who eventually found even Unitarianism too conservative for his humanistic tastes, and the editor of a weekly religious magazine titled—what else?—*Unity*.[30] When Wright set up his Taliesin Fellowship in the 1930s, he included as part of its ritual activities a Sunday-morning gathering at which the assembled community listened to classical music, readings from favorite authors, and rambling lectures about architecture, life, and morality by Wright himself. It was like nothing so much as a Unitarian service, a ritual gathering at which his uncle Jenkin and the other Lloyd Joneses would surely have felt right at home.

ECHOING EMERSON

Unitarianism exercised an influence on the intellectual life of nineteenth-century America that was out of all proportion to the number of people who formally declared their allegiance to its doctrines. This was partly because, as the liberal successor of New England Congregationalism, it dominated the area around Boston, a city that was home to far more than its share of the nation's intellectual elite. For much of the nineteenth century, many of Boston's most prominent thinkers and artists called themselves Unitarians; indeed, the Harvard Divinity School essentially served as a Unitarian seminary. Because Unitarians so eagerly embraced the progressive intellectual movements of their day, declaring their confidence that there need be no necessary conflict between liberal religion and the beliefs of an increasingly secular age, it is easy from the perspective of the twentieth century to forget their faith and regard them as merely secular. The denomination aligned itself with romanticism, humanism, and liberalism—the secular trinity that would help lay the foundations for modernity as the twentieth century would know it. Indeed, one of the most important early expressions of American romanticism—the group of writers and artists who called themselves Transcendentalists—began with a technical dispute among New England Unitarians.[31] Unitarianism served as an important vehicle for introducing romantic idealism into the mainstream of American thought, which is why the convergence of these two movements in the thinking of Frank Lloyd Wright was no accident. Much of his understanding of them in fact flowed from a common source, and the name of that source was Ralph Waldo Emerson.

Nothing serves as a better gauge of how far twentieth-century Americans have drifted from their nineteenth-century roots than the spectacular decline of Emerson's popularity. Today, he is read mainly as a mandatory assignment in college classrooms on the few occasions when he is read at all, and most people find him far less accessible than such writers as Henry David Thoreau, Walt Whitman, or John Muir, all of whom regarded themselves as his followers. Yet no American writer enjoyed more universal acclaim in the nineteenth century; none was more influential or widely read than this renegade Unitarian minister turned popular lecturer and romantic philosopher. To understand the language and ideas of Frank Lloyd Wright today, one cannot avoid a serious encounter with Ralph Waldo Emerson. This is true despite the fact that Wright himself did not lay great stress on Emerson's contributions to his thought: following his usual practice of obscuring his greatest intellectual debts lest they seem to diminish his own originality, Wright did not even mention Emerson's name among the thinkers whose work he had "long ago consulted and occasionally remembered" in writing *An Autobiography*.[32]

Some have argued that Wright came to his knowledge of Emersonian ideas only indirectly, through Louis Sullivan's affection for Walt Whitman. Certainly Wright was himself a fan of Whitman and read the poet's work regularly to the apprentices in the Taliesin Fellowship.[33] But it was Emerson, not Whitman, who throughout Wright's childhood had served as high priest in the intellectual and spiritual pantheon of the Lloyd Joneses. His sister Maginel tells a wonderful anecdote about the family's piano, which Wright—exaggerating as always—described as a Steinway. She knew with absolute certainty that her brother was wrong about this, because she associated the piano with a revealing childhood confusion on her part. "I know very well that it was an Emerson," she wrote, "because I remember the awe and admiration I felt, believing a man of that name could build pianos and write books, too—books that one's mother, father, aunts, and uncles were always quoting: 'As Mr. Emerson says.'"[34] If they agreed about nothing else, William and Anna Wright shared a passion for Emerson, and Anna even taught classes about his work during her years in Oak Park.[35] It would hardly seem to matter, then, how Wright acquired his familiarity with the sage of Concord; what does matter is that no voice echoes more resoundingly in Wright's own prose than Emerson's.

Emerson, for instance, gave license to Wright's fiercely defended conception of himself as iconoclast, individualist, genius. The architect's self-centeredness and willful refusal to march to anyone else's beat had powerful roots in his family psychodrama, but also conformed to Emersonian notions of personal integrity. Self-reliance was a favorite Emersonian theme that had deep resonance for Wright. "To believe your own thought," Emerson wrote, "to believe that what is true for you in your private heart is true for all men,—that is genius."[36] Particularly in the years after 1909, when he abandoned his family to embark on a scandalous love affair with another man's wife, Wright embraced almost to the point of caricature the romantic image of genius that is so much a part of Emerson's thought. The elaborate myth that Wright constructed in his autobiography of a lone genius fighting against great odds and nearly universal opprobrium to defend his architecture against intellectual philistines, as well as the attack he mounted against conventional morality for not accepting his love affairs, his loose ways with money, and his "honest arrogance"[37]—all of these, in Emersonian terms, could serve as proofs of the independence, originality, and integrity that revealed true genius. "Whoso would be a man," wrote Emerson, "must be a nonconformist. He who would gather immortal palms must not be hindered by the name of goodness, but must explore if it be goodness. Nothing is at last sacred but the integrity of your own mind."[38]

Here was a philosophy that could justify Wright's unconventional lifestyle at the same time that it endorsed his artistic mission. In Emerson's thought, the lone search of individual genius to find original meaning in the world began with the radical Protestant impulse of Unitarianism to know God directly, without reliance on biblical prophecy, but extended far beyond formal religion to all of art and life. "Let me admonish you, first of all," Emerson had told the graduating class of the Harvard Divinity School in 1838, "to go alone; to refuse the good models, even those which are sacred in the imagination of men, and dare to love God without mediator or veil. . . . Thank God for these good men, but say, 'I also am a man.' Imitation cannot go above its model. The imitator dooms himself to hopeless mediocrity."[39] To give in to conventional wisdom, to succumb to the opinion of the world, to imitate someone else's creation, could only adulterate and betray one's own genius. "The objection to conforming to usages that have become dead to you," Emerson wrote, "is, that it scatters your force. It loses your time and blurs the impression of your character."[40] Wright said much the same thing to his apprentices at Taliesin, declaring that nothing was more detrimental to an architect's vision than "to have deep in his heart one wish and to have to conform to the conditions and demands of another. That's what makes a bad marriage and will also make a bad architect. . . . Really to believe in something is the greatest boon, I think, and to believe wholeheartedly in it and to serve it with all your strength and your might is salvation, really."[41]

But Emerson's influence on Wright went much deeper than simply to serve as a role model for romantic genius. When Wright spoke of his search for an "organic" architecture, a way of building that would look to nature for its models and inspiration, he was using the word *nature* in a peculiarly Emersonian sense that is much less familiar today than it was in the nineteenth century. It is precisely here that we are most likely to misunderstand Wright's thought. The crude popular view today is that romantics like Emerson or Thoreau, or for that matter Wright, celebrated the beauty of nature in a literal sense much as many modern environmentalists do, believing that the world's creatures and landscapes are intrinsically beautiful in their own right. In fact, raw nature was much less compelling for most nineteenth-century romantics than it is for modern nature-lovers. The romantics regarded plants and animals and the rest of creation as the outward manifestations of an all-encompassing spiritual unity whose name was God. It is a textbook truism to say of romanticism that one of its principal tasks was to secularize Judeo-Christian values by relocating onto nature the sublime transcendence that had once been reserved for the deity. But this statement can just as easily be inverted, for the secularization of God was also the sacralization of Nature. This is why Wright could declare: "I think Nature should be spelled with a capital 'N,' not because Nature is God but because all that we can learn of God we will learn from the body of God, which we call Nature."[42]

Once we recognize that romantic conceptions of nature were fundamentally religious, we can begin to understand that for romantics like Emerson and Wright, nature's value was primarily spiritual. Indeed, nature acquired its meaning for them only in relation to the human soul and the divine spirit of which the soul was a manifestation. "Every natural fact is a symbol of some spiritual fact," said Emerson.[43] The multitudes of natural forms were only so much dead matter until touched by spirit, and so it was the role of human beings—especially artists—to breath life into matter by relating it to the whole of creation and thereby giving it spiritual meaning. "Nature is a sea of forms radically alike and even unique," declared Emerson. "A leaf, a sunbeam, a landscape, the ocean, make an analogous impression on the mind. What is common to them all,—that perfectness and harmony, is beauty. The standard of beauty is the entire circuit of natural forms,—the totality of nature. . . . Nothing is quite beautiful alone; nothing but is beautiful in the whole. A single object is only so far beautiful as it suggests this universal grace."[44]

The role of the artist in relation to this all-encompassing universal spirit was to distill its virtues into a concentrated vision so that the resulting work of art would serve as a microcosm for the beauty of the whole. Emerson's metaphor for this was the alembic, the laboratory glassware that chemists and alchemists had long used to distill and concentrate liquids. "The poet, the painter, the sculptor, the musician, the architect," he wrote, "seek each to concentrate this radiance of the world on one point, and each in his several work to satisfy the love of beauty which stimulates him to produce. Thus is Art, a nature passed through the alembic of man. Thus in art, does nature work through the will of a man filled with the beauty of her first works."[45] The highest expression of this artistic impulse was the human love of beauty, which found its roots in the graceful forms of organic nature but drew its true inspiration from the spiritual essence that lay behind and beyond those forms. Indeed, Emerson went so far as to argue that the world existed more than anything else to act as a mirror in which the soul could see beauty reflected back as the foremost expression of God's presence in the world. "The world thus exists to the soul," he wrote, "to satisfy the desire of beauty. This element I call an ultimate end. No reason can be asked or given why the soul seeks beauty. Beauty, in its largest and profoundest sense, is one expression for the universe. God is the all-fair. Truth, and goodness, and beauty, are but different faces of the same All."[46] Natural beauty was of value only insofar as it reflected divine beauty. "Beauty in nature is not ultimate. It is the herald of inward and eternal beauty, and is not alone a solid and satisfactory good. It must stand as a part, and not as yet the last or highest expression of the final cause of Nature."[47] That final cause was spirit, which could be found only in the soul's awareness of its own divine nature. Following Emerson, one could thus believe that art was a truer, richer, more organic expression of nature's beauty than were the natural forms on which it was modeled: indeed, if one wanted truly to encounter Nature, one could do so more readily in Art than in nature itself.

Wright's beliefs about nature and art were wholly congruent with Emerson's, which is why we are so apt to misunderstand his arguments on behalf of an *organic* or *natural* architecture if we interpret these words according to their most common meanings in our own time. The great principle that the Lloyd Joneses had held up in their struggle to defend "Truth Against the World" was Unity. Their offspring would turn their own Emersonian ideas against them by arguing that the family had overemphasized "the beauty of TRUTH" and "did not so well know the truth of BEAUTY."[48] In the name of truth and beauty alike Wright followed Lloyd Jones traditions in attacking contemporary artists and critics who embraced too literal an understanding of nature's meaning:

I began to see that in spite of all the talk about Nature that "natural" was the last thing in this world they would let you be if they could prevent it. What did they mean when "they" used the word nature? Just some sentimental feeling about animals, grass and trees, the out-of-doors? But how about the nature of wood, glass and iron—internal nature? The nature of boys and girls? The nature of law? Wasn't that Nature? Wasn't nature in this sense the very nature of God?

Somehow I had always thought when I read the word "nature" in a book or used it in my own mind that it was meant that interior way. Not the other measly, external way. "Fools!" They have no sentiment for nature. What they really mean by "nature" is just a sentimentalizing of the rudimentary animal.[49]

For Wright, the purpose of art and architecture was not slavishly to copy external nature, but to use it in the way Emerson recommended, as the occasion for exploring inner nature and thereby expressing universal spirit. For the artist, nature was raw material awaiting transformation into some greater vision of a still more divine ideal. "Nature is not fixed but fluid," Emerson had declared. "Spirit alters, moulds, makes it. The immobility or bruteness of nature, is the absence of spirit; to pure spirit, it is fluid, it is volatile, it is obedient. Every spirit builds itself a house; and beyond its house a world; and beyond its world, a heaven. Know then, that the world exists for you. . . . Build, therefore, your own world. As fast as you conform your life to the pure idea in your mind, that will unfold its great proportions."[50] It would be hard to imagine a clearer statement of the mission—artistic, moral, and religious—that Frank Lloyd Wright pursued with such passion throughout his long life. His house, his world, his heaven, would eventually extend from Taliesin to Broadacre City to produce a visionary statement of the architectural and aesthetic space that, in Wright's eyes, could serve as the ideal canvas for a truly American democracy.

Wright learned from Jenkin Lloyd Jones and other members of his family how to defend his artistic vision in the language of a sermon; he learned from Emerson the sacrament of beauty and spirit, which became for him the moral content of that sermon. It is thus no accident that his polemics on behalf of an "organic architecture" are so often expressed in words that are overtly moralizing. The unity of truth, beauty, nature: this for Wright was the very name of God.[51] "Beauty is the mark God sets upon virtue," Emerson had written. "Every natural action is graceful."[52] Wright openly expressed his allegiance to this principle by declaring: "I believe that Emerson was right when he said, 'Beauty is the highest and finest kind of morality.' . . . If you are attuned, and you love sincerely, harmony, rhythm and what we call beauty, instinctively what is ugly will become offensive to you."[53] Ugliness was not merely a violation of aesthetic values; it was an offense against God, a sin. "There is not, nor ever was, room in right living for the ugly. Ugliness in anything is the incarnation of sin, and sin is death—ugliness is death."[54] To avoid this sin meant answering to a catechism of unity in which the most sacred terms were all finally synonymous. "The sort of expression we seek," Wright wrote, "is that of harmony, or the good otherwise known as the true, otherwise known as the Beautiful."[55] These were the principles to which Wright invariably appealed in trying to make sense of his life and work. However much he might stray from them or use them to rationalize actions whose motives were sometimes less pure, however arrogantly and self-righteously he might wield them to condemn those with whom he disagreed, there is no reason to doubt the moral passion with which he embraced them. They were quite literally his religion.

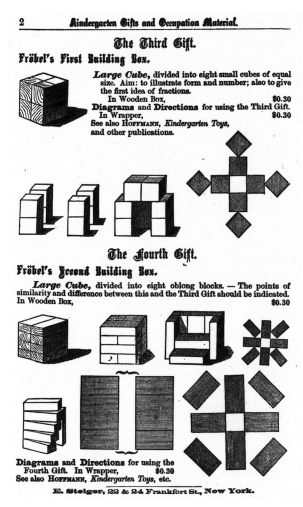

The Third Gift.

Fröbel's First Building Box.

Large Cube, divided into eight small cubes of equal size. Aim: to illustrate form and number; also to give the first idea of fractions.
In Wooden Box,   \$0.30
Diagrams and **Directions** for using the Third Gift.
In Wrapper,   \$0.30
See also HOFFMANN, *Kindergarten Toys*, and other publications.

The Fourth Gift.

Fröbel's Second Building Box.

Large Cube, divided into eight oblong blocks. — The points of similarity and difference between this and the Third Gift should be indicated.
In Wooden Box,   \$0.30

Diagrams and **Directions** for using the Fourth Gift. In Wrapper,   \$0.30
See also HOFFMANN, *Kindergarten Toys*, etc.

E. Steiger, 22 & 24 Frankfort St., New York.

Figure 3: Friedrich Froebel's blocks, as depicted in *Kindergarten Gifts and Occupation Material*, 1876

TOWARD A GRAMMAR OF STYLE

Emerson did not, of course, invent romantic idealism. He served as its most prolific and popular missionary in the United States, and was almost surely the ultimate source for Wright's moral philosophy, but he was by no means alone in transmitting romantic ideas to Wright or to American culture generally. Romanticism had many roots on both sides of the Atlantic, permeating nineteenth-century life in so many ways that one encounters it everywhere. It was, for instance, the foundation of the often cited kindergarten training that Anna Wright gave her son. In 1876, while visiting the Centennial Exposition in Philadelphia, she saw a display of educational playthings called "Gifts"—in the form of colored strips of paper, two-dimensional geometric grids, and wood spheres, blocks, and pyramids (figure 3). All were designed so that mothers and schoolteachers could train children following the educational philosophy of Friedrich Froebel, the German inventor of the kindergarten, who had developed an elaborate series of exercises designed to educate a child's sensory experience of the world. Like other American mothers of her day, Anna was much enamored with Froebel's system and went so far as to seek formal training so that she could educate her son following the German educator's methods. In

later years Frank Lloyd Wright regularly cited the Froebel Gifts as one of the most profound influences on his approach to architecture. "I give you my word," he would say, "all those things are in my hands today—the feeling for those maple forms."[56]

Scholars have spent considerable energy demonstrating that Wright's buildings can be derived from Froebelian forms.[57] As the architect himself noted—probably in part as a way to claim prior inspiration for a method Le Corbusier had championed—Wright's habit of designing on a modular plan directly paralleled the formal exercises in which Froebel encouraged children to arrange wood blocks on a two-dimensional grid to form geometric patterns and miniature structures. "There," Wright said, "is the modular system that has been back of every design I ever made."[58] Froebel helped nurture Wright's lifelong fascination with a small collection of geometric shapes, different combinations of which can be used for periodization of almost his entire oeuvre: the line and the spiral, the circle and the sphere, the square and the cube, the triangle and the tetrahedron. Prairie houses, Larkin Building, Unity Temple, California Romanzas, Fallingwater, Johnson Administration Building, Usonian houses, Guggenheim: in the long parade of Wright's prodigiously diverse structures one has little trouble imagining him in a perennial childhood game of combining and recombining simple wood blocks, the most basic of geometric forms, as a way displaying his own incredible ability to push them to the furthest limits of artistic expression. "When you had mastered the interplay of those things upon one another," he said of the Froebel blocks, "when you had taken them by different angles and revolved them to get subordinate shapes, there you got a perfect language of form."[59]

The Froebel blocks cannot by themselves, of course, explain Wright's later brilliance in manipulating interior and exterior space. Not only was it long after his kindergarten training that he eventually developed his mature style, but many other influences were at least as important in shaping the particulars of his aesthetic vision. In this respect, attempts to show that Froebel's blocks can be rearranged to mimic Wright's structures are a little beside the point. The significance of the blocks in fact lies much deeper, as Wright's allusion to a perfect language of form suggests.[60] Froebel did not design his kindergarten exercises simply to give his young pupils an analytical tool for breaking complex shapes into their constituent parts and assembling them again into new structures. He intended that children begin to associate different shapes with well-defined symbolic meanings. He wrote of the sphere, for instance, that "the spherical is the symbol of diversity in unity and of unity in diversity."[61] Wright was arguing from this general Froebelian perspective when he declared that "certain geometric forms have come to symbolize for us and potently to suggest certain human ideas, moods, and sentiments—as for instance: the circle, infinity; the triangle, structural unity; the spire, aspiration; the spiral, organic progress; the square, integrity."[62] The Froebel blocks permitted a child to explore not just the innate physical properties of different shapes, but their relationship to the underlying spiritual meaning of the cosmos, and it is here that we will discover their most important influence on Frank Lloyd Wright.

For Froebel, Euclidian geometry expressed a Platonic order, and the endlessly shifting patterns of his blocks were but guises of the Universal One. Listening to him describe the most important goal of his pedagogy, one instantly recognizes the idealist voice of nineteenth-century romanticism:

In all things there lives and reigns an eternal law. . . . This law has been and is enounced with equal clearness and distinctness in nature (the external), in the spirit (the internal), and in life which unites the two. This all-controlling law is necessarily based on an all-pervading, energetic, living, self-conscious, and hence eternal Unity. . . . A quietly observant human mind, a thoughtful, clear human intellect, has never failed, and will never fail, to recognize this Unity. This Unity is God. All things have come from the Divine Unity, from God, and have their origin in the Divine Unity, in God alone.[63]

The American textbooks on which Anna Wright probably relied in transmitting Froebel's ideas to her son made clear that mere geometry was hardly the most important lesson she should be trying to teach. As one declared, the exercises were "intended as an aid to secure the union between mother and child, between God and the world."[64] Another announced with some frustration: "Hundreds of well-meaning friends of the Kindergarten who have not had time to look beneath its surface, still class Froebel's Gifts with the trivial playthings of the toy-shop. . . . Froebel's Gifts are serious things, freighted with life, endowed with a soul, and not to be handled irreverently without injury to the thoughtless culprit."[65] Their final, most cosmic lesson was one that young Frank Lloyd Wright had been imbibing from his Unitarian family for as long as he could remember. "This is the soul of Froebel's gifts: *Unity in Universality, and Universality in Unity—One in All, and All in One.*"[66] We can almost see Anna Wright, Jenkin Lloyd Jones, and Ralph Waldo Emerson nodding in agreement.

Froebel helps us understand yet another important way in which Wright's relationship to nature subtly differs from our own. The German pedagogue was adamant that his young pupils not make drawings or any other artistic representations directly from real objects until after they had spent long months working through his formal geometric exercises. The idea, as Wright described it, was that a child "should not be allowed to draw from nature, to imitate the look of objects until he had mastered the fundamental forms of nature."[67] In this way kindergarten children would come to understand the ideal Euclidian geometries that organized and structured the exterior surfaces of the world, enabling them to recognize the "shapes that lay hidden behind the appearances all about."[68] Wright had learned from Emerson the primacy of inner spiritual nature as reflected in his own soul; he learned from Froebel that inner nature had a Euclidian grammar. This helps explain why an architect who consistently described his work as "organic" or "natural" could just as consistently refuse to include naturalistic designs in his structures, apparently preferring highly abstract patterns that on the surface seemed much more artificial. The vast majority of Wright's decorative motifs are geometric abstractions designed not so much to look like the natural forms

Figure 4: Frank Lloyd Wright. Tree of Life stained-glass window, Darwin D. Martin House, Buffalo. 1902–04

they represent as to capture the *essence* of those forms. The best-known examples are stained-glass, cast-concrete, and copper plant motifs that have come to be associated with individual Wright buildings: the tulips at Wright's Oak Park House and Studio of 1889–98; the sumac at the Susan Lawrence Dana House in Springfield of 1902–04; the hollyhock at the Aline Barnsdall House in Los Angeles of 1916–21; the Spanish moss at Auldbrass Plantation in Yemassee, South Carolina, of 1938–42; the Tree of Life at the Darwin D. Martin House in Buffalo of 1902–04 (figure 4).[69] In choosing to decorate his "organic" houses with such abstract designs, Wright was declaring his allegiance to Froebel. Both men sought an ideal language that could capture the inner meaning of outward forms to reveal the cosmic unity of nature and spirit.

Euclidian geometry may have been the grammar of that language, but beyond mere grammar—beyond the Froebel blocks—was the more challenging question of the particular vocabulary and the chosen style in which Wright himself would try to speak. Here a number of leading nineteenth-century art critics and architectural theorists helped him add flesh to the bare bones of Froebel's geometry. From the English critic John Ruskin, for instance, he found explicit support for the idea that artists should convey not just the natural appearance of an object, but its meaning for the artist's soul.[70] Ruskin taught that "all most lovely forms and thoughts are directly taken from natural objects," so that the artist should always turn to nature for inspiration. And yet he also declared that art must abstract from nature to convey its deepest truths.[71] This was especially the case with architecture,

Ruskin wrote, which "delights in Abstraction and fears to complete her forms."[72] An artist should distinguish between mere imitation and truth. "There is a moral as well as material truth," Ruskin wrote, "a truth of impression as well as of form—of thought as well as of matter; and the truth of impression and thought is a thousand times the more important of the two."[73] By using signs and symbols that conveyed deep emotional meaning even though devoid of any natural likeness, an artist could represent the highest truths. Not to strive for those truths was to violate artistic integrity. "Truth," wrote Ruskin in an aphorism that echoed the Lloyd Jones family motto, "cannot be persisted in without pains; but is worth them."[74]

Similar lessons came from Eugène-Emmanuel Viollet-le-Duc, the great French architect and theorist whose *Dictionnaire raisonné* made such a deep impression on the young Wright that he later called it "the only really sensible book on architecture in the world."[75] Unlike Ruskin, who was adamantly opposed to the use of machine-made objects or new construction materials such as cast iron, Viollet-le-Duc encouraged architects to explore any tools and materials that technology had put at their disposal, demanding only that they employ those materials honestly.[76] When Wright repeatedly wrote of the need for architects to make their work conform to "the nature of materials," he was relying on Viollet-le-Duc as one of his chief authorities. Most of all, though, the French architect gave Wright a concrete architectural restatement of the abstract idealist philosophies the young man had imbibed from so many sources during his youth. In the long entry on style in the *Dictionnaire raisonné*, for instance, Viollet-le-Duc argued that "no creative work . . . can truly live unless it possesses what we call style." And how did one achieve this key to artistic greatness? The young Wright would surely have recognized the language in which the French architect stated his response: "*Style,*" he wrote, "*is the manifestation of an ideal based on a principle.*"[77]

To achieve style, Viollet-le-Duc declared, the architect must go to nature and observe it closely to discover the principles that already existed in the order of the universe. "Architecture, this most human of creations," he wrote, "is but an application of principles that are born outside of us. . . . Gravitational force existed before we did; we merely deduced the statics of it. Geometry, too, was already existent in the universal order; we merely took note of its laws, and applied them. The same thing is true of all aspects of the architectural art; proportions—indeed, even decoration—must arise out of the great natural order whose principles we must appropriate in the measure that human intelligence permits us to do so."[78] Starting from this premise, Viollet-le-Duc set out to demonstrate how the laws of geometry could be used to derive the structures of natural crystals (Wright would surely have recognized in this an almost identical exercise that Froebel had his kindergarten pupils perform) and that the laws of these crystals could, in turn, be used to discover the most natural and appropriate principles for handling architectural materials.[79] Applying these basic principles, one could then assemble all of a building's parts into a unified whole by subordinating them to a common architectural scale. "What is the scale?" Viollet-le-Duc asked. "It is the relation of all the parts to unity."[80]

One other author whose influence Wright explicitly acknowledged from his early years as an architectural apprentice was the English critic Owen Jones, whose book *The Grammar of Ornament* contained hundreds of sample decorative patterns from the great civilizations of human history. Anna Wright's kindergarten textbooks had been similarly filled with designs for the child to imitate with his Froebel blocks, but Jones's designs were far more complex and beautiful, awash in bright colors and geometric patterns. After checking the book out from his uncle's church library, Wright bought a packet of onionskin paper and traced the ornaments for many evenings. As with Viollet-le-Duc's *Dictionnaire raisonné*, he was searching in Jones for a vocabulary in which to express his personal vision. But Jones offered more than just a collection of pretty designs. He, too, was in search of principles and offered thirty-seven numbered "propositions" as formal rules for his *Grammar of Ornament.* "I read the 'propositions,'" Wright wrote forty years later, "and felt the first five were dead right."[81] Jones argued that the decorative arts existed to serve architecture, which must in turn reflect and serve the material and spiritual needs of its age. Architecture and decoration should be combined so as to produce "fitness, proportion, harmony, the result of all which is repose." Jones's fifth proposition had an especially familiar ring to it: "That which is beautiful is true; that which is true must be beautiful."[82] Jones also offered more specific advice, which added further syntax to Wright's own Euclidian grammar. "All ornament," he argued, "should be based upon a geometrical construction," and "every assemblage of forms should be arranged on certain definite proportions; the whole and every particular should be a multiple of some simple unit."[83] The specific propositions may have been new, but the principles behind them already seemed quite natural to the young architect.

Wright read these and other authors in his restless search to define his own architectural voice, his own expression of an ideal based on a principle, and in 1900 he synthesized what he had learned in an essay titled "A Philosophy of Fine Art," one of the least well known but most important of his career. In it he centered his theory of art on the doctrine of "conventionalization."[84] The artist, he declared, must do more than merely imitate nature; he must see "with a prophetic eye." His job was to distill natural beauty into its "conventional" essence, so that, for example, the decorative lotus on an ancient Egyptian temple would long survive the natural flower that had inspired it. Through this "rare and difficult process," Wright said, the flower's "natural character was really revealed and intensified in terms of stone, gaining for it an imperishable significance, for the Life principle of the flower is translated to terms of building stone to satisfy the Ideal of a real 'need.' This is Conventionalization, and it is Poetry."[85] The purpose of such abstract ornamentation was far more than simply to clothe a building with superfluous decoration. In Wright's view, the task of art was to conventionalize the state of nature—define its symbolic meaning—lest civilization forget its own roots and decay. "Of all Art, whatsoever," Wright declared, "perhaps Architecture is the Art best fitted to teach this lesson, for in its practices this problem of 'conventionalizing' Nature is worked out at its highest and best. . . . A work of Architecture is a great coordination with a distinct and vital organism, but it is in no sense naturalistic—it is the highest, most subjective, conventionalization of Nature known to man, and at the same time it must be organically true to Nature when it is really a work of Art."[86]

THE DANCE OF OUTWARD FORMS

Having placed Frank Lloyd Wright in the context of Emerson, Froebel, Viollet-le-Duc, and other romantic idealists, it finally becomes possible to understand what he meant when he called for an "organic" architecture. In arguing that architecture should strive as much as possible to be natural without being naturalistic and should emulate the principles of nature without imitating its forms, he was joining some of the most influential thinkers of his time. Thus he could write in 1896: "Say to yourself: my condition is artificial. So I cannot copy Nature and I will not slavishly imitate her, but I have a mind to control the shaping of artificial things and to learn from Nature her simple truths of form, function, and grace of line. Nature is a good teacher. I am a child of hers, and apart from her precepts cannot flourish."[87] One way to think about Wright's long career is to regard him as a man whose aesthetic theory and moral philosophy were more or less complete by the first decade of the twentieth century. One gets very little sense that he changed his mind thereafter about anything that really mattered to him, despite the fact that his architecture continued to evolve along strikingly diverse lines and his personal life underwent several major upheavals. Throughout it all, his core principles remained rigidly intact. But because the grammar of his thought was ultimately Platonic and sought its expression in the endless multitude of forms in which a shape-shifting nature clothed itself, it could accommodate virtually any vocabulary Wright chose to adopt. And so this most unbending and single-minded of men could also be astonishingly protean in his ability to assimilate new forms. Organic unity was the key to organic diversity: the unchanging inward principles were the still point of a turning world, a stage for the kaleidoscopic dance of outward forms.

For this reason, any search for the specific vocabularies in which Wright designed his buildings means rummaging widely to look for eclectic influences large and small. Some were quite fundamental, constituting such deep obsessions that they operated almost as core principles themselves, changing their form but always recapitulating their deeper meanings. Here one thinks of such basic materials as limestone and raw wood, to which Wright always returned, and of certain spatial devices—the concealed entrance, the central hearth, the constricted passage leading to releasing space, the opposition between tree house and cave, prospect and refuge.[88] Others seem to have resulted from chance encounters with people or materials or ideas that for whatever reason stuck with Wright long enough to leave a mark on at least a few of his buildings. Some of these were passing fancies, often involving experimental new materials like the individually cast concrete blocks of the California Romanzas, the glass tubing at the Johnson Administration Building, the corrugated fiberglass at Beth Sholom. Others seem to have been partly the expressions of Wright's unfailing competitiveness with other architects, as when he sometimes hurried to outdo the European modernists at their own game. But whereas the story of Wright's design grammar keeps circling back to a common idealist center, any comparable story about his different design vocabularies necessarily wanders over much broader terrain, feeling more like a whimsical treasure hunt in uncharted waters than an unswerving pilgrimage to a known shrine.

Where will we find the chief sources for Wright's favorite aesthetic tropes? These, too, for the most part came early. One of the most important was the Wisconsin landscape itself, especially the rolling countryside around the Lloyd Jones family farms where Wright eventually built Taliesin.[89] A region where fields and scattered woodlands mingle easily amid low hills and gentle valleys, southwestern Wisconsin was a classic pastoral landscape, neither wholly artificial nor wholly wild. As a boy, Wright spent long hours exploring the terrain to read in it "this marvelous book-of-books, Experience, the only true reading, the book of Creation." For the rest of his life he believed that "from sunrise to sunset there can be nothing so surpassingly beautiful in any cultivated garden as in these wild Wisconsin pastures."[90] The boy learned the common weeds and trees he encountered, and later declared—following Emerson and Viollet-le-Duc—that "the secret of all styles in architecture was the same secret that gave *character* to the trees."[91] Despite repeated rebellion at the hard physical labor his uncles demanded of him, Wright's later descriptions of his summers in the Helena Valley are openly sentimental. Even the repetitive farm work, which he often hated, eventually became a kind of metaphor for the rhythmic patterns of music and of "the obvious poetry in the mathematics of this universe"[92]—though he also not so sentimentally told an apprentice that farming was "all pulling tits and shoveling shit."[93]

Southwestern Wisconsin is, first and foremost, a sedimentary landscape in which limestone and sandstone take turns serving as bedrock for the general topography.[94] The limestone in particular has thin horizontal bedding planes that fracture the rock and give it a rectilinear appearance that resembles nothing so much as rough masonry. For a child already accustomed to looking for the underlying geometries of nature, the lesson of this blocklike stone must have seemed a striking confirmation of Wright's kindergarten training. "See the principle that 'builds,' in nature, at work in stone," he wrote. "Geometry the principle, busy with materials. . . . Read the grammar of the Earth in a particle of stone!"[95] No building material was more evocative for Wright than limestone. He had his masons lay it according to a regularly irregular formula so that the resulting walls would mimic the original strata of the quarries from which it came (figure 5).[96] So strong was his attraction to this effect that he sometimes forced other materials into the same pattern. Thus, the sandstone at Fallingwater, which in its original form has little horizontal bedding, is laid in such a way as to make it virtually indistinguishable from a Wisconsin limestone.[97] One could argue that the same is true of Wright's favorite trick in masonry walls of using brick-colored mortar to disguise vertical joints and raking out horizontal joints to mimic the natural strata of sedi-

Figure 5: Frank Lloyd Wright. Detail of house and steps, Taliesin III, Spring Green. 1925

mentary rock.[98] Indeed, the much-vaunted horizontality that characterizes the buildings of Wright's Prairie period surely owes at least as much to the geology of midwestern limestones as it does to the flatness of midwestern prairies.

But there is another property, subtler and less obvious than horizontal bedding planes, which limestone and sandstone share. Both rocks erode easily, so that when they appear as outcrops on the crests of hills, they have a weathered, ancient appearance. "In Wisconsin," Wright said, "erosion has, by way of age, softened everything."[99] This soft quality is familiar to anyone who has lived in a well-weathered sedimentary landscape, lending it a gentle, homelike feel that can only be described as domestic. No one has described this quality more movingly than W. H. Auden in his poem "In Praise of Limestone," which begins: "If it form the one landscape that we the inconstant ones / Are consistently homesick for, this is chiefly / Because it dissolves in water."[100] The result, Auden wrote, is a region of "short distances and definite places," whose inhabitants, "accustomed to a stone that responds," easily become "Adjusted to the local needs of valleys / Where everything can be touched or reached by walking."[101] This was Wright's ideal landscape, where one could gaze from atop the weathered outcrops across woodlots and cornfields to farms nestled in their protective valleys. The themes of prospect and refuge that recur so frequently and profoundly in his mature architecture are everywhere present in such a place. When Wright built Taliesin on a hillside near his uncles' farms, he placed it—the shining brow—to make it seem like

an outcrop itself. To inhabit a limestone landscape was to be surrounded by bubbling springs, meandering streams, eroding slopes, dissolving stone, the signs of a terrain visibly responding to the flow of time and malleable to human hands and human dreams—a fundamentally forgiving, nurturing place. One of Auden's most striking passages about the homelike qualities of this landscape could almost have been written to describe Wright himself:

What could be more like Mother or a fitter background
*   For her son, the flirtatious male who lounges*
Against a rock in the sunlight, never doubting
*   That for all his faults he is loved; whose works are but*
Extensions of his power to charm? From weathered outcrop
*   To hill-top temple, from appearing waters to*
Conspicuous fountains, from a wild to a formal vineyard,
*   Are ingenious but short steps that a child's wish*
To receive more attention than his brothers, whether
*   By pleasing or teasing, can easily take.*[102]

There is one other aspect of this scene that speaks to Wright's aesthetic vision and his larger attitudes toward nature. When Wright first knew the Helena Valley as a child, it was still on the cusp of a closing frontier, a place that had ceased to be wild during the lives of Wright's own grandparents. The human and the natural seemed comfortable neighbors here, and this came to be Wright's model as well. If one arranges American cultural conceptions of landscape along an abstract continuum—from city to suburb to pastoral to wild—then Wright's preferred spaces lay between the two poles, shifting from suburb toward pastoral in the years after his ignominious flight from Oak Park.[103] Wright had little use for nature in the raw but was also increasingly hostile to cities, and so he was drawn to middle landscapes, to worked countrysides that had been domesticated and made beautiful by the human labors upon them. When forced to build in any other setting, his impulse was to turn his buildings inward, sheltering them with protective walls, recessed windows, and overhanging eaves as in his suburban Prairie houses. In the case of truly urban sites such as those of Unity Temple, the Johnson Administration Building, or the Guggenheim Museum, he shut out the surrounding environment altogether and replaced it with a beautiful inner space that was wholly artificial.

Only in places like the Helena Valley did he wholly open his structures to their surroundings.[104] Taliesin looked out not on wild nature, but on fields and pastures—a classic pastoral retreat. Wright devoted almost as much attention to shaping the grounds of his estate—planting orchards, adding a millpond, constructing new farm buildings, maintaining the fields—as he did on the house itself.[105] For the whole of his life, he tried to situate his structures in an ideal space that mimicked this one. "When selecting a site for your house," he advised his clients, "there is always the question of how close to the city you should be, and that depends on what kind of slave you are. The best thing to do is go as far out as you can get. . . . Go way out into the country—what you regard as 'too far'—and when others follow . . . move on."[106]

In thus recommending a pastoral landscape as the ideal site for his houses, he was also recapitulating the contradictions of the American frontier experience, in which the migrations of those who sought new homes and wide open spaces eventually reproduced the very crowding they sought to flee. His urban utopia, Broadacre City, would be the ultimate embodiment of this paradox, proposing a complete decentralization of urban life. "We can go forward to the ground," he wrote, "not the city going to the country but the country and city becoming one."[107] That in such a setting Wright himself would almost surely have felt compelled to move on as his neighbors pressed in on every side was a contradiction he never resolved, perhaps because he did not live long enough to see it happen to the valley that had inspired this vision of a natural city.

Wright did not, of course, launch his architectural career in the Helena Valley, despite his early efforts helping construct the Lloyd Jones family chapel. For his first quarter-century of professional practice he worked in a far more urban setting, Chicago, and this too certainly left its marks on his aesthetic vocabulary. When he arrived there in 1887, it was very much a city on the make, its downtown still enjoying the extraordinary building boom that followed the Great Fire of 1871. No doubt because of that boom Chicago was a place where architects often seemed larger than life, veritable culture heroes who were single-handedly remaking the city in their own image. When Henry Blake Fuller wrote his classic novel *With the Procession* about Chicago in the 1890s, he included an architect among its principal characters to reflect the special role such men were playing in the city.[108] Among those who embraced this romantic image of the architect as hero, none did so more self-consciously than Louis Sullivan. The young Wright soon managed to gain a position with Sullivan's firm, which was then at work on the Auditorium Building of 1886–90, one of the most famous of the tall office buildings that were transforming the Chicago skyline. For the next half-decade, Wright served as chief assistant to the man whom he would call *Lieber Meister* for the rest of his life.

The extent of Sullivan's influence on Wright is today rather difficult to assess. Certainly Wright is unusually generous in acknowledging the training he received from Sullivan, who gave him his first extensive experience in running a large architectural firm. It was Sullivan and his partner Dankmar Adler who introduced Wright to the engineering technologies that were so dramatically transforming architecture in the late nineteenth century. Sullivan's own most distinguishing trademark—the almost erotically florid vegetative surface decorations with which he covered his buildings—appeared only briefly in Wright's work. One sees echoes of this ornamental influence in Wright's William H. Winslow House in River Forest, Illinois, of 1893–94 (plates 9–13), but he rapidly moved on to the much more geometric patterns for which he later became famous—patterns that would seem to owe more to Froebel, Owen Jones, and the Arts and Crafts movement than to Sullivan's ornamental practice. But stripped of their surface decorations, Sullivan's buildings shared this basic concern for geometric expression and so were of a piece with the other intellectual influences that were shaping Wright's aesthetic sensibility.

Sullivan's most important influence on Wright may have been both more mundane and more cosmic. He educated his young protégé in the nitty-gritty details of architectural practice, helped finance the construction of Wright's House in Oak Park of 1889–90 (plates 5–7, 21–26), and unintentionally launched his independent career. In the realm of ideas, Sullivan was as steeped as Wright in Emersonian romanticism, regarding himself as a disciple of Walt Whitman. His own dearest wish was to fulfill the romantic vision of the architect as universal artist, heroic individual, and prophet of democracy, while also embodying the no less romantic role of the artist as cultural critic. For Wright, Sullivan was first and foremost a model of the artist striving for original style, refusing to compromise with the reigning orthodoxies of his day (in this, both men looked for inspiration to the example of Henry Hobson Richardson). Sullivan also spoke and wrote in an oracular prose that tried to emulate Whitman—admittedly with modest success—and it is perhaps from him that Wright acquired some of his own literary style and ambition. Although Wright later asserted that he never actually read Sullivan's 1924 *Autobiography of an Idea* (a statement that is itself evidence to the contrary), its parallels with Wright's *An Autobiography* are striking enough to make this claim almost laughable.[109] In Sullivan, Wright recognized a kindred spirit who also worshipped where nature and spirit met—at the divine altar of Unity.

Sullivan gained his fame by designing tall office buildings; Wright, by designing houses. In fact, both were contributing to the new urban landscape of late-nineteenth-century America, for the downtown in which Sullivan worked was the necessary counterpart to Wright's suburban neighborhoods. The commercial buildings of the central business district provided the workplaces for commuters (most of them men), who left their children and spouses (most of them women) in the comfortable houses on large lots that distinguished new suburbs such as Oak Park, River Forest, and Riverside. Even the names of these places suggested the image of pastoral retreat that their developers were trying to promote. The suburb was meant to embody domesticity, a place to which harried businessmen could retreat at day's end, where families could nurture children in isolation from the crowds, dangers, and vices of the city. Wright's houses were intended to serve this domestic ideal, and many of their most familiar features—the central hearth, the sheltering eaves, the windows from which a person could see without being seen—were metaphors for enclosure to protect the sanctity of the family. In 1896–97 Wright embellished and helped publish a book titled *The House Beautiful*, written by William C. Gannett, a Unitarian minister who was a close friend of his uncle Jenkin. In that book Gannett described an ideal house whose purpose was to embody the principle of family love, and situated that house in "A world of care without; / A world of strife shut out; / A world of love shut in!"[110] He argued that it should nurture the spirit no less than it sheltered the body. "A home," Gannett declared, "should be home for all our parts. Eyes and ears are eager to be fed with harmonies in color and form and sound; these are their natural food as much as bread and meat are food for other parts." If an architect could feed the soul in these ways, he would make of the home "a building of God, a house not made with hands."[111] Wright's lifelong architectural commitment to the domestic ideal is surely, in part, a product of the Chicago suburbs where he raised—and then abandoned—his own family.

Gannett's book reflected another influence that touched Wright in Chicago. By the 1890s the city was home to a group of artists who were deeply influenced by the Arts and Crafts movement that William Morris and others were promoting in England.[112] Dedicated to preserving traditional artisanal relationships to craft production, Morris's movement had fostered communities of artists who worked together in all mediums—printing, glassware, pottery, textiles, furniture, and not least architecture—as a way of retrieving skills that might otherwise be lost to machine technologies. Their collective work had a profound effect on Wright, and *The House Beautiful*, which he produced on a handpress with his client William H. Winslow, was an expression of that influence. Although Wright never embraced Morris's communitarian values or his socialist politics, he did gather around himself a group of artists working in different mediums to produce the sculptures, murals, and stained glass that so distinguished his Prairie school houses. Later, the Taliesin Fellowship upheld this early commitment to the decorative arts, and Wright's books echoed Arts and Crafts printing traditions right up to the end of his life. Wright, of course, broke with Morris (and with John Ruskin) in defending the virtues of machine production, but he did so in the service of more fundamental values—the integrity of materials, the unity of form and function, the belief that even the most mundane object should be made beautiful—that he shared with the Arts and Crafts movement.[113] Wright's furniture and ornamentation clearly owed much to Arts and Crafts influences, and even his early houses owed something: flatten the roof of a Tudor revival building, remove its vertical members, and it is not hard to see what is left as a transitional step on the way to a Prairie house.

Among the most important Chicago influences on Wright's design vocabulary, however, is one he tried hard to hide and for which we therefore have the least documentation. In 1893 Chicago played host to the World's Columbian Exposition, one of the most remarkable fairs ever held in America. Under the influence of the architect Daniel H. Burnham, one of Sullivan's leading rivals, the fair's managers adopted neoclassical Beaux-Arts motifs for the buildings of its central Court of Honor. The result was the "White City," a magnificent vision of architectural beauty that would help spur a classical revival throughout the United States for at least the next three decades. Architectural historians ever since have used the fair as a benchmark in the story of modern architecture. Most have agreed with Louis Sullivan that it represented a kind of setback—Sullivan would have called it an unmitigated disaster—for the new forms of architecture that he and other members of the Chicago school had tried to pioneer.[114] Wright himself certainly agreed that the fair's aesthetic was a step in the wrong direction, and he opposed all such revivalism as essentially hostile to his own search for an organic architecture that would spring from American soil.[115]

But whereas Sullivan always viewed the fair as the beginning of the end for his own career, it was much more of a starting point for Wright, in two important ways. One is by now well known. At the World's Columbian Exposition, Wright almost surely visited Japan's Ho-o-den exhibit (figure 6), a reconstructed temple on a rustic island set well off from the formal axes of the classical main fairgrounds. Wright had already encountered Japanese art in the print collection of his first employer, the Chicago architect Joseph Lyman Silsbee, and probably elsewhere as well, given the general Western interest in Japanese culture during the late nineteenth century. Until then, though, he had never actually seen a Japanese building. We will never know how he reacted to the Ho-o-den, whether it came as a sudden revelation of new architectural possibilities, or simply planted the seed of an idea that would not finally flower for another seven years. But there can be no doubt about the many parallels between Wright's mature style and Japanese domestic architecture. The open floor plan, the flowing interior space partitioned with movable screens, the light-colored panels outlined with dark wooden strips, the generous fenestration with its attendant abundance of light, the overhanging eaves, the shallow roof, and the overall feeling of a building half-tempted to float free from its foundations with apparent indifference to the ordinary demands of gravity—all of these were elements that Wright surely absorbed into the core vocabulary of his Prairie houses.[116]

Wright himself went well out of his way to deny all this, which in his case is usually a good sign that the thing being denied may represent an influence so deep that it threatened his own heavily defended sense of originality. Perhaps as a way of acknowledging his debt without admitting its direct architectural significance, Wright repeatedly asserted that it was Japanese *prints*, not buildings, that had affected his mature style. "I have never confided to you," he told the Taliesin Fellowship in 1954, "the extent to which the Japanese print per se as such has inspired me. I never got over my first experience with it and I shall never probably recover. I hope I shan't. It was the great gospel of simplification that came over, the elimination of all that was insignifi-

Figure 6: Ho-o-den, World's Columbian Exposition, Chicago. 1893

Figure 7: Katsukawa Shunsho. The Actor Ichikawa Danjuro V. c. 1777–86. Brocade print. Formerly collection Frank Lloyd Wright

cant."[117] Wright became a great collector of Japanese art (figure 7) and published a major essay on its significance in 1912, claiming for it the same lessons of antinaturalism and formalism that he associated with Froebel's pedagogy. "A Japanese artist," he declared, "grasps form always by reaching underneath for its geometry. . . . The forms, for instance, in the pine tree (as of every natural object on earth), the geometry that underlies and constitutes the peculiar pine character of the tree—what Plato meant by the eternal idea—he knows familiarly. The unseen is to him visible."[118] No other people, he argued, had more completely committed themselves to conventionalizing their morals and their vision of nature into an integrated whole, making the entirety of Japanese civilization "a true work of Art."[119] In this, Japan served as the most perfect possible example of the integrity and unity that Wright believed to be the object of his own art. "No more valuable object lesson was ever afforded civilization than this instance of a people who have made of their land and the buildings upon it, of their gardens, their manners and garb, their utensils, adornments, and their very gods, a single consistent whole, inspired by a living sympathy with Nature as spontaneous as it was inevitable."[120]

The Ho-o-den would have been lesson enough for Wright to take away from the World's Columbian Exposition, but there may have been one other lesson so deep that it has not heretofore been much noticed by scholars. It was simply this: the fair was *temporary*. The extraordinary buildings that arose beside Lake Michigan on the south side of Chicago had been called into being to realize an ideal vision of

perfect architectural beauty (figure 8). Whether or not one agreed with that vision—whether one was drawn to the Beaux-Arts classicism of the Court of Honor, or to Louis Sullivan's polychromatic Transportation Building (figure 9) or to the exotic Oriental structures of the Midway Plaisance or to the elegant Ho-o-den itself—was almost beside the point. If there was no concern about the permanence of such structures, one could call them into being as if by the wave of a magician's wand, constructed of steel and clad in plaster to give them the appearance, if not the substance, of eternal beauty. Wright later objected to such illusions as a dishonest use of materials, but he can hardly have failed to notice the extraordinary effects that could be achieved architecturally—the amazing array of forms that could be paraded before the eyes of an awestruck audience—if solidity and permanence were not the paramount goals. The materials used at the fair would, for the most part, never have survived a midwestern winter, but that hardly mattered to the millions who were struck dumb by what the architects had achieved there. Virtually everyone who saw the White City regarded it as one of the wonders of the age. A British journalist who visited it just before it was scheduled to be torn down was typical in declaring, "Nothing that I have ever seen in Paris, in London, in St. Petersburg, or in Rome, could equal the effect produced by the illumination of these great white palaces that autumn night." They left on the mind "an impression of perfect beauty."[121]

For all their grandeur and glory, the buildings of the fair were meant to express an ideal that could not have been realized had they been required to last for a long time. Like all the great nineteenth-century fair architecture, from the 1851 Crystal Palace forward, they were follies, achieving wonderful effects at the expense of permanence.[122] They enabled their builders to play with the latest materials and technologies, showcasing the miracles that new ideas and inventions could achieve. As such, they expressed a number of high ideals: progress, improvement, the achievements of science and art, the genius of heroically creative individuals, the onward march of civilization, and the triumph of mind, spirit, and will. But among the most profound lessons of the fair was one that could be expressed only as a paradox. On the one hand, the Exposition's goal was to point toward the future by inventing a fantasy world—a White City—that was as yet beyond the outer limits of human possibility: it attempted to embody, however briefly and beguilingly, an eternal ideal. On the other hand, the very fact that the fair's buildings could not survive, that they would be dismantled once the crowds had left and would henceforth live only in memory, was itself a metaphor for all human creation. However gloriously one might seek an ideal, one could never finally and permanently attain it. Even the Acropolis was now a noble ruin. Since all architecture would eventually suffer a similar fate, one could reasonably ask whether it was better to strive after the illusory hope of designing a building that would last forever, or to point toward an ideal so compelling that it would survive the building that expressed it. Certainly Japanese architecture did not include permanence among its highest goals, and the same was true of the White City. Its purpose was to showcase technological and aesthetic possibilities that would influence

Figure 8: View from the Peristyle, World's Columbian Exposition, Chicago. 1893

Figure 9: Adler and Sullivan. Golden Doorway, Transportation Building, World's Columbian Exposition, Chicago. 1893

the course of history itself. In so doing, it implicitly asked whether the architect's most important achievement should be the physical structure or the impact that such a structure might make upon the human mind. The fair suggested that it might be possible to leave a profound impression on the collective cultural memory with "demonstration" buildings capable of resonating through a thousand subsequent works even if they did not themselves survive the ebb and flow of time.[123] We will never know whether Frank Lloyd Wright consciously pondered such questions as he stood before the Ho-o-den and wandered about the Court of Honor, but his later practice suggests that he knew full well the expressive possibilities of an architecture that flirted, follylike, with impermanence.

THE RIDDLE OF A LEAKY ROOF

One great legacy of the World's Columbian Exposition for Wright, therefore, was the lesson that every building, no matter how humble or small, could enjoy the expressive freedom of the folly and also profoundly influence the structures of architects working far in the future. The buildings of the Exposition had achieved a unique playfulness and freedom by pretending that time did not exist, and they did so in such a way as to affect the course of American architecture for the next thirty years. Like all follies—like all temporary buildings that revel in their own evanescent opportunities—the fair gave its builders the chance to try experimental ideas, explore extreme effects, and express their most exuberant visions in ways that would not have been possible under any other circumstances. Certainly Sullivan's grand entrance to the Transportation Building went beyond anything he had attempted in more permanent structures, and the same was true for many other architects and engineers whose works ranged from the great Ferris Wheel to the Court of Honor itself. Wright himself experienced the pleasures of folly

architecture when, less than three years after the fair, he erected the Romeo and Juliet Windmill near his aunts' school in the Helena Valley (plate 49). Although he intended the structure to be permanent and it held up reasonably well over the years—albeit with significant restoration and eventual reconstruction—it shared with the buildings of the fair a clear sense that its utilitarian function was merely an excuse for its extravagantly elegant, playful, even ribald form. It would have been right at home on the Midway Plaisance in Chicago.

Throughout his career Wright was drawn to fantasies such as this one, many of which he must have known were not likely to be realized. Some, like the wildly exaggerated Tudor of the Nathan G. Moore House in Oak Park of 1895, or the vaulting Crystal Palace–like skeleton of the remodeled Rookery Building lobby of 1905, or the explicit follies of Chicago's Midway Gardens of 1913–14 (plates 133–144), actually did come into being. Many more remained ideas on paper, memories without physical expression: The Mile High Illinois skyscraper of 1956, the Doheny Ranch Resort of 1923, the Cottage Group Hotel and Sports Club for Huntington Hartford of 1946–48, the Marin County Fair Pavilion of 1957–59 (see plates 198–199, 316–318, 341–342, 388). Broadacre City and the Usonian houses were more constrained in their impulses, but they too sought to serve as visionary templates transmitting a Wrightian legacy to the landscapes and memories of the future. Built or unbuilt, all such designs expressed the visionary joy of folly architecture, all were made as much of memory as of masonry and mortar, and all served as demonstration buildings whose purpose was to leave Wright's unmistakably personal mark on all who would follow in his footsteps.

Looking at Wright's drawings of such projects today, it is hard to believe that he really imagined they would ever be built. But because one could easily say the same of so many other Wright buildings that *did* come to fruition, one must be very careful not to draw the wrong conclusion about the meaning of these fantasy projects. Above all, Wright sought the freedom to express his own creative genius as an artist. During his years at Oak Park, when he was still trying to uphold a conservative suburban lifestyle not unlike that of his bourgeois neighbors, Wright for the most part reined in his more playful side. He built structures that for all their originality still upheld Gannett's traditional family values, still conformed to many ordinary expectations about domestic architecture, still usually managed to be built more or less within his clients' budgets. After fleeing the staid environs of Oak Park, however, Wright's impulse toward more exuberant structures began to play a greater role in his work. The possibilities that he had first discovered in the follies of the 1893 Exposition increasingly encouraged him to explore the endlessly plastic manipulations of geometry and form that were the core of his idealism. If we wish to answer the riddle of his leaky roofs, it is here, to the folly and the imperatives of romantic individualism, that we must finally turn.

As I suggested at the outset, the riddle is more profound than it first seems. The practical failings of Wright's buildings are so numerous that one cannot hope to catalogue them in an essay of this size. Although the interruption of Herbert Johnson's dinner party by Wingspread's leaking roof is undoubtedly the most famous example of these failings, it is hardly the most dramatic. When members of the Beth Sholom Synagogue (plates 372–375) held their first High Holy Days celebration in 1960, water literally poured onto their heads from the rain outside, requiring the congregation to move elsewhere. The rabbi confessed that he was a nervous wreck each time he had to plan a service or a wedding, and jokesters in Philadelphia began to ask, "Why go on the Water Wagon? Join Wright's Beth Sholom and get your water free."[124] Workers at the Johnson Administration Building became so accustomed to the leaks from its Pyrex glass-tubing skylight that they were never without five-gallon buckets near their desks to catch the drips—though buckets could not protect them when the glass itself occasionally descended to the floor.[125] And yet falling tubing was nothing compared to the problems that parishioners faced at Wauwatosa's Greek Orthodox Church (plates 376–379). There, Wright's blue tiled dome experienced frost heaving within a few years of its being completed and began to leak. The roof's accumulated moisture gradually loosened the two-inch asbestos insulation behind the church's interior ceiling, which began to sag in 1965. On Easter Sunday 1966, a large section of the ceiling collapsed, fortunately at a time when the sanctuary was unoccupied. The asbestos insulation was eventually replaced with urethane foam, which provided a more effective vapor barrier, but not before so much moisture damage had been done to the dome's exterior tiles that they too had to be replaced with a more durable material at considerable expense.[126]

Such stories, alas, are only the tip of the iceberg. In the case of these three buildings, Wright was working with unusual materials, so it is hardly surprising that they did not perform quite as originally anticipated. But leaks occurred even when he worked with more traditional materials, especially when he wished to stress a building's horizontality. We have already seen that by diminishing the pitches of the

Figure 10: Frank Lloyd Wright. Unitarian Church, Madison. 1945–51. Interior view with buckets for collecting water

roofs for houses in temperate latitudes, he increased the likelihood that they would have to carry their winter snow burdens for longer periods. At the same time, he eliminated the attic so as to increase the height of public rooms, which could now soar right to the top of the building—through the space that the attic had formerly occupied.[127] In the process, he failed to recognize that the attic existed in vernacular architecture to serve several important functions. Most obviously, it enabled the roof to be more steeply pitched—but then, Wright was no fan of pitched roofs during his Prairie years. (Later, he sometimes used steep pitched roofs for aesthetic effect, as at Beth Sholom and the Unitarian Church, but leaks remained a persistent problem.) The attic provided extra storage space—but Wright was generally opposed to cluttering his designs with the kind of chaos that usually accompanies storage. Finally, it served to contain the extreme swings of temperature and moisture that occur at the tops of most buildings—but Wright was for some reason not always attentive to the importance of vapor barriers and ventilation in the outer shell of his houses. The result was that Wright's roofs could experience problems from many different sources. The copper roof of the Unitarian Church (figure 10) has leaked from rain and snow, and sometimes simply from the moisture that the congregation itself exhales while breathing in the room beneath this natural vapor barrier. The flat-roofed Usonian houses have had moisture problems as well. When, for instance, the new owner of the first Herbert Jacobs House in Madison of 1936–37 (plates 241–245) sought to restore it in the 1980s, he discovered severe structural damage in the roof where inadequate insulation had encouraged frequent leaks and condensation from the repeated freezing and thawing of poorly drained snow.[128]

Roofs were not the only places where these sorts of design problems could occur. Wright's frequent wish to make his buildings appear to defy gravity produced a lifelong love affair with the cantilever, which he often extended farther from its structural supports than conservative engineering practice advised. Although he loved to boast that he knew more about such matters than the engineers, and although few of his cantilevers have actually failed, deflections have been common and occasionally severe. Edgar J. Kaufmann nervously commissioned several engineering studies to determine whether the sags and cracks in Fallingwater's famous cantilevers (plates 234–240) might pose a serious threat to the building's safety, and one gets the feeling that he was never completely reassured on this point.[129] Not long after it was completed, the choir loft in Madison's Unitarian Church had deflected downward by more than a foot and needed extensive structural repair; the cantilevered eave over the building's entrance today sags so much that those over six feet are in serious danger of bumping their heads on it. The third-floor roof of the Robie House is similarly deflected downward by many inches.[130] Any number of Wright buildings have had to have discreet props added to hold up their sagging cantilevers. Some of the worst problems are at Taliesin itself, where Wright's lack of money often led him to adopt less than optimal solutions to the design problems he faced. Walking along the building's eastern terraces, for instance, which initially appear to be made of solid stone, one detects an odd springiness underfoot. The reason becomes clear when one looks below and sees that flagstones have been laid directly on wooden joists, which have not fared well from this treatment. The south terrace beyond Wright's own bedroom, as of 1992, was on the verge of collapse and required extensive reconstruction before it could safely be used again. Sags and deflections such as these are the norm at Taliesin, and the total bill for repairing them is estimated in the tens of millions of dollars.

Wright's game of chicken with the force of gravity was matched by other refusals to accommodate the surrounding environment. These seem especially perplexing when one considers his reputation as an "organic" architect whose highest goal was to design buildings that would be "naturally" suited to their sites. On the one hand, Wright could display extraordinary environmental sensitivity in the siting of his buildings, practicing passive solar architecture long before it even had a name. Whenever possible, he oriented his houses so that three of their four sides would receive full sun for part of the day; moreover, he tried to extend his eaves just far enough so that they would provide shade in summer but permit direct lighting from the lower midwinter sun.[131] On the other hand, he was also capable of introducing at the Jacobs House an innovation called the carport which did away with the four walls of a garage as a way of saving money (and presumably of using yet another cantilever—which has, inevitably, sagged and needed repair). To introduce a garage without walls to the cold winter climate of Wisconsin, and worse, to place it on the northwest corner of its building, where it must bear the brunt of winds and drifting snow, does not seem a particularly sensitive response to the environment.

Similar indifference to winter cold is reflected in Wright's regular use of single-paned glass, his intense dislike for double-hung windows, his habit of butting glass directly against stone or masonry, where caulking will regularly fail, and the general difficulty of keeping his buildings warm. Herbert and Katherine Jacobs reported that their house could be *very* cold in the early years, and Wright's decision in the 1930s to migrate semiannually between Wisconsin and Arizona must surely reflect his tacit admission that it was a losing battle to try to keep Taliesin warm.[132] Environmental problems such as these were by no means limited to houses that had to survive a northern winter. Wright placed La Miniatura, his beautiful house for Mrs. George Madison Millard, on the floor of a desert arroyo despite being warned of the attendant danger of floods (plates 178–181). When the inevitable happened, he excused himself by declaring that no one had seen such rain "in fifty years."[133] The danger at Fallingwater was more calculated, and most visitors would probably agree that the risk was well worth running, but it too has suffered damage from floods.[134]

When his mind was set on a particular architectural effect, Wright could be as unwilling to compromise with a building's inhabitants—his clients—as he was with its natural environment. The uncomfortableness of his furniture is so legendary that even he complained of having been "black and blue in some spot, somewhere, almost all my life from too intimate contact with my own early furniture."[135] Owners of Wright houses frequently found them difficult to decorate because their architect had so forcefully imposed his unitary vision upon them. Ordinary furniture and ornament just did not look right, and even Wright's own furniture could be arranged in only a limited number of ways to suit the space. When owners did the best they could with the furniture they possessed, Wright complained that "very few of the houses . . . were anything but painful to me after the clients brought in their belongings."[136] His preferred solution was for them to throw most of their old things away. He told Herbert and Katherine Jacobs, when he saw their original possessions: "This stuff is all prehistoric, and it will have to go."[137]

But perhaps Wright's most important refusal to compromise with the needs of his clients was financial. His frequent and seemingly willful inability to complete his buildings within their promised budgets was nothing less than extraordinary. Wright was quite shameless about underestimating costs. When told that the original architect for the Johnson Administration Building had estimated that it might cost about $300,000, Wright "snorted and said it was too damn much money for the job and he could do a better functional job in more appropriate manner for a lot less."[138] In the end, his building cost nearly $900,000, admittedly for reasons that were not entirely in the architect's control.[139] The most extreme cases of Wright's exploding budgets—the Johnson Building, Fallingwater, the Guggenheim Museum—involved clients who could afford to pay Wright's ballooning expenses, but others were by no means spared. He promised the Madison Unitarians that their new church would cost $60,000; the final bill was $213,487.61, and that did not include the large amounts of volunteer and donated labor that were needed to finish it.[140] Beth Sholom and the Wauwatosa Greek Orthodox Church experienced comparable increases.[141] In the case of the Usonian houses, which were designed to carry a much lower price tag, Wright was somewhat more successful at coming in close to budget, though even there he frequently set up circumstances that pushed his clients into paying more than they had intended. When, for instance, he designed the first house for the lot that Herbert and Katherine Jacobs had purchased for it, he so filled the property that they instantly recognized they would have to double the size of their lot.[142] Later, he frequently fell into the habit of blaming any problems with such buildings on his clients' inability to pay for better materials or more features. Some were so persuaded by this argument that they felt apologetic about complaining.[143]

The reasons for Wright's cost overruns were manifold. Some were common to virtually all modern architecture. The impulse to design innovative forms using radically new materials could hardly help but entail steep learning curves that were bound to be costly, which is why Wright was hardly alone among major modern architects in underestimating expenses (or in designing roofs that leaked, for that matter) —he merely committed the sin more consistently and unapologetically than most. His blueprints could be notoriously difficult to interpret, and this, combined with his unusual designs, meant that contractors wasted much time and money trying to figure out how to work from them. Worse, Wright constantly modified his plans as new ideas occurred to him on the construction site, and this too inevitably jacked up costs. He did not hesitate to offer an extremely low estimate in order to gain a contract; then, once the client was hooked, he offered any number of reasons why changes in the plan would entail increased costs. Money apparently meant very little to him, as his son's description makes clear: "He carried his paper money crumpled in any pocket—trousers, vest, coat or overcoat. He would have to uncrumple a bill to see its denomination. He never counted his change. He never put his money into interest-bearing investments. . . . He either paid too much or too little for everything"—if, one might add, he paid at all.[144] In Wright's view, apparently, the client's money was a means to the artist's end, with consequences that could be expensive only for the client. One early Wright patron summed up the problem with the following advice: "Better take warning and be *very* careful in your dealings with him. If he is sane, he is *dangerous*."[145]

It is worth mentioning one additional problem with Wright's buildings that also has important financial implications. They were not just expensive to build; they also have proved to be remarkably costly to keep up. All their many problems—the leaks, the sags, the failing materials—of course entail repair costs. Wright's affection for using expensive or unusual building materials that are not easily replaced has not helped either. Jeffrey Chusid, the architect in charge of restoring the Samuel Freeman House in Los Angeles of 1923–24 (plates 187–191), described the problems he is facing in trying to deal with its twelve thousand concrete blocks, of which perhaps a thousand or more have experienced serious deterioration: "Remember how Tolstoy begins *Anna Karenina* by saying that every happy family is alike, but every unhappy family is unhappy in its own special way? Well, in this house we have twelve thousand unhappy families."[146]

But there is another source of costs that is more surprising and more interesting. In many instances, Wright apparently did not try to anticipate the ways in which his buildings would require regular maintenance of their mechanical systems. As a result, he rendered some of their most basic utilities almost inaccessible, dramatically escalating costs when something did in fact go wrong with them. Even so simple a matter as changing a light bulb could cause problems. At the Johnson Building, for instance, the incandescent bulbs of the Great Workroom were located between two layers of glass tubing with no easy way to gain access to them; a fifteen-foot-high wheeled scaffold had to be kept in the room so that tubes could be removed and bulbs replaced.[147] At the first Jacobs House, the radiant heating system beneath the floor had never been wholly successful, but when its cast-iron pipes finally began to leak, there was no way to gain access to them. The only solution was to remove the entire floor and start over.

The Greek Orthodox Church's congregation made a similar discovery when it sought to clean the ventilation conduits in its building: the conduits were more constricted than usual, had unexpected bends in them, and Wright had left no way to get at them. Special devices had to be employed to clean them mechanically. Many other problems have surfaced as well. The congregation holds one of the nation's largest fund-raising festivals each year, and the bulk of the money it raises goes toward maintaining Wright's difficult structure. As a result of experiences like these, many of the church's members are more than a little jaded about Frank Lloyd Wright, and some even regard their building as a great albatross. They are surely not alone. Surveying the hundreds of Wright buildings that still stand and seeing the many ways in which they are now decaying, one realizes that the cost of fully restoring them is astronomical. It would unquestionably run to hundreds of millions of dollars, and could easily exceed a billion.

And so one returns to the riddle of these many leaky roofs. What do they tell us about this greatest of all American architects? Surely Wright's high Emersonian ideals—his pleas for honesty and truth in the service of an organic architecture whose integrity would rest on nature's own principles—are more than a little inconsistent with his personal behavior and the practical failings of his buildings. How could an organic architect fail to respond to so basic an environmental constraint as the need for a house to fend off winter's cold or the need for its roof to shed water? How could a man of integrity so frequently fail to pay his bills and so often mislead his clients about the bills they themselves would have to pay? How could an artist so devoted to nature surround himself with so much artifice? How could a man so committed to truth so frequently lie? Were these mere inconsistencies, foolish and otherwise, or were they deep contradictions, hypocrisies even, in the very soul of Frank Lloyd Wright?

By now, the answers to such questions should be reasonably clear. Wright remained throughout his life the romantic he had been since childhood. As such, he brought a romantic's vision and romantic's scale of values to the practical challenges of his life. "Trust thyself," Emerson had taught. "Great men have always done so, and confided themselves childlike to the genius of their age, betraying their perception that the absolutely trustworthy was seated at their heart, working through their hands, predominating in all their being."[148] More than anyone or anything else, Wright trusted himself. Steeped in a tradition that saw the genius as a visionary individual doing battle with the forces of blind convention (Truth Against the World), he felt wholly justified in ignoring the niceties of conventional behavior—the foolish consistencies—if they got in the way of his higher truths. Lesser men might think him arrogant, but in his own eyes he was bearing righteous witness to the truth of his own vision. "I am telling you now the truth," he declared in the final year of his life:

No man who believes in himself and who is not pretentious, who is not trying to swindle you out of your eyeteeth pretending that he is something that he isn't, no such man, if he is sincere, is arrogant. We have come to mistake this thing we call arrogance, mistake the sureness of one's self, the faith in one's self which rejects the inferior, which will not countenance interference or destruction. . . . It is not arrogance. I am not an arrogant person and I never was. But I am a person who believes in what I believe in, and I am always willing to fight for what I believe in, and I am never willing to take less than what, to me, is the best.[149]

Romantic genius, artistic iconoclast, heroic individualist: these were the labels Wright attached to himself, these the standards against which he measured his own behavior. When he told clients to throw away their belongings or when he cajoled them into spending far more than they had ever intended on their houses, he was serving his vision of an ideal truth. Given his own perennial indifference to money, one can almost imagine that he literally had trouble regarding it as real. When he underestimated costs, he may sometimes have fooled himself as much as he did his clients, for the money (perhaps even the client) was just a means to an end. Indeed, Wright went so far as to suggest that money actually acquired its value by enabling his genius to create, and was as good as worthless if not pressed into the service of some higher good. "Money," he told his apprentices, "becomes valuable because you can do something with it. If you take away all the creative individuals, all the men of ideas who have projected into the arena of our lives substantial contributions, money would not be worth anything."[150] All of his behavior is consistent with this principle, however convenient and self-serving the uses to which it could be put. From his own point of view, much of what is most troubling about Wright can be explained as part of his single-minded struggle to overcome any obstacle that might prevent his vision from being realized.

Above all else, Wright's vision served beauty. When he quibbled with Sullivan's dictum that "form follows function," suggesting instead that "form and function are one," he was in fact revealing that when push came to shove his own true passion was form more than function.[151] What he admired in the Arts and Crafts movement was its commitment to crafting all objects in such a way as to render them beautiful. What he loved about Japan was the idea of a culture in which every human action and every human object were integrated so as to make of an entire civilization a work of art. In pursuit of beauty, he sought to subordinate all elements of his architecture to a consistent style that would express their underlying unity. No matter how radically his individual buildings may differ from each other, they all express his struggle for aesthetic consistency, his habit of seizing a single abstract theme and recapitulating it with endless variations as if in a Beethoven symphony. This man who could sometimes seem so inconsistent in his personal and professional life in fact held up consistency as the highest ideal of his architecture. "Consistency from first to last," Wright declared, "will give you the result you seek and consistency alone."[152] The vocabulary in which he sought to achieve this consistency was geometrical, so that Fallingwater, to take an obvious case, is an almost obsessive rumination on the possibilities of the cantilever, from the basic structure of the suspended floors right down to the treatment of the bookshelves. "You must be consistently grammatical," Wright said, for a building "to be understood as a work of Art."[153] Geometry was the key to grammatical consistency, which was in turn the key to aesthetic unity, which was in turn the key to beauty, which was in turn the key to God.

But consistency alone was not enough; it was only of value if coupled with the new. By itself, consistency would kill creativity, producing yet another of the lifeless, backward-looking traditions that were the death of art. Newness was proof of creative genius, and *consistent* newness was the best proof of all. Just as he tried hard not to seem influenced by anyone else's style, Wright had a restless urge to keep inventing new styles lest he start repeating his own too often. His boastfulness and his competitive need to claim priority over all other architects were surely tied to this horror of repetition. So was his love affair with new technologies, his willingness to experiment with virtually any new material that came his way so he could claim that he, Frank Lloyd Wright, was the first architect ever to have employed it. Describing to his apprentices the many innovations he had supposedly made in constructing the Larkin Building—air conditioning, plate-glass windows, integral desk furniture, suspended toilet bowls, and so on—he concluded, "I was a real Leonardo da Vinci when I built that building, everything in it was my invention."[154]

Wright's love of new technologies was matched by a desire to use old technologies in new ways. His fascination for the new and his need to show off his unsurpassed talents as an architectural virtuoso undoubtedly help explain his tendency to demand so much of his materials, daring to test their limits almost to the point of failure if it meant achieving effects he could claim as uniquely his own. The sags in Wright's cantilevers are but the logical complement to his perennial testing of limits in the search for new expression. Wright's defenders sometimes claim that he was simply ahead of his time, that the materials did not yet exist that could do what he wished them to do, and that this explains some of the problems with his buildings. Nothing in Wright's career supports this argument. Had he lived to be able to take advantage of the newer technologies and stronger materials of our own day, he would surely have pushed them to their limits as well. The proof he demanded of his genius was to go where no architect had ever gone before, and that meant accepting risks that few others were willing to take. If the cost of gambling on greatness was some leaky roofs, badly heated rooms, sagging cantilevers, and unhappy clients, then Wright was more than willing to pay the price.

Wright combined all these creative qualities—his exploration of new technologies, his invention of new styles, his striving for maximum expressive effect, his search for grammatical consistency in all his buildings—with a remarkable playfulness. There was something child-like about the man even in his late eighties—a powerful sense of romance and an unabashed enthusiasm for his own creations. In one sense, he never ceased being the flirtatious male of Auden's poem, lounging in the sunlight and performing for mother with seemingly effortless grace. But for all his self-centeredness, he also had a remarkable ability to sweep others up in his vision. Long before the ground for a new building had even been broken, Wright had conjured for his audience a beguiling fantasy of the ideal form that building would represent. No one has described this seductive power of Wright's better than his son John. His father's talent, he said, was to build "a romance about you, who will live in it—and you get the House of Houses, in which everyone lives a better life because of it. It may have a crack, a leak, or both, but you wouldn't trade it for one that didn't." This would be true, John said, even if Wright were building you a chicken coop. "He weaves a romance around the gullibility of the chicken and the chicanery of the human being—and you get the Coup of Coops in which every chicken lives a better life on its own plot of ground. You may crack your head or bump your shins on some projecting romanticism, but life will seem richer, the air clearer, the sunshine brighter, the shadows a lighter violet. You will gather the eggs with a dance in your feet and a song in your heart, for your coop will be a work of art, not the cold logical form chasing the cold logical function."[155]

The romantic spirit that Wright brought to all his buildings may point at once to the deepest secret of his architecture and the most profound reason for his leaky roofs. In the end, the leaks and sags did not much matter to him. Although his practical goal was to strive as hard as he could to make his structures conform to the vision in his mind, form mattered more than function to him, and the vision behind form mattered most of all, far more than did its physical incarnation. The building itself would invariably fall short, and could only be an approximation of the Platonic ideal that lay behind it. This may explain why Wright was so willing to modify his buildings even when they were under construction, and why he apparently felt no compunction about altering them once they were complete. Taliesin itself underwent innumerable revisions, with walls and windows and doors and rooms being added and subtracted on an almost monthly basis. No building seemed permanent to Wright, because none could reflect for more than an instant the multifaceted geometric ideal that was in his mind. Perhaps this is why he was apparently so undisturbed when one or another of his buildings was torn down. "I have learned not to grieve long," he wrote, "now that some work of mine has met its end." He took comfort from the fact that its image would survive in photographs, and these would spread its memory "as an idea of form, to the mind's eye of all the world."[156] It was the lesson of the folly: the architect could

not help but be a builder in the sand, and his works could not hope to escape what Wright called "the mortgage of time . . . on human fallibility foreclosed."[157] Buildings, like their architects, were mortal, and so they leaked and sagged and aged and eventually passed away. But like the White City, which had leapt into being for but a single summer to realize a dream on the shore of Lake Michigan, it was possible for "an idea of form" to live far longer in "the mind's eye of all the world." If an architect aspired to immortality, he had best seek it in the realm of memory, spirit, and eternal ideals, not mortal matter.

Wright finally staked his claim to greatness on the mind's eye as his best defense against the mortgage of time. "The product of a principle," he declared, "never dies. The fellows who practise it do, but the principle doesn't."[158] However inconsistent he may have been about other aspects of his life, he never wavered from this chief article of faith: an organic architecture, like a life well lived, must serve the principles that give order to nature and meaning to the human spirit. "We learn," Emerson had written, "that the dread universal essence, which is not wisdom, or love, or beauty, or power, but all in one, and each entirely, is that for which all things exist, and that by which they are."[159] However cleverly an architect might manipulate natural materials, however brilliantly he might combine wood and stone and mortar to create breathtakingly beautiful space, his truest creation was not material but spiritual. "Spirit creates," wrote Emerson. It "does not build up nature around us, but puts it forth through us, as the life of the tree puts forth new branches and leaves through the pores of the old."[160] Where nature and spirit met, there one would find the principles one sought, the lessons that would reveal the secrets of trees and flowers and buildings and even of the architect's own soul. "The principles that build the tree," declared Wright, "will build the man."[161] If such language today seems alien to us, if architectural critics now sometimes dismiss Wright's high-blown romantic words as unreliable guides to his architectural practice, this may be because we have forgotten the ideals that were ultimately more important to him even than buildings. The secret of Wright's architecture, he would surely have reminded us, will not be found on its surface but in its heart. If we wish to find it for ourselves, we must make our own way to the unity he managed to discover in so many corners of his universe: in the romantic words of a Concord preacher, in the geometric lessons of a kindergarten toy, in the gentle prospects of a Wisconsin landscape, in the evanescent beauty of a Japanese temple that was also a playful folly in the midst of a dream city—perhaps even in the persistent leaks of Wright's own roofs.

NOTES

The author would like to thank Diana Balmori, Nan Fey, John Holzhueter, Jeffrey Limerick, Cesar Pelli, Peter Reed, Terence Riley, and Vincent Scully for helpful comments on an earlier draft of this essay.

1. Ralph Waldo Emerson, "Self-Reliance," in *Ralph Waldo Emerson: Essays and Lectures* (New York: Library of America, 1983), p. 265. It is consistent with the spirit of this famous remark that it is often misquoted as referring to a foolish *inconsistency.

2. Frank Lloyd Wright, *An Autobiography* (1932; rev. ed., New York: Duell, Sloan and Pearce, 1943), pp. 107–08.

3. John Lloyd Wright, *My Father Who Is on Earth* (New York: G. P. Putnam's Sons, 1946); reprint ed., *My Father, Frank Lloyd Wright* (New York: Dover, 1992), p. 74.

4. Wright, *Autobiography*, p. 31.

5. In one of his earliest pronouncements on the goals of domestic architecture, Wright argued: "There should be as many types of homes as there are types of people, for it is the individuality of the occupants that should give character and color to the building and furnishings." Frank Lloyd Wright, "The Architect and the Machine" (1894), in Bruce Brooks Pfeiffer, ed., *Frank Lloyd Wright: Collected Writings*, vol. 1 (New York: Rizzoli, 1992), p. 23.

6. Frank Lloyd Wright, *The Natural House* (1954; reprint ed., New York: New American Library, 1970), p. 68.

7. Bruce Brooks Pfeiffer, ed., *Frank Lloyd Wright: His Living Voice* (Fresno: Press at California State University, 1987), p. 186.

8. The most famous furniture-rearranging story is that of Herbert Johnson, whose wife Irene Johnson never forgave Wright for the insult. See Samuel C. Johnson, "Mr. Wright and the Johnsons of Racine, Wis.: Reminiscences of 'Wingspread' and Its Architect," *AIA Journal* (January 1979), reprinted by the Johnson Foundation. Herbert and Katherine Jacobs were told by Wright that most of their existing furniture was "prehistoric" and would "have to go." Herbert Jacobs with Katherine Jacobs, *Building with Frank Lloyd Wright: An Illustrated Memoir* (1978; reprint ed., Carbondale: Southern Illinois University Press, 1986), p. 1.

9. For clients' reports on the experience of working with Wright, see Jacobs and Jacobs, *Building with Frank Lloyd Wright*; and Paul R. and Jean S. Hanna, *Frank Lloyd Wright's Hanna House: The Client's Report*, 2nd ed. (Carbondale: Southern Illinois University Press, 1987). See also Brendan Gill, *Many Masks: A Life of Frank Lloyd Wright* (New York: G. P. Putnam's Sons, 1987), pp. 189–90.

10. For a sample of Wright's lectures on this theme, see Pfeiffer, *His Living Voice*, passim, but esp. p. 78. Wright's son John has described his father's teaching abilities as follows: "Dad, with his uncanny genius in architecture, is not a good teacher. . . . Dad has always told his students that they could learn from his school but that he could not teach them anything. But I can see now that his teaching, even though apparently without method, had a very definite one. He taught me not to say 'Old Antique' by laughing at me when I said it. I had to analyze the phrase myself before I knew why he laughed." John Lloyd Wright, *My Father*, p. 131.

11. This last word occurs in Wright's earliest extant essay, "The Architect and the Machine"; see Pfeiffer, *Collected Writings*, vol. 1, p. 26.

12. For an authoritative telling, see Johnson, "Mr. Wright and the Johnsons."

13. When I inquired about whether the church had any photographs of such leaks, the minister replied that I was welcome to come take one myself "on any rainy day."

14. Cited in Gill, *Many Masks*, p. 375.

15. Ibid., p. 335.

16. On this theme, see Emerson, "Self-Reliance," *Essays and Lectures*, p. 260: "Trust [thy]self: every heart vibrates to that iron string. Accept the place the divine providence has found for you, the society of your contemporaries, the connection of events. Great men have always done so, and confided themselves childlike to the genius of their age, betraying their perception that the absolutely trustworthy was seated at their heart, working through their hands, predominating in all their being."

17. Alfred Lord Tennyson, "Flower in the Crannied Wall," in *The Poems and Plays of Alfred Lord Tennyson* (New York: Modern Library, 1938), p. 721. Wright used these lines as the frontispiece for his design of the fine-art edition of William C. Gannett, *The House Beautiful* (River Forest, Ill.: Auvergne Press, 1896–97); he also had Richard Bock inscribe them on the famous statue of the muse of architecture that Wright originally designed for the Susan Lawrence Dana House in Springfield and later reproduced as a central icon at Taliesin. Narciso G. Menocal has discussed the poem in a way that complements my own argument in "Taliesin, the Gilmore House, and the 'Flower in the Crannied Wall,'" in Narciso G. Menocal, ed., *Wright Studies, Vol. 1: Taliesin 1911–1914* (Carbondale: Southern Illinois University Press, 1992), pp. 66–69.

18. Wright, *Autobiography*, p. 11.

19. Pfeiffer, *His Living Voice*, pp. 69–70; see also pp. 169–70. Wright used almost exactly these words to describe his father's teachings about music: see, for instance, Wright, *Autobiography*, pp. 12–13, and also p. 47.

20. Wright described his father "composing" (the editorializing quotation marks are Wright's), pencil in his mouth, "weird" black smudges on his face, and asked: "Was music made in such heat and haste as this, the boy wondered?" Wright's own answer to this rhetorical question was clearly no. Wright, *Autobiography*, p. 13.

21. Maginel Wright Barney, *The Valley of the God-Almighty Joneses: Reminiscences of Frank Lloyd Wright's Sister* (1965; reprint ed., Spring Green: Unity Chapel Publications, 1986), p. 64.

22. Wright, *Autobiography*, p. 49.

23. Barney, *Valley of the God-Almighty Joneses*, p. 151.

24. John Lloyd Wright, *My Father*, p. 100.

25. Meryle Secrest, *Frank Lloyd Wright: A Biography* (New York: Alfred A. Knopf, 1992), p. 79.

26. Wright, *Autobiography*, p. 16.

27. John O. Holzhueter has discussed Wright's relationship to Unitarianism in an unpublished lecture, "Frank Lloyd Wright, Unitarianism, and Community," delivered at the First Unitarian Society, Madison, Wisconsin, September 29, 1992. Meryle Secrest also emphasizes this theme in her biography.

28. The Reverend Max Gaebler, longtime minister of the First Unitarian Society in Madison, is my source for the story about Wright's wanting the word *Unity* to appear on its pulpit. After being persuaded by his wife to abandon his Baptist beliefs for Unitarianism, Wright's father served for a brief time as the founding secretary of the Madison congregation; consistent with the rest of his troubled career, though, he failed to receive the call to a Unitarian pulpit.

29. "Meet Mr. Frank Lloyd Wright: A Conversation with Hugh Downs," broadcast May 17, 1953, reprinted in Patrick J. Meehan, ed., *The Master Architect: Conversations with Frank Lloyd Wright* (New York: Wiley-Interscience, 1984), p. 49; a slightly different version appears in "A Conversation," reprinted in Frank Lloyd Wright, *The Future of Architecture* (1953; reprint ed., New York: New American Library, n.d.), p. 29.

30. Wright's sister Maginel remembered Jenkin's "sonorous voice in the pulpit, august and cadenced with magnificent rolling r's. We children used to play church and imitate him." Barney, *Valley of the God-Almighty Joneses*, p. 99. To compare Jenkin's rhetorical style with that of his nephew, see Thomas E. Graham, ed., *The Agricultural Social Gospel in America: The Gospel of the Farm by Jenkin Lloyd Jones,* Studies in American Religion, vol. 19 (Lewiston, N.Y.: Edwin Mellen Press, 1986). Many of Wright's Taliesin "sermons" have been recorded, and a sample can be heard as well as read in Pfeiffer, *His Living Voice*.

31. A key event in the Transcendentalist revolt against more traditional Congregationalist and Unitarian beliefs was Ralph Waldo Emerson's scandalous address to the graduating class of the Harvard Divinity School (then called Divinity College), delivered on July 15, 1838. It is today read primarily as a document of American romanticism, but in fact it was mainly written to contribute to a very particular theological debate about biblical authority versus direct personal revelation as the best source of religious inspiration. Emerson, "An Address Delivered Before the Senior Class in Divinity College, Cambridge," *Essays and Lectures*, pp. 73–92.

32. Wright, *Autobiography*, p. 561; for one of Wright's few references to Emerson, see p. 17. Wright did go so far as to include a long passage from Emerson's essay on farming as an appendix to *The Living City*, and Emerson's name appears among the great thinkers Wright listed on his Broadacre City display as having been among its inspirations.

33. Pfeiffer, *His Living Voice*, p. 65, says Whitman was "a prime favorite" of Wright's; see also Randolph C. Henning, ed., *"At Taliesin": Newspaper Columns by Frank Lloyd Wright and the Taliesin Fellowship, 1934–1937* (Carbondale: Southern Illinois University Press, 1992). Brendan Gill also seems to think that Whitman was more important than Emerson in influencing Wright's thought, though he arrives at this conclusion because he finds both Whitman and Wright muddled and sloppy in their intellectual reasoning; he apparently believes Emerson to have been a much more rigorous thinker. Anyone who knows Emerson well will probably find this a curious description of so mystical, protean, and shape-shifting a philosopher. Gill, *Many Masks*, p. 339. Vincent Scully also emphasizes the poet's influence; see Vincent Scully, Jr., *Frank Lloyd Wright* (New York: Braziller, 1960), p. 12.

34. Barney, *Valley of the God-Almighty Joneses*, pp. 59–60.

35. Gill, *Many Masks*, p. 39; Secrest, *A Biography*, p. 225.

36. Emerson, "Self-Reliance," *Essays and Lectures*, p. 259.

37. Meehan, *Master Architect*, p. 55.

38. Emerson, "Self-Reliance," *Essays and Lectures*, p. 261.

39. Emerson, "An Address," *Essays and Lectures*, p. 89.

40. Emerson, "Self-Reliance," *Essays and Lectures*, p. 263.

41. Pfeiffer, *His Living Voice*, p. 203.

42. Gill, *Many Masks*, p. 22.

43. Emerson, "Nature," *Essays and Lectures*, p. 20.

44. Ibid., p. 18.

45. Ibid., pp. 18–19.

46. Ibid., p. 19.

47. Ibid. The Unitarian basis for these Emersonian ideas, and hence their links to the principles Wright imbibed from the Lloyd Jones family religion, can be clearly seen in the following passage: "Each creature is only a modification of the other; the likeness in them is more than the difference, and their radical law is one and the same. A rule of one art, or a law of one organization, holds true throughout nature. So intimate is this Unity, that, it is easily seen, it lies under the undermost garment of Nature, and betrays its source in Universal Spirit. For it pervades Thought also. Every universal truth which we express in words, implies or supposes every other truth. *Omne verum vero consonat.* It is like a great circle on a sphere, comprising all possible circles; which, however, may be drawn and comprise it in like manner. Every such truth is the absolute Ens [Absolute Being] seen from one side. But it has innumerable sides." Ibid., p. 30.

48. Wright, *Autobiography*, p. 16.

49. Ibid., p. 89. The year before he died, Wright was still saying much the same thing: "We use the word 'nature' in a very careless way. Nature to us is the cows in the fields and the winds and the bees and the trees, unfortunately. But the theory of nature goes deep into the character of whatever it is. What is the nature of this thumb of mine—or anything else you want to

take to investigate—what is the nature of it? There lies the very essence of its character; the very essence of that thing, which by study, you come to know." Meehan, *Master Architect*, p. 234.

50. Emerson, "Nature," *Essays and Lectures*, p. 48.

51. Carl Sandburg once chided Wright for using words such as *beauty*, *truth*, and *ideal*, which made his prose so abstract and difficult to follow, arguing that Wright would be more readily understood if he would get "down to brass tacks and talk about barns and nails and barn doors." Wright's reply was revealingly Emersonian: "Those words—romance, poetry, beauty, truth, ideal—are not precious words nor should they be *specious* words. They are elemental human symbols and we must be brought back again to respect them by using them significantly if we use them at all, or go to jail." Frank Lloyd Wright, "In the Cause of Architecture, IX: The Terms," *Architectural Record* 64 (December 1928); reprinted in Pfeiffer, *Collected Writings*, vol. I, p. 310.

52. Emerson, "Nature," *Lectures and Essays*, p. 16.

53. Pfeiffer, *His Living Voice*, p. 68.

54. Frank Lloyd Wright, "A Philosophy of Fine Art" (1900), in Pfeiffer, *Collected Writings*, vol. I, p. 39.

55. Ibid., p. 41.

56. Cited in Meehan, *Master Architect*, p. 216. See also Wright, *Autobiography*, pp. 14–15.

57. The early work on this subject is by Grant Carpenter Manson: "Wright in the Nursery: The Influence of Froebel Education on the Work of Frank Lloyd Wright," *Architectural Review* 113 (June 1953), pp. 349–51; and idem, *Frank Lloyd Wright to 1910: The First Golden Age* (New York: Van Nostrand Reinhold, 1958), pp. 5–10. It has been discussed more recently in greater detail in R. C. MacCormac, "Froebel's Kindergarten Gifts and the Early Work of Frank Lloyd Wright," *Environment and Planning* B, no. I (1974), pp. 29–50; and idem, "Form and Philosophy: Froebel's Kindergarten Training and the Early Work of Frank Lloyd Wright," in Robert McCarter, ed., *Frank Lloyd Wright: A Primer on Architectural Principles* (New York: Princeton Architectural Press, 1991), pp. 99–123. See also Jeanne S. Rubin, "The Froebel-Wright Kindergarten Connection: A New Perspective," *Journal of the Society of Architectural Historians* 48 (March 1989), pp. 24–37, and letters responding to same, ibid. (December 1989), pp. 413–17. Manson and McCarter are usefully criticized in Edgar Kaufmann, Jr., "'*Form* Became *Feeling*,' A New View of Froebel and Wright," in Kaufmann, *9 Commentaries on Frank Lloyd Wright* (New York: Architectural History Foundation, 1989), pp. 1–6. The link between Froebel's system and Wright's architecture was discussed as early as 1900: see Robert C. Spencer, Jr., "The Work of Frank Lloyd Wright," *Architectural Review* 7 (June 1900), pp. 61–72; reprinted in H. Allen Brooks, ed., *Writings on Wright: Selected Comment on Frank Lloyd Wright* (Cambridge, Mass.: MIT Press, 1981), pp. 105–10.

58. Meehan, *Master Architect*, p. 217.

59. Pfeiffer, *His Living Voice*, p. 32.

60. Despite problems with his historical argumentation, Edgar Kaufmann, Jr. is right to stress this point in his "*Form* Became *Feeling*."

61. Friedrich Froebel, *The Education of Man*, trans. W. N. Hailmann (New York: D. Appleton, 1899), p. 169.

62. Frank Lloyd Wright, *The Japanese Print: An Interpretation* (Chicago: Ralph Fletcher Seymour, 1912); reprinted in Pfeiffer, *Collected Writings*, vol. I, p. 117.

63. Froebel, *Education of Man*, pp. 1–2.

64. Maria Kraus-Boelte and John Kraus, *The Kindergarten Guide, Vol. I: The Gifts* (New York: E. Steiger, 1877), p. 37. It seems likely that this book may best reflect the particular methods that Anna Wright followed in performing Froebelian exercises with her son. See Manson, *Wright to 1910*, p. 5.

65. W. N. Hailmann, *Law of Childhood, and Other Papers* (Chicago: Alice B. Stockham, 1889), p. 43.

66. Ibid., p. 42; italics in original. That Frank Lloyd Wright

fully understood this idealist goal of Froebel's system is suggested by his description of it in the very last interview he ever gave, just six days before he died: "All teachers," he declared, "should study and learn Plato, and then take it on to the children. A child should begin to work with materials just as soon as he is able to hold a ball. By holding a ball, a child gets a sense of the universe and there is a closeness to God. The ball or sphere leads the child to other geometric shapes: the cone, the triangle, the cylinder. Now he is on the threshold of nature herself. . . . A new world is opened to him." Cited in Meehan, *Master Architect*, p. 313.

67. Pfeiffer, *His Living Voice*, p. 32.

68. Wright, *Autobiography*, p. 14.

69. The most thorough discussion of Wright's decorative style is by David A. Hanks, *The Decorative Designs of Frank Lloyd Wright* (New York: Dutton, 1979). Less analytical, but lavishly illustrated, is Carla Lind, *The Wright Style: Re-creating the Spirit of Frank Lloyd Wright* (New York: Simon & Schuster, 1992).

70. References to Ruskin are relatively few in Wright's work—more often than not, Wright linked him with William Morris as a representative of the Arts and Crafts ambivalence about the machine—so that it is hard to judge how direct the English critic's influence on the young architect may have been. Wright may have been covering his tracks in this case, or he may have been exposed to Ruskinian ideas indirectly, for instance, in the writings of Viollet-le-Duc, which we know he read closely. My own inclination is to suspect that Wright read some of Ruskin's work and acquired some of it indirectly, but that it was so much of a piece with so many other idealist sources one detects in Wright's work that general osmosis may be as likely an explanation as any.

71. John Ruskin, *The Seven Lamps of Architecture* (2nd ed., 1880; reprint ed., New York: Dover, 1989), p. 105.

72. Ibid., p. 124.

73. John Ruskin, *Modern Painters*, vol. I (1843), quoted in Robert L. Herbert, ed., *The Art Criticism of John Ruskin* (Garden City, N.Y.: Doubleday, 1964), pp. 10–11.

74. Ruskin, *Seven Lamps of Architecture*, p. 31.

75. Wright, *Autobiography*, p. 75; cf. John Lloyd Wright, *My Father*, p. 69, which also includes a long extract from Viollet-le-Duc's *Discourses on Architecture*.

76. See, for instance, M. F. Hearn, ed., *The Architectural Theory of Viollet-le-Duc: Readings and Commentary* (Cambridge, Mass.: MIT Press, 1990), p. 187. For Ruskin's belief that cast iron and any machine-made ornament represented "deceits," see Ruskin, *Seven Lamps of Architecture*, p. 35.

77. Eugène-Emmanuel Viollet-le-Duc, *The Foundations of Architecture: Selections from the Dictionnaire raisonné* (1854), trans. Kenneth D. Whitehead (New York: Braziller, 1990), p. 233; italics in original.

78. Ibid., p. 235.

79. "Crystals are proof of nature's architectural principle." Frank Lloyd Wright, "In the Cause of Architecture III: The Meaning of Materials—Stone" (1928); reprinted in Pfeiffer, *Collected Writings*, vol. I, p. 270; this passage was omitted from the original *Architectural Record* article.

80. Hearn, *Architectural Theory of Viollet-le-Duc*, p. 229.

81. Wright, *Autobiography*, p. 75.

82. Owen Jones, *The Grammar of Ornament* (1856; reprint ed., London: B. Quaritch, 1910), p. 5.

83. Ibid.

84. Wright, "A Philosophy of Fine Art" in Pfeiffer, *Collected Writings*, vol. I, pp. 39–44. The *Oxford English Dictionary* attributes the first occurrence of the verb "conventionalize" to John Ruskin in 1854.

85. Ibid., p. 43. In this passage, Wright was echoing Owen Jones's thirteenth proposition: "Flowers or other natural objects should not be used as ornaments, but conventional representations founded upon them sufficiently suggestive to convey the

intended image to the mind, without destroying the unity of the object they are employed to decorate." Jones, *Grammar of Ornament*, p. 6.

86. Wright, "A Philosophy of Fine Art," in Pfeiffer, *Collected Writings*, vol. I, p. 43.

87. Frank Lloyd Wright, "Architect, Architecture, and the Client" (1896), in Pfeiffer, *Collected Writings*, vol. I, p. 31.

88. One of the most suggestive analyses of these devices is by Grant Hildebrand, *The Wright Space: Pattern and Meaning in Frank Lloyd Wright's Houses* (Seattle: University of Washington Press, 1991). The literature here is enormous: other important works surveying these very general Wrightian themes include Henry-Russell Hitchcock, *In the Nature of Materials: The Buildings of Frank Lloyd Wright, 1887–1941* (1942; reprint ed., New York: DaCapo, 1973); Manson, *Wright to 1910*; Scully, *Frank Lloyd Wright*; H. Allen Brooks, *The Prairie School: Frank Lloyd Wright and His Midwest Contemporaries* (Toronto and Buffalo: University of Toronto Press, 1972); John Sergeant, *Frank Lloyd Wright's Usonian Houses: The Case for Organic Architecture* (New York: Whitney Library of Design, 1976); McCarter, *A Primer on Architectural Principles*; and Paul Laseau and James Tice, *Frank Lloyd Wright: Between Principle and Form* (New York: Van Nostrand Reinhold, 1992).

89. An ahistorical but provocative Jungian reading of this subject is given by Thomas H. Beeby, "Wright and Landscape: A Mythical Interpretation," in Carol R. Bolon, Robert S. Nelson, and Linda Seidel, eds., *The Nature of Frank Lloyd Wright* (Chicago: University of Chicago Press, 1988), pp. 154–72. A more historicized interpretation is that of Jonathan Lipman, "The Architecture of Arcadia," in *The Wright State: Frank Lloyd Wright in Wisconsin* (Milwaukee: Milwaukee Art Museum, 1992), pp. 11–31. Wright's biographers emphasize his relationship to the Wisconsin landscape as well.

90. Wright, *Autobiography*, p. 26.

91. Ibid., p. 27.

92. Ibid., p. 40.

93. Gill, *Many Masks*, p. 48.

94. Wisconsin limestones have a high magnesium content and are technically known as dolomites; in the text I use the more familiar, generic term.

95. Wright, "Meaning of Materials—Stone," in Pfeiffer, *Collected Writings*, vol. I, p. 275.

96. Ibid., p. 274.

97. For illustrations of the effect and of the original appearance of the sandstone, see Edgar Kaufmann, Jr., *Fallingwater: A Frank Lloyd Wright Country House* (New York: Abbeville Press, 1986), esp. pp. 29, 31, 36–45, 58, 76–77. Wright explicitly compared Fallingwater with Taliesin in his interview with Hugh Downs (see Meehan, *Master Architect*, p. 37), and Donald Hoffmann, writing of Fallingwater, was so taken by the similar stonework of the two buildings that he mistakenly assumed Taliesin's masonry to be sandstone. See Donald Hoffmann, *Frank Lloyd Wright's Fallingwater: The House and Its History* (New York: Dover, 1978), p. 18.

98. The Heurtley House (1902) is a particularly striking example of this effect, which is very common in Wright's brick buildings.

99. Meehan, *Master Architect*, p. 44.

100. W. H. Auden, "In Praise of Limestone," *Selected Poetry of W. H. Auden* (New York: Modern Library, 1959), pp. 114–17.

101. Ibid.

102. Ibid., p. 115.

103. A polemical and now quite dated reading of Wright's antiurbanism can be found in Morton and Lucia White, *The Intellectual Versus the City: From Thomas Jefferson to Frank Lloyd Wright* (Cambridge, Mass.: Harvard University Press and MIT Press, 1962), pp. 189–208. A more balanced view can be found in Robert Fishman, *Urban Utopias in the Twentieth Century: Ebenezer Howard, Frank Lloyd Wright, Le Corbusier* (New York: Basic Books, 1977), pp. 89–160.

104. Taliesin achieves privacy despite the openness of its plan and fenestration by its height and distance from prying neighbors; Fallingwater, which is perhaps the least private of Wright's houses, relies on its remote site to perform the same service.

105. On the landscape of Taliesin, see Walter L. Creese, *The Crowning of the American Landscape: Eight Great Spaces and Their Buildings* (Princeton: Princeton University Press, 1985), pp. 241–78.

106. Wright, *Natural House*, p. 134.

107. Ibid., p. 135.

108. Henry Blake Fuller, *With the Procession* (1895; reprint ed., Chicago: University of Chicago Press, 1965).

109. Wright, *Autobiography*, 561; Louis Sullivan, *The Autobiography of an Idea* (1924; reprint ed., New York: Dover, 1956).

110. Gannett, *The House Beautiful*. In the first and last of these excerpts Gannett is quoting another author, but I have been unable to determine the original source. Wright was still quoting Gannett as late as the 1950s, when he prominently displayed a passage from *The House Beautiful* in the auditorium of the Unitarian Church in Madison.

111. Ibid.

112. The best essay on Chicago's Arts and Crafts community is by Richard Guy Wilson, "Chicago and the International Arts and Crafts Movements: Progressive and Conservative Tendencies," in John Zukowsky, ed., *Chicago Architecture, 1872–1922: Birth of a Metropolis* (Munich: Prestel-Verlag, 1987), pp. 209–27. See also Nikolaus Pevsner, *Pioneers of Modern Design: From William Morris to Walter Gropius* (London: Penguin, 1936; 1975); Peter Stansky, *Redesigning the World: William Morris, the 1880s, and the Arts and Crafts* (Princeton: Princeton University Press, 1985); Gillian Naylor, *The Arts and Crafts Movement: A Study of Its Sources, Ideals and Influence on Design Theory* (1971; reprint ed., London: Trefoil Publications, 1990); Leslie Greene Bowman, *American Arts and Crafts: Virtue in Design* (Los Angeles: Los Angeles County Museum of Art, 1990); and Elizabeth Cumming and Wendy Kaplan, *The Arts and Crafts Movement* (London: Thames and Hudson, 1991).

113. As its very title suggests, Wright's most famous single essay, "The Art and Craft of the Machine" (1901), is at once a criticism of the Arts and Crafts movement for its hostility to the machine, and a defense of the movement's underlying values. Wright reprinted the essay throughout his career and revised it many times, but the standard version is probably the one printed in Pfeiffer, *Collected Writings*, vol. 1, pp. 58–69.

114. Sullivan's classic account can be found in his *Autobiography of an Idea*, pp. 317ff.

115. Wright, *Autobiography*, pp. 125–28.

116. Grant Carpenter Manson's discussion of the Ho-o-den influence (*Wright to 1910*, pp. 34–41) remains among the best we have, despite his evident discomfiture at the heated denials of his still-living subject. See also Dimitri Tselos, "Exotic Influences in the Architecture of Frank Lloyd Wright," *Magazine of Art* 46 (April 1953), pp. 160–84. Vincent Scully followed Tselos in pointing out the parallels between the Ho-o-den and the Ward W. Willits House (1902–03), which many regard as Wright's first true Prairie style house (Scully, *Frank Lloyd Wright*,

p. 17). At the Susan Lawrence Dana House (1902–04), Wright's debt to Japan seems explicitly acknowledged in his treatment of the roof. For a classic discussion of Japanese domestic architecture itself, see Atsushi Ueda, *The Inner Harmony of the Japanese House* (1974), trans. Iwanami Shoten (Tokyo: Kodansha International, 1990).

117. Pfeiffer, *His Living Voice*, p. 32.

118. Wright, *The Japanese Print*, in Pfeiffer, *Collected Writings*, vol. 1, p. 118.

119. Ibid., p. 119.

120. Ibid.

121. William T. Stead, "My First Visit to America: An Open Letter to My Readers," *Review of Reviews* 9 (1894), pp. 414–15.

122. The word *folly* today carries mainly a negative meaning in English, so that the *Penguin Dictionary of Architecture* defines it as "a costly but useless structure built to satisfy the whim of some eccentric and thought to show his folly; usually a tower or a sham Gothic or classical ruin in a landscaped park intended to enhance the view or picturesque effect." John Fleming, Hugh Honour, and Nikolaus Pevsner, *Penguin Dictionary of Architecture* (Harmondsworth: Penguin Books, 1972), p. 100. Nineteenth-century usage of the word still carried more of the sense that its French cognate, *la folie*, maintains as one of its standard meanings: a structure built solely for pleasure at a villa or rural retreat, intended to express a caprice and serve as the site for romantic rendezvous. In the text, I intend my usage to convey some of this older, more favorable connotation.

123. Terence Riley rightly encouraged me to stress the role of the Exposition in teaching Wright the importance of "model" or "demonstration" buildings as a way of influencing public memory and cultural values.

124. Patricia Talbot Davis, *Together They Built a Mountain* (Lititz, Penn.: Sutter House, 1974), p. 147.

125. Jonathan Lipman, *Frank Lloyd Wright and the Johnson Wax Buildings* (New York: Rizzoli, 1986), p. 169.

126. John Gurda, *New World Odyssey: Annunciation Greek Orthodox Church and Frank Lloyd Wright* (Milwaukee: Milwaukee Hellenic Community, 1986), p. 114.

127. Grant Hildebrand describes these changes well in *The Wright Space*, pp. 15–27; for Wright's own celebration of these innovations, see Wright, *Natural House*, pp. 32–33.

128. James Dennis, "Restoring Jacobs I," lecture delivered in Madison, Wisconsin, September 24, 1992. Sergeant, *Frank Lloyd Wright's Usonian Houses*, pp. 27–30, says that the overall experience of most Usonian owners has been positive, but for some reason fails to mention the roofs. Eugene R. Streich, "An Original-Owner Interview Survey of Frank Lloyd Wright's Residential Architecture" (1972), in Brooks, *Writings on Wright*, pp. 35–45, claims that the thirty-three original owners of Wright buildings he interviewed complained of "very few" leaks.

129. Kaufmann, *Fallingwater*, pp. 49–54; Hoffmann, *Frank Lloyd Wright's Fallingwater*, pp. 41–48, 56–57.

130. Hildebrand, *The Wright Space*, p. 177; on pp. 176–77 Hildebrand supplies a long list of significant deflections in Wright structures.

131. Wright, *Natural House*, p. 150.

132. On heating problems at the first Jacobs House, see Jacobs and Jacobs, *Building with Frank Lloyd Wright*, pp. 54, 59–60.

133. Wright, *Autobiography*, p. 249.

134. Kaufmann, *Fallingwater*, pp. 62–63.

135. Wright, *Natural House*, p. 37.

136. Ibid.

137. Jacobs and Jacobs, *Building with Frank Lloyd Wright*, p. 15.

138. Jack Ramsey to Herbert Johnson, July 19, 1936, as quoted in Lipman, *Johnson Wax Buildings*, p. 12.

139. Ibid., p. 157.

140. Mary Jane Hamilton, *The Meeting House: Heritage and Vision* (Madison: Friends of the Meeting House, 1991), p. 26.

141. See Davis, *Together They Built a Mountain*; and Gurda, *New World Odyssey*.

142. Jacobs and Jacobs, *Building with Frank Lloyd Wright*, p. 17.

143. Ibid., p. 60. The standard explanation for leaks at the Unitarian Church is that the roof is supposedly a thinner gauge of copper than Wright originally intended, and this rationale has been offered for other leaky Wright roofs as well. But an engineering report in 1993 revealed that the roof was built precisely to Wright's specifications, which were well below industry standards of the day.

144. John Lloyd Wright, *My Father*, p. 92.

145. W. E. Martin to D. D. Martin, September 19, 1905, as quoted in Gill, *Many Masks*, p. 159.

146. Jeffrey Chusid, conversation with author, November 9, 1992.

147. Lipman, *Johnson Wax Buildings*, p. 169.

148. Emerson, "Self-Reliance," *Essays and Lectures*, p. 260.

149. Meehan, *Master Architect*, p. 240.

150. Pfeiffer, *His Living Voice*, p. 74.

151. John Lloyd Wright, *My Father*, p. 120.

152. Wright, "The Architect and the Machine," in Pfeiffer, *Collected Writings*, vol. 1, p. 22.

153. Wright, *Natural House*, p. 182.

154. Pfeiffer, *His Living Voice*, p. 31.

155. John Lloyd Wright, *My Father*, p. 121.

156. Wright, *Autobiography*, p. 312.

157. Ibid., p. 31. Wright was here referring not to the fair but to two domed buildings he had known as a student in Madison, both of which he saw destroyed within a few years of each other.

158. Pfeiffer, *His Living Voice*, p. 28.

159. Emerson, "Nature," *Essays and Lectures*, p. 41.

160. Ibid.

161. Frank Lloyd Wright, as quoted in Gill, *Many Masks*, p. 22.

ANTHONY ALOFSIN

FRANK LLOYD WRIGHT AND MODERNISM

Frank Lloyd Wright's architecture spanned a seventy-two-year career that began in the late 1880s and continued until his death in 1959. From the start of his independent practice, in or about 1893, Wright's work went through several phases and focused on such themes as nature, organicism, the midwestern Prairie, modernism, and the search for an American identity through architecture. His designs ranged widely from apartment buildings and single-family houses for middle-class families to elaborate estates for a rich elite. They included commercial and industrial buildings, religious buildings, speculative developments, and entire new community plans. His clients often were independent, enterprising, and freethinking individuals who were willing to gamble on Wright's daring ideas. His design systems utilized basic geometric shapes—squares, circles, and triangles—anchored by grids and proportioned according to the materials and methods of construction that constituted his buildings. He related the meaning of his work to the order of nature, believing that the correlation of physical form to nature would elevate the spiritual condition of humankind. His buildings and designs were metaphors for technology, nature, and democracy. And all his work occurred in relation to the evolution of modernism, although at times he vehemently denied it.

Wright barely acknowledged modernism as the major cultural phenomenon of his lifetime. Reducing an artistic interest in simplification to sources in the Japanese wood-block print, he stated: "The gospel of elimination preached by the print came home to me in architecture as it came home to the French painters who developed 'Cubisme' and 'Futurisme.' Intrinsically it lies at the bottom of all this so-called 'modernisme.'"[1] But the modernism that Wright dismissed provided the cultural context for his career. The complex phenomenon of modernism encompassed literature, the visual arts, music, and politics, and its preoccupations ranged widely to include perceptions of space, time, myth, parody, the quest for originality, the role of the outcast, attacks on religion, the subversive function of language, and the effects of fragmentation. Despite this diversity of attitudes and even contradictions, there appear to be some fundamental interests common to modernism in all the arts, namely functionalism, abstraction—a new language of form—and a social program.[2]

In pursuing functionalism—the concept that there is a rational relationship between the form of an object and its purpose—Wright identified form and function as one and the same. This implied that building structure, materials, and method of construction melded together to create an organic whole suited to human needs. Like other modernists he rejected realism for abstraction—creating a distinctive

formal language. When we look at the totality of his oeuvre, we see in his form language a remarkable coherence, continuity, and recurrence of motifs. Although ornament can be abstract, many modern architects not only rejected abstract form for a new language of ornament but also repudiated the concept of ornament itself. Wright's abstract form language made him different from most other modernists: instead of eliminating ornament, he celebrated it.

Despite his claims of being influenced only by Japanese wood-block prints and his mentor Louis Henri Sullivan, he constantly absorbed, transformed, and reacted against the contemporary world around him in America and Europe. The political and social motivations for his work were rooted in a distinct belief in defining a democratic America. For Wright, as for European modernists, architecture was a tool for social reform.

Thus, two running dialogues—one articulated visually, the other ideologically—occurred simultaneously throughout his career. One was situated within his work and among his own designs; the other took place between his work and the culture outside it. Discussed together, they provide a path for exploring what made Wright modern as well as a means for understanding modernism itself.

ORGANIC ARCHITECTURE

In the latter half of the nineteenth century the effort to create a modern architecture began to coalesce from disparate ideas centered on the machine and the role of architecture in society. In America these efforts were identified with the development of the skyscraper, especially in Chicago, which provided the immediate context for Wright's early architectural formation. Bound into the technological development of tall buildings was the hope that a new modern architecture would also represent an American identity and set of values distinct from those of European modernism.[3]

Wright was a key player in the development of modern architecture yet constantly at odds with it. He shared the goals of many other modernists, yet his work was often very different. In order to assess what constituted this difference and what made his work modern we must first examine Wright's concept of organic architecture. For Wright true modern architecture and organic architecture were synonymous. His concept of organic architecture evolved from a set of architectural principles in the 1890s into a lifestyle by the 1930s. The best synoptic statement of his early ideological position is found in his essay "In the Cause of Architecture," which he claimed to have written in 1894, although he first published it in *Architectural Record* in 1908.[4]

Wright formulated six major design principles in defining organic architecture. The first was that simplicity and repose should be the measures of art. Achieving these qualities required the elimination of all that is unnecessary, including interior walls. Consequently, he wrote, a building should have as few rooms as possible; openings should be integrated into the structure and form (becoming a kind of "natural ornamentation"); detail and decoration should be reduced; and appliances, fixtures, pictures, and furniture should be integrated into the structure.

Wright's second principle called for as many different styles of houses as there were styles of people. This allowed the expression of the client's individuality (albeit through designs that were recognizably Wright's). Having multiple styles also obviated the perennial question of historical styles, which had preoccupied architects throughout the nineteenth century. At the start of the twentieth century and thereafter the question was moot. The answer—to build in a modern style—caused the debate to shift from the selection of a style to what architecture itself should represent: the collective values of society or the values of an individual artist.

The third principle correlated nature, topography, and architecture. Wright said: "A building should appear to grow easily from its site and be shaped to harmonize with its surroundings."[5] His designs for the rolling and gentle hills of the Midwest were characterized by low, sloping roofs, sheltering overhangs, and terraces. If a building had no natural features to draw upon, he believed it should be as unobtrusive as possible.

Wright's fourth principle called for taking the colors of buildings from nature and adapting them to fit harmoniously with the materials of buildings. Wright applied the term *conventionalization*, a method of abstracting form to its essentials, to color and to plant forms as sources of design motifs.[6]

The fifth principle called for expressing "the nature of materials." Wood should look like wood, showing its grain and natural color, with the same verity applying to brick, stone, and plaster. Wright considered these materials inherently "friendly and beautiful." Implicit in the concept of the nature of materials was the idea of structure. An honest modern architecture would express the structural system of its buildings: load and support could be read from a building.

Wright's sixth principle called for spiritual integrity in architecture. He believed buildings should have qualities analogous to the human qualities of sincerity, truth, and graciousness. Reflecting ideas current in the Arts and Crafts movement, Wright unabashedly stated that buildings should be lovable and bring joy to people. These traits in architecture would produce, over time, a far more important value than the expression of a style in fashion. Wright maintained that integrity of human values and architecture could only be achieved by the use of the machine, "the normal tool of our civilization," for which new "industrial ideals" would be required.[7]

Wright's organic principles provide the fundamental links between him and other modern architects. They establish the basic tenets of his architecture: functionalism, technology, metaphysics, social purpose, and an evolving language of architectural forms.

Wright's principles for an organic architecture were not static; they shifted, sometimes subtly, during his career, and to speak of them precisely we must tie them down in time.[8] By 1909 they had provided verbal formulations of some of Wright's great contributions to architecture: open interior planning; emphasis on the horizontal; masterful play of plastic compositions; integration of structure, material, and site into a symbolic representation of dwelling; a new sense of space; and the celebration of the freedom of the individual and new social patterns. The Larkin Company Administration Building (plates 65–73), Unity Temple (plates 74–82), the Ward W. Willits House (plates 46–48), the Susan Lawrence Dana House (plates 34–41), the Avery Coonley House (plates 87–95), and the Frederick C. Robie House (plates 100–106)—all built in the first decade of the century in America—became standard-bearers in the history of modern architecture.

BEFORE 1900

In Wright's architecture of the late nineteenth century we see certain tendencies of modern architecture at a time when some of his contemporaries employed the latest technology in revivals of classical architectural styles. His call for a break with the past and his rejection of revivalism had been stimulated by the functionalism of the Chicago school, led by Louis Sullivan in the 1880s. Sullivan and his followers searched for a rational architecture that expressed the purpose of a building while retaining some elements of classical organization. Its focus was the tall building, and American technological developments in skyscrapers were seen internationally as a distinct modern development.

Agreeing with Sullivan, Wright denigrated the World's Columbian Exposition in Chicago of 1893 as having drastically set back American architecture and blamed this regression on the teachings of the Ecole des Beaux-Arts, which reinforced the revival of classicism against the pursuit of functionalism and the skyscraper. Just as Sullivan had replied to the classical onslaught with the stunning design of the Transportation Building at the Exposition, he made the 1893–94 William H. Winslow House in River Forest, Illinois (plates 9–13), his own statement about the direction needed for an American architecture. It was his first independent commission, and already included the formal elements that would characterize his mature early work: a tendency toward simplification, increased interior openness, a base that connected the house to the earth, a central zone on the facade behind which were the elaborate entry and living room, and a broad, sheltering roof with wide overhang. It showed that he wanted his buildings to symbolize ideas and social values rather than mere technology. Even at this early date he foresaw that modern principles of design had the potential of creating exciting and dramatic spaces, particularly inside buildings. The symmetry of the front facade expressed the house's identity as a home and created a sense of repose, while the large windows communicated a sense of openness within. The rear exterior expressed a different purpose: it deviated from symmetry and took on a varied expression, with the mass of the house breaking into parts that corresponded to the functions they contained, including a porch, conservatory, and kitchen.

Nevertheless, whether by his own choice or in response to pressures from his clients, in the late 1880s and throughout the 1890s Wright did experiment with abstract and simplified versions of historical styles in designs for Chicago, Oak Park, and the surrounding communities. The James Charnley House, designed in 1891–92 while he was employed by Adler and Sullivan, was a successful attempt to reduce the morphology of the Renaissance villa to simplified masses (plate 8). The George Blossom House of the following year reworked the fashionable colonial revival style. The 1893 residence for Walter Gale in Oak Park explored the Queen Anne style. The first Hillside Home School of 1887 for Wright's aunts near Spring Green, Wisconsin, and his own house in Oak Park of 1889–90 (plates 5–7, 21–26) demonstrated his grasp of the Shingle style. He used a spare neo-Gothic for the Robert Roloson Apartments (1894), a Tudor idiom for the Nathan Moore House (1895), and mastered the grand classical gesture in his 1893 project for the Milwaukee Library and Museum.

But the turning away from historical styles was an international phenomenon of the new machine age, and the Arts and Crafts movement provided the first links among modern developments in America, Great Britain, and the Continent. Wright and his contemporaries shared the motivations of the Arts and Crafts movement, but they had different ideas about the role of the machine. Embodying technology as a whole, the British Arts and Crafts adherents, led by William Morris, saw the machine as a dehumanizing factor in modern life, whereas Wright saw the machine as an ally and a quintessential tool for the expression of democracy precisely because it could liberate individuals from the drudgery of repetitive labor.[9]

With a fiery intensity inherited from a family of radical preachers Wright proclaimed the arrival of the machine age. The tall office building was a perfect task for machine technology. He pointed to the steel frame that allowed buildings to express their purpose without pretense. He maintained that Morris's followers were working with outmoded ideas and did not fully understand the call for simplicity: until they grasped the nature of the machine and found an appropriate vocabulary for expressing it, they should work as social reformers and not as architects.[10]

Wright regarded the machine not as an object, but as a metaphor for the age and for processes of production. This allowed him to explore modern materials—concrete and steel, glass, and, later, plastics—but to avoid making buildings that resembled machines. At the end of the nineteenth century, machine production featured mill work that seemed to Wright to be most rational when it was simple, with square and rectangular sections that minimized waste. Its gang saws produced thin slabs of stone that could be put together in a variety of patterns and eliminated the imprisoning of stone in solid blocks. The casting of metal—another machine process—could produce forms that were suitable expressions of their production processes, not imitations of wood forms cast in metal. Although the same milling techniques could produce turned and circular objects, Wright preferred rectilinear shapes for the principal vocabulary of his architecture at this time.

For Wright the machine was integral to the social role of architecture; this view linked him to other modernists. His program was that of a reformer, but he did not believe that the material improvement of society was enough. He believed that architecture should assist in the spiritual rejuvenation of people, and this in turn made him sympathetic to another emerging modernist tendency: a belief in the rejuvenating power of non-Western art. Like other artists Wright recognized that much could be learned from people of other cultures, particularly China and Japan. These exotic cultures, along with many primitivist sources, were considered unsullied by Western materialism. Increasingly, "primitivist" architecture was associated with folk art, nativism, and simplicity but often implied an exotic aspect. Exotic architecture differed from that which referred to primitive sources by its connotations of complexity and foreignness—a fascinating otherness. Emulating exotic and primitive architecture provided many modernists a way of rejecting decadent Western values and replacing them with values that seemed simple and pure. Wright himself made little distinction between the exotic and the primitive, and generally used the word *primitive* in his writings even when he alluded to exotic sources. This lack of distinction also reflected his belief in a universality of forms common to all older cultures, and in their "unerring" appreciation of beauty. The "Renaissance-of-the-Primitive," as Wright later called it, provided an antidote to historicism in art.[11] Japanese art had provided a paragon of non-Western taste, which had stimulated European artists in Paris and Vienna since the reopening of Japan in the 1860s. Starting as a collector and aficionado, Wright became a leading American dealer in Japanese prints. His Japanism formed an aspect of an interest in the exotic that was latent in his early designs and found more literal expression in his work of the first two decades of the new century.

The broad appeal of Japanism lay in the purity of its aesthetic. Its simplicity, bold flat areas of color, and repetitive patterns spoke simultaneously of nature and abstraction. While Wright probably saw the Japanese pavilions, the Japanese bazaar, and the Ho-o-den at the World's Columbian Exposition, he attempted to avoid any literal expression or imitation of Japanese architecture. Though his buildings would have similarities to Japanese architecture, Wright's interest in Japanism was always subject to abstraction and to experimental analysis.

WRIGHT'S SYNTHESIS: 1900 TO 1909

At the turn of the century Wright synthesized his vision of the machine age into an architecture that focused on the conceptual integration of plan, section, and detail into a plastic space defined by an ideology. It pushed forward into axioms the use of the free plan with its spatial continuity, the expression of the inherent qualities of materials, and the integration of buildings with their sites. Through an abstraction that came from his amalgamation of Japanese aesthetics and the existing domestic vernacular, including details of Tudor and Arts and Crafts styles, he produced a simplicity that denied the validity of late Victorian architecture in America and launched a revolution in domestic design. The impact of this triumph was not to be recognized in America for decades. Nevertheless, Wright's efforts produced the great houses of the Prairie period in Oak Park and nearby communities: the Ward W. Willits (Highland Park, 1902–03), B. Harley Bradley (Kankakee, 1900), Warren Hickox (Kankakee, 1900), William Fricke (Oak Park, 1900), E. B. Henderson (Elmhurst, 1901), Frank Thomas (Oak Park, 1901), and Arthur Heurtley (Oak Park, 1902) houses (see plates 44–48). They ranged in materials from brick to stucco with more modest designs for rustic settings executed in board-and-batten. While several were similar in plan and organization, they varied in the types of roofs that covered them. Pitched, gabled, or flat-roofed, they tended to focus on the hearth as the physical and symbolic center of domestic life.

In subsequent commissions for single-family houses for upwardly mobile clients—the Susan Lawrence Dana House in Springfield, Illinois, of 1902–04 (plates 34–41); the Darwin D. Martin House in Buffalo, New York, of 1902–04 (plates 55–59); the William R. Heath House in Buffalo of 1905; the F. F. Tomek House in Riverside, Illinois, of 1907; and the Avery Coonley House in Riverside of 1906–08 (plates 87–95)—Wright was able to continue to explore the integration of building fabric, structure, and ornament into total designs of rich spatial complexity. These houses balanced the themes of his prescription for organic architecture, combining his interests in functionalism, technology, spatial development, creation of a modern form language, and metaphysical experience. These homes were the *built* manifestation of his reformist social program for the betterment of a growing middle class. The processes of abstraction explored in these works inevitably led him to develop the modern form language that governed everything from the mass of his buildings to their ornament.

Wright developed a family of styles that bore little resemblance to the individual styles of other modern architects. He often described his own architecture by roof types, but his work can be organized as well by plan types and dominant materials.[12] His form language can also be broken down into families of motifs—most notably by examples of his ornament. Identifying this form language as we examine his architecture helps us to see the continuities in his work and to go beyond simply calling everything he designed "organic architecture."

While Wright initially defined his architecture in domestic projects, he first explored his ideas in major civic, commercial, and religious architecture during the first decade of the twentieth century. The Larkin Company Administration Building, completed in Buffalo in 1906 (plates 65–73), became one of the most important representations of modernism in Wright's career. It was the first great machine of Wright's new organic architecture, embodying principles of functionalism with its client's moralistic program extolling the virtues of industrious labor.[13] Its shafts were conduits for "conditioned" air and contained fire stairs, while its balconies were devoted to well-lit clerical

work areas. The central shaft of space with its clerestory lighting became a design strategy that Wright used shortly thereafter at Unity Temple in Oak Park (1905–08), and later at the Solomon R. Guggenheim Museum in New York (1943–59).[14]

The Larkin Building served as the administrative headquarters for an immense mail-order business that sent soap and other household products throughout America. The growing company's new building housed its executive and support facilities adjacent to its manufacturing plant. Although initial reception in America was hostile, the building was one of the most progressive buildings of the time in this country and in Europe.[15] The building's function radiated from the simplicity of its massing, the centrality of the great space of the Light Court, or atrium, and the correlation of space, circulation, and amenities for its workers to the business functions of commerce. In his use of specially designed furniture Wright created the first work stations. Acknowledging the needs of the building's workers, he provided social spaces for employees. And all was set in a moralizing atmosphere of wall slogans celebrating the value of the work ethic.

Unity Temple (plates 74–82) demonstrated the modernist belief in technology through its expression of the nature of its material: concrete.[16] It paralleled developments in France by Auguste Perret and Tony Garnier, and although there were other buildings of concrete in America, Unity Temple was the first major building to synthesize its technology, function, and meaning so effectively. Although intended for a congregation of four hundred Unitarians, the design had to accommodate a meager budget. Wright divided the activities of the congregation in half, with the church consisting of Unity Temple for worship—square in plan—and Unity House, a parish house with a Greek-cross plan. Reinforced concrete was chosen as the material, and the building was erected by the contractor Paul F. P. Mueller. The result was a monument to the unity of form and purpose, fused in a new physical expression that had no contemporary counterpart.

Unity Temple demonstrated one of the more significant principles of modern architecture: that the space within a building is its primary reality. In contrast to the simple abstract space of the great central hall of the Larkin Building, Wright here broke the rigid separation of wall and ceiling planes to create a complex space by means of a deeply coffered ceiling and continuous planar surfaces whose restless movement was countered by a network of linear trim. Space was woven into both vertical and horizontal dimensions, resulting in what Wright termed "plasticity."[17]

To these early modernist icons must be added Wright's Yahara Boathouse project of 1905 for Madison, Wisconsin, and the Frederick C. Robie House in Chicago of 1908–10 (plates 83, 100–106). As the history of modern architecture has been written to date, they have assumed a special status as precursors of the abstract and functionalist architecture that defined the modern movement. Described as years ahead of their time, they have been said to have had a particular influence on European modernists.[18]

The Robie House owes the beginning of its fame to its recognition by Europeans as *Dampfer*, or steamship, architecture.[19] Wright gave it

Figure 1: Frank Lloyd Wright. Larkin Company Administration Building, Buffalo. 1902–06. Perspective (detail); print on paper. The Frank Lloyd Wright Foundation. As published in *Ausgeführte Bauten und Entwürfe von Frank Lloyd Wright*, 1910

no special importance when he published it in 1910–11, but to Europeans it was a startling image of sliding parallel horizontal masses hugging the ground. Designed for an inventor who made bicycle parts, the house had integrated mechanical and electrical systems, responded to its local climate, and provided extraordinary privacy for its setting on a cramped urban block. Like the slick and efficient steamship, it was a symbol of the machine age. Both it and the Yahara Boathouse were steps along the path of abstraction that Wright had launched around 1900. The Yahara project was a minor pause, the Robie House more of a climax than Wright knew when he sailed for Europe in October 1909, leaving the completion of the details, including furnishings, to others.

THE MODERNISM OF THE "PRIMITIVE": 1910 TO 1922

Even if Wright's career had ended in 1909 he still would be considered the first eminent American modernist. But it did not end, despite a fundamental rupture that occurred in his personal life. Around 1905 he had fallen in love with Mamah Borthwick Cheney, who along with her husband, Edwin, had been Wright's client and friend. By 1909 Wright had decided to leave his wife, Catherine, and six children and travel with Mamah Cheney to Europe; there he planned to produce two synoptic publications of his work. *Ausgeführte Bauten und Entwürfe von Frank Lloyd Wright* and *Frank Lloyd Wright: Ausgeführte Bauten*, published in Berlin in 1910–11 by Ernst Wasmuth, have traditionally been said to have had an immediate influence on modern architects in Europe, especially in Germany (figure 1).[20] However, the history of their influence is far more complex than published accounts indicate. Wright had intended the publications to be primers for a democratic American architecture, and their impact in Europe was

incidental to his intentions. Most important in spreading news of Wright's work were the Dutch architects, notably Hendrik Petrus Berlage, the leading modernist in the Netherlands, who had actually visited Wright's buildings.[21] Historians have repeated accounts of Wright's immediate impact on Dutch and German architecture, but he was in fact more affected by Austrian Secessionist developments during his trip abroad than the Europeans were by his work.[22] Having seen the great monuments of Western architecture, Wright was especially stimulated by his encounter with the work of the Secessionists, particularly in Vienna, to start exploring archetypal motifs of non-Western cultures. Japanism, an interest that Wright and the Secessionists shared, led to an interest in Mayan, African, Oceanic, and folk traditions, as well as an interest in Egypt and the Near East. These investigations opened the primitivist phase of his work.

Wright described, some years after the fact, how he encountered Secession art and how he saw his work and Sullivan's as the only parallels to it in America: "I came upon the Secession during the winter of 1910. At that time Herr Professor Wagner of Vienna, a great architect, the architect Olbrich of Darmstadt, the remarkable painter Klimt of Austria and the sculptor Metzner of Berlin—great artists all—were the soul of that movement. And there was the work of Louis Sullivan and of myself in America."[23] In 1911 Wright compared himself to the recently deceased Joseph Maria Olbrich, the former star of the Vienna Secession. He also acknowledged the German sculptor Franz Metzner, who sought an abstraction of the human figure—the "conventionalization" of the flesh—just as he did; Metzner's sculpture (and that of his student Emilie Simandl) became a model for Wright's sculpture at Midway Gardens in Chicago of 1913–14 (plates 133–144). His relationship to the Secession in Europe was remarked on by Harriet Monroe, editor of *Poetry* magazine, who called Wright America's leading Secessionist.[24]

Upon his return to America in 1910 Wright began a new search for a modern language of form, pursuing architectural directions that Europeans had begun to turn from but which no one in America recognized. Precisely at the time when the use of ornament had begun to come under attack and Secession architects began to turn to their classical roots as a means of finding continuity between new and old, Wright concentrated on expanding ornament with primitivist and exotic references and further exploring the internal logic of pure geometry. Like many other Chicago architects, Wright had known Secession designs from architectural periodicals, but only after his contact with them did his ornament receive such intense treatment. He had long used the simple forms of the circle, triangle, and square as units of composition, as had Sullivan, but they tended to be derived from the abstraction, or "conventionalization," of plant forms. In his primitivist phase he abstracted the human figure and developed more purely nonrepresentational forms, as if he were probing beneath the forms of nature to explore pure structure itself. Many of these motifs, such as frets, keys, scrolls, and squares within squares, were found nearly universally; the forms persisted while their symbolic meanings differed. Furthermore, his new ornament differed from that of earlier work: it covered more surface area and was more densely composed. Wright believed that by returning to archetypes in nature, he would avoid the pitfalls of historical imitation and allow the indigenous character to emerge. To Wright this was a way for architecture to fulfill its social purpose: by manifesting indigenous form it expressed the democratic, collective identity of a people. The richness of his primitivist ornamentation later became the principal factor separating him from the stripped-down, bare aesthetic of the modern movement of the 1930s.

Wright's work after the Prairie period has not been well understood. His buildings and projects, such as Midway Gardens in Chicago, the Imperial Hotel in Tokyo of 1912–23, and Hollyhock House, the Aline Barnsdall residence in Los Angeles of about 1916–21 (plates 133–144, 151–163, 165–169), have not been previously considered together in terms of his attempts to define a modern language of form. By seeing primitivism as a source of artistic renewal, Wright was taking part in an important preoccupation shared by modern artists in Europe, among them Pablo Picasso and Georges Braque. No longer did *primitive* have a pejorative meaning. For Wright and other artists, the primitivist world was the last bastion of pure culture in which religion and art were one. He came to his interest in primitivism, however, through his own personal search for artistic renewal, in which his travels to Europe had played an important role.

Two ironies characterized Wright's work at this time: for his enriched language of ornament he turned to the archaic sources of non-Western architecture, and while he pursued experimental designs, he also continued to utilize the compositional methods, vocabulary, and aesthetics of the Prairie period. Taliesin I, Wright's house and studio near Spring Green, Wisconsin, begun in 1911, initially had a special place in his primitivist period. It reached back to archaic origins in architecture and in Wright's ancestry, but utilized the Prairie idiom to create a mythic residence and a home for Wright and Mamah Cheney. It was also a studio for architecture, with resident draftsmen, an office to receive clients in, an art gallery, a farm, and a place where Wright could identify himself with the land of his ancestors. First built in 1911, Taliesin burned down in 1914 and in 1925, and was each time rebuilt and enlarged, resulting in three versions of the complex (plates 122–132).

The archaic quality of Taliesin I comes from references to the mythic Welsh poet Taliesin and all the associations of art, renewal, and freedom that were connected with him in many forms. To capture the spirit of myth Wright used the original materials of architecture itself: stone, wood, and plaster. His house was set along the edge of a hill, framing its top, or brow, providing a direct reference to Taliesin, whose name means "shining brow." The house turned at its entry, connecting at right angles to a studio and an adjacent apartment and farm buildings. All the other structures were interconnected with low-pitched roofs, and interspersed among them and the hill was a series of courtyards. The details and overall treatment of Taliesin recalled Wright's Prairie houses, but the total effect was more private, personal, and—to the extent that a house can embody such feelings—magical. Here the Prairie ethos ended and Wright's primitivist experiments started.

The experiments began with ornament, spread to his use of figural sculpture, and eventually created a new mode of making plans that produced nonrectilinear designs. Having grasped, in his work up to 1910, the power of space to affect experience, he now turned to the symbolic possibilities of combining abstract pattern and the human figure. Consistent with his belief that modern architecture should have spiritual content, Wright attributed metaphysical meaning to the primary elements of geometry. In *The Japanese Print*, published in 1912, he associated the circle with infinity, the triangle with structural unity, the spire with aspiration, the spiral with organic process, and the square with integrity.[25] These elements had always been the compositional units of his architecture but took on new roles in his unprecedented synthesis of a symbolic architecture.

In this phase Wright's architecture was marked by his interest in the development of a form language embodying spiritual and social values in contradistinction to spatial and technological developments. In any case, the spaces of his major primitivist works—Midway Gardens and the Imperial Hotel—have been destroyed, and to understand his work of this period we must resort to multiple readings of his buildings through their iconography rather than their spatial achievement. Integral to that iconography is his interest in the nature of materials, particularly concrete, in natural materials transformed in function, and in the effort to represent indigenous social values. With layers of meaning describing his architecture, an ambiguity characteristic of modernism itself is present. The famous windows Wright designed for the Avery Coonley Playhouse in Riverside of 1912, commissioned by Mr. Coonley's wife, Queene Ferry Coonley, were a sign of his new emphasis on a symbolic program that turned away from the abstraction of plants to pure forms (plates 112–114). The windows were the beginning of a study in primary forms that correlate with the simple forms of circles, triangles, and squares Austrian modernists had used to cover surfaces of buildings, furniture, and objects. Another example is the skyscraper Wright designed for *The San Francisco Call*, which combined his experience with tall buildings at the Adler and Sullivan office with motifs similar to those used by the Secessionists (figure 2). The entry and the window openings above it contained the motif of the multiple frame (one square within another), a basic pattern that Olbrich had used in his Wedding Tower, completed in 1908 for the Grand Duke of Hesse in Darmstadt (figure 3). Had Wright's high-rise structure been built, it would have been the first Secessionist skyscraper in America.

Midway Gardens, an entertainment complex with summer and winter gardens built in Chicago in 1914, became the centerpiece of Wright's works featuring ornament and sculpture (plates 133–144). In it he sought to define a unique expression of American architecture that synthesized foreign and exotic references, ranging from German beer gardens and Secessionist sculpture to a magical aura that evoked Egyptian, Mayan, and Japanese cultures.[26] In addition to a rich spatial complexity that linked inside to outside, it contained an unparalleled iconographic program in its ornamentation. Wright's Midway Gardens sculptures, executed with the collaboration of the sculptor Alfonso

Iannelli, provided strong links to the work of Franz Metzner and the Vienna Secession. Both sculptors rendered the human body as if it were a prismoidal form. For Wright the human figure represented in pure geometry created a harmony with the pure forms of his building designs so that both figure and building were generated by the same shapes. Wright attributed symbolic meanings to these representations at Midway Gardens, calling his sculptures Cube, Sphere, and Triangle in a way that was analogous to Metzner's student Emilie Simandl calling her sculptures Painting, Sculpture, and Architecture.[27]

The cast-concrete tiles of the Midway Gardens building facades, and the glazing patterns, became testing grounds for Wright's processes of rotating basic geometric shapes to create pattern. By stopping before the rotation was complete, Wright created a dynamic asymmetry that he called the Dancing Glass pattern (plate 143). It added a vigor to his surfaces that went beyond the symmetrical patterns of his previous work. This dynamic diagonality in ornament became a new formal element in his design vocabulary.

Simultaneous with the work on Midway Gardens in 1913, Wright began designs for the Imperial Hotel in Tokyo (plates 151–163). He had been initially approached in 1911 for the commission to design a luxury hotel near the imperial palace in Tokyo, to accommodate foreign visitors and provide modern standards of Western taste. In this immense work Wright attempted to integrate traditional Japanese culture, including temple precinct planning, with the complex program of an international hotel. Beset by delays and natural disasters, the commission was not completed until 1923, and required that Wright spend much time in Japan. By the time of its completion, it had allowed for the richest development of ornament that Wright ever achieved. In the first design (plate 151) Wright explored his version of what he perceived as the latest modern architecture of Europe, the late planar surfaces of the Secession. The roof became a series of stacked planes, similar to Josef Hoffmann's treatment of the Austrian Pavilion in Rome of 1910–11.[28] The walls were shear surfaces with punctures for windows. The H-shaped plan, sometimes misunderstood as a "regression" to Beaux-Arts planning principles, was more closely related to the long tradition of enclosed temple courtyards and aristocratic residences. As his design proceeded it required further abstraction in order to find a suitable modern expression for the hotel's motifs, materials, and functions and, at the same time, to link it to tradition. Retaining the original floor plan, he began a series of studies, focused on the central pavilion of the hotel, in which he explored more literal applications of oriental architecture: the roofs now recalled pagodas and the walls became canted. When finally constructed, the building was an extraordinary hybrid, combining the up-to-date technology of radiant electric heaters and an "innovative" structural system with an extraordinarily rich program of murals, sculpture, and patterns carved in *oya*, a volcanic tufa that had previously been used for utilitarian purposes.

Once again Wright sought to define the machine age by an original use of materials and technology while searching for a traditional contextual idiom. The artistic experimentation that was taking place was little recognized at that time. The building became famous for sur-

Figure 2: Frank Lloyd Wright. The San Francisco Call Building, San Francisco. Project, c. 1913. Perspective (detail); pencil on tracing paper. The Frank Lloyd Wright Foundation

Figure 3: Joseph Maria Olbrich. Entrance, Wedding Tower, Darmstadt. 1905–08

viving the great Kanto earthquake of 1923, and Wright and others attributed this to his structural design. Although the efficacy of the structural system has been seriously challenged, the building was perceived to have survived because of its engineering, and as news spread around the world nothing could have been a higher accolade for a modern building than to triumph over nature because of its rational technology. In the popular view the Imperial Hotel was modern because of its building technology, a point Sullivan made in one of the last articles he wrote before his death.[29] Its ornament, when discussed later by critics, was seen as romantic, strange, and even decadent.

The culminating design of the series was Wright's Hollyhock House for Aline Barnsdall (plates 165–169). The building has been compared to Mayan architecture, but if we accept that it has several meanings, it could also be seen as an exploration of Amerindian motifs, primordial shelter, and massing resulting from concrete technology. The overall impression is one of exoticism, romanticism, and delight. Here Wright used forms employed ten years earlier by the Austrian Secessionists and designers from the Wiener Werkstätte, such as Hoffmann and Kolo Moser, but not without a certain irony. Modernists celebrated technology above all, and contemporary classical buildings hid their modern engineering, but Wright's technology was used to express an exotic language rather than technology itself. He explored a primitivism that had motivations similar to those of European avant-garde painters and sculptors, but his efforts were in no way synchronized with theirs. His interest here predated the successful commercial adaptations of the exotic sources, particularly those of the Maya, Aztec, and Amerindian, that became central to the more theatrical American Art Moderne movement of the late 1920s. Thus Wright explored a more serious romantic primitivism, while the modernist mainstream moved forward with increasing dematerialization and elimination of representational content.

1920S: THE END OF PRIMITIVISM AND RISE OF A NEW OBJECTIVITY

Upon his return from Japan in 1922, Wright pursued architecture mainly in designs for Southern California that continued for a brief time to reflect the primitivism he had perfected at the Imperial Hotel, further developed the form language of his ornament, and explored the mass production of building elements. Wright had called the Hollyhock House a "California Romanza," but the term applies to many of his buildings of the 1920s and supports his principle that modern architecture should be an architecture of romance, of spirited joy.[30] In spite of the legacy of Spanish and Mexican culture in California, Wright intended to amalgamate the climate, lifestyle, and indigenous materials of the region into his version of a distinct American culture.

Wright achieved this goal through his romantic interpretation of the site, materials, and program requirements of his buildings. The design for his own dwelling in Death Valley, California, of 1921–24 was a highly metaphorical interpretation of primal elements of earth, water, and fire. Burrowed into the ground for protection from the heat, this project for a desert compound resembled a mythic cave, or a clay pot, and featured water as the primary symbolic element. His unbuilt designs for the development of a summer colony at Lake Tahoe, California, of the same years (plates 172–173) included floating barges, and tentlike cabins with siding that referred to the forests in which they were situated. The board-and-batten construction, articulated with his multiple framing motif (with one layer laid on another in recessed planes) for the cabins and houseboats, became an example of Wright's notion of delight; the barges were even given names such as Fallen Leaf.

The grandest romantic vision of this period was the 1923 design for the Doheny Ranch Resort in the Beverly Hills area of Los Angeles (plates 198–199, 402). This project showed Wright moving from the exoticism of his earliest primitivist work to a romantic vision specifically formulated for the sunny California life. The site was prime real estate consisting of tall, relatively treeless hills that rose toward the east and offered a view of the Pacific Ocean to the west. For this landscape Wright created a kind of Xanadu, with buildings bridging ravines, winding roads in harmony with the contours of the land, arched portals, and terraces opening to views. He envisioned a concrete-block system for the entire complex, much like that for individual dwellings of the same period in the hills of Los Angeles and Hollywood.

At the same time Wright translated the asymmetrical diagonality that had enriched his ornamental schemes into explicit diagonals in his plans. Challenged by new sites, new building programs, and accommodating new lifestyles, Wright's designs began to engage the landscape freely and to allow for new spatial configurations (triangles, octagons, hexagons, and trapezoids). Into this mix he added basic new plan strategies using nonrectilinear geometry, asymmetry, and diagonals. Alone among practitioners in America, Wright explored these compositional methods, which produced a vibrant asymmetrical diagonality in his building plans. Although he continued to use the square, he now added regular and irregular polygons as basic planning tools. Ultimately, he supplemented the use of polygons, such as hexagons and diamonds, with circles and ellipses. In his designs of the early 1920s for a Kindergarten and Playhouse for Aline Barnsdall, called the Little Dipper (plate 171), and the Desert Compound and Shrine for A. M. Johnson (plate 196) Wright inserted into his floor plans the diagonality that had evolved in his ornament at the Imperial Hotel and Midway Gardens. For the shrine and compound, intended for a site in Death Valley, Wright envisioned strange and exotic elevations.

The use of the diagonal also allowed for responses to irregular terrain. Ocotillo, the Frank Lloyd Wright Desert Camp in Chandler, Arizona, of 1929, demonstrated how diagonal orientation could respond to a circulation system, to a site with complex topography, and even to distant views. He had gone to the desert with his draftsmen to design the San Marcos-in-the-Desert Resort, in which diagonal planning was the central means of composition. The unexecuted plan, for Dr. Alexander Chandler, used outreaching wings, shifting in angles, to engage the landscape, and diagonality reiterated itself in the crystalline

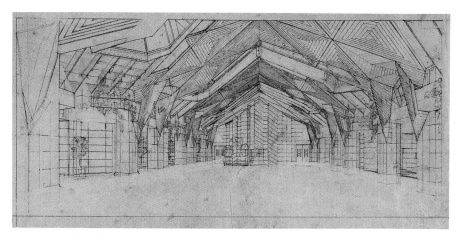

Figure 4: Frank Lloyd Wright. San Marcos-in-the-Desert Resort, Chandler, Arizona. Project, 1928–29. Interior perspective, dining room; pencil and color pencil on tracing paper. The Frank Lloyd Wright Foundation

Figure 5: Hans Poelzig. Salzburg Festival Theater. Project, 1920–22. Interior perspective. Whereabouts unknown

forms that resulted. The design for the dining room featured angular forms (figure 4). Resembling a more abstracted version of the great banquet hall at the Imperial Hotel, the interior is also reminiscent of the crystalline structures that had fascinated German Expressionist architects, such as Bruno Taut or Hans Poelzig (figure 5).

Wright's dynamic diagonals allowed a means not only of engaging buildings with the landscape but of creating plan configurations that used polygons as modules. In his project for the Steel Cathedral for New York City of 1926 (plates 207–208), a crystalline plan utilized the multiple rotation of triangles and polygons to create a variety of podlike spaces. Consistent with Wright's principle that the plan, section, and elevation share the same generating concept, the cathedral's verticality was defined by triangles and polygons, compositionally, and glass and steel, materially, that would have had it rise 1,500 feet and become the tallest modern building in the world.

The use of rotational geometry also became the means of articulating the St. Mark's-in-the-Bouwerie Towers of 1927–31 (figure 6; plates 211–214), conceived as a series of identical income-producing properties for the church headed by Wright's friend the Reverend William Norman Guthrie. Each building's internal rotations allowed for irregular room configurations and for the complex to respond to the triangular site on which towers were to be located. With this design, Wright created a prototype of the modern office building that he was to pursue in various projects for the next thirty years. As a unit, it became a model of the tall building, which could be arranged loosely on a site at St. Mark's-in-the-Bouwerie or linked, as in Wright's scheme for the Grouped Towers (plates 215–216) in Chicago, or at the Crystal Heights complex in Washington (plate 321). Compared to a tower by Sullivan, the St. Mark's-in-the-Bouwerie Tower shows how far Wright had moved. Compared with a tower by Ludwig Mies van der Rohe (figure 7), it shows two diverging strands of modernism. Wright modulated the surface to control light and create an allusion to the machine; Mies dissolved the wall into a shifting plane of glass so that uncontrolled light poured into the building.

By this time in Europe several manifestations of modernism in

architecture had begun to lose ground. Since the end of World War I the Secession in Austria had entered a slow-moving phase of classicism, and Expressionism struggled forward principally through the designs of Erich Mendelsohn, while its other practitioners, such as Hans Poelzig, became increasingly peripheral. The Dutch movement had split into two camps: those forming an expressionistic Amsterdam school and those who followed the objective lines of J. J. P. Oud and De Stijl.[31] During the 1920s Wright was exploring potential directions for modern architecture that had no equivalent in America and a very complex relationship to developments in Europe. His awareness of the evolving modern movement in architecture—later known in America as the International Style—was enhanced by a stream of young European architects who came to work with him. The European presence in Wright's office had begun with the arrival of the Czech Antonin Raymond in 1916. He had studied at the Technical College in Prague, where Jan Kotera held a position similar to that of Otto Wagner in Vienna, training a generation of architects. Kotera had gone to the Louisiana Purchase Exposition in St. Louis in 1904 and saw buildings by Wright, but Raymond appears to have learned of Wright's work only after arriving in the United States. In 1919 he went to Japan with Wright to work on the Imperial Hotel and remained there, establishing his own office in 1920.[32] The Austrian Rudolph M. Schindler worked for Wright from 1917 through 1921, then intermittently until 1923.[33] In December 1919, while Wright was in Japan, Schindler was put in charge of Wright's California practice and work on the Barnsdall House. In 1923 Werner M. Moser, a member of a famous Swiss family of architects, came to work for Wright; he returned to Switzerland in 1928 to become a founding member of the Congrès Internationaux d'Architecture Moderne (CIAM). After Schindler's departure from Wright's office, his Austrian friend Richard Neutra arrived. He had met Schindler in 1912, and knew of Wright's work through his Wasmuth publications. Neutra worked for Mendelsohn in 1921–22, contacted Wright in 1921, arrived in America in 1923, and worked for Wright at Taliesin from fall 1924 to January 1925, precisely the time during which Mendelsohn visited Wright.

Disregarding the prior arrivals of apprentices Raymond, Schindler, Moser, and Neutra, Wright welcomed Mendelsohn as "the first European to come and seek him out and truly find him."[34] Indeed, Mendelsohn, who had learned of Wright from Neutra, was the first famous German architect to make the pilgrimage and actually meet the master.[35] Mendelsohn's Einstein Tower in Potsdam (figure 8) had just been completed, and his office was one of the most successful in Berlin.[36]

Mendelsohn became, as Berlage had been earlier, Wright's most distinguished architectural connection to Europe in the mid-1920s. Their meeting had two results: interest about Wright reawakened in Germany, and Wright became more aware of European developments. Mendelsohn saw in the intimate angularity and abstraction of Wright's work a synthesis of expressionist tendencies, a viewpoint he described in articles that he published in Europe.[37] Mendelsohn's articles on Wright and the ensuing critical response resulted in a new round of publications, additional visitors, and competition between the Dutch and Germans. One of the first indications of this reawakening was that Wasmuth had reissued in 1924, apparently without Wright's permission, a reduced edition of his folio monograph.[38] The original Wasmuth folios of 1910–11 were by that time out of date and out of print, but the situation was soon corrected, in part, by two new books, one by the Dutch architect and editor H. Th. Wijdeveld and the other by the German architect and writer Heinrich de Fries.[39] In them he published his post-1910 designs in Europe long before they were published in America; in several cases they were never published in America during his lifetime. The result was that European modernists saw a version of Wright's modernism while Americans relied on old memories from the Prairie period or nothing at all.

The 1925 Dutch publication, *The Life-Work of the American Architect Frank Lloyd Wright*, consisting of most of the articles by Wright and others that had appeared in the same year in the journal *Wendingen*, became known by the name of the journal, and marked a high point of interest in Wright's work.[40] He later said it was his favorite publication of his work.[41]

Wright admired the Wendingen publication, even though Oud, in one of the articles, claimed that Wright's influence in Europe had not been "a happy one in all respects."[42] According to Oud, despite its "exotic peculiarities," the simplicity of motifs, expression of structure, and integration with its sites had made Wright's work immediately convincing. Indeed, Oud lamented that Wright's work had been too influential on the modern developments in Europe. It had seduced architects, encouraged them to emulate form (Wright's) over function, and weakened the role of Cubism (favored by Oud and other exponents of the New Objectivity), which had developed parallel with Wright's work "in complete independence of Wright."[43] Oud had defined the core of the problem of Wright's influence on Europe: images of his architecture commingled with distinct European developments so that the differences of each were blurred. Not only did Wright ignore this warning, but so did historians who subsequently replicated the myth of Wright's influence in Europe without alluding to its problematic nature.

Figure 6: Frank Lloyd Wright. St. Mark's-in-the-Bouwerie Tower, New York. Project, 1927–31. Model

Figure 7: Ludwig Mies van der Rohe. Glass Skyscraper, Berlin. Project, 1922. Model

Heinrich de Fries's monograph, *Frank Lloyd Wright: Aus dem Lebenswerke eines Architekten*, of 1926 was the first new book on Wright in Germany in sixteen years. De Fries attempted to show what made Wright modern by describing how he opened the space of interiors. He also assessed Wright's recent work: he saw in the speculative development project for Lake Tahoe a "unity of landscape and water, of solid and moveable building, of light, beach, sun, people and plants" brought to poetic heights. He defended this design and the grandiose development project for the Doheny Ranch Resort against accusations of their being fantasies, claiming that visionary schemes were a proper domain of all artists.[44] At the same time de Fries pointed out what appeared to many critics as a limitation of Wright's work, that his designs were essentially for an elite class to which Wright himself apparently belonged. This underlines the intense social consciousness that was part of the European debate on modernism. In de Fries's assessment, Wright was a socially conscious architect concerned with problems of minimum human requirements—as were European modernists—but also an architect of nature whose preoccupation with space, plants, and water led to a higher spiritual goal.[45]

In 1925–26 Wright used these publications to address the modern movement in Europe, but in 1928 he employed a more direct means of commenting on the emerging International Style by reviewing the English translation of Le Corbusier's *Towards a New Architecture*. Wright was receptive to several of that architect's principles: that the clean lines and surfaces of airplanes, ships, and certain machines create new models of modern beauty, and that "styles" are dead.[46] His variances with Le Corbusier's ideas concerned both interpretation and intention. While both believed the machine age demanded its distinct expression, Le Corbusier defined the house as a *machine à habiter*, and Wright rejected the notion that buildings should appear to be machines. He believed buildings should have the efficiency of machines,

Figure 8: Erich Mendelsohn. Einstein Tower, Potsdam. 1920–25

but their appearance should be the result of organic processes.[47] He was one of the first practitioners to sense the potential sterility of functionalist architecture looking too machinelike. In a refutation of Le Corbusier's concept that a house is a machine for living, Wright later argued that just because people lived in the machine age did not mean their houses should resemble machines, and said that the machine age might be "in danger of being sterilized—castrated by a factory-aesthetic."[48]

There were other shared beliefs as well as fundamental differences between Wright and Le Corbusier. Both believed that the machine age heralded a new era for humanity and that architecture had a responsibility to represent the new age, to inculcate social values, and to cease imitating historic styles. Their differences concerned the formal expression of an architecture of floating planes compared with one of cantilevered masses anchored to the earth, the collective European vision of community compared with Wright's for the individual, and the alleged rationality of functionalism compared with a metaphysical interpretation of architecture. Thus the battle was launched between two visions of modernity: Wright's was that of an individual on behalf of individualism, the European vision was formulated in several countries to establish a collective identity in a stripped-down International Style.

It is not surprising that Europeans questioned Wright's commitment to a social program during the 1920s. When they saw illustrations of his project for the San Marcos-in-the-Desert Resort, they assumed Wright was designing for a leisure class. The assumption was correct, except that Wright may have believed that the provision of an upwardly mobile middle class with a distinctive modern American architecture was fulfilling a social obligation, and with few commissions during the 1920s, he, like most architects, seized any work he could get. Also, it was difficult to grasp that for Wright the provision of delight—the California Romanza—was *part* of his social program of architecture. Furthermore, despite the increasing number of speculative schemes for would-be developers, Wright never lost sight of the need to provide economical housing types.[49]

While he increasingly became aware of the differences between his

organic architecture and the European modern movement, he continued to explore his own evolving language of form in work consisting of studies of materials and technology put into the service of romance and individualism, and the spatial development that ensued. In the mid-1920s Wright resumed his series of articles titled "In the Cause of Architecture," which he had started in 1908. Thirteen articles, appearing in *Architectural Record* in 1927 and 1928, pursued ideas Wright had promulgated earlier, and added a new emphasis on materials. In "The Logic of the Plan," he provided one of his few explanations of how to compose a building plan using a grid whose unit dimensions were determined by the dimensions of construction—a brick produced one dimensioned unit, a square tile another. To his early approval of the machine, he added comments on standardization and fabrication, and essays on the modern use of materials in terms of both their inherent nature and the particular appropriateness to modern technology of steel, glass, concrete, and sheet metal. His essay on the role of labor, however, remained unpublished. Had it been printed, Europeans may have seen Wright, with his socialistic leanings, as more politically correct.

Wright's persistent interest in the potentialities of the machine age focused in the 1920s on his Textile Block houses, built using a system of blocks with metal rods tying them together, much as a textile is woven. The system had the potential of being economical, expressive of rich "conventionalized" surface pattern and modern technology, and, ultimately, useful for mass housing. In Japan, Wright had had a nearly unlimited supply of raw material and labor, but when he returned to America he needed to transfer the process of hand-carving to the casting of multiple units. The patterns for *oya* blocks at the Imperial Hotel were similar to the patterns for concrete textile blocks for his houses in Southern California, although the processes of manufacturing and the material differed. His Southern California houses for Mrs. George Madison Millard (La Miniatura), John Storer, Samuel Freeman, and Charles E. Ennis, all of 1923 and 1924 (plates 178–195), provided opportunities to explore the possibilities of cast ornament using the concrete block. Cast at the building site, they represented the idea of bringing manufacturing to the locus of work and also allowed for variations that could arise from having a different pattern cast at each location. This went against the European modernists' interest in fabricating standardized building parts in factories.

These explorations of technology were soon affected by a change in Wright's form language. As he responded to the incipient International Style he simplified his surface patterns, a shift that marked the end of his primitivist phase. Operating as if he were in direct competition with European modernism's increasing planar abstraction, by the end of the 1920s Wright provided his own version of a planar, spare architecture in his designs for a terraced apartment building in Los Angeles for Elizabeth Noble of 1929–30 (plates 224–225). A perspective view shows the building conceived as a piling of smooth masses articulated by surface indentation, not surface texture. This elimination of the rich organic textural patterns that had preoccupied Wright for fifteen years was also seen in the large concrete-block house Westhope, which he designed in 1928–31 for his cousin Richard Lloyd Jones (plates 219–223). His drawings for this house in Tulsa, Oklahoma, resemble engineering diagrams in which details are signs for technology. Corners have windows consisting of two panes of glass butted together at right angles without mullions, as seen earlier in the Freeman House. All surface pattern was eliminated. Rectangular and cubic volumes were now defined by flat ceiling and floor planes. Even the representation of the design in an axonometric view utilized a modernist graphic mode.

During this period Wright's imagery of modern architecture superseded other, more dramatic, developments in his centralized interior spaces. One building that conveyed a complex image, utilized technology, but also formed an immense interior space was Wright's 1924–25 project for the Gordon Strong Automobile Objective and Planetarium at Sugarloaf Mountain, Maryland (plates 209–210). Reminiscent of the ziggurat and the organic model of the chambered nautilus, the building provided an "objective" for travelers in automobiles and allowed them to ascend in their cars to the top of a spiral where they could observe nature around them and later view a representation of the heavens in the vast planetarium embedded within the building. Drawn with heavy crayon or broad pencil, some studies of this project resemble Mendelsohn's expressionistic sketches. The romantic image of the building thus celebrates the automobile as the symbol of the machine age while finding an expression for it in the organic world.[50]

THE 1930S

As was often the case, critical events in Wright's personal life intersected with his evolving definition of modern architecture. His marriage to Olgivanna Hinzenberg in 1928 provided a stability that allowed him to focus on the emerging International Style, to continue his critique of American life with a new focus on the evils of the city, and to assemble around him a fellowship that would support his work and ideology for the rest of his career. The Taliesin Fellowship, as it became known, served as a professional office, a school, and a communal family that was essential to the propagation of Wright's ideas.

The Fellowship provided Wright and his wife a means to extend the architectural concept of organic architecture into a lifestyle. Student apprentices worked in the gardens and fields of Taliesin, performed chores, and built buildings as well as drafted to create a total approach to understanding architecture. They came in direct contact with nature and the processes of making architecture. Numerous young people from around the world were attracted to the Fellowship, largely through the reputation and charisma of Frank Lloyd Wright. With this young and energetic work force, paid in food and lodging, Wright could tackle architectural projects of any scale. In addition, he found a totally supportive audience for his ideas.

As the 1930s began Wright intensified his critiques of the modern movement and the International Style through public lectures, articles and books, exhibitions of his work, and new building designs. The decade closed with two of his greatest works and most profound comments on the issues that formed this modernist controversy: Fallingwater, for Edgar J. Kaufmann, and the S. C. Johnson & Son, Inc. Administration Building, known as the Johnson Wax Building.

Wright was aware of both Art Deco revivalism, which had a tremendous impact in America, and the extreme rationalism of the International Style in Europe. His sympathies, however, lay elsewhere—with the expressionism embodied in Mendelsohn's work—and in 1930 he recommended that Mendelsohn's article "Das neue Berlin" be considered a good summary of the German point of view compared with his own.[51] Wright may have been reciprocating Mendelsohn's extensive efforts in promoting his work in Europe, but it is equally likely that he saw in Mendelsohn's work the romance that was missing elsewhere. Wright attacked other aspects of the modern movement in lectures at The Art Institute of Chicago, following his Kahn Lectures on Modern Architecture at Princeton University in 1930. His argument focused on the emerging International Style and the skyscraper, two antagonists he pursued relentlessly. Wright called International Style buildings "cardboard houses" and accused their proponents of evading the basic issues of the nature of materials, the "depth" of a fully three-dimensional architecture, and integral ornament.

A key element of his answer to the International Style was the idea of Usonia, an acronym for the United States of North America,[52] first developed in his Princeton lecture on the city. Usonia was an idealized location for which Wright was to design building types ranging from residences to farms and automobile service stations to civic buildings. Broadacre City was intended to represent the built version of the ideal. Communities called Usonia I and Usonia II were planned for Lansing, Michigan, and Pleasantville, New York (only the latter project was built, with the first three houses designed by Wright). Combining his attack on skyscrapers with a notion of the city as outmoded, Wright stated that the city was tyrannized by the skyscraper, which exacerbated traffic and brought serious overcrowding and exploitation of the citizenry, now reduced to a mob of huddled masses, or a "mobocracy," as he called it. Wright added an issue that related to urban crowding, the question of optimum density, and placed it in the Jeffersonian context that was fundamental to all of his philosophy: "Even the small town is too large. . . . Ruralism as distinguished from Urbanism is American and truly Democratic."[53]

Wright also took the opportunity to recast his own image as the leading figure of modern architecture in a reading of his essay "The Art and Craft of the Machine." Although he claimed it was the essay he had written twenty-seven years earlier, Wright had totally revised his text in 1930. The thrust of his lecture was the same, but he updated it with language that made him appear far more prescient than he had been, and he added the key concept of space, another tenet of modern architecture: "Space is more spacious, and the sense of it may enter into every building, great or small."[54] While Wright pressed the themes of technology as the moving force for the machine age, he returned in his updated lecture to the ideas, but not the forms, of primitivism. While these ideas had been abandoned by European modernists, Wright raised a call to what now appears as multiculturalism when he advocated looking to "those human nature-cultures of the red man, lost in backward stretch of time, almost beyond our horizon—the Maya, the Indian—and of the black man, the African—we may learn from them. Last, but not least, come the men of bronze, the Chinese, the Japanese—profound builders of the Orient."[55] Also, when the lectures were published Wright recast the representation of some of his designs by having his draftsmen redraw them in a bold graphic style that made them appear as precursors of the black-and-white renderings of the International Style (figure 9). These altered representations added to the general perception of Wright as a forerunner of the modern movement.[56]

Like other American and European modernists Wright associated the social program of architecture with a political position. But in elevating the individual over the community his ideological viewpoint was antithetical to that of the socialists and communists of the modern movement. Political liberty implied possibilities for liberty in the arts. A new people, Americans required a new architecture independent of historical imitation. However, instead of a unique national identity the modern American identity would consist of the variant identities of its individuals.

Meanwhile Wright's self-promotion moved forward with the publication of *An Autobiography* in 1932. Despite his unrelenting complaint that he was continually ignored in America, from 1930 onward he was increasingly recognized as a giant of American architecture and a central figure of modernism, and his autobiography was praised. The book's charm and vitality were responsible for attracting many young people to study and work with Wright in the coming decades. George Howe, one of the preeminent International Style interpreters,

Figure 10: Frank Lloyd Wright. Broadacre City. Project, 1934–35. Model (detail)

described Wright as "without doubt the dominating figure in the architectural world today."[57]

While his autobiography summarized his life experiences, his project for Broadacre City synthesized his critique of modern life and was his most elaborate response to urban congestion and modernist utopian plans. Conceived first in theoretical terms immediately after the stock market crash of 1929, Broadacre City was Wright's project for a new way of living in the American landscape. The theory of Broadacre City, first fully published in his 1932 book, *The Disappearing City*, took physical form in the midst of the Depression through a three-dimensional twelve-by-twelve-foot model built in 1934–35 (plate 404), which was first presented to the public in an exhibition with ten smaller collateral models at Rockefeller Center on April 15, 1935.[58]

It described a four-square-mile settlement for 1,400 families that was organized by its transportation system and zones of activity. Highways and feeder roads were arranged to maximize convenience in getting to work and leisure activities and to provide safety. It accommodated farming, small-scale manufacturing, and residential areas. Standard elements were: farms "correlated" with production and sale; nonpolluting factories; decentralized schools; monorails; a controlled traffic system with separation of classes of vehicular traffic; warehouses incorporated into highway structures; and cost-saving houses, described as "generally of prefabricated units," with much glass, "roofless rooms," and rooftop gardens. Residents would live in a variety of dwelling types, with each family having its own acre of land. Wright provided for the individual through small factories, farm cooperatives, hotels, controlled traffic systems, vehicles that combined the automobile with flying machines (Wright's so-called aerotors), and design centers with communal arrangements for artisans supported by industry and the community. The prevailing ethos was that small was good: "small farms, small factories, small homes for industry, small schools on home grounds, all working in coordination."[59] Although Wright attacked skyscrapers as the bane of urban life, he thought they

Figure 9: Frank Lloyd Wright. Larkin Company Administration Building, Buffalo. 1902–06. Perspective, c. 1930 (detail); pencil and ink on paper. The Frank Lloyd Wright Foundation

Figure 11: Le Corbusier and Pierre Jeanneret. Voisin plan, Paris. Project, 1925. Model (detail)

had a place as singular objects in the landscape of Broadacre City. Furthermore, Broadacre City was to extend throughout the nation: every man, woman, and child deserved to own an acre of ground as long as he or she used it or lived on it, and every adult, Wright argued, was entitled to own at least one automobile. According to Wright, the design "presupposes that the city is going to the country" and that the "country" would consist of four sections of land on which "the hills come down to the plains and a river flows down and across the plain."[60] Thus Wright was relying on the traditional systems of American land division: a full section (the township of the official public-land survey), subdivided into acre units, with the 640 acres of the section having a density of about 2.2 families per acre.

Broadacre City shared with other modernist visions a set of beliefs in rational solutions to problems of planning. These included a call for central administration, an emphasis on transportation networks, a focus on the machine as a metaphor for industrial technology, and the provision of discrete zones for leisure and work activities. But the differences in approach between Wright and Le Corbusier (the latter in his Voisin plan, for example) were significant (figures 10 and 11). While most European solutions focused on *Zeilenbau*—linear block housing—Wright's used multiple building types, with an emphasis on detached residences, in a treatment of the landscape that once again appears romantic in contrast to the strict rationalism of European efforts. In marked contrast to Le Corbusier's planning schemes, Wright's vision, with its accompanying manifestos, was pointedly political and social. Moreover, Wright conceived of his scheme in relation to the landscape, while Le Corbusier defined his in relation to the city in an attempt to unite nature and the city. Wright's political and conceptual approach also differed from the more focused planning concepts and varied political camps promoted by German planners. Yet Broadacre City appeared to serve a one-class system. There was only an enlightened democratic throng, directed by the only aristocrat, the architect, in a system that might be called an "architocracy."[61]

While Wright was debated in Europe, he was seen in America in contradictory terms. He was both criticized from the modernist perspective and lionized as the greatest American architect. His relationship to the modern movement was typified by the view of Catherine K. Bauer, a protégée of Lewis Mumford and co-curator of the housing component of The Museum of Modern Art's landmark presentation of the International Style, the exhibition *Modern Architecture: International Exhibition.*[62] After touring the modern buildings in Germany, France, Norway, and the Netherlands, and reflecting on Wright's role in the modern movement, she asserted that "the best contemporary European architects . . . have gone beyond him."[63] But, according to her, the path from Art Nouveau to the current "international spirit of rationalism" could not have been traveled so quickly without Wright.

This 1932 exhibition provided Wright with one of the best opportunities to combine his ideological critique with alternative architecture. As has been well established the epochal event played a fundamental role in bringing a perception of the new architecture that had developed in Europe in the 1920s to America in the early 1930s. Philip Johnson and Henry-Russell Hitchcock, the curators, endeavored to portray Wright's role in the modern movement as that of an elder statesman, who was somewhat passé, but Wright rejected this role. Wright agreed to stay in the exhibition only if Johnson and Hitchcock would publish "Of Thee I Sing," his reply to the International Style. In the article, which appeared in *Shelter* magazine, Wright pilloried Hitchcock, Johnson, and Alfred H. Barr, Jr., the Museum's founding director and the third collaborator on the exhibition, as a "self-elected group of formalizers" who were in part responsible for reducing the International Style to an aesthetic formula that would "stultify this reasonable hope for a life of the soul."[64] Despite the fact that five years later Wright returned from visiting Russia with praise for many architectural developments there, he saw these "communistic" tendencies of the International Style as an affront to democracy.

While Wright's portion of the exhibition included a sample of his work from the Prairie period and Westhope, the more recent Richard Lloyd Jones House, his 1931 project for a House on the Mesa (figure 12;

Figure 12: Frank Lloyd Wright. House on the Mesa, Denver. Project, 1931. Model

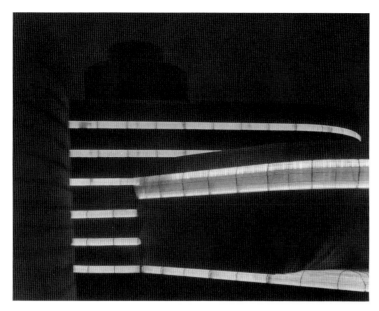

Figure 13: Frank Lloyd Wright. S. C. Johnson & Son, Inc. Administration Building, Racine. 1936–39. Night view

plates 226–228) provided an ideal foil to the examples of the International Style. Intended originally for a site in Denver, it was soon incorporated into Broadacre City as a basic housing type. It showed a vision of modern life that shared some aspirations of other modernists, but was significantly different. The house expressed its technology and modern materials by having a shell of concrete with glass and sheet-copper screens. The roofs, like those of International Style buildings, were defined as cantilevered, flat slabs. But the shifting masses were articulated with Wright's distinctive vocabulary: the square-within-a-square motif became the framing device for the small lake adjoining the house, and a fountain, consisting of a receding stack of layered planes, repeated the motif. Acknowledging the lake and nearby foliage, the house responded to the landscape more than other International Style buildings tended to do. Also, the house had no pretense to modesty: costing $125,000, it was a luxury product for a wealthy elite in the midst of the Depression. The size of the house and the powerful shifting of masses created a dramatic interplay of solids and voids—an elegance that made the economical intentions of the International Style appear pallid.

While Wright waged a polemic in his writings, lectures, and exhibitions, he achieved an unparalleled demonstration of his principles of modern architecture in his buildings and projects throughout the 1930s. The decade culminated in the completion of some of the most recognized buildings of his career since the Imperial Hotel: the S. C. Johnson & Son, Inc. Administration Building in Racine, Wisconsin, of 1936–39; Fallingwater, the Edgar J. Kaufmann House in Mill Run, Pennsylvania, of 1934–37; and the Honeycomb House for Paul R. and Jean S. Hanna in Palo Alto, California, of 1935–37 (plates 234–240, 254–260, 264–267, 270–274). The buildings themselves made a better argument for his ideas than had all the polemics and protestations.

Following the remarkable synthesis of the Larkin Building, Wright's design for the Johnson Administration Building produced a

new standard of representation for modern corporate America. It expressed its function as an administrative headquarters in a lyrical brick building in which light became as important an articulating device as space (figure 13). More an organism than a machine for industry, as the functionalism of European modernists would have it, the building was Wright's answer to modernist streamlining, especially in its corners, which formed an organic curve related to nature, as in many of Mendelsohn's works (figure 14).

The Johnson Administration Building turned in on itself in an attempt to create an idealized environment, just as the Larkin Building had thirty years earlier. Now no moralistic statements were necessary: the business of science, channeled into commerce, had become the moral imperative, and Wright found its architectural expression. The key to the creation of this interior realm was the use of the open plan for offices and the incorporation of lighting from above (plate 259). Unlike other modernists, who might have been tempted to span the Great Workroom with trusses, Wright invented a column to support the roof that also allowed a soft light to pour into the interior. The column had the form of a lotus seen from below the surface of water. Recalling ideas he had articulated much earlier, Wright translated a form from nature into a structural element by incorporating a screen of steel mesh into the narrow neck of the column. The combination of steel and concrete, using only enough material required to support its load, allowed the column to be slender. The capital, or lotus pad, expressed the distribution of the weight carried in its flared-out shape, recalling as well the logic of nature's plant forms. The result was a gorgeous union of form and function. Incredulous building inspectors were amazed when Wright had a test column loaded to withstand immense weights. Few, if any, modern architects in 1936 had pursued with such relentless intensity the search for a relationship among nature, technology, and modern expression.

Not only did Wright triumph by finding the perfect organic metaphor for his structural system with the design of this building: he virtually resurrected his national and international reputation as a modern architect. The immediate acclaim of the building as a monumental expression of modern architecture was so great that it gave the impression—erroneous, as we have seen—that Wright's creativity had been in limbo for the previous twenty years.

Wright's ultimate response to the International Style at the domestic level was Fallingwater, a house for Edgar J. Kaufmann. It used the modernist vocabulary of floating planes, but everything about it contradicted the functionalism of the style: its color, its definition by and of the landscape, its framing of vistas from within, and its metaphorical interpretation of human confrontation with nature, symbolically summed up in the stairs that descend from the living room to the water. Each material—stone, glass, concrete—was assigned a function, yet each was consonant with the site over a waterfall.

The house was intended as a weekend retreat for Kaufmann, his wife, Liliane, and son, Edgar, Jr., who had become one of Wright's apprentices. Approaching from a country road and passing over a bridge spanning Mill Run, a visitor had to search for the entry, a clue that he or she was about to experience something extraordinary. Once inside the house, under the low entry ceiling, the visitor's gaze moves inevitably on a diagonal across the living room and out over the water, through the trees, and into the sky. This ethereal sense of soaring is at once countered by the primal character of the stone floor, with the boulder on which the house is sited protruding through it into the room and by an immense hearth with a great, spherical, swinging caldron. All the essential elements of life confront the visitor at once: earth, air, sky, and water. At the same time, the massing of the building, with its protruding trays, forms abstractions of the native stone ledges of the stream and the surrounding terrain. Wright wanted these cantilevered trays to be covered in gold leaf, which would have glinted through the woods like lacquer on a Japanese box or like the water itself. Although ultimately painted a tan color, they embody the dramatic difference between Wright's approach to modern architecture and that of his peers. His distinctive concept of the organic bound nature and technology: the effect was one of dynamic contrast between the floating suspension of the cantilevered trays and their heaviness. His contemporaries, on the other hand, sought to reduce the planes of their buildings to the thinnest possible sheets of material. Both positions gave technology the role of directing the expression of modern form, but Wright linked that expression with an abstraction of nature.

Fallingwater was a high point in Wright's evolving language of form and space. He also had achieved other successes in more modest residences that formed part of his larger—organic and social—vision of American community: Usonia. From this point on the manifestations of Wright's modern architecture occurred for the most part in the piecemeal execution of the disparate elements of Usonia. His pursuit of the Usonian house had reached a new synthesis in the first scheme for the Malcolm Willey House of 1932–34 (plate 229). Its use of masonry mass and cantilevered balconies with lapped siding provided a basic model for the Usonian houses to come. Even Fallingwater owed it a debt in the cantilevering of its floors. Wright's house for Herbert Jacobs in Madison, Wisconsin, of 1936–37 (plates 241–245) provided another basic Usonian model. While it utilized a simple Cartesian grid to organize the various zones of sleeping, recreation, and work space—as the kitchen was now called—Wright also continued to use his methods of diagonal planning, particularly in dramatic landscapes with rugged terrain. His design of the Hanna House, using a "honeycomb" floor pattern of hexagons, synthesized these principles (plate 271). Like the Jacobs House, it became a prototype for Usonia.

The contributions of Wright's evolving modern architecture had begun to receive the massive recognition in America he had always craved. The immediate coverage of his work played an important role in propagating his ideas. This must have given Wright the impression that he was finally making progress in the promotion of organic architecture as the true modern architecture for America. The Museum of Modern Art played an important role in promoting Fallingwater, by lending its cultural imprimatur to the building before it was even finished and publishing a small pamphlet with stunning photographs.[65] Simply put, Fallingwater was the most powerful response to

Figure 14: Erich Mendelsohn. Schocken Department Store, Chemnitz. 1928–30

the International Style any architect had built. The use of cantilevered, planar slabs thrust from an escarpment created a metaphorical dialogue between building and site and between architecture and nature that had no European equivalent.

Along with the Johnson Administration Building, Fallingwater catapulted Wright into the public view as never before. The text and many of the photographs that were in The Museum of Modern Art pamphlet on the house came from the extraordinary compilation of Wright's work that filled the entire issue of *Architectural Forum* in January 1938. It was the first comprehensive treatment of Wright's work in an American architectural journal since 1908, and it became the precedent for several issues that followed through the 1950s. From this time forward the publication of Wright's architecture in professional architectural journals and popular magazines became the most powerful tool for disseminating the ideas of Wright to an upwardly mobile American middle class. His acknowledgment in the popular press confirmed his earlier accomplishments as a brilliant architect, and set the stage for his role in the last two decades of his life as the undisputed American master of modern architecture.

THE 1940S

Enthusiasm for the modern movement, as it was translated into the International Style, grew in America during the 1930s, as progressive architects attacked traditionalists. But dissenting voices, such as those of the architects Paul Nelson and Karl Lundberg-Holme, were also heard in addition to that of Frank Lloyd Wright. Nelson declared, on the completion of Pierre Chareau's Maison de Verre in Paris, that modern architecture was dead.[66] The 1940s, however, marked the beginning of a broader and more basic reassessment of the modern movement and Wright's role in it.

One such reconsideration occurred with The Museum of Modern Art's exhibition of Wright's work in 1940–41. Planned and installed by Wright, the show was praised by his admirers but criticized by others as lacking coherence. For unclear reasons, Wright blocked the publication of the exhibition catalogue even though it had been intended as a tribute to him.[67] The exhibition in New York was held in conjunction with an exhibition at the Institute of Modern Art in Boston. Joseph Hudnut, dean of the Harvard Graduate School of Design and one of the most brilliant architectural educators in America, wrote a perceptive foreword that went to the heart of Wright's program, calling it a fusion of analytical experiment and invention with a poetic stream of feeling and intuition. Grasping how Wright's interest in the metaphysics of architecture separated him from the modern movement, Hudnut commented on Wright's designs: "With all their assertion of modernity they do not exist in a modern world integral with our time, our way of life. They are interwoven, not with industry and social experiment but, rather, with the earth upon which they rest; and that transcendental spirit which inhabits meadow and hill, stream and tree, seems also at times to inhabit them."[68]

In May 1943 Harvard's Fogg Museum of Art exhibited Wright's work, along with that of three other masters of modern art: Maillol, Picasso, and Stravinsky.[69] Relinquishing his antiacademic bias, Wright lent drawings, models, and photographs, and The Museum of Modern Art provided supplementary materials. Selected by Wright and others, the exhibited materials were representative of Wright's production as a modern artist. Wright's masterpieces—the Johnson Administration Building and Fallingwater—were placed at the forefront of the canon, but a wide spectrum of recently completed work was also featured, including photographs and drawings of Usonian houses and Taliesin West, Wright's winter quarters in Scottsdale, Arizona, begun in 1937–38 (plates 278–283). Except for the Robie House and Unity Temple, no works of the Prairie period were shown, with the curious exception of the Francis W. Little House in Deephaven, Minnesota, of 1912–14. The Usonian house was emphasized, especially Usonia I of 1939, for a group at Michigan State College, which included the Goetsch-Winckler, Erling P. Brauner, C. D. Hause, and C. R. Van Dusen houses in Lansing and Okemos, Michigan.

Meanwhile, Wright had begun to be recognized in Great Britain for his role in modern architecture. In 1941, two years after his first lectures there, he was awarded the King George Gold Medal of Architecture. An anonymous reviewer in the London magazine Country Life stated that his work, while highly impressive, was difficult to reduce to a single idea and that its impact in Europe was second-, third-, and even fourth-hand. The critic pointed out several modern factors traceable to Wright: the free-plan principle; the interpenetration of house and garden; decentralization in regional planning; and the idea of buildings growing out of the earth, taking their materials and form from their sites. According to the reviewer, these factors differed from the goals of younger architects who believed that in this scientific age synthetic materials and intellectual and social needs must be explored "rather than rocks and tree-trunks."[70] Each of these assertions about Wright, however, was problematic: there were no simple lines of influence between Wright and other modernists, who often pursued themes parallel to Wright's. The free plan had been explored by Adolf Loos,

Mies van der Rohe, and Le Corbusier; the relationship of the house to the garden by Alvar Aalto and Mies van der Rohe; decentralization was part of ideas such as Le Corbusier's Ville Radieuse and various American ideas of regional planning, such as Arthur Coleman Comey's diamond-shaped grids. Furthermore, the assumption that all younger architects were totally alienated from nature was simplistic. Nevertheless, the perception of Wright's contributions confirmed his tendencies, and pointed to the overlaps and incongruities between his ideas and those of other modernists.

Although World War II slowed all advances in construction, the 1940s proved to be one of the most productive periods of his career, one in which his architecture became truly national and increasingly international in scope. His work showed a continuing interest in function and technology, and in their metaphorical expression. The Factory for the USA Defense Plant in Pittsfield, Massachusetts, of 1941–42 was one of his most minimal designs. Reflecting the austerity of wartime and his organizational concept for the Johnson Administration Building, the factory's administration was separated from its production facility, yet both were connected by a central entry. The structural system used lotus columns as had the Johnson Building. Unlike the curving streamlined forms of the latter, the Pittsfield factory would have appeared from the exterior to consist of stacks of planes, receding in size like a flattened stepped pyramid. Within these forms were open plans with immense spaces analogous to those in such works of Mies van der Rohe's as Crown Hall at Illinois Institute of Technology in Chicago.

In the S. C. Johnson & Son, Inc. Research Laboratory Tower in Racine of 1943–50 Wright showed his interpretive approach to function. Calling it a heliotrope, which implied that, like a plant, it moved with the sun, Wright created a facility that was more a stunning image of modernity than a practical building. Using the tap-root system of construction, as proposed for the St. Mark's-in-the-Bouwerie project, with its central core from which floors were suspended, he freed the wall to allow marvelous illumination (plates 261–266). However, the small floor areas and the inability of the building to expand contradicted the functional requirements of scientific experimentation: movable and flexible spaces for different experimental needs. Wright also used the tap-root concept for the Rogers Lacy Hotel project in Dallas of 1946–47 (plates 331–332). Enclosing one of the first great multistory atrium spaces (an idea that would later become popular in hotel construction), the exterior walls were composed of a scalelike skin of triangular glass panels. Filled with glass-wool insulation, they filtered light into the interior, and some could also be opened for natural ventilation. The accommodation of light for solar heating became the theme of Wright's Solar Hemicycle, the second house he designed for Herbert Jacobs in Middleton, Wisconsin, of 1943–48 (plates 311–314). Utilizing segments of a circle in plan, the house was an early example of passive solar heating and earth-berm insulation.

Wright's metaphorical interpretations of technology and materials were integral with developments in his language of form and ornament in the Usonian houses, which became diversified and flourished in the

1940s. The plans can be described as linear, L-shaped, and clusters with lines appended, with each configuration composed of simple units that use either right angles or polygons. The roofs are flat or pitched with overhangs. While some houses for Usonia, such as the Lloyd Lewis House in Libertyville, Illinois, of 1939–41 and the John C. Pew House (a modest version of Fallingwater) near Madison, Wisconsin, of 1938–40 (plates 246–250), used the strategies of earlier Usonian houses with roots in the Willey House, others, such as the Rose Pauson House in Phoenix, Arizona, of 1938–41 and Eaglefeather, the Arch Oboler House, a project for Malibu, California, of 1940–41 (plates 289, 291–292) took their building materials directly from their sites. These houses used desert rocks cast into walls. This technique of "desert masonry" became a standard construction method using pieces of the landscape itself for building materials as a means of organic integration.

Angular planning continued to be an important means of organizing a modern dwelling or an entire complex. Taliesin West in Scottsdale, Arizona, the winter home he started building in 1937 for himself and the Fellowship (plates 278–283), used diagonal planning, and desert masonry provided the walls for experimental buildings that were originally roofed with light canvas. When published in the early 1940s, Taliesin West effectively conveyed Wright's success at integrating buildings with their sites and taking their inspiration from them. He continued to use primary forms, particularly circles and segmental circles, for the plans of his Usonian houses.[71] Ellipses provided the plan of the Lloyd Burlingham House, designed for El Paso, Texas, in 1941–43 (plates 298–299). Circles were employed at every scale, from ornament to entire complexes, as can be seen in Wright's first designs for Pittsburgh Point Park Civic Center of 1947–48 (plates 322–324). At the Auldbrass Plantation for C. Leigh Stevens in Yemassee, South Carolina, of 1938–42 Wright demonstrated the use of the hexagonal unit in a plan with asymmetrical, angular planning techniques (plates 293–297). The wooded site was reflected in the rustic treatment of battered walls to convey the sense of romance Wright considered necessary for modern architecture. His project for Meteor Crater Inn, a visitors station at Sunset Crater National Monument, Arizona, of 1947–48, also to have been built of desert masonry, gave a more primordial image, as he carried the viewer out over the edge of the massive crater to contemplate the impact of an extraterrestrial force (plate 315). Spirals continued to play a role in Wright's repertory of modern forms, as at the V. C. Morris Gift Shop in San Francisco of 1948–49 (plates 345–347). Defying the modernist expectation that a building announce its function, the ramp was housed in a cavelike exterior with no relationship of interior to exterior.

In addition to interpreting function and expanding his form language, Wright explored new building types required of modern life, many of which had not received much attention from architects. Most of these appeared in Wright's vision of Broadacre City as it continued to develop in the 1940s. The Adelman Laundry project for Milwaukee of 1945 was streamlined, but unlike the streamlining of the early 1930s, it looked like a machine-molded plastic object (plate 365). Other works exceeded the traditional idea of the building type and included such inventions as automobile service stations that had apartments for their owners; a truck, called a "Dinky Diner," that converted into a mobile feeding station; and several modern automobiles, including one with a cantilevered roof.

The elaboration of Wright's architectural vocabulary in the 1940s was harnessed to conditions brought on by World War II. In the early 1940s there was much speculation about what form modern housing would take once the war ended. Unlike many other architects who believed that housing could be built in factories and shipped to sites, Wright thought that the house of the future would be mass-produced but not standardized. He favored the standardization of building parts, such as sheet-metal screens, but not whole buildings. Assembly-line production could produce variety for a wide range of choices, thus assuring individuality. The Wrightian postwar economical house would have built-in furniture and would be as high in quality as an expensive one. Wright's position was that standardized buildings would suffer from a lack of individuality, although for other modernists, such as Walter Gropius, standardization satisfied the needs of the masses for more economical housing.

The issue of the collective versus the individual became more visible in the immediate postwar period when the collaborative movement became a leading factor. The political ambitions of collective efforts, which had begun to infiltrate American architectural circles in the 1930s, emerged triumphant through revamped professional training in the 1940s. Although Joseph Hudnut had formulated the concepts of collaborative design education around 1936 at Columbia and Harvard, Walter Gropius, whom Hudnut brought to Harvard in 1937, became most identified with the team approach to design.[72] It was an obvious development for Gropius, who in 1919 had founded the Bauhaus in Germany, where he had foreseen collaborative design as a key means of renewing industrial production. Collaboration implied that architects, landscape architects, and city planners would work together to create an efficient vision of the modern world. This view increasingly gained importance in the profession, and its triumph was anathema to Wright. Instead of considering collaborative design in which all partners were equal, he maintained his role as chief architect, supported by his Taliesin Fellowship. From his perspective, the facelessness of group design that he had anticipated in the 1930s had now come to pass with devastating consequences: "There are two kinds of slums—the slum that is a physical matter, and the slum that is a matter of the soul. We seem to be trying to trade the first for the second."[73]

Wright's vision of an alternative to a soulless mass architecture could be seen in a project for clustered wartime housing in Pittsfield, Massachusetts. The Cloverleaf Housing Project of 1942 (plate 406) was so designated because each unit had a lobe-shaped garden, and a cluster of the four units resembled a cloverleaf in plan. The units had sun decks and, as noted on one of the drawings, provided "modern motorcar convenience at home with the ground." Wright further identified them as "Usonian Houses for the USA," but despite his intentions, they were only built as isolated examples in Ardmore, Pennsylvania.

The conclusion of World War II gave people hope, enthusiasm, and a willingness to reassess where they had been and where they were going. Modern architecture was part of this reassessment, and Wright's role in it was put into perspective as having been crucial to its development, but somehow apart. In discussing Wright's work and theories the critic J. M. Richards pointed out that "though his work developed in sympathy with the modern movement elsewhere, he was never really of it."[74] He had rejected all theories and aesthetics that would impose an image from the outside. He wanted modern architecture to be more human not less. Wright had been seen as "a crank and an impractical romantic, partly because of the unfashionable strain of mysticism that accompanied his own exposition of his beliefs."[75] But, according to the critic, by the mid-1940s an important change had occurred so that Wright's work was now seen to have a new importance: "There is a feeling now, since modern architecture has matured a bit, that it must somehow get closer to simple human needs and aspirations; that the time has come for it to be less abstract—and, in fact, to value more highly those very qualities that Wright has always stood for: naturalness, a sympathetic relationship to the landscape, a sense of the quality of live materials that are friendly to the touch."[76] Hudnut echoed this theme when he wrote his essay, "The Post-Modern House."[77] Coining a term that would become important thirty years later, Hudnut had grown alarmed at the results of Gropius's approach to reducing all problems to technology and function. Hudnut's subsequent writings called for championing the human spirit in architecture as an antidote to the faceless architecture of functionalism.[78]

The postwar reassessment of Wright also provided an opportunity to clarify old misunderstandings. In 1949 Philip Johnson finally replied to Wright's attacks on the International Style of the previous twenty years. He began his response by acknowledging Wright's position: "In my opinion, Frank Lloyd Wright is the greatest living architect . . . the founder of modern architecture . . . the most influential architect of our century."[79] He acknowledged that Wright "invents new shapes using circles, hexagons and triangles to articulate space in new ways." But Johnson defended his position and that of The Museum of Modern Art by claiming that they had fought functionalism. Furthermore, he attacked Wright's principles as being "impossible to teach in the conventional, institutional way."[80] Despite Johnson's insightful claim, Wright's dream of modern architecture finally flourished in American culture, representing a singular vision of the modern in his buildings, the print media, and even in film.

Along with the broad dissemination of Wright's ideas of modern architecture was the confirmation of his contributions to the most salient aspect of modernism: continuous space. In his classic book *Space, Time and Architecture: The Growth of a New Tradition,* Sigfried Giedion, the secretary-general of CIAM, art historian, and supporter of Gropius, codified the role of space in modern architecture by identifying it with Einstein's theory of relativity and technological innovation to create the zeitgeist of modernism.[81] But in the 1940s Bruno Zevi reoriented the definition of modern architecture by placing the idea of continuous space above technical construction, social theory, and what he called "modern taste."[82] Zevi, who introduced the concept of organ-

ic architecture to Italy as a distinct branch of modern architecture, identified Wright as the master of modern space and defined Wright's organic architecture along two principles: the integration of his buildings as living organisms and their particular function with respect to man.[83]

Wright had provided ample confirmation of these ideas for Zevi and his other admirers with the unveiling of his model for the Solomon R. Guggenheim Museum in 1946 (plate 303). Culminating his pursuit of space as the inner reality of architecture, the Museum took sixteen years to complete (1943–59) and underwent several important design changes (plates 301–310). The Guggenheim embodied Wright's lifelong interest in architectural archetypes. His use of the ziggurat-shaped spiral of the Gordon Strong Automobile Objective as a point of departure was no coincidence: the ziggurat was a three-dimensional translation of the spiral and thus a primordial organic form. Amazingly, Wright turned the ziggurat on its head to create the outwardly expanding interior space of the museum.

Wright's boldness, as demonstrated at the Guggenheim, came from seeing the same language of forms existing at every scale. At this point, as he approached the age of eighty, all his work had come together so that motifs and methods were interchangeable. The asymmetrical diagonal that had appeared in his relief panels at Midway Gardens became the plan strategy for an entire complex at Florida Southern College, partially realized in Lakeland, Florida, beginning in 1938 (plate 284). The use of circles as motifs allowed for an immense variety of designs, ranging from ones that explored technological innovation to those that continued his interest in the romance of architecture. His design for Seacliff, the V. C. Morris House of 1944–46 (figure 15), used concentric circles to form a series of cylinders that cascade down the side of a palisade in San Francisco. Facing the Pacific Ocean, the house formed a promontory jutting from the edge of the earth like a boulder shaped by the architect. The Cottage Group Hotel for Huntington Hartford, intended for Runyon Canyon in Hollywood of 1946 (plate 316), recalled the San Marcos-in-the-Desert Resort with its angular wings, but pivoted around a crystalline form that resembled a snowflake. This vision of dwellings embedded into the landscape continued the romantic image of his Doheny Ranch Resort project designed twenty-five years earlier. An even more romantic image of building and landscape that also used circular forms was the second project for Huntington Hartford, the design of a Sports Club in 1947 (plates 317–318). Thrusting the sports complex over the landscape, as at the V. C. Morris House, Wright used a massive angular wedge of masonry as the support for a series of shallow basins used for entry, sports facilities, game rooms, viewing platforms, and a swimming pool with water cascading to the canyon below. The saucer-shaped basins recurred throughout the 1940s and in the 1950s, often as roof forms. Floating over the edges of walls, with no indication of their means of support, these saucers were an indication of a new weightlessness in Wright's architecture.

Circles, partial circles, and ellipses—elements that defined the vertical dimensions of interior spaces—convey an illusive quality in his

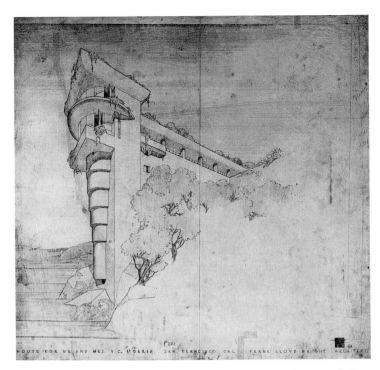

Figure 15: Frank Lloyd Wright. Seacliff, V. C. Morris House, San Francisco. Project, 1944–46. Perspective, first scheme; pencil, color pencil, and ink on tracing paper. The Frank Lloyd Wright Foundation

late work: a lightening of structure and building mass. This can be seen in the drawing showing the interiors of Pittsburgh Point Park Civic Center, and, at a smaller scale, it is visible in the interior of the living room of Crownfield, the Robert F. Windfohr House in Fort Worth, Texas, of 1948–50 (plate 344; later proposed to a Mexican cabinet minister and to Arthur Miller and Marilyn Monroe). How the ceiling is supported seems irrelevant. On the exterior, the circles under the eaves recall an inverted arch, but they resemble more a thin material nipped or punched at its edges. These treatments defy the call for tectonic logic that had been a central idea of modern architecture. The circles and the ceiling suspended in air impart the feeling of a floating world that increasingly preoccupied Wright in his last decade.

THE 1950S

Organic architecture was still the only true modern architecture for Wright by the last decade of his life, yet the definition of the term had changed in subtle ways. Some of those changes are apparent in one of his last synopses on the subject. At the age of eighty-six, Wright coined a lexicon of nine terms to define organic architecture.[84] Each term, he maintained, had been misused and misunderstood. He indicated that *nature* is not just living matter but the interior essence of materials, plans, or feelings. *Organic* refers to the relationships of parts to wholes, connoting integral and intrinsic qualities. *Form follows function* remained a sterile slogan for Wright's enemy, the International Style; it only made sense for Wright if "form and function are one."[85] *Romance* stands for the creative force expressed by the inspired individual and the embodiment of poetry in form. *Tradition* does not

require imitation of precedent, but a sense of belonging, as a robin belongs to a genus of birds. *Ornament* is the making of poetry, an emotional expression that is integrated into architecture and reveals and enhances the structure of building. *Spirit* is the essential life force within an object, not the imposition of a divine presence on high. The *third dimension* is the depth that is intrinsic to a building. And *space* is the "continual becoming: invisible fountain from which all rhythms flow to which they must pass. Beyond time or infinity. The new reality which organic architecture serves to employ in building. The breath of a work of art."[86]

To these nine terms, Wright added a tenth: *democracy*, the national ideal defined as the gospel of individuality. Confirming his lifelong Jeffersonian stance, he saw the government of American democracy as a protector of its people, not a controller of them through its policy. In a summation of the various political oppositions that culminated with the onset of the Cold War in the early 1950s, Wright saw democracy as "the opposite of totalitarianism, communism, fascism or mobocracy."[87] In Wright's mind mobocracy had long assumed the role of the enemy from within. It was the herd instinct that produced mediocrity in American life; organic architecture, with its emphasis on individuality, would be the antidote.

What remains remarkable about this lexicon is, first, the tenacity of Wright's ideas; he had articulated some of them fifty years earlier, others emerged in his twenty-five years of attacks on the International Style. Throughout is the conviction that architecture is the core of American democracy. Second, Wright's definition of organic architecture shows its metaphysical basis. Increasingly, he emphasized that architecture was the manifestation of spiritual conditions, paralleling in his ninth decade his own transition from a physical to a spiritual state. Nature, function, ornament, depth, and space all express intrinsic spiritual qualities. However, by the mid-1950s he felt that modern architecture had failed to communicate these qualities: "Thus modern-architecture is organic-architecture deprived of a soul."[88]

The work of Wright's late career can be examined within the framework of a seemingly dematerialized and metaphysical architecture, whose ultimate public presentation was the traveling exhibition *Sixty Years of Living Architecture*. The largest exhibition of his career, it began in Philadelphia at Gimbels department store in 1951 and traveled worldwide for three years to Florence, Zurich, Paris, Munich, Rotterdam, Mexico City, Los Angeles, and New York. Complemented by his last comments on organic architecture and his book, *A Testament*,[89] this exhibition of a lifetime provides the background for seeing how the themes of Wright's modernism played out.

Wright's late works were characterized by a paradox. On the one hand, some buildings that had been designed much earlier were finally realized, but their conceptual contribution seemed to have already been made, or they contradicted a prime objective of organic architecture by being transferred in time, space, and location to different clients. As such, they were built examples of elements of Broadacre City, but achieved outside the Usonian vision that Wright had defined. Instead of being nowhere and everywhere, they ended up somewhere. The persistence of Wright's ideas is seen in his design for a first version of a project for the Point View Residences of 1952–53 (plate 339). An unexecuted project for the Edgar J. Kaufmann Charitable Trust, it was an adaptation of the Elizabeth Noble Apartments of 1929–30. Conceived as a reply to the International Style, the Noble project had been deliberately one of the starkest designs of Wright's career. In adapting the design for a Pittsburgh site, Wright continued his rebuttal by adding what had been in those days least regarded: ornament, seen in the articulated balconies, and nature, visible in the plantings hanging over the balconies, and added in the rendering by Wright himself to the surrounding landscape. Wright's reprise of such earlier motifs as the lotus column is seen in the Lenkurt Electric Company factory project in San Carlos, California, of 1955–58, conceptually derived from the Johnson Administration Building. The Lenkurt design used pyramids of glass between the tops of the lotus columns to allow light inside and to provide a jewel-like effect at night.

On the other hand, mixing innovations with recurring ideas, Wright continued to explore technology and building materials. Tensile structures and tap-root cores with cantilevered floors continued to be used. Wright's ambition to erect a skyscraper (taller than the Johnson Research Laboratory Tower) with a tap-root core and cantilevered floors was finally realized in the 1952–56 H. C. Price Company Tower in Bartlesville, Oklahoma (plates 333–338). Bringing to fruition the 1927–31 design of the towers for St. Mark's-in-the-Bouwerie, the building consisted of a combination of offices and apartments, using superimposed floor plans, rotated about the core, to define living and work zones. An interior view shows a vision of life within a Price Tower apartment that combined office units and apartments and allowed for a dramatic vertical interior space. The exterior of the building demonstrates Wright's concept of the organic curtain wall, a screen composed of the quintessential modernist materials, sheet metal and glass, both of which are coordinated to create colorful lively sun shades. But as the model for a new modern building type, Price Tower was a Pyrrhic victory. Its cost made it the most expensive building for its size in America.[90] And, contrasting with the typical modern office building modeled on Mies van der Rohe's Seagram Building in New York of 1958, the small floor area made it functionally impractical.

Wright's other late skyscraper designs for Chicago, The Golden Beacon Apartment Building of 1956–57 and The Mile High Illinois project of 1956 (plates 340–342), demonstrated the use of modern materials on the curtain wall and altered each facade in response to the sun. Instead of being glass boxes, Wright's designs contradicted the frequent modernist practice of making every facade the same regardless of a building's orientation. Wright's use of the triangle elaborated into a diamond, as in The Mile High skyscraper, produced angular projections that recalled the fins on automobiles in the 1950s. At the same time, The Mile High was a polemic, perhaps tongue-in-cheek, that made fun of the interest in making skyscrapers taller. Wright seemed to thumb his nose at other architects by saying, in effect, "If you want a tall building then design a truly tall one—and I will show you how."

Wright's sculptural use of concrete continued in his San Francisco Bridge project of 1949–53 (plates 329–330). This concrete "butterfly-wing" bridge appeared to distribute its load in a rational manner, as did the structures of such architect-engineers as Pier Luigi Nervi and Eduardo Torroja, but the design was more plastic and made associations to organic forms, ranging from fleshy plant forms to bones. Wright also used heavy concrete arch forms in his second scheme for the Monona Terrace Civic Center, Madison, Wisconsin, of 1954–56, where the thin support of the arches at the lowest levels of the project shows his increasing interest in dematerialization.

Wright's tensile structures also confirm the lightening up of his designs. From the earlier cantilevers of the Prairie designs and throughout his periodic pronouncements about organic architecture, the concept of the tensile structure had been a core means of achieving a modern aesthetic in the machine age. When steel was used with concrete it provided a synergistic effect that allowed cantilevers, a key element in Wright's designs. The synergy had provided the necessary strength and curving forms of the lotus columns of the Johnson Administration Building. But in Wright's late work, beginning in the 1940s, he increasingly used steel in the form of cables. Building elements would be suspended by cables in tension, as in the project for a Self-Service Garage in Pittsburgh of 1949 (plates 327–328), which used an immense concrete mast to support the floors that held automobiles. Wright's sketches—entirely in his own hand—for a New Sports Pavilion for Harry S. Guggenheim, in Belmont Park, New York, of 1955–58 show the dematerialization of the building's structure, as does the project for the Marin County Fair Pavilion in California (plate 388).[91] But such buildings are only structurally viable if the masts holding the cables are laterally stable. Wright's masts appear too thin to serve their function. Either they are undeveloped—which is doubtful since the rest of the design is highly detailed—or they are part of a distinctly evolved approach to Wright's final vision of modern architecture. Unlike work executed over decades, in the later work we inevitably must ask, How do these buildings stand up?

As technological advances continued, the development of synthetic materials boomed. Delight in new materials, combining their potential for expressing unconventional building, continued the modernist ethos of pursuing the nature of materials to reveal the spirit of the age. Added to the canonical modernist materials of steel, concrete, and glass were plastics and exotic materials. New materials seemed to call for new configurations and building shapes. In his circular, domed structures for the Fiberthin Air Houses for the U. S. Rubber Company of 1956–57 (plate 409), Wright utilized his predilection for circles and spheres in a scheme that now recalls the work of R. Buckminster Fuller, among others.

Wright's language of modern forms continually returned to the wide repertory of motifs and plan strategies that he had assembled throughout his career. Wright's Boulder House for Liliane and Edgar J. Kaufmann, a project for Palm Springs, California, of 1951, used a plan consisting of partial ellipses with curving pod-shaped roofs and circular masonry fireplaces (plate 351). Unbuilt, it contrasted with the design by Richard Neutra (Wright's employee in the 1920s) that the Kaufmanns had executed in Palm Springs in 1946 (figure 16). While Neutra's design was taut, with "pristine coolness" in its elegant rectilinearity, Wright's project was more romantic.[92] It formed one of the ongoing series that used partial ellipses, including the Robert Llewellyn Wright House, a design for the architect's youngest son in Bethesda, Maryland, of 1953–57 (plates 352–354).

In his last years Wright continued to use the same design methods and motifs at various scales. Regardless of size, the configurations tended increasingly toward simple shapes. The plan of the Annunciation Greek Orthodox Church, Wauwatosa, Wisconsin, of 1955–61 (plates 376–379), a figure of overlapping and congruent circles, can be seen as analogous to the configuration Wright used for a simple sign for the Henry Wallis gatehouse in 1901 at Lake Delavan, Wisconsin. The entire building for his design for Trinity Chapel in Norman, Oklahoma, of 1958 is simply a spire, widened at its supports, of interlocking triangles.

In continuing to explore the potentialities of building technology, materials, and a modern form language, Wright's designs provided models for rich and middle-class clients as well as public institutions. The Prefabricated Houses for the Marshall Erdman Company in Madison, Wisconsin, of 1955–59 and the Grandma House for the Harold C. Price family in Paradise Valley, Arizona, of 1954–55 (plates 360–363) were intended for people of upper income levels. For people with moderate incomes, Wright proposed the Usonian Automatic, intended to provide a means, using the principles of the Textile Block system, by which an owner could build his or her own house. Instead of relying on contractors to erect the buildings, the clients could assemble the materials, with a bit of help, and put them in place so that the house would "automatically" rise. This recalled the old American tradition of the barn raising. Although a number of these houses were built (examples include the Arthur Pieper House in Paradise Valley, the W. B. Tracy House in Normandy Park, Washington, of 1954–56, and the Benjamin Adelman House in Phoenix of 1951–53), the Usonian Automatic system did not become widespread (see plates 355–359). It was too cumbersome, too expensive, and most Americans no longer had the time or motivation to erect their own houses.

The projects for great public buildings envisioned a vast realm, yet they focused inward. They tended to define their own local context, lay outside any existing urban condition, and gave priority to the automobile. Wright offered to the state of Arizona a new capitol building (plates 383–385); the drawings hint at the kind of delight he achieved at Midway Gardens. Ironically, this sense of delight occurred within an interior world. Perhaps the arid, hot climate dictated the interior focus, but Wright's civic projects were generally self-contained realms. His building complex for the Marin County Civic Center in San Rafael, California, of 1957–62 (plates 386–392), another built example of Wright's late dematerialized vocabulary, was a suburban seat of government, accessible principally by automobile. And the completed vision of the ultimate landscape for such buildings was to be seen in Wright's updated version of Broadacre City—*The Living City*, published in 1958, one year before his death (plate 411).

Figure 16: Richard Neutra. Edgar J. Kaufmann House, Palm Springs. 1946

Wright's sketches for the design of the Fine Arts Center, Arizona State University, Tempe, of 1959 (plate 393) were a collage of the circular themes that preoccupied his work in the last decade. William Wesley Peters, who finished supervision of the project, claimed that a remarkable technological feat had occurred in acoustic design. But the building is more striking for its antitectonic image. The attenuated columns holding the arches of the auditorium veer as far as possible from a rational interpretation of the conditions of load and support. The nature of materials and logic of the machine are absent. Wright wanted outrigger wings to connect the building to the pod roofs of elliptical garages. The auditorium becomes an object floating in a sea of circulating automobiles, isolated from the life of the university and city it was intended to serve. Confirming how modern architecture by the late 1950s had achieved its ambition of isolating the object from its context, the auditorium floated outside a Broadacre City that never would be. Regardless of the precise causes, the result implied delight for the individual in an increasingly ill-defined public realm. Wright seemed to be achieving one of his long-standing visions for modern architecture: individualism triumphed, but at what cost?

The reduction of the tectonic character of many of Wright's buildings was a final refutation of modernist ideology. Wright had maintained that modern architecture interpreted structure metaphorically—other modernists, with the notable exception of Mies van der Rohe, were more literal in intending their designs to express structure, not interpret it. But increasingly there appeared to be less structure to interpret, and Wright's buildings experienced a dematerialization that had not been present earlier.

Despite the contradiction of a basic principle, Wright steadfastly adhered to his vision that modern architecture should speak to the emotions and express metaphysical forces. His design of the Rhododendron Chapel for the Edgar J. Kaufmann Family at Mill Run, Pennsylvania, of 1951–52 (plate 371) used triangular units to create a truncated crystal that may have been serene during the day and that glowed like a

Figure 17: Frank Lloyd Wright. Beth Sholom Synagogue, Elkins Park. 1953–59. Perspective (detail); pencil and color pencil on tracing paper. The Frank Lloyd Wright Foundation

Figure 18: Bruno Taut. House of Heaven. 1920. Perspective. Whereabouts unknown

quartz prism at night. His various designs for Baghdad, Iraq (plates 380–382), may have been his last Romanzas, dedicated in an inscription on a drawing to the early sources of civilization: "Sumeria, . . . Larsa, and Babylon."

Wright tried throughout his career to include the serenity of worship in the joy of architecture. Although places of worship are intended by their function to embody spiritual pursuits, they do not automatically achieve that joy of living that Wright insisted be an element of modern architecture. In his last few years Wright had several commissions for religious buildings, but perhaps the most successful was the Beth Sholom Synagogue in Elkins Park, Pennsylvania, of 1953–59 (plates 372–375), which perfectly integrated structure, materials, building technology, and purpose. The building was intended to symbolize, in its imagery, the rock from which Moses descended with the Ten Commandments. Entering the synagogue, a worshiper could feel as if he or she had entered the interior of a glowing crystal, at whose metaphorical center was the word of God.

Yet compared to other modern religious buildings, Beth Sholom stood entirely apart (figure 17). If it resembled any other modern buildings, it would be the expressionist architectural fantasies of Bruno Taut (figure 18). Was Wright returning to the primitivism of his work of the 1920s? Probably not. Something else was occurring: Wright's own spiritual path charted directions that were increasingly outside the mainstream of modern architecture. By the end of his career Wright's architecture conveyed a dematerialization of form; ironically, it was dematerialization that the early proponents of the modern movement had sought in their architecture of thin, floating planes. Their objective had been to create a new aesthetic that required the reduction of ornament, the primacy of function, and the disappearance of depth.

Wright's dematerialization took on an entirely different character; in contrast to the work of other modernists, his architecture retained a physical depth while it became less tectonic. It breathed spiritual intention often at the cost of rationality of structure or the development of detail.

When Henry-Russell Hitchcock reviewed The Museum of Modern Art's 1940–41 Frank Lloyd Wright retrospective, he raised the fundamental questions that still apply to the impact of Wright's modernism: Does his work lead to the broad directions that affect American architecture at large? Or is the architecture of Frank Lloyd Wright the product of a unique genius, like that of Michelangelo, which only finds itself, if at all, absorbed in the hands of lesser artists? Since his death in 1959, the answer has clearly been that, despite his fame, his work did not divert the mainstream of American culture.

As Wright pointed out, any architecture expresses the moment of its creation, regardless of whether it is innovative or imitative. Space as the quintessential modernist experience is no longer an ethos, but space remains an essential quality of architectural enclosure, as do proportion and scale. Its successful achievement still seems elusive to most architects, and its experience by people occurs almost by chance. Wright's achievements may still serve as lessons of spatial integration, if only we can discern how to understand and adapt them. In the end, we did not build Usonia; no system of mass housing follows his models. Broadacre City remains a polemical model as the decentralization of cities has brought a host of problems. Yet the need for a spiritual dimension to architecture, a joy of living, in an age of despair is as strong now as ever, and Wright's breathing the spirit of life into architecture is an example the future could embrace.

NOTES

This essay is dedicated to the pioneers in the study of Frank Lloyd Wright: Grant Carpenter Manson, Henry-Russell Hitchcock, and Edgar Kaufmann, Jr. In addition, I wish to thank Thomas S. Hines, Dana Hutt, Christopher Long, Margo Stipe, and Patricia Alofsin for reading and commenting on the text.

1. Frank Lloyd Wright, *An Autobiography* (London, New York, and Toronto: Longmans, Green, and Co., 1932), p. 204.

2. In this essay I assume that *modernism* defines these tendencies, along with a self-conscious break with the past in a search for new forms of expression in the arts. While *modern* can also imply whatever is contemporary, I use the term to characterize the break with traditional forms and techniques—a break that emphasized boldness, experimentation, and originality.

3. European modernists were increasingly aware of American advances in technology. Modernist architects and writers in the first decade of the twentieth century had a broader base and a more immediate impact in Germany than in any other country. In the 1920s and 1930s the German view of modern architecture catalyzed an organized approach identified as the modern movement. For a standard, if not canonical, view of the movement see Nikolaus Pevsner, *Pioneers of Modern Design: From William Morris to Walter Gropius*, 3rd ed. rev. (1960; reprint ed., Harmondsworth: Penguin Books, 1978), p. 17; first published in 1936 under the title *Pioneers of the Modern Movement* by Faber and Faber, London; 2nd ed. published in 1949 by The Museum of Modern Art, New York.

4. Frank Lloyd Wright, "In the Cause of Architecture," *Architectural Record* 23 (March 1908), pp. 155–221; reprinted in Frank Lloyd Wright, in Frederick Gutheim, ed., *In the Cause of Architecture: Essays by Frank Lloyd Wright for Architectural Record 1908–1952* (New York: Architectural Record Books, 1975). This article was the first of a series using the same title that was to be reprised over the next twenty years.

5. Ibid., p. 55.

6. Conventionalization was a method of abstraction used by architects and artists during the nineteenth century. The concept generally applied to abstracting motifs from plants for contemporary graphic designs.

7. Wright, "In the Cause of Architecture" (1908), p. 55.

8. See, for example, "In the Cause of Architecture, Second Paper," *Architectural Record* 35 (May 1914), pp. 405–13, where Wright modulated his definition of organic architecture: "By organic architecture I mean an architecture that *develops* from within outward in harmony with the conditions of its being as distinguished from one that is *applied* from without" (Gutheim, *Essays*, p. 122). He also reorganized his principles slightly in the Kahn Lectures, given at Princeton University in 1930, and in Wright, *Autobiography*, passim; see Frank Lloyd Wright, *Modern Architecture, Being the Kahn Lectures for 1930* (Princeton: Princeton University Press, 1931).

9. In "The Art and Craft of the Machine," a lecture given at Hull House in Chicago in 1901, Wright asserted that the machine—the symbol of technology—was the "great forerunner of Democracy" because it liberated the individual and it would be a vital aid to architects who used it intelligently. He made several subsequent versions of this famous lecture. I refer here to the paper actually delivered in 1901 and published in Bruce Brooks Pfeiffer, ed., *Frank Lloyd Wright: Collected Writings*, vol. 1 (New York: Rizzoli, 1992), p. 59.

10. According to Wright, "Artists who feel toward Modernity and the Machine now as William Morris and Ruskin were justified in feeling then, had best distinctly wait and work sociologically where great work may still be done by them." Pfeiffer, *Collected Writings*, vol. 1, p. 64.

11. See Frank Lloyd Wright, "Introduction," in *Ausgeführte Bauten und Entwürfe von Frank Lloyd Wright* (Berlin: Ernst Wasmuth, 1910), n.p. In a slightly revised version Wright observed: "It would seem that appreciations of fundamental beauty on the part of primitive peoples is coming home to us today in another Renaissance to open our eyes so we may cut away dead wood and brush aside the accumulated rubbish-

heaps of centuries of false adoration. This Renaissance-of-the-Primitive may mean eventual return to more simple conventions in harmony with Nature. Primarily we all need simplifying, though we must avoid a nature-ism. Then, too, we should learn the more spiritual lessons the East has power to teach the West, so that we may build upon these basic principles the more highly developed forms our more highly developed life will need if the Machine is to be a safe tool in our hands." Frank Lloyd Wright, "The Sovereignty of the Individual," an introduction to a brochure for his exhibition at Palazzo Strozzi, Florence, 1951; reprinted in Edgar Kaufmann, Jr. and Ben Raeburn, *Frank Lloyd Wright: Selected Writings and Buildings* (New York: Meridian Books, 1960), p. 88.

12. See "List of Plates" and "Introduction" in Wright, *Ausgeführte Bauten und Entwürfe*.

13. For the definitive work on the Larkin Building see Jack Quinan, *Frank Lloyd Wright's Larkin Building: Myth and Fact* (New York: Architectural History Foundation, 1987).

14. Edgar Kaufmann, Jr., "Wright, Frank Lloyd," *Macmillan Encyclopedia*, vol. 4, p. 437.

15. While Wright's houses and other buildings demonstrated an enthusiasm for the machine age that had become the first axiom of modern architecture, his trail-blazing efforts had little immediate impact in America. Meanwhile, the Europeans at the turn of the century were preoccupied with finding an appropriate expression for the times. Drawing on the Arts and Crafts traditions, theories of Eugène-Emmanuel Viollet-le-Duc and Gottfried Semper, and their own perceptions of contemporary life, the Austrians Otto Wagner and Adolf Loos, the Belgian Henry Van de Velde, the Italian Futurists Filippo Tommaso Marinetti and Antonio Sant'Elia tried to define an architecture for the machine age. But most of the Secession, Jugendstil, Art Nouveau, and Italian "Liberty" designers sought this expression without making a fundamental break with the traditional methods, materials, and social structures that had characterized the late nineteenth century. They were interested in finding a continuity with the past—a situation that would dramatically change with the more radical development of the modern movement in the 1920s and 1930s.

The major developments of modern architecture in Europe during the early 1900s occurred in the Secession movements, which in Vienna reached their zenith around 1904, and in Dutch architecture. In Germany political antagonism toward the Austro-Hungarian empire created an interest in finding an architecture and design that would be competitive in international markets. The Germans considered their architecture more rational and functional than that of the Austrian Secessionists, whose elaborately ornamental designs were seen as decadent.

Nevertheless, it was in Germany that the call for simplicity and the rationalization of ornament coalesced into developments that would be important during the next several decades. The Deutscher Werkbund was formed in 1907, and architects postulated that the new architecture would be *sachlich*, meaning objective, matter-of-fact, and relevant, a term we can consider parallel to Wright's concept of organic. *Sachlich* meant durable and flawless work. For its adherents, modern architecture and design required "the attainment of an organic whole rendered *sachlich*, noble, and if you will, artistic by such means." Pevsner, *Pioneers of Modern Design*, p. 35.

The means of achieving *Sachlichkeit*, however, were subject to a debate that Wright would resume long after Europeans thought it had concluded: does standardization or individualism guide the expression of machine art? Hermann Muthesius and Van de Velde debated the issue of standardization versus individualism at the annual meeting of the Deutscher Werkbund in Cologne in 1914, which resulted in a schism within the modern movement. Wright had long before decided that individualism was the guiding impetus for the creative artist, as was the individual character of the client for the architect.

16. In the Monolithic Bank project of 1901 Wright first explored the massive form that results from the use of concrete.

17. For "plasticity," see Edgar Kaufmann, Jr., "Frank Lloyd Wright: Plasticity, Continuity and Ornament," *Journal of the*

Society of Architectural Historians (March 1978); reprinted in idem, *9 Commentaries on Frank Lloyd Wright* (New York: Architectural History Foundation, 1989), pp. 119–34.

18. For the history of the project and the impact of Wright's travels to Japan, see John O. Holzhueter, "The Yahara River Boathouse," in Paul Sprague, ed., *Frank Lloyd Wright and Madison* (Madison: Elvehjem Museum of Art, 1990), pp. 37–44. This influence also applies to Wright's Thomas P. Hardy House in Racine, Wisconsin, also designed immediately after his return from Japan. On a drawing for this house, which is in the format of a Japanese scroll, Wright added: "To Hiroshige."

In the design of the boathouse Pevsner and Hitchcock saw a precedent for the planar architecture that characterized the early developments among modernists (particularly Dutch) seeking a New Objectivity in their architecture. An attributed date of 1902 added to the impression of Wright's foresight, but the project was misdated and actually designed in 1905. See ibid.

19. See Donald Hoffmann, *Frank Lloyd Wright's Robie House: The Illustrated Story of an Architectural Masterpiece* (New York: Dover, 1984).

20. See Frank Lloyd Wright, *Ausgeführte Bauten und Entwürfe von Frank Lloyd Wright* (Berlin: Ernst Wasmuth, 1910), and *Frank Lloyd Wright: Ausgeführte Bauten* (Berlin: Ernst Wasmuth, 1911).

21. For a history of the Wasmuth publications and a study of Europe's influence on Wright in the 1910s, see Anthony Alofsin, *Frank Lloyd Wright: The Lost Years, 1910–1922* (Chicago and London: University of Chicago Press, 1993).

22. These facts do not mean the Wasmuth publications had no influence in Europe, but Wright's work became a far more important subject of debate in the 1920s and 1930s, the heroic period of the modern movement.

23. Wright, *Kahn Lectures*; reprint ed. (Carbondale: Southern Illinois University Press, 1987), p. 32.

24. Harriet Monroe, "The Orient an Influence on the Architecture of Wright," *Chicago Daily Tribune* (April 12, 1914), sec. 8, p. 8.

25. Frank Lloyd Wright, *The Japanese Print: An Interpretation* (Chicago: Ralph Fletcher Seymour, 1912; reprint ed. New York: Horizon Press, 1967), p. 16.

26. "In a scene unforgettable to all who attended, the architectural scheme and color, form, light and sound had come alive. Thousands of beautifully dressed women and tuxedoed men thronged the scene. And this scene came upon the beholders as a magic spell. All there moved and spoke as if in a dream. They believed it must be one. Yes, Chicago marveled, acclaimed, approved. And Chicago came back and did the same, marveling again and again and again. To many it was all Egyptian. Maya to some, very Japanese to others." Frank Lloyd Wright, *An Autobiography*, 2nd ed. (New York: Duell, Sloan and Pearce, 1943), pp. 190–91.

27. For a more thorough discussion of Wright's sculpture see Alofsin, *The Lost Years*, ch. 6.

28. See Josef Hoffmann's Austrian Pavilion, Rome, 1910–11; illus. in *Der Architekt* 17 (1911); and Eduard F. Sekler, *Josef Hoffmann: The Architectural Work*, translated by the author, catalogue translated by John Maass (Princeton: Princeton University Press, 1985).

29. Louis H. Sullivan, "Reflections on the Tokyo Disaster," *Architectural Record* 55 (February 1924), pp. 113–18. See also idem, "Concerning the Imperial Hotel, Tokyo, Japan," *Architectural Record* 53 (April 1923), pp. 332–52.

30. Wright, *Autobiography*, 2nd ed., p. 224.

31. A fundamental development occurred as the modern movement began to coalesce in Europe around 1922 when the emergence of the New Objectivity (*Neue Sachlichkeit*) began to codify what ten years later would come to America as the International Style. Recalling the plea for *Sachlichkeit* in the first decade of the century, this call for a New Objectivity brought with it, regardless of claims to the contrary, implications for a

modern style. This development started a revision that began to relegate to the sidelines modern experiments in expressionism, the late Secession, exoticism, and primitivism. Developments that implied rationality, science, and simplicity reflected in the use of primary colors, thin floating planes, flat roofs, and no ornament came to the forefront. After 1922 the rational vocabulary of the New Objectivity in Germany and Holland, along with the ideas of Le Corbusier, ascended eventually to dominate the modern movement. The floating planes and austerity of the New Objectivity contrasted with Art Deco, which the Exposition des Arts Décoratifs in Paris of 1925 had codified in France and which provided a major stylistic trend in America.

32. See Antonin Raymond, *An Autobiography* (Rutland, Vt., and Tokyo: Charles E. Tuttle, 1973), pp. 46–53, 65–77.

33. See August Sarnitz, *R. M. Schindler, Architect: 1887–1953* (New York: Rizzoli, 1988), pp. 16–17; and David Gebhard, *Schindler* (New York: Viking, 1971–72; reprint ed., Salt Lake City: Peregrine Smith, 1980).

34. Oskar Beyer, ed., *Erich Mendelsohn: Letters of an Architect* (London, New York, and Toronto: Abelard-Schumann, 1967), p. 73.

35. Ibid., p. 71. Kuno Francke, who was living in America, did not meet Wright, nor did Bruno Möhring and H. P. Berlage when they came to America and saw Wright's buildings.

36. On his travels in October 1924 Mendelsohn visited the Larkin Building, and incidentally came to Ann Arbor on October 28 to see Emil Lorch, Eliel Saarinen, and Karl Lundberg-Holme. After meeting Wright in Spring Green, Mendelsohn went to Oak Park and saw the Coonley House with Barry Byrne, Wright's former apprentice, and Midway Gardens in Chicago. Mendelsohn's letters indicate a strong mutual admiration, and Mendelsohn joined Wright's cause by contributing a poetic tribute that appeared in the journal *Wendingen*. Mendelsohn also wrote a series of articles that were published in the Dutch journal *Architectura*, reprinted from the newspaper *Berliner Tageblatt*, for which he was both architect and correspondent. See Erich Mendelsohn, "Das Schiff," *Architectura* 29 (April 18, 1925), pp. 145–46; and idem, "Frank Lloyd Wright," *Architectura* 29 (April 25, 1925), pp. 153–57. Mendelsohn's *Wendingen* text came from a discussion in the presence of Fiske Kimball and Werner Hegemann, the editor and city-planning expert who had visited the United States, on the subject of the "Victory of Young Classicism over the Functionalism of the 90's," published in *Wasmuths Monatshefte für Baukunst* 9, no. 6 (1925). Mendelsohn's text was reprinted in *Wasmuths Monatshefte für Baukunst* 10, no. 6 (1926), pp. 244–46, and subsequently attacked by Leo Adler in the next issue, *Wasmuths Monatshefte für Baukunst* 10, no. 7 (1926), pp. 308–9.

37. Beyer, *Mendelsohn: Letters*, pp. 16–18. Citing the organicism of nature and the unity of living as the goal of housing, Adolf Rading included illustrations of Wright's Coonley House and Taliesin II, rebuilt after the 1914 fire, in his "Die Typenbildung und ihre städtebaulichen Folgenrungen," in Fritz Block, ed., *Probleme des Bauens* (Potsdam: Müller & Kiepenheuer Verlag, 1928), p. 80. The illustration had been previously published in Heinrich de Fries, ed., *Frank Lloyd Wright: Aus dem Lebenswerke eines Architekten* (Berlin: Ernst Pollak, 1926). Werner Hegemann continued the debate about the appropriateness of Wright's architecture as a German model and challenged Mendelsohn's accusation of Le Corbusier as merely "literary" in approach by saying the epithet applies to Wright as well. Werner Hegemann, "Bermerkungen, Baumeister, 1, Frank Lloyd Wright," in *Die Weltbühne* 25, no. 26 (June 25, 1929), p. 982 (courtesy Christanne Crasemann Collins).

38. Frank Lloyd Wright, *Ausgeführte Bauten und Entwürfe von Frank Lloyd Wright*, 2nd ed. (Berlin: Ernst Wasmuth, 1924).

39. Aware of the competition to publish his work, Wright had an opportunity to take full advantage of the situation by carefully apportioning which projects would be published in the spate of imminent publications. These publications were crucial in updating and disseminating Wright's work, and the prominence he gave certain buildings and projects points to the aesthetic ideas he wanted to communicate in his buildings.

40. H. Th. Wijdeveld, ed., *The Life-Work of the American Architect Frank Lloyd Wright* (Santpoort, Netherlands: C. A. Mees, 1925); 2nd ed., under the title *The Work of Frank Lloyd Wright: The Life-Work of the American Architect Frank Lloyd Wright, With Contributions by Frank Lloyd Wright*, The Wendingen Edition (New York: Horizon Press, 1965).

41. Olgivanna Lloyd Wright, "Introduction," ibid.

42. J. J. P. Oud, "The Influence of Frank Lloyd Wright on the Architecture of Europe," ibid., p. 86.

43. Ibid., p. 88.

44. De Fries, *Aus dem Lebenswerke*, p. 34.

45. One of the reviews of de Fries's *Aus dem Lebenswerke* highlighted some of these issues. The appearance of the review in the *Frankfurter Zeitung* indicates that the debate about Wright had expanded from the architectural press to the newspapers. Wright kept a copy of the review in one of his scrapbooks; whether he commented on its contents is not known. In the review Grete Dexel, wife of the art critic Walter Dexel, expressed the social consciousness of the European modernist when she stated that Wright's open letter, "To his European Co-Workers," which appeared in *Wendingen*, as well as his "An die europäischen Kollegen," in *Werk* 13 (1926), pp. 375, 377–80, said little, that de Fries was overenthusiastic, that the Tahoe and Doheny projects were designed for an elite rich class, and that Wright was aligned with class interests that made his work strongly antisocial: "We all know that Frank Lloyd Wright has decisively influenced the European building of today. Some of his country houses (villas) and ground plans are found in every book on new architecture and shown to us in slides in every pertinent lecture. Nevertheless, Wright's work is also by a wide margin not yet understood by the better informed." Grete Dexel, in *Frankfurter Zeitung* (December 12, 1926); reprinted in Walter Dexel, *Der Bauhausstil—Ein Mythos Texte 1921–1965* (Starnberg: Joseph Keller Verlag, 1976), pp. 91–92, 175. More appealing and more important from the critic's point of view were the Textile Block houses; they could more easily be seen as parallel to European modernists' efforts in their search for economical mass-building techniques.

46. Frank Lloyd Wright, "Towards a New Architecture," *World Unity* 2 (September 1928), pp. 393–95.

47. Just as Wright had articulated architectural principles for modern life in his concepts for organic architecture, Le Corbusier had enunciated in 1927 "five Points of a New Architecture," specifically based on reinforced concrete and all the programs of modern industrial society. The vocabulary consisted of *pilotis* (freestanding columns), roof garden, free plan, free facade, and ribbon windows. Within these elements Wright could see his own tendencies, but rather than acknowledge their parallel development in the work of Le Corbusier and other members of the modern movement, he thought that they derived directly and exclusively from his own work and claimed that the basis of all Le Corbusier's ideas was present long ago: "All Le Corbusier says or means was at home here in architecture in America in the work of Louis Sullivan and myself—more than twenty-five years ago and is fully on record in both building and writing here and abroad." Wright, "Towards a New Architecture," p. 393.
Le Corbusier must have seen Wright's work, at least when he obtained a copy of Wright's *Ausgeführte Bauten* for Auguste Perret during World War I. See Alofsin, *The Lost Years*, p. 101.
Furthermore, Wright assumed that Le Corbusier's planar aesthetic was referring to a two-dimensional architecture while Wright saw American developments as three-dimensional. In Wright's view, the emphasis on surface and mass in France neglected *depth*: "It is this quality of *depth* that alone can give life or purpose to the other two dimensions and result in that integrity in Architecture that makes building no less organic than the tree itself." Wright, "Towards a New Architecture," pp. 394–95.
Wright's perception of Le Corbusier's architecture as merely surface and mass suffered from the same problem that European modernists confronted in his work: to see architecture from photographs was to see it in two dimensions. Books and articles provided the supplementary means of conveying theory and polemics, but the reality of architecture, particularly its space, was available only to those who directly experienced it.

For Wright depth integrated all the other elements of architecture—length, width, thickness—but for them to be meaningful they had to have a "spiritual interpretation." This extension of the physical into the metaphysical meant that length connoted "continuity"; width, "breadth"; and thickness, "depth." Le Corbusier's results, Wright claimed, would in the end be picturesque: "a plea for another kind of picture-building. It is only more appropriate now to leave off all the 'trimming' and keep all severely plain." Nevertheless, Wright ended his review with accolades that he rarely gave to any architect, saying, "I wish everyone engaged in making or breaking these United States would read the Le Corbusier book." Part of Wright's motivation may have been ironic; part was the belief that in order to have an impact in the United States, American ideas—and notably his own—first had to be recognized in Europe and then exported back: "So, welcome Holland, Germany, Austria, and France! What you take from us we receive from you gratefully." Ibid., p. 395.

48. Frank Lloyd Wright, "The Logic of Contemporary Architecture as an Expression of This Age," *Architectural Forum* 52 (May 1930), p. 638.

49. The critiques of these projects capture some essential points about how European modernists understood and misunderstood Wright's architecture. Misunderstood were Wright's continuing efforts—even amid projects for the wealthy elite like Barnsdall and Doheny—to find solutions to middle-class housing. Ironically, the very system of the Textile Block houses that de Fries was publishing had the potential for mass housing, a fact that he overlooked. Also, de Fries failed to grasp how much Wright was a social outcast and not a standard member of the middle class, but an artist who argued for democratic principles. Understood was the perception of Wright's vision of social transformation not merely as the coordination of technology (machine and materials) and society but as a spiritual transformation. Recalling the manifestos of the avant-garde and the Bauhaus before 1922, in particular, Wright's ideas about the future called for a renovation of soul not merely building trades. The American context for this call forced Wright to operate in a culture foreign to his own, where classical styles still formed the models of architecture. Wright's development of an organic whole encompassing health, quality of life, factories, country houses, and even the landscape consequently made him appear as "unamerican as possible." De Fries, *Aus dem Lebenswerke*, p. 30. The debate among European modernists focused on the following questions: How socially motivated was Wright in his architecture? What was his relation to American culture and society? Was he an exoticist indebted to China and Japan, a romantic poet, or a devoted rationalist?
The limited credit that Wright gave Le Corbusier was short-lived, as oblique references to gas-pipe railings and houses on stilts peppered Wright's subsequent critiques. Just as Wright and Olbrich had been comparable around 1910, Wright and Le Corbusier now became the paragons of comparison, representing a broad European movement played against a singular American one. As some European modernists looked over his work as it appeared in numerous new European publications, they were revolted by what they considered his decadence. Included in that group was the young American architectural historian Henry-Russell Hitchcock, whose introduction to the first French monograph on Wright excoriated his ornament. See Henry-Russell Hitchcock, "Introduction," in *Frank Lloyd Wright* (Paris: Cahiers d'Art, 1928).

50. According to Edgar Kaufmann, Jr., the project "celebrated modern technology with, for Wright, unprecedented vigor." Edgar Kaufmann, Jr., "Frank Lloyd Wright's Years of Modernism, 1925–1935," *Journal of the Society of Architectural Historians* 24 (March 1965), pp. 31–33.

51. "Frank Lloyd Wright and Hugh Ferriss Discuss This Modern Architecture," *Architectural Forum* 53 (November 1930), pp. 535–38.

52. For Wright's use of the term *Usonia* in 1927, see Frederick Gutheim, ed., *Frank Lloyd Wright on Architecture: Selected Writings* (New York: Duell, Sloan and Pearce, 1941), p. 100.

53. Wright, *Kahn Lectures*, p. 109.

54. Wright incorporated the revised "Art and Craft of the Machine" into his lecture "Machinery, Materials and Men"

(ibid., p. 20). Referring in 1936 to Wright's essay and believing it had been written earlier, Nikolaus Pevsner considered Wright's position in 1901 "almost identical with that of the most advanced thinkers on the future of art and architecture today." Pevsner, *Pioneers of the Modern Movement*, pp. 31–32. While no one in America spoke with such vehemence about the machine, this statement made him appear to be the forerunner of the Italian Futurists, notably Sant'Elia and Marinetti.

55. Wright, *Kahn Lectures*, p. 4.

56. The Yahara Boathouse was redrawn, along with the Robie House, Winslow House, and Larkin Building. By adding early dates, Wright gave the misleading impression that these buildings presaged the new architecture not only in style, but also in method of representation.

57. George Howe, "Creation and Criticism: Two Book Reviews," *Shelter* 2 (April 1932), p. 27. See also note 1.

58. These details of the traveling exhibition of the Broadacre City model, made in 1935 in preparation for publication in issues of his magazine, *Taliesin*, come from Wright's archive, ms. 2401.164. See also Anthony Alofsin, "Broadacre City: The Reception of a Modernist Vision," *Center: A Journal for Architecture in America* 5 (1989), pp. 8–43; and Frank Lloyd Wright, *The Disappearing City* (New York: William Farquhar Payson, 1932).

59. "Models New Type of City for Self-Contained Group," *The New York Times* (March 27, 1935), p. 16.

60. John Sergeant, *Frank Lloyd Wright's Usonian Houses: The Case for Organic Architecture* (New York: Whitney Library of Design, 1976), p. 123, n. 11.

61. The display of Broadacre City was only one of several exhibitions that played a significant role in allowing Wright to criticize the modern movement and to present his work as an alternative. A traveling exhibition in Europe, opening at the Akademie der Künste in Berlin in 1931, provided the first documented major exhibition of his work in Europe. The exhibition subsequently went to Amsterdam, Auvers, Brussels, Stuttgart, as well as American cities. An anonymous American critic, writing in *Art News* about the Berlin exhibition, summed up Wright's place in international modernism and the reactions against his modern designs of the past two decades. See "Models by Frank Lloyd Wright in Berlin Exhibition," *Art News* 29 (August 15, 1931), p. 16. Despite Wright's persistent claims of being ignored in his homeland, the critic described Wright as "America's great architect" and the "spiritual father of the present international development." Wright was "the first to consider revolutionary conceptions and methods" whose efforts resulted in "freeing architecture, the mistress art, from the bonds of traditionalism." However, the critic claimed that in his later work, while honest and simple in principle, there was a problem: "The romantic nature of these elements clashes with the new materials—concrete and steel—in the use of which Wright was so far in advance of his contemporaries." In sum, the rich experiments in ornament were seen as inappropriate expressions of the modern materials of the machine age. Regardless of the fact that concrete is a plastic moldable material, the perception implied that flat-surfaced concrete blocks were more modern than patterned blocks. Furthermore, romanticism was seen as incompatible with rationalism, assuming that science and technology could be the equivalent of individualist expression.

The exhibition further stimulated debate about Wright's role in the modern movement. Often before they had appeared in America, Wright's most recent designs—Ocotillo, San Marcos-in-the-Desert, the third version of his home Taliesin, the skyscraper for St. Mark's-in-the-Bouwerie—were published in Europe, where they could be analyzed, interpreted, and misinterpreted. One of Wright's proponents, Siegfried Scharfe, a German architect who knew Wright and his work personally because he had been a guest professor at the University of Wisconsin, translated Wright's essays and promoted organic architecture in Germany. Commenting on the 1931 Berlin exhibition, Scharfe explained that it was difficult to understand Wright's concept of organic architecture because his career had been so long and had changed over time. Scharfe compared Wright's organic architecture to the organic order of nature and portrayed his buildings as a compromise between the "gothic" attitude of modernists who sought to express structure and the pure abstraction of Le Corbusier and Walter Gropius. Repeating Wright's preoccupations, Scharfe suggested that issues for evaluating modernism concerned the machine, tradition, and individuality. See Siegfried Scharfe, "Frank Lloyd Wright," *Baugilde* 13 (July 25, 1931), pp. 1164–71.

62. See Henry-Russell Hitchcock et al., *Modern Architecture* (New York: The Museum of Modern Art, 1932), a catalogue of the exhibition, also issued in a trade edition as *Modern Architects* by W. W. Norton, New York. See also Henry-Russell Hitchcock and Philip Johnson, *The International Style: Architecture Since 1922* (New York: W. W. Norton, 1932); and Terence Riley, *The International Style: Exhibition 15 and The Museum of Modern Art* (New York: Rizzoli, 1992).

63. Catherine K. Bauer, "The Americanization of Europe," *The New Republic* 67 (June 24, 1931), p. 154.

64. Frank Lloyd Wright, "Of Thee I Sing," *Shelter* 2 (April 1932), p. 11.

65. Edgar Kaufmann, Jr. was associated with The Museum of Modern Art's architecture and industrial design programs in various capacities from 1938 to 1955.

66. See Paul Nelson, "Maison de Verre," *L'Architecture d'Aujourd'hui* 9 (November–December 1933), pp. 9–11.

67. See Alfred H. Barr, Jr., [Letter to the editor] *Parnassus* 13 (January 1941).

68. Joseph Hudnut, "Foreword," *Frank Lloyd Wright: A Pictorial Record of Architectural Progress* (Boston: Institute of Modern Art, 1940), n.p.

69. See *Masters of Four Arts: Wright, Maillol, Picasso, Strawinsky* (Cambridge, Mass.: Fogg Museum of Art, 1943).

70. "A Major Prophet of Architecture," *Country Life* 89 (January 18, 1941), p. 49.

71. Circular planning was widely used in these designs, including the Galesburg Country Homes, partially realized in Galesburg, Michigan, of 1946–49 and the Sol Friedman House in Pleasantville, New York, of 1948–49, which also had a tap-root column to support the carport.

72. On Hudnut see Anthony Alofsin, "The Arrival of Walter Gropius in America: Transformations of a Radical Architect," in *Walter Gropius e l'habitat del novecento* (Rome: Effelle Editrice, 1987), pp. 48–66; and idem, *An Arrival of Modernism: Architecture, Landscape Architecture, and City Planning at Harvard 1893–1952* (Carbondale: Southern Illinois University Press, 1994).

73. "Slum of the Soul," *Architectural Forum* 80 (January 1944), pp. 104, 106.

74. J. M. Richards, "Organic Architecture," *The Listener* 36 (December 12, 1946), pp. 837–38.

75. Ibid.

76. Ibid., pp. 836–37.

77. Joseph Hudnut, "The Post-Modern House"; reprinted in Joseph Hudnut, *Architecture and the Spirit of Man* (Cambridge, Mass.: Harvard University Press, 1949), pp. 108–19.

78. Another sign of the reassessment of modern architecture was the symposium "What Is Happening to Modern Architecture?" held at The Museum of Modern Art on February 11, 1948. Several distinguished historians, architects, and critics as well as their younger colleagues debated the role of modern architecture. The discussions were supposed to focus on two camps: proponents of the International Style and those who had reacted to it by forming more humanistic approaches—the "New Empiricism" in England and the "Bay Region" school in America. But the arguments were dominated by those who promoted styles and standards and those who denounced all labels and isms. Where did Wright fall? Alfred Barr recalled the view promulgated in the International Style exhibition that Wright was "the most important single source of the style, but also . . . the magnificent living example of romantic individualism." Alfred H. Barr, Jr., "What Is Happening to Modern Architecture?" *Museum of Modern Art Bulletin* 25, no. 2 (Spring 1948), p. 7. But he also implied that Wright himself had been influenced by the International Style since 1932. Christopher Tunnard claimed that a modern architecture inspired by concepts of space or materials, such as Wright's, was too limited because it lacked a positive sense of style that could be called beautiful. At the same time, Lewis Mumford recalled, with ambivalence, that the Johnson Administration Building created a luxurious monumentality that might lead to the future of modern architecture.

79. Philip Johnson, "The Frontiersman," *Architectural Review* 106 (August 1949), p. 105.

80. Ibid., p. 106.

81. Given as the Charles Eliot Norton Lectures at Harvard in 1938–39, Sigfried Giedion's *Space, Time and Architecture: The Growth of a New Tradition*, was published in 1941 by Harvard University Press, Cambridge, Mass., and became the principle text for the curriculum on modern architecture through the 1960s.

82. Bruno Zevi began with *Verso un'architettura organica* (Rome: Einaudi, 1945). It was followed in 1947 by *Vita e opere di Louis H. Sullivan* (Milan: Poligono, 1947); and *Frank Lloyd Wright* (Milan: Il Balcone, 1947); 2nd ed., 1954, from which I quote: "The story of modern architecture is the story of modern technical construction, the story of modern social theory, the story of modern taste (*gusto moderno*). But in a more specific sense, it is the story of a new concept of continuous space" (p. 13, my translation).

83. Ibid., p. 21.

84. Frank Lloyd Wright, *The Future of Architecture* (New York: Horizon Press, 1953), pp. 320–25.

85. Ibid. The statement—dated Taliesin, May 20, 1953—was written three days after an interview with Hugh Downs for the National Broadcasting Company.

86. Ibid., pp. 323–24.

87. Ibid., p. 325.

88. Frank Lloyd Wright, "Organic Architecture Looks at Modern Architecture" *Architectural Record* III (May 1954), p. 154

89. Frank Lloyd Wright, *A Testament* (New York: Horizon Press, 1957).

90. See "Prairie Skyscraper," *Time* 61 (May 25, 1953), p. 94.

91. This dematerialization also applies to the partially executed design for the Pilgrim Congregational Church, Redding, California, of 1958, as well as to the Hanley Aircraft Hangar project for Benton Harbor, Michigan of 1958–59, among other projects.

92. Thomas S. Hines, *Richard Neutra and the Search for Modern Architecture* (Oxford: Oxford University Press, 1982), p. 204. See esp. fig. 250, p. 211.

KENNETH FRAMPTON

MODERNIZATION AND MEDIATION: FRANK LLOYD WRIGHT AND THE IMPACT OF TECHNOLOGY

For the private person, living space becomes for the first time, antithetical to the place of work. The former is constituted by the interior; the office is its complement. The private person who squares his accounts with reality in his office demands that the interior be maintained in his illusions. This need is all the more pressing since he has no intention of extending his commercial considerations into social ones. In shaping his private environment he represses both. From this spring the phantasmagorias of the interior. . . .

About the turn of the century, the interior is shaken by the art nouveau. *. . . It represents art's last attempt to escape from its ivory tower, which is besieged by technology.* Art nouveau *mobilizes all the reserves of inwardness. They find their expression in a mediumistic line-language, in the flower as the symbol of naked vegetal nature confronting a technically armed environment. The new elements of iron building, girder forms, preoccupy* art nouveau. *In ornamentation it tries to win back these forms of art. Concrete offers it the prospect of new plastic possibilities in architecture. About this time the real center of gravity of living space is transferred to the office. The de-realized individual creates a place for himself in the private home.* Art nouveau *is summed up by* The Master Builder—*the attempt by the individual to do battle with technology on the basis of his inwardness leads to his downfall.*

Walter Benjamin, 1936 [1]

Technology has sociological ramifications that invariably extend beyond the development of any particular technique. Application and reaction follow each other in quick succession: a new technology is perfected and applied, new markets emerge, demographic changes occur, traditional cultures are undermined, and a new system of values comes into being. These, in turn, are subject to other vicissitudes, and the entire cycle begins all over again. Having to respond to technological and cultural transformations, which he himself did nothing to engender, Frank Lloyd Wright was caught in just such a vortex of dynamic change. Thus the first major monument of his career—the Larkin Company Administration Building in Buffalo, completed in 1906 (plates 65–73)—would have been unthinkable without the advent of modern hygiene, the development of the postal service, the invention of the typewriter, the telegraph, the railroad, the streetcar, and all the paraphernalia of the modern mail-order business, together with its mode of marketing and the concentration of low-paid clerical labor that it had to have at its disposal. It is, of course, Wright's response to

these innovations that particularly interests us, and yet we sense that we cannot adequately characterize the nature of his reaction without taking into consideration the scope of the technological spectrum to which he was exposed.

TECHNOLOGICAL LEGACY, 1831–1915

Like the Froebel Gifts that, at the age of nine, he received from his mother after her visit to the 1876 Philadelphia Centennial Exposition, the micro- and macro-elements of the modern world were already in place by the time Wright joined the Chicago office of Dankmar Adler and Louis Henri Sullivan in 1888. Moreover, as the historian Sigfried Giedion and others have remarked, a great deal of modern technology and much of the modernizing thrust that went with it first saw application in Chicago, the city that later became the proving ground for Wright's apprenticeship. In terms of techno-economic development, the rise of Chicago dates from its consolidation as a rail hub and from the building of the enormous stockyards south of the city in 1865. However, the building boom that marks the emergence of the modern city did not begin until after the destruction of a large sector of Chicago's urban fabric by fire in 1871. In the aftermath of this disaster, the city increased its population from 800,000 to 2,000,000 over the next forty years, with Wright initiating his own practice at the height of this demographic wave with the realization of the William H. Winslow House in River Forest, Illinois, in 1893–94 (plates 9–13). Significantly, this was also the year in which Wright's moonlighting compelled him to leave Sullivan's employ. As it happened, 1893 had also seen the triumph of pompier classicism in the World's Columbian Exposition on the shores of Lake Michigan.

This exhibition proved crucial to Wright in a number of ways. First, as he never tired of reiterating, it announced the demise of the midwestern Prairie style and heralded, instead, the rise of the Ecole des Beaux-Arts that was to dominate the American scene for the next four decades. Second, it made at least two indelible impressions on his mind: the Japanese Ho-o-den pavilion, his first direct experience of the exotic "other" to which he aspired throughout his life, and Daniel H. Burnham's pastiche Beaux-Arts city, which demonstrated for the first time the feasibility of creating an urban microcosm de novo. Burnham's exhibition was already the city-in-miniature, which Wright was to recast in different forms throughout his early career, from his Wolf Lake Amusement Park project of 1895 (plates 19–20) to the Imperial Hotel in Tokyo of 1912–23 (plates 151–163).

Figure 1: McCormick horse-drawn grain binder, c. 1890

With the exception of Cyrus McCormick's reaper (1831)[2] and the balloon frame system of construction of 1833 (figures 1 and 2), much that was key to modern technology was realized in the entrepreneurial whirlwind that blew through Chicago between Wright's birth in 1867 and 1890, the year that Adler and Sullivan's Auditorium Building was completed on the lakefront. Wright found himself, at twenty-three, ensconced in the Auditorium tower as Sullivan's right hand. The previous two decades had seen much that was totally new, ranging from Frederick Law Olmsted's perfection of the American suburb, in his Riverside, Illinois, plan of 1869 to the birth, a few years later, of the meat-processing industries that led to the fortunes of Philip Armour and Gustavus Swift. The completion of the transcontinental rail link at Promontory Point, Utah, on May 10, 1869, virtually coincided with the establishment of the Pullman Palace Car Company and with George Pullman's perfection of the sleeping car, thereby assuring the means for comfortable transcontinental travel for the first time.

Building technology underwent comparable changes during the same period, from Frederick Baumann's so-called Chicago foundation system, his "method of isolated piers" of 1873,[3] which provided for safe bearing on the city's spongy soil, to William Le Baron Jenney's development of the wide-span Chicago window, together with his perfection of fireproof steel-frame construction. Both techniques were successfully demonstrated in Jenney's Fair Department Store, realized in Chicago in 1891. Adler and Sullivan were equally on the technological cutting edge at this time, as may be judged by their introduction of "conditioned air" into the various auditoriums that they built from the early 1880s on. In their Auditorium Building, refrigerated or warm air was introduced into the principle volumes through registers in the floor or under the seating. The air was sucked into the building through a ten-foot-diameter fan and then passed over heating coils in winter and blocks of ice in summer. A similar system was installed at virtually the same time in Carnegie Hall in New York, built to the designs of the consulting engineer Arthur R. Wolf. This was but one of a number of technological devices pioneered in the 2,500-seat Auditorium Building (figure 3), as Dankmar Adler later testified: "The architectural and decorative forms found in the auditorium are unconventional in the extreme and are determined to great extent by the acoustic effects to be attained. . . . A series of concentric elliptical arches effect the lateral and vertical expansion of sound from the proscenium opening to the body of the house. The soffits and faces of these elliptic surfaces are ornamented in relief, the incandescent electric lamps and the air inlet openings of the ventilating system forming an essential and effective part of the decoration."[4]

Assisted by the young German émigré engineer Paul F. P. Mueller, Adler was clearly the master technocrat of his day, with an expertise that ranged from his use of Scott Russell's isacoustic (equal hearing) curve[5] to determine the acoustical profile of the auditorium, to his adoption of Baumann's foundation system for the undercroft of the Auditorium Building. It was Mueller who modified this system to produce a set of "floating" foundations to carry the weight of the structure. Situated close to the edge of the lake, the system served as the prototype for the clustered piles that Mueller later employed in the antiseismic footings of Wright's Imperial Hotel in Tokyo (figure 4). Mueller took the precaution of prestressing the foundation under the Auditorium tower by loading it with pig iron, a ballast that was progressively withdrawn as the tower rose in height. The concrete-and-asphalt tanking of a basement set seven feet below the level of the lake is yet another indication of the sophisticated technology to which Wright was heir at the turn of the century.

Reinforced concrete was being pioneered in a number of places in the United States around this time, first with the realization of William E. Ward's all-concrete house at Port Chester, New York, in 1877, and then with the work of Ernest L. Ransome, who perfected the reinforced-concrete frame as a comprehensive trabeated system for industrial application in his four-story flatted factory built at Greensburg, Pennsylvania, in 1901. Ransome was followed by C. A. P. Turner who, in

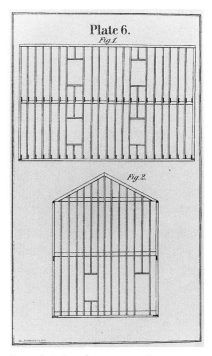

Figure 2: Balloon frame construction

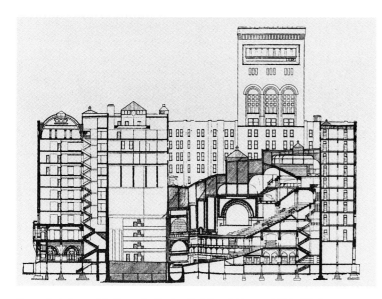

Figure 3: Adler and Sullivan. Auditorium Building, Chicago. 1886–90. Section

his Johnson-Bovey Building, erected in Minneapolis in 1906, successfully demonstrated the first flat, beamless, two-way reinforced-concrete slab, supported on mushroom-headed columns.[6] In the interim, the first concrete-framed skyscraper had been built by a Ransome licensee: the 1903 Ingalls Building in Cincinnati, Ohio. The alacrity with which Wright followed these pioneering achievements is borne out by his own precocious use of a reinforced-concrete frame in his brick-faced E-Z Polish factory of 1905, the year the American Concrete Institute was founded.

The repertoire of modern technology included many other techniques—ranging from communication devices such as the telegraph (1856), the telephone (1876), and the typewriter (1878) to the optimization of repetitive machine-shop production—that were common practice by the time Wright entered his apprenticeship.[7] Among other predisposing inventions were Elisha Graves Otis's safety device for passenger elevators (1853), without which high-rise structures could never have been erected, and Thomas Alva Edison's carbon-filament incandescent lamp (1881), which enabled electric light to become a standard feature of metropolitan life by the turn of the century. Moreover, the commutational interdependence of the metropolis and the suburb could not have emerged as it did in Chicago in the late nineteenth century without a number of diverse developments, such as the electric streetcar (1884) and the economical production of rolled plate glass (1887), this last being crucial to the development of the Chicago window and to the progressive realization of the first fully glazed curtain-wall facade as this appeared in S. S. Beman's Brunswick (Studebaker) Building in Chicago of 1895.[8] To this list must be added the accumulation of sanitary services that were an inseparable part of modern building production: the water closet (1778), the universal provision of piped water (1880), and the chemical clarification of sewage (1894). Five years before the turn of the century, two-pipe ventilated plumbing, with its full complement of modern bathroom appliances, had become standard in Chicago, while built-in vacuum-cleaning systems completed the repertoire of hygienic devices for domestic buildings. Wright installed just such a system in the house that he designed for the bicycle manufacturer Frederick C. Robie in Chicago in 1908–10.

The improvement of milling machinery around 1876 facilitated large-volume, high-speed precision work in wood, and this, together with the emerging scientific management of building processes, permitted the rapid erection of a large number of suburban homes in the last two decades of the century. We must also note the concomitant increase in the extent of the railroad infrastructure, which attained some two million miles of track by the turn of the century, virtually a seven-fold increase since the Civil War. It is ironic that this mileage should have peaked at the very moment when Henry Ford assembled his first automobile (1896).[9] Another twenty years elapsed, however, before Ford mass-produced the Model T in his Highland Park plant. In the late 1890s, when the rail infrastructure was at its height and mass ownership of the automobile had yet to emerge, Wright turned to the railroad as the only available means of mass transit, which no doubt accounts for the prominence of the rail spur in his proposal for Wolf Lake Amusement Park.

THE AMERICAN WOMAN'S HOME, 1869–1909

Inspired by Catherine Beecher and Harriet Beecher Stowe's book *The American Woman's Home* of 1869,[10] the American household reform movement stressed the rationalization of the kitchen through the provision of convenient storage and continuous work surfaces, a practice long deployed in the design of ships' galleys. Thereafter the ergonomic kitchen was repeatedly brought to public notice, first in E. C. Gardner's *Houses and How to Make Them* of 1874, and then in Christine Frederick's articles for the *Ladies' Home Journal* and in her book *Household Engineering: Scientific Management in the Home* (1915). As its productivist title suggests, Frederick's volume extolled the virtues of Frederick W. Taylor's production engineering principles, as first set forth in his book *The Principles of Scientific Management* of 1911. This drive toward the reform of domestic space was part of a comprehensive concern for familial welfare that came from different quarters: from the Nation Household Economics Association, founded by the Women's Congress at the Chicago World's Columbian Exposition of 1893, and from such pioneering social workers as Jane Addams and Ellen Gates Starr, who established their first settlement for the poor, Hull House, in Chicago in 1889. Last, but by no means least, there were the University of Chicago's schools of educational reform and social research, of which John Dewey, Robert Park, and Charles Horten Cooley were prime movers, Cooley being the first person to develop the concept of the neighborhood unit, in his book *Social Organization* of 1909.[11] All of this progressive activity was complemented by a general concern for improving domestic culture, as set forth in the pages of certain periodicals, among them Edward Bok's *Ladies' Home Journal*, Eugene Klapp's *House Beautiful*, and Gustav Stickley's *The Craftsman*. The readers of these journals constituted the principal audience to which Wright appealed in the talks that he gave at the turn of the

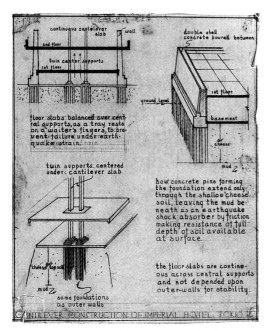

Figure 4: Frank Lloyd Wright. Imperial Hotel, Tokyo.
c. 1912–23. Structural diagrams; ink and pencil on
tracing paper. The Frank Lloyd Wright Foundation

century at the University Guild, Evanston, The Art Institute of Chicago, and above all at Jane Addams's Hull House, the site of his seminal address of 1901, "The Art and Craft of the Machine."

Wright empathized with the urban-suburban lifestyle of his Oak Park and River Forest clientele, as they commuted back and forth between bustling downtown Chicago and the bucolic tranquility of the dormitory suburb. In his "Promotional Brochure for the Practice of Architecture" of 1898 he alluded quite categorically to the way in which he would divide his time between mornings in his downtown office and afternoons spent in the tranquility of Oak Park, where he could, as he put it, concentrate free from the distractions of the city.[12] Wright's privileging of the suburb at the turn of the century seems to have guaranteed his initial success. Thus he had no reason to doubt his decision to abandon the field of high-rise office construction and give his full attention to the middle-class hinterland of the garden city to which he would make a critical contribution over three decades, beginning with the model houses he published in 1901 in the *Ladies' Home Journal*—A Small House with "Lots of Room in It" and A Home in a Prairie Town (plates 42–43)—and concluding with his Usonian houses of the late 1930s.

Until 1909, when he decamped with Mamah Borthwick Cheney, the wife of his client Edwin Cheney, Wright was able to accept the dichotomous interdependence of the city and suburb. The commutation between the masculine reality of the Loop and the feminine dream of the suburb was no longer an option once Wright was ostracized from the Oak Park community in which he had lived for eleven years. He was forced back to the land, so to speak, in order to reground himself in a form of preindustrial agricultural self-sufficiency, as this could still be found in the pioneer domain of the Midwest. In short, Wright returned to the agrarian stronghold of his Welsh émigré fore-

bears in Spring Green, Wisconsin, where he had previously built his aunts' Hillside Home School in 1901–03 (plates 50–52). To this he now added his own house—Taliesin, or Shining Brow—the first phase of which was under construction from 1911 to 1914 (plates 122–124). For the rest of his life Wright lived as a farmer-architect. He thereby attempted to restore the homestead to its agrarian origin, liberating it from the corrupting influence of the city and its divided labor.

As far as progressive domestic planning was concerned Wright's point of departure stemmed from the earlier prototypes advanced by E. C. Gardner in his *Illustrated Homes . . .* of 1875 and from the Shingle style houses of Bruce Price and McKim, Mead and White of the 1880s. Wright was hardly alone in this endeavor, however, for a number of Prairie school architects attempted to found a new domestic tradition, among them Robert C. Spencer, Jr., whose Voyseyesque design, A Shingled Farmhouse, was exhibited at the Chicago Architectural Club in March 1900. This was surely a response to Wright's, equally Arts and Crafts–like A. K. McAfee House for Kenilworth, Illinois, of 1894. The close-knit character of all this activity in the late 1890s can hardly be overestimated. According to the historian H. Allen Brooks: "Chicago was among the earliest and most important centers of arts and crafts activity in America. . . . By the mid-nineties the arts and crafts came into existence at Hull House, and it was there, on 22 October 1897, that the Chicago Arts and Crafts Society was founded. Among the charter members were those architects of the Prairie School who had their offices in Steinway Hall—Hunt, Perkins, Spencer, and Wright . . . and within a few months the Society was participating in the 1898 annual exhibition of the Chicago Architectural Club, where it had more exhibits than did its host."[13]

Despite Spencer's sophistication in turning to C. F. A. Voysey as the most evolved protomodernist of the English Arts and Crafts movement, it is clear that Wright was the superior designer, in part because of his feeling for proportion and in part because of his strikingly unorthodox use of horizontally raked brickwork, which set his work apart. That this was quite self-conscious is suggested by his precise specification of the exterior finishes to be employed in the Isidore Heller and Joseph Husser houses in Chicago of the late 1890s. The specifications called for their varying finish in buff Roman brickwork—so-called Tiffany bricks—with raked joints to emphasize the horizontal grain (plates 30–33).[14]

While the exterior finishes of the Prairie school usually ran to plaster of a light ocher hue, combined with rough-sawn stained wood, which either represented the building's structure or served as its trim, Wright favored a tactile expression using a single material, as in his Heller and Husser houses (plates 30–33) or in his so-called River Forest clapboard style. This style was first broached in the Romeo and Juliet Windmill at Spring Green, Wisconsin, in 1896 (plate 49) and subsequently elaborated in the River Forest Golf and Tennis clubs (1898 and 1906; see plate 54), the Charles Ross House, Lake Delavan, Wisconsin (1902), and the summer cottage built for George Gerts in Whitehall, Michigan, in 1902. In every instance, we encounter a three-foot stud module, with boarded sheathing and horizontal battens at one-foot intervals, the latter capping the seams and performing the same rhythmic function as the projecting brick courses that modulate the facade of the all-brick Arthur Heurtley House in Oak Park of 1902.

In Wright's 1901 address "The Art and Craft of the Machine" he first tried to show how a new kind of "woven" civilization could be derived from a judicious rationalization of traditional construction:

The new will weave for the necessities of mankind, which his Machine will have mastered, a robe of ideality no less truthful. . . .

Now let us learn from the Machine.

It teaches us that the beauty of wood lies first in its qualities as wood; no treatment that did not bring out these qualities all the time could be plastic, and therefore not appropriate—so not beautiful, the machine teaches us, if we have left it to the machine that certain simple forms and handling are suitable to bring out the beauty of wood and certain forms are not; that all wood carving is apt to be a forcing of the material, an insult to its finer possibilities as a material having in itself intrinsically artistic properties, of which its beautiful markings is one, its texture another, its color a third.

The machine, by its wonderful cutting, shaping, smoothing, and repetitive capacity, has made it possible to so use it without waste that the poor as well as the rich may enjoy to-day beautiful surface treatments of clean, strong forms that the branch veneers of Sheraton and Chippendale only hinted at, with dire extravagance, and which the Middle Ages utterly ignored.

The machine has emancipated these beauties of nature in wood; made it possible to wipe out the mass of meaningless torture to which wood has been subjected since the world began, for it has been universally abused and maltreated by all peoples but the Japanese.[15]

But Wright no sooner projected houses as "woven" forms in wood or brick than he turned in the opposite direction, namely to monolithic concrete construction as it appears in his Monolithic Bank project, published in *The Brickbuilder* in 1901 (plates 28–29). This project explores the pre-Columbian syntax[16] that he later adopted for Unity Temple in Oak Park of 1905–08, a building in which Wright attempted to reconcile the woven with the cast inasmuch as the resultant space was "plaited" on the interior, as the shell of the building was cast on the exterior. This composite condition was expressed not only through the cast, crotcheted decoration of the external concrete piers, rising between the leaded clerestory lights of the church, but also through the internal freestanding piers, the orthogonal, gridded skylight, the three-dimensional chandeliers built up of wood spars, and the overall banded decoration of the interior volumes. A similar hybrid form, part cast, part woven, appeared in Wright's third *Ladies' Home Journal* house, A Fireproof House for $5000, published in 1907, the choice of concrete in this instance being ostensibly a response to the technological and economic pressures of the moment:

Changing industrial conditions have brought reinforced concrete construction within the reach of the average homemaker. The maximum strength peculiar to the nature of both concrete and steel is in this system

utilized with great economy. A structure of this type is more enduring than if carved intact from solid stone, for it is not only a masonry monolith but it is interlaced with steel fibers as well. . . .

The walls, floors, and roof of this house are a monolithic casting, formed in the usual manner by means of wooden false work, the chimney at the center carrying, like a huge post, the central load of floor and roof construction. Floors and roof are reinforced concrete slabs approximately five inches thick if gravel concrete is used. The roof slab overhangs to protect the walls from sun, and the top is waterproofed with a tar and gravel roofing pitched to drain to a downspout located in the chimney flue, where it is not likely to freeze. To afford further protection to the second-story rooms from the heat of the sun, a false ceiling is provided of plastered metal lath hanging eight inches below the bottom of the roof slab, leaving a circulating air space above, exhausted to the large open space in the center of the chimney. In summer this air space is fed by the openings noted beneath the eaves outside.[17]

Aside from his skill as an artist, this text testifies to his exceptional ingenuity as a space-planner and, above all, his ability to arrange for all four sides of the house to be identical so that, as in Unity Temple, it would be possible to economize in the use of formwork. A similar pragmatic logic will lead him to ventilate the ceiling space and to use outward-opening casement windows rather than the neocolonial sash.

Of the three prototypical houses that Wright designed for the *Ladies' Home Journal* at the turn of the century, the first two versions, framed in wood, are capped with sloping roofs of varying pitch, as befits their *tectonic* structure, whereas in the *stereotomic* fireproof version, the concrete roof, integrally cast with the rest of the house, remains flat and drains inward toward the central chimney stack. The fact that this third version was eventually realized as a balloon frame in no way diminishes the prototypical character of its form, for it was typical of Wright's pragmatic attitude to change the constructional system if that was the only way to realize the work. Despite his occasional opportunism, comfort was a major concern for Wright, and to that end he was always eager to install the latest in mechanical services, although his enthusiasm in this respect sometimes outstripped his technical know-how, as in the installation of gravity-fed hot-air heating in the William Greene House in Aurora, Illinois, of 1912.[18]

Wright's capacity for responding with sensitivity to varying climatic conditions is particularly noticeable in the Frederick C. Robie House of 1908–10 (plates 100–106), wherein, as Reyner Banham has observed, environmental balance was maintained in part through built-in radiant heating and in part through cross ventilation.[19] The latter was complemented by venting the roof space in high summer with a special shaft integrated into the central chimney stack. Wright attempted to integrate mechanical services throughout, so that they were largely invisible. Thus the radiators were carefully integrated into the fabric, irrespective of whether they were set into the upstands or recessed into the floor, and covered with flush-fitting brass grills where the south windows came down to the floor. Either way the continuous fenestration was paralleled by dropped ceilings in fretted woodwork

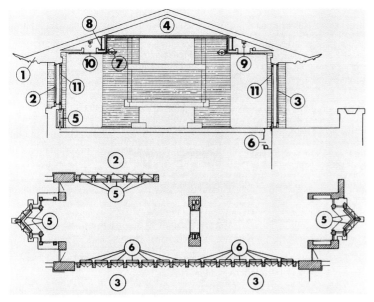

Figure 5: Environmental provisions, section and partial plan, Frederick C. Robie House: 1, roof overhangs; 2, opening windows; 3, glazed doors; 4, roof space; 5, radiators under windows; 6, radiators in floor; 7, glass globes; 8, steel beam; 9, dimmer-controlled bulbs; 10, lighting grills; 11, hinged screens

with concealed lighting above (figure 5). Heat rising from these fittings may well have contributed to the convection of air up through the roof space; and in this regard, as Wright indicated, a special air shaft let into the chimney played a crucial role: "The gently sloping roofs grateful to the prairie do not leave large air-spaces above the rooms, and so the chimney has grown in dimensions and importance and in hot weather ventilates the circulating air-spaces beneath the eaves through openings easily closed in winter."[20] Such was the ingenuity of Wright's response to the extremes of the midwestern climate some twenty years before Willis H. Carrier and others succeeded in reducing the size of the standard air-conditioner to the scale of a small domestic unit.[21]

The sectional subtlety of Wright's Robie House did not end with this, however, for as Banham has remarked, Wright extended its eaves to the exact extent that was necessary to prevent the sun's rays from striking the continuous glazing on the south face in high summer. At the same time, the sectional profile of the living-room balcony and forecourt was such as to assure both visual and acoustical privacy, while still affording a more distant view of the Midway Plaisance on the other side of the street. In this way, Wright put his self-imposed standards for domestic privacy to a severe test on a dense urban site, in a canonical work that was the last house of the Prairie series.

As the architectural historian Leonard Eaton has shown, Wright's clients were all members of an "inner-directed" middle-class clan.[22] They ranged from professionals in the service industry to entrepreneurs in small-scale enterprises and inventors, together with a small number of self-made manufacturers, all of whom Wright once characterized as having "unspoiled instincts and untainted ideals."[23] While being of fairly conservative, nonliterate dispositions, both culturally and politically, they all were, like Wright himself, extremely sociable, which surely accounts for the large living rooms incorporated into their

houses. Two other characteristics were also frequently in evidence: the men were often amateur musicians and the women engaged in progressive politics.[24] At the same time, with the singular exception of Avery Coonley, none was from an aristocratic or monied background. Even more surprising, given Wright's acquaintances at the University of Chicago, almost none of his clients was an academic, save those who sponsored the ill-fated University Heights, Como Orchards Summer Colony project for Darby, Montana, of 1909–10 (plate 399). Wright's clients were mainly the makers of things rather than the accumulators of wealth or wisdom, to invoke Thorstein Veblen's distinction,[25] and in this regard the bronze founder William H. Winslow and the bicycle merchant-cum-inventor Frederick C. Robie were both typical Wrightian clients of the Prairie period.

The two most important patrons in Wright's early career from among his River Forest friends were the aforementioned Winslow and the real-estate speculator Edward Carson Waller, who were closely associated with each other. While Winslow was Wright's first major client for a private house, Waller (for whom Wright never succeeded in building a house) played an equally important role, for it was Waller who commissioned the Wolf Lake Amusement Park of 1895, the Rookery remodeling of 1905, and the Francisco Terrace Apartments of 1895; and it was Waller's son, Edward, Jr., who became Wright's client for Midway Gardens of 1913–14 (see plates 19–20, 133–144).[26]

Winslow embodied in his own persona Wright's ideal of the self-made, cultivated technocrat: he was an amateur lawyer, cabinetmaker, musician, photographer, typographer, and printer. The best-known product of his expertise in this last regard was his publication of William C. Gannett's *The House Beautiful* in 1896–97, with page decorations by Wright and typography by himself. Winslow exercised all these talents while running the Winslow Brothers bronze- and iron-casting foundry, located in the industrial zone that separated Oak Park from downtown Chicago. As Eaton has written:

Both he and his brother Francis made contributions to the bronze-and iron-casting process, and they invented the Winslow window, a pioneering variety of the movable sash. They also worked on a flash boiler for the steam automobile. This was an immediate concern, since they both drove steam cars. Winslow was, in fact, an inventor and a man who all his life was fascinated by things mechanical. His daughter recalls her childhood as being filled with mechanical devices. These included elaborate swings and gymnastic apparatus and an auto turntable in the garage, which she and her brothers used as a merry-go-round, somewhat to their parents' displeasure.[27]

PRISMATIC LIGHT, 1897–1910

Winslow and Waller exercised an influence on Wright that went far beyond the normal role of a client. Aside from their aforementioned patronage, this took a particular form in their foundation of the American Luxfer Prism Company in 1897, with Wright's plumbing consultant E. C. MacHarg.[28] That this venture had a particularly intimate character is borne out by the fact that at one time all these men had their business premises in John Root's Rookery Building in the Loop of 1885–87, the glazed foyer of which, faced with Luxfer prisms, was redesigned by Wright in 1905. It appears that the prism concept itself originated with Augustin Fresnel's invention of dioptric and catoptric lenses in the early 1820s, these lenses becoming universally available thereafter for use in lighthouse lantern construction.[29] The basic prism, as produced by the Luxfer company, consisted of four-by-four-inch glass tiles of varying thicknesses that were variously profiled on one face, so as to refract light back into the depth of the space. Obviously such a device could be seen as having a wide application in overdeveloped, downtown areas such as the Chicago Loop, with its high-rise office buildings and its overshadowed light wells of which the Rookery foyer was a typical example. Prior to the invention of the Luxfer Prism proper, glass lenses were bonded together through lead or zinc cames, which reduced the net size of the glazed area. As a means of overcoming this disadvantage Winslow invented a system known as "electroglazing" in the year the company was founded. Stipulating that his patent should apply to prismatic window glass and vault lights, and that this glass should have projecting, refracting ribs on its inner surface, Winslow's official patent went on to describe the system by which he had been able to fuse an assembly of such prisms into a single glazed surface, reinforced by a grid of copper ribbons holding the mosaic in place. Referring to the prism as a "glass tile," Winslow's 1897 patent reads:

The method of forming tile-sections into a body, which consists in bringing the several sections nearly together edge to edge, but with an open space between, interposing a foundation cathode electrical conductor comprising a loose skeleton frame of relatively strong material between such edges but so as still to leave a space to be filled between such edges, then subjecting the whole to the process of electro-deposition while the parts are in such a position, and thus depositing a homogeneous mass of metal between the tile edges until the tile edges are permanently secured together by the engagement of the conductor and mass of deposited metal with each other and with the tile and between the edges thereof.[30]

By placing a grid of prisms in a shallow acid bath and inserting a wire ribbon into their interstices Winslow was able to achieve a tight joint between the copper and the glass through electrolytic action. The deposition of copper onto the aforementioned cathode was continued until a dumbbell of metal was formed holding each prism in place, the fused joint being so tight as to render further weatherproofing unnecessary. The company announced the perfection of this technique in 1897 by publishing a booklet that provided the potential user with the necessary data showing how an optimum penetration of natural light could be obtained in each instance. Proffering a wide range of lenses, it recommended the most suitable prism section to be employed in each case. The brochure went so far as to suggest movable light-refracting canopies, although it seems that none was ever constructed. Electro-glazing soon came to be applied to some of the most progressive works of the period, including Wright's Isidore Heller House of

1897 (plates 30–31), Sullivan's Gage Building of 1899, and his later Schlesinger and Mayer Store (Carson, Pirie, Scott), completed in 1904. Both with and without electro-glazing the Luxfer Prism principle was sufficiently successful during the first decade of its existence to ensure the development of branches of the company in England and Germany. The most serious drawback to the process was that it was relatively slow and rather expensive, and this, plus the general increase in the use of artificial light, rendered the process and the prism obsolete by the late 1920s.

As far as its influence on Wright was concerned, the Luxfer Prism venture was important on a number of levels (see plate 27). First, both the product and the process furthered Wright's interest in the use of extensive areas of glass, both decorative and otherwise. Second, it provided Wright with direct craft commissions, most notably the design of so-called "signature plates" for the various lights that the company installed. Last, but not least, it was one more example of the latent potential of modern technology to yield unprecedented methods for constructing heterogeneous elements out of unconventional materials. To the extent that electro-glazing was a woven fabric, we may note its subsequent transposition as a principle to the scale of entire buildings—in the concrete-block houses that Wright built in California in the 1920s and even more directly in his totally glazed National Life Insurance Company Building in Chicago of 1924–25 (plate 205).

THE CITY IN MINIATURE, 1901–1922

With the opening of its own, admittedly short-lived, opera house in 1902, Oak Park was already close to becoming an ideal garden city, although Wright realized that such communities could hardly be assured of a civic identity by simply proliferating one freestanding house after another. His first attempt to develop a higher civic sense within suburbia came with A Home in a Prairie Town for the *Ladies' Home Journal* of 1901, which was laid out on a quadruple-block system (plate 42). This was the system that he later adopted, in modified form, for his so-called Noncompetitive Plan for City Residential Land Development of 1913–16 (plate 400). Wright seems to have posited this hypothetical model suburb for the outskirts of Chicago as an alternative to the Haussmannian grandeur of Daniel Burnham's Commercial Club Plan for Chicago of 1909.[31]

In principle, this microcosmic suburban town, fed by electric streetcars, was a synthesis of the Prairie typology that he had developed to date, including the Francis Apartments and Lexington Terrace Apartments of 1895 and 1901–09, respectively (plates 17–18, 60–62), the Quadruple Block Plan for C. E. Roberts of 1900–03 (plates 394–395), the Larkin Company Administration Building in Buffalo of 1902–06 (plates 65–73), Unity Temple in Oak Park of 1905–08 (plates 74–82), and the City National Bank and Hotel built in Mason City, Iowa, in 1909–11 (plates 107–108). Variations on these building types were here depicted as being integrated into a green fabric that was more articulated as a civic entity than Raymond Unwin's garden city, founded in Letchworth, England, in 1907.

Influenced by the Chicago school of urban sociology and by a revisionist consensus shared by such intellectuals as Addams, Dewey, Cooley, Veblen, and Robert Park, Wright's diminutive neighborhood unit may be regarded as an apotheosis of American Progressivism.[32] It was organized in such a way as to encourage the spontaneous formation of Cooley's primary social groups, namely the family, the kindergarten, and the neighborhood unit. Influenced by the elaborate Chicago park system initiated by Le Baron Jenney, Wright's park city was designed to facilitate a pattern of social interaction capable of compensating urban migrants for the loss of their small-town roots. In his ideal city-suburb, workers' low-rise high-density housing would be combined with clusters of single-family houses, the whole being interwoven like a carpet, together with the necessary educational and recreational facilities. The aim was to raise the level of the society through a process of spatial acculturation. As Roger Cranshawe has remarked, this was the last reformist effort to transcend the hegemony of industrial capitalism through bourgeois moral reform, and in this regard it is no surprise to find that Wright conceived of the church in his diminutive ideal city as nondenominational.[33]

Both Midway Gardens in Chicago of 1913–14 and the Imperial Hotel in Tokyo of 1912–23 (plates 133–144, 151–163) may be seen as further condensations of Wright's microcosmic city, and it is ironic that this romantic vision of a new kind of civic form, rivaling the great non-Eurocentric civilizations of the past, should attain its initial realization in a beer garden and a hotel. Be this as it may, Midway Gardens, festooned with colored balloons, evokes, like Wright's earlier Wolf Lake Amusement Park, an all but hallucinatory image of the future. In this festive display of civic glory and in the sculptural ornamentation of its garden court and suspended terraces Wright attempted to transcend the all too populist aspect of its consumerist character. Assisted by a team of artists acting under his direction—the cabinetmaker George Niedecken, the mosaic designer Blanche Ostertag, the glass artist Orlando Giannini, and the sculptors Richard Bock and Alfonso Iannelli—Wright sought to overcome through the total work of art (*Gesamtkunstwerk*) the expanding privatization and commercialization of the modern world. Following Sullivan's heroic example, he attempted to create an absolutely unprecedented architecture appropriate to the emerging destiny of the new world. This much is declared as an intent with overwhelming pride and confidence in his description of Midway Gardens, which appeared in the 1925 Wendingen publication of his complete works:

Imagination will vivify the background and expression of modern life, as truly and more universally and richly than was ever before seen in the world,—even in the aesthetic background of the Moors or the Chinese.

The sneer of "factory aesthetics" goes by its mark. It is the Imagination that is new challenged, not the Memory.

When the industrial buildings of a country are natural buildings, and vital expressions of the conditions underlying their existence—the domestic architecture of that country will be likewise true. . . .

Beauty may come abide with us in more intimate spirit than ever

graced and enriched the lives of the masterful-few in the ancient "Glory that was Greece" and the "Grandeur that was Rome" if we master the Machine in this integral sense. It is time we realized that Grecian buildings have been universally overrated as Architecture: They are full of lies, pretence and stupidity. And the Roman architecture, but for the nobility of the structural arch, a thing now dead,—was a wholly debased version of the better Greek elements that preceded it.[34]

While Greece and Rome are deprecated, this revealing text, written by Wright when he was nearly sixty, glorifies the orient in general and Islam and China in particular as the only valid heritage for a revitalized modern civilization. At the same time, mechanized production and industrial aesthetics are jointly seen as the occidental catalyst with which to re-create a culture of comparable richness.

THE MAGNESITE MACHINE, 1902–1906

By the turn of the century Wright had already posited the idea of the building as a machine, most notably in the Larkin Company Administration Building, designed and realized for Darwin D. Martin in Buffalo between 1902 and 1906 (plates 65–73). In order to exclude the harsh industrial environment in which it was situated, Wright conceived of this structure as an introspective microcosm with which to compensate for the general absence of any kind of public realm in what was rapidly becoming a totally privatized, productional world, exacerbated in its effect by the ever-escalating amortization of both plant and equipment. All of this accounts in different ways for the fundamentally inward character of the Larkin Building, a structure in which, while one could not look out, a considerable amount of light entered the office space from above and from the sides. An equally introspective approach can be found in all of Wright's subsequent public buildings, as though the immediate environment surrounding any civic work could no longer be experienced as a significant public realm. By contrast, his private domestic works remained open to a continual exchange with the benevolent natural environment by which they were usually surrounded.

The Larkin commission arose from the necessity of providing the company's expanding mail-order business with more efficient space and from the desire of Martin's idealistic office manager, William R. Heath, to house his 1,800 employees, mostly women, in an efficient, but nonetheless dignified and morally uplifting, environment. Wright answered this program with five floors of offices arranged around four sides of a top-lit atrium, thereby imparting a *horizontal* dimension to the internal space. The resultant feeling of lateral communality, so to speak, was balanced by the aspiring verticality of the central void.

Influenced by Sullivan's Wainwright Building of 1886–90 and stemming ideologically from his seminal essay "The Tall Office Building Artistically Considered" of 1896,[35] the Larkin Building was evidently not just one more isolated office structure. Like the top-lit galleria or department store from which it derived its section, the Larkin Building was permeated by diffused light descending from above. In this way Wright was able to create a self-sufficient world that not only afforded recreational and educational facilities for its employees, as is evidenced by the lounge, library, restrooms, and classrooms incorporated into the annex, but also provided the staff with facilities for lunching together on the fifth floor, not to mention the option of taking a lunchtime stroll within the conservatory and roof garden above (figure 6). For Wright, as for Martin and Heath, the place of work, like the family hearth, was to be rendered as a place of sacrament, hence the inscriptions that adorn the more prominent parts of the structure at every juncture (figure 7), from the highest spandrels of the atrium that were inscribed with moralistic legends such as "Ask and It Shall Be Given You / Seek and Ye Shall Find Knock / and It Shall Be Opened unto You," to Richard Bock's stone-faced wall fountain at the Seneca Street entry, bearing the words, "Honest Labor Needs No Masters / Simple Justice Needs No Slaves." High under the laylight of the atrium, forty-two virtuous words, embossed in gold, spelled out the ethical slogans of the entire enterprise, including the revolutionary "Liberty, Equality, Fraternity."[36] While the disingenuousness of such sloganeering could hardly have been lost on the more sophisticated of Heath's "office force," an atmosphere of heroic dedication and civic decorum prevailed throughout, as is confirmed by the surviving photographs of the building in its heyday. This conscious evocation of an Emersonian aura was greatly enhanced by the installation of an organ at the north end of the fifth floor that, aside from

Figure 7: Frank Lloyd Wright. Detail of Light Court, Larkin Company Administration Building, Buffalo. 1902–06

bestowing an ecclesiastical atmosphere, also afforded the employees an instrument for the occasional concert either at lunchtime or in the evening.[37] This unusual feature, the whim of the client rather than the architect, inadvertently recalls the precedent for the Larkin scheme in Wright's own work, namely his proposal for the Abraham Lincoln Center in Chicago of 1898–1905 (plates 63–64), designed for his uncle the Reverend Jenkin Lloyd Jones. In this project a three-story church at grade was to have been capped by three floors of offices above, partially lit by a central atrium.

By displacing the circulation and service ducts to the four corners of the Larkin Building, Wright was able to create a bureaucratic machine of unprecedented efficiency, a structure that became the second fully air-conditioned office building in the world, the first having been Le Baron Jenney's Chicago National Bank, erected in Chicago in 1901. In addition to ducts for air, gas, water, waste, electricity, and a built-in vacuum-cleaning system, many other fittings were specially designed by Wright to facilitate the operation of the building, including built-in metal filing cabinets set beneath double-glazed fixed windows, wall-hung water closets and suspended magnesite partitions, and finally, mobile steel office furniture running on castors that raised it above the floor in order to facilitate cleaning. Apart from the semivitreous cream-colored facing bricks used to line the interior wall, the building was finished throughout in fireproof magnesite cement, imported from Greece. The extent to which this was used for every auxiliary component is borne out in Wright's own description of 1906: "Stairs, floors, doors, window sills, copings, capitals, partitions, desk tops, plumbing labs, all are of this material and are worked 'in situ'

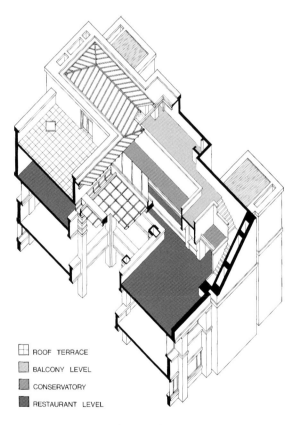

☐ ROOF TERRACE
☐ BALCONY LEVEL
☐ CONSERVATORY
☐ RESTAURANT LEVEL

Figure 6: Axonometric diagram of upper floors, Larkin Company Administration Building

without seams or joints with sanitary curves at all wall surfaces, finishing as hard and durable as iron, as light in color as the brick work and, not the least valuable of its properties, light in weight."[38] At its peak, this "machine-for-working-in" handled five thousand letters a day. The looms of the textile industry had been replaced, as it were, by Remington typewriters and Graphophones, and textile production had been displaced by the handling of information. And while the open work space, with its regimented desks, was nothing short of panoptic in every respect, with a red light indicating when an operator was out of work, Wright and the Larkin executives did their best to transcend this new form of alienated labor and to advance the rationalized office structure as a new "social condenser."[39] At the same time, for Heath, the Larkin Building, together with its staff, remained the physical embodiment of the industrial demiurge, which, like water flowing downhill and turning a water wheel, feeds the wheels of commerce.[40] The furniture itself seemed grounded in the principles of F. W. Taylor's scientific management, since, as Frank Duffy has observed, the hinged chair cantilevering off the desk on a swivel system "allowed only a minimum of movement, an eloquent indication of the abdication of freedom on the part of the clerk in the early years of Taylorism."[41]

THE TEXTILE TECTONIC, 1915–1924

Notwithstanding his occasional recourse to reinforced-concrete construction, Wright invariably adopted a plaited approach toward architectural form; one that not only depended on the interpenetration of tartanlike grids, as in the brick house that he designed for Darwin D. Martin in 1902–04 (plates 55–59), but also one that stemmed from the interwoven assembly of different structural components regardless of whether they were of light-timber or heavy-masonry construction. As we have seen, the first of these modes gave rise to his so-called River Forest style, based on a three-foot modified balloon-frame module, with battens covering the horizontal joint at thirteen-inch intervals. In principle, Wright returned to this method in 1915 in his prototypical designs for the so-called American System Ready-Cut House made for the Milwaukee builder Arthur L. Richards, who founded American System-Built Houses in that year (plate 176).[42] Following the rupture with his Oak Park clientele in 1909 and realizing that, in any event, this privileged middle class was beginning to lose its capacity to build on a lavish scale, Wright turned his attention toward the permutable, modular aspects of mechanical reproduction as these might be applied to the housing needs of the society at large. At this juncture he opted for rationalized modes of production based on existing mill sizes rather than for specially designed prefabricated forms as self-contained hermetic systems. And yet despite his ingenious adaptation of the balloon frame to the Ready-Cut method and the construction of a considerable number of Ready-Cut houses in the Milwaukee area during the first year of operation, the company was dissolved in the late summer of 1917. We may obtain some idea of the technical aspects of this system from Richards's insistence that the main framing members should

not be interrupted by openings, and that windows should be so placed to assure cross lighting and cross ventilation.[43] He went on to state that the kitchens and roof spaces should be well ventilated and that as far as possible all the furniture should be built-in. Aside from assuring value for money and durability, Wright praised the virtues of the method in 1916 in terms that recalled his Hull House address of 1901:

The American System-built house is not a ready-cut house but a house built by an organization systematized in such a way that the result is guaranteed the fellow that buys the house. I want to deliver beautiful houses to people at a certain price, key in packet. If I have made progress in the art of architecture, I want to be able to offer this to the people intact. I think the idea will appeal also to the man in the street. Every man would love to have a beautiful house if he could pay for the tremendous amount of waste usually involved in building such a house. The American [System] plan you see, simply cuts out the tremendous waste that has in the past made house building on a beautiful scale possible only to the very rich.[44]

When Wright first fully tackled fair-faced reinforced-concrete construction in Unity Temple, he was already oriented toward devising the most economical means possible for achieving a homogeneous cast-in-place form (figure 8). Thus, he wrote in retrospect:

Why not make the wooden boxes or forms so the concrete could be cast in them as separate blocks and masses, these . . . grouped about an interior space. . . .

The wooden forms or molds in which concrete buildings must at that time be cast were always the chief item of expense, so to repeat the use of a single one as often as possible was desirable, even necessary. Therefore a building all four sides alike looked like the thing. This, in simplest terms, meant a building square in plan. That would make their temple a cube, a noble form.[45]

Notwithstanding the geometrical form of Unity Temple, Wright was prompt to recognize that, due to its inherent lack of articulation, monolithic concrete could hardly be rendered as an articulate tectonic surface. Thus, even as late as 1928, we find him writing that it is not easy "to see in this conglomerate, a high aesthetic property, because, in itself it is amalgam, aggregate, compound. And cement, the binding medium, is characterless."[46]

Wright's acknowledgment of this lack of character brought him to consider the possibility of replacing concrete with reinforced, monolithic concrete-block construction built up out of stack-bonded prefabricated units. As he wrote in his famous confessional, *An Autobiography*, of 1932: "The concrete block? The cheapest (and ugliest) thing in the building world. It lived mostly in the architectural gutter as an imitation of 'rock face' stone. Why not see what could be done with that gutter-rat? Steel wedded to it cast inside the joints and the block itself brought into some broad, practical scheme of general treatment then why would it not be fit for a phrase of modern architecture? It might be permanent, noble, beautiful. It would be cheap."[47]

For all its self-evident simplicity the idea proved difficult to realize

Figure 8: Frank Lloyd Wright. Unity Temple, Oak Park. 1905–08. Under construction

in an economical form, for while Wright was prompt to realize that concrete blocks could be erected readily by unskilled labor, the man-hours required to cast, stack, reinforce, and cement-grout the blocks proved to be much greater than initially envisioned. While the price varied, it was certainly more expensive than traditional construction, partly because of its prototypical character and partly because of the vested interests of the building industry, which, aided and abetted by bureaucracy, stood in the way of a more general adoption of such a system. So pervasive was this official resistance that the four concrete-block houses Wright built in the short space of two years in the Los Angeles region were all completed without an official building permit.

Designed for Mrs. George Madison Millard, for whom he had previously built a house in Highland Park, Illinois, in 1908, the first concrete-block house, known as La Miniatura (plates 178–181), was built in Pasadena out of concrete walls made up of two, three-and-one-half-inch-wide, concrete tile screens separated by one inch of air space. While variously adapted in the subsequent block houses built over the space of a year, the basic unit always remained the same, namely sixteen-by-sixteen-inch precast blocks (figure 9). As Wright put it: "I finally had found a simple mechanical means to produce a complete building that looks the way the machine made it, as much at least as any fabric need look. Tough, light, but not 'thin'; imperishable; plastic; no unnecessary lie about it anywhere and yet machine-made, mechanically perfect. Standardization as the soul of the machine here for the first time may be seen in the hand of the architect, put squarely up to the limitations of imagination the only limitation of building."[48]

Wright seems to have first envisioned monolithic block construction around the time that Unity Temple was completed. This can be seen in the prefabricated block house that he designed for Harry E. Brown in Geneva, Illinois, of 1906. In the decade that followed he increasingly used patterned block and tile formations of various kinds, first in the tiling applied to the exterior of the Avery Coonley House in Riverside, Illinois, of 1906–08 (plates 87–95), and then in the ornamental concrete blocks that made up the cornice of the A. D. German Warehouse in Richland Center, Wisconsin, of 1915–20 (plates 146–147), and in similar blocks applied to Midway Gardens, completed in

1914. Wright may have first posited repetitive, steel-wire-reinforced concrete-block construction, assembled out of identical rectangular units, in the compound and shrine that he designed for A. M. Johnson in Death Valley, California, of 1922–25 (plate 196). In terms of both panoramic form and programmatic grandeur this Egyptoid structure was as exotic in its cultural aspirations as the house and theater that Wright designed at the same time for Aline Barnsdall on her estate, Olive Hill, overlooking Los Angeles in 1916–21 (plates 164–170). However, Barnsdall's Hollyhock House was not built in concrete block, so that the full proof of the textile system did not occur until the realization of La Miniatura, of which Wright wrote in noticeably environmental terms in 1932: "We would make the walls double of course, one wall facing inside and the other wall facing outside, thus getting continuous hollow spaces between, so the house would be cool in summer, warm in winter and dry always."[49] In the same text Wright referred to himself as a "weaver," thereby stressing once again his conception of the Textile Block as an all-enveloping woven membrane and suppressing, by implication, those complementary structural members that were essential to its erection—namely, those reinforced-concrete beams and columns, and even the occasional wooden lintel or rafter floor, that were necessary to the horizontal continuity of the system. This technical inconsistency is emphasized by the fact that in almost all of the block houses the floor depths do not quite coincide with the vertical modular dimension.

With its patterned, perforated glass-filled apertures La Miniatura already embodied the essential syntax of the Textile Block system that would be employed, with subtle variations, in each of the subsequent houses. With the exception of the Samuel Freeman House in Los Angeles of 1923–24 (plates 187–191), where the blocks run into open glass corners and where the muntins seem to extend directly from the joints between the blocks, Wright's subsequent California block houses, the John Storer and Charles E. Ennis houses of 1923–24 (plates 182–186, 192–195), add little to the basic syntax of the Millard House. With the exception of this first prototype, in which Wright cast the blocks from wood molds, the textile blocks were invariably made from metal patterns, filled with a dry, compacted concrete mix.[50] The blocks were then wet-cured for ten days prior to their assembly. Wherever possible Wright attempted to introduce decomposed granite from the site into the mix from which the blocks were cast, in order to achieve a particularly intrinsic, not to say mystical, union between nature and culture, although this incorporation of imperceptible amounts of organic material proved to be detrimental to the durability of the construction.[51]

Whether they were simply indented, freely perforated, or filled with glass, Wright employed three different patterns in his blocks: radially symmetrical, symmetrical, and asymmetrical.[52] This variation, plus the different degrees of visual permeability, afforded a wide range of alternative permutations with which to express different tectonic conditions and to vary, in a more general sense, the superficial rhythm and scale of mass-form. In the Millard prototype Wright attempted to solve all the different junction conditions to be encountered in the work:

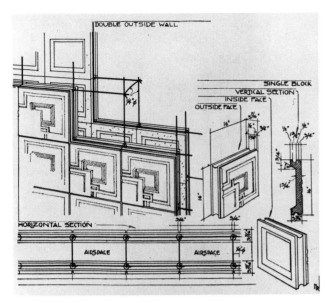

Figure 9: Frank Lloyd Wright. Textile Block construction system.
c. 1923. Print. The Frank Lloyd Wright Foundation

the reentrant corner, the freestanding wall, and the end corner condition. In all of this Wright conceived of the built-up columns and piers as fragments of the overall system. We should note, however, that the system was not as "automatic" as Wright may have implied, since in the Freeman House some forty percent of the blocks were mitered at the corners.[53]

Wright's last concrete-block house in this series was erected in Tulsa, Oklahoma, in 1928–31 for his cousin Richard Lloyd Jones (plates 219–223). It already appears to be a transitional work, since here, the hitherto finely woven fabric of the square textile block is abandoned in favor of a larger rectangular unit, laid up as walls or monumental piers. Wright's unrealizable ideal of a building without windows is relinquished here in favor of an alternating pattern of piers and slots where solid and void are equally matched. This passage from the sixteen-inch-square pattern of the Los Angeles houses to the fifteen-by-twenty-inch plain-faced, stack-bonded block pattern of the Lloyd Jones House produces a paradoxical decrease in the apparent mass, the true scale being lost through the partial suppression of floor heights. However, apart from permitting a consistent alignment between block courses and window transoms, the larger block displayed other advantages, from the saving of labor in the process of laying it to the filling of the hollow cores with substantial amounts of cement and steel reinforcement to produce integrated reinforced-concrete piers of much greater strength or, alternatively, to provide voids for the accommodation of ventilation ducts and piped services.

THE PAGODA AND THE ZIGGURAT, 1924

In 1924 Wright returned to the theme of the modern office building artistically considered, only this time he treated it as a translucent mass that rose as much in height as it extended in depth. In this unrealized project for the National Life Insurance Company in Chicago he demonstrated once again his penchant for tectonic reversal: he treated the glazing as though it were a form of textile block interwoven with copper mullions and hung off a structural core of cantilevered concrete construction so as to form a tessellated curtain wall (plate 205). As we have already seen, Wright's earlier connection to the American Luxfer Prism Company seems to have been a direct inspiration for this invention. Conceived nearly thirty years after his project for the curtain-walled Luxfer Prism Office Building of 1896–97 (plate 27) and twelve years after his second essay in high-rise construction, his twenty-story, Sullivanian, brick-clad skyscraper project for *The San Francisco Call* company in 1913, Wright elaborated this thirty-one-story building as a castellated, glass-and-sheet-metal high-rise. Almost as tall as the thirty-four-story, steel-framed, stone-faced Chicago Tribune Tower then under construction, this project was clearly intended to be read as a challenge to Raymond Hood's Gothic Revival design. The comprehensive technological character of this naturally ventilated, prefabricated counter-proposal is evident from Wright's description of it in 1928:

The exterior walls, as such, disappear—instead are suspended, standardized sheet-copper screens. The walls themselves cease to exist as either weight or thickness. Windows become in this fabrication a matter of a unit in the screen fabric, opening singly or in groups at the will of the occupant. All windows may be cleaned from the inside with neither bother nor risk. The vertical mullions (copper shells filled with nonconducting material), are large and strong enough only to carry from floor to floor and project much or little as shadow on the glass may or may not be wanted. Much projection enriches the shadow. Less projection dispels the shadows and brightens the interior. These protecting blades of copper act in the sun like the blades of a blind.

The unit of two feet both ways is, in this instance, emphasized on every alternate vertical with additional emphasis on every fifth. There is no emphasis on the horizontal units. The edge of the various floors being beveled to the same section as is used between the windows, it appears in the screen as such a horizontal division occurring naturally on the two-foot lines. . . .

Being likewise fabricated on a perfect unit system, the interior partitions may all be made up in sections, complete with doors, ready to set in place and designed to match the general style of the outer wall screen.

These interior partition-units thus fabricated may be stored ready to use, and any changes to suit tenants made over night with no waste of time and material.

The increase of glass area over the usual skyscraper fenestration is only about ten per cent (the margin could be increased or diminished by expanding or contracting the copper members in which it is set), so the expense of heating is not materially increased. Inasmuch as the copper mullions are filled with insulating material and the window openings are tight, being mechanical units in a mechanical screen, this excess of glass is compensated.

The radiators are cast as a railing set in front of the lower glass unit of this outer screen wall, free enough to make cleaning easy.[54]

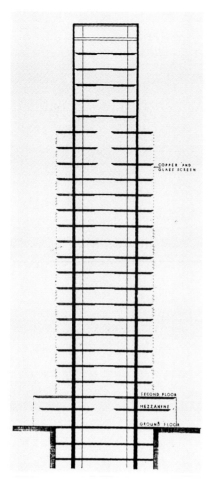

Figure 10: Frank Lloyd Wright. National Life
Insurance Company Building, Chicago.
Project, 1924–25. Section

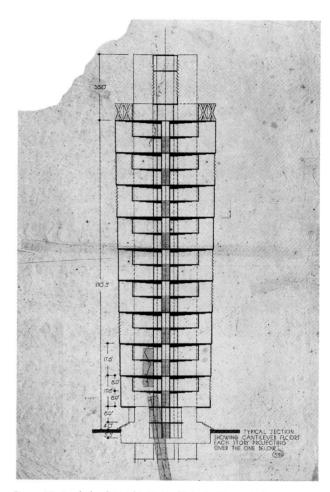

Figure 11: Frank Lloyd Wright. St. Mark's-in-the-Bouwerie Tower,
New York. Project, 1927–31. Section; ink on tracing paper.
The Frank Lloyd Wright Foundation

Wright conceived of this internal, treelike cantilevered structure as a composite, four-column symmetrical system supporting cantilevered floors that were linked by a slab of shallower depth spanning between the points of contraflexure (figure 10). Where this slab was omitted at the higher levels, it yielded a central atrium similar in scale and character to the Larkin Building. As the architectural historian M. F. Hearn has argued, this project was particularly significant for the way in which it extended Wright's debt to Japanese culture. After noting that Wright's previous skyscraper proposal of 1913 had been predicated on rather conventional framing techniques, Hearn suggested the pagoda as the prototype for the high-rise form that Wright was to adopt twelve years later:

As is well known, Wright had espoused a special interest and regard for the architecture of Japan since seeing the Ho-o-den at the Columbian Exposition in Chicago in 1893. There can be no doubt that during the years when he resided primarily in Japan (1917–1922), while working on the Imperial Hotel, he was both interested and attentive when he had the opportunity to see something new to him in Japanese architecture. (He acknowledged, for instance, that he got the idea for the heated floors of his Usonian houses from Baron Okuda's "Korean room," with its warm-air ducts beneath the floor.) Therefore, when the occasion for an

excursion to major sites of Japanese religious architecture arose, he would certainly have welcomed it. One of the most likely candidates for such an experience would have been the oldest sanctuary in Japan, the Horyu-ji shrine near Nara, preserved from the seventh and eighth centuries. Waiting there for Wright's attention was a feature in the pagoda that had been consciously adopted from China to help the tower withstand the shock of earthquakes; a rigid central member, or "heart pillar," acting as a mast.[55]

Once adopted, the pagoda concept appeared elsewhere in Wright's work, notably in the St. Mark's-in-the-Bouwerie Towers for New York of 1927–31 (figure 11; plates 211–214) and in a linear complex of apartment towers designed for Chicago in 1930 (plates 215–216). Wright returned to the concept again after World War II in the S. C. Johnson & Son, Inc. Research Laboratory Tower of 1943–50 (plates 261–267) and the H. C. Price Company Tower, completed at Bartlesville, Oklahoma, in 1956, three years before his death (plates 333–338). These last works established beyond any doubt the structural feasibility of the concept, above all perhaps the fourteen-story research tower, which was the first building ever to cantilever its floors from a hollow central concrete core containing a cylindrical elevator, utilities, and stair (figure 12).

In the 1920s Wright's work assumed a peculiarly prophetic cast.

Wright not only anticipated the corporate office complex but became increasingly preoccupied with the mass ownership of the automobile during a period when it was growing seven times as fast as the population. This unprecedented admass phenomenon manifested itself in his architecture with the appearance of a ziggurat form, which he projected as a so-called Automobile Objective to be built on the top of Sugarloaf Mountain in Maryland (plates 209–210). This work was commissioned by the entrepreneur Gordon Strong, who wanted to build a tourist attraction catering exclusively to motorists. With its car ramps facing out over a vast panorama and its interior lined with restaurants and shops, Wright's spiraling cantilevered concrete construction, was wrapped around the hemispherical concrete shell of a planetarium some two hundred feet in diameter. The whole was evidently intended to function as a viewing platform, both inside and out. While this project was never realized, its spiral form reemerged in yet another transposition in Wright's Solomon R. Guggenheim Museum, first sketched out in 1943 as a literal ziggurat, spiraling upward toward the top. In the very same year he inverted the spiral to form what he playfully called a "taruggiz," that is to say, a ziggurat in reverse (plates 301–310). It is typical of Wright's perennial orientalism that both of these tectonic paradigms of the mid-1920s—the pagoda and the ziggurat—should have their origins in the East: in China and Persia.

THE USONIAN DOMUS, 1932–1939

Wright's return to his midwestern roots led to the final phase of his textile tectonic: the Usonian house that prevailed in his work as a continuous domestic type right up to his death in 1959. This generic brick-and-timber domestic prototype first appeared in his Malcolm Willey House in Minneapolis of 1932–34 (plate 229). That Wright was aware of the breakthrough that this work represented is borne out by the following passage: "Now came clear *an entirely new sense of architecture*, a higher conception of architecture . . . space enclosed. . . . This interior conception took architecture away from sculpture, away from painting and entirely away from architecture as it had been known in the antique. The building now became a creation of interior space in light. And as this sense of the interior space as the reality of the building began to work, walls as walls fell away."[56]

Double-sided and triple-layered, these walls were of lightweight wood construction, comprising seasoned twelve-by-seven-inch timber boards affixed to a continuous plywood core to yield a striated wall, composed of horizontal recesses inside and out, as opposed to the projecting cover battens of Wright's River Forest style. Woven at more than one scale, the Usonian house was more generally conceived as a three-dimensional gridded cage in which two-by-four-foot and four-foot-square modular units yielded spatial layers that were interwoven, so to speak, with thirteen-inch vertical intervals governing the position of all the horizontal elements, including window transoms, door heights, bookshelves, built-in furniture, and even the brick coursework of the central chimney stack. The walls were given a spatial warp and woof into which, as Wright put it, in the sixth point of his *Architectural*

Figure 12: Frank Lloyd Wright. S. C. Johnson & Son, Inc. Research Laboratory Tower, Racine. 1943–50. Under construction

Forum manifesto of 1938, furniture, pictures, and bric-a-brac could readily be accommodated.[57] That the typical Usonian dwelling consisted of a three-dimensional matrix made up of interlocking locational fixes and layers is borne out by Wright's typical provision of three separate plan cuts: one at floor level, one at door-head or clerestory height, and one at roof level. Needless to say, such sophisticated information required considerable site supervision for, as John Sergeant has remarked, from this point onward Wright's millwork was conceived as kind of intricate basketry.[58]

As in the Ready-Cut system, Wright eliminated field labor as much as possible and reduced waste in the cutting of timber by adopting a module that corresponded to standard mill dimensions and the typical eight-by-four sheet. At the same time, since almost all of the Usonian houses were of a single story, Wright was able to exploit the thermal flywheel effect of the cast-concrete slab on which the house was invariably grounded. Such an inert mass tended by its very nature to be warmer in winter and cooler in summer than the average wood floor. Wright evidently saw this provision as a natural evolution of the gravity heating system that he first encountered in Japan in 1919. With serpentine, small-bore heating pipes cast into the slab, the typical Usonian dwelling, even when boosted with an open fire, tended to be just comfortable in the winter rather than overheated, and Wright openly admitted that in severe weather people would simply have to put on more clothes.[59] In high summer the ubiquitous clerestory window system provided ample cross ventilation, as did the chimney flues, while deep overhangs shielded the large areas of full-height glass from sun penetration in the middle of the day. Many liberative spatial sequences were built into the volume of the typical Usonian dwelling, including fairly ample wall storage (the thick-wall concept), continuous seating, and the close physical and visual proximity of the kitchen to the dining-living area. In the Herbert Jacobs House in Madison, Wisconsin, of 1936–37 subtle zones of microspace are distributed throughout the house for every conceivable activity (plates 241–245).

From the beginning, Wright conceived of the Usonian system as a kit of parts that had to be assembled according to a particular sequence. His growing recognition of the socioeconomic need for many people to build their own houses led him to standardize many of the details in the Usonian system, and these, quite naturally, were repeated with variations from one house to the next. Borrowing its sequence and method of assembly from aspects of traditional Japanese house construction, the typical Usonian dwelling was built in a particular order. At each stage, this sequence can be seen as incorporating each of Gottfried Semper's generic elements as set forth in his *Four Elements of Architecture* of 1851, although we have no evidence that Wright was consciously aware of Semper's text.[60] Thus, in the process of casting the floor slab and building the brick chimney, we might arrive at the first two elements of Semper's anthropological paradigm, namely the earthwork and the hearth. This would be followed by the third Semperian element, the essential carpentry component of the framework and the roof, while the whole would then be enclosed by the application of the screenlike fourth element, namely the infill wall or *die Wand*, as Semper referred to it.

THE STREAMLINED ATLANTIS

Wright's ultimate essay in cantilevered concrete construction came with the remarkable house that he built for Edgar J. Kaufmann at Mill Run, Pennsylvania, between 1934 and 1937 (plates 234–240). In retrospect, this house may be seen as a condensation of the essential tectonic of Wright's National Life Insurance Company project in that the concrete cantilevered core of the office building now becomes the visible body of the entire work, while its tessellated curtain-wall was transformed into the horizontal steel glazing that served as an infill between the concrete upstands of the house. Thus what had been essentially translucent and vertical in the Chicago project, became transparent and horizontal at Mill Run. His insistence on smoothly flowing tiered forms turned Wright toward a kind of dramatic streamlined expression that, in effect, became his complex response to the alternative modern styles being disseminated at the time: the so-called International Style and Art Deco form.

Wright's drive to juxtapose nature and culture as explicitly as possible took on a particularly dramatic character in this house in the projection of an eighteen-foot clear-span concrete cantilever over the crest of a waterfall, from which it derived its renowned name, Fallingwater. Wright wrote: "There in a beautiful forest was a solid, high rock ledge rising beside a waterfall, and the natural thing seemed to be to cantilever the house from that rock bank over the falling water."[61] However natural this may have seemed to Wright, it was almost beyond the capacity of reinforced concrete to perform such a feat, let alone the various bureaucrats and engineers who supervised its construction— including William Wesley Peters and Mendel Glickman, who acted as Wright's engineers.[62] Thus, despite the twenty-four-inch structural depth, consisting of upstand beams set at forty-eight-inch centers, rein-

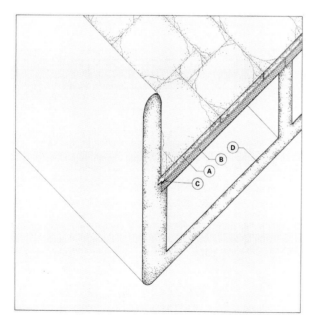

Figure 13: Diagram of balcony detail, Fallingwater, Edgar J. Kaufmann House: A, flagstone paving; B, two layers of gypsum block; C, lead flashing; D, concrete slab

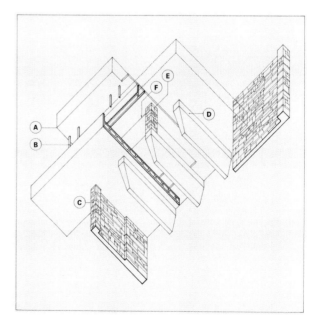

Figure 14: Diagram of framing plan, Fallingwater, Edgar J. Kaufmann House: A, cantilevered balcony; B, steel posts; C, masonry pier; D, concrete piers resting on rock; E, stone columns resting on concrete piers; F, concrete slab

Figure 15: Frank Lloyd Wright. Window detail, Fallingwater, Edgar J. Kaufmann House, Mill Run. 1934–37

forced with one-inch-diameter steel bars, and carrying a soffit slab seven inches deep, insufficient allowance was made for deflection, given the span and load, so that an all but imperceptible sag developed at the end of the cantilever.[63] The inevitable settlement cracks that followed were equally disquieting to client and architect, and Wright once remarked that he thought that the floors of Fallingwater were too heavy.[64] He and his engineers deeply regretted their failure to exploit the full depth of the balustrading as structural trusses, although it is unlikely that this could have been achieved without compromising the overall illusion of floor planes miraculously floating in space.

It is interesting to note that Wright reduced the weight of his cantilevered terraces by laying flagstone paving directly onto gypsum block panels spanning between the concrete ribs of the terrace structure (figure 13). The support of the main cantilever in part on a rough-coursed fieldstone wall and in part on three massive reinforced-concrete bolsters rising from the rock bed and tapering up toward the soffit (figure 14), came together in such a way as to create the aura of a modern mountain lodge. This feeling for rusticated modernity would be reinforced by building the hearth of the house over a rock outcrop in the living-room floor and by allowing the horizontal metal-framed glazing to enter directly into the fieldstone walls (figure 15). Wright concluded this romantic tour de force with the suspension of a concrete stair leading down to a thin platform hanging just above the surface of the waterfall (plate 237). His wish to finish the entire house in gold leaf, once again betrayed his antipathy to concrete, but this grotesque extravagance was resisted by Kaufmann, and Wright finally settled for painting the exposed concrete surfaces in yellow-ocher cement-based paint.[65]

Momentarily abandoning the pagoda, the ziggurat, and the concrete cantilever, Wright turned in 1931 to a uniquely hybrid applica-

tion of mushroom-column construction in which, by greatly expanding and flattening the diameter of the mushroom cap, the flat slab as such is virtually eliminated. This lily-pad hypostyle-hall typology was first proposed by Wright for the Capital Journal Building in Salem, Oregon, of 1931–32 (plates 252–253). There an eight-by-eight, dendriform-columned, double-height hall is envisioned as housing the printing and editorial space of a local newspaper.[66] As in the National Life Insurance Company project, the exterior membrane is reduced to a translucent curtain wall, which in this instance assumes the form and rhythm of the fenestration in the Richard Lloyd Jones House. Wright totally abandoned this quasi–Art Deco reference in his next dendriform proposal, namely, the S. C. Johnson & Son, Inc. Administration Building at Racine, Wisconsin, of 1936–39 (plates 254–260, 264–267). Jonathan Lipman's account of the unique character of Wright's structural invention can hardly be improved upon:

Wright called the columns "dendriform"—tree-shaped—and he borrowed from botany to name three of their four segments: stem, petal, and calyx. The base of each column is a seven-inch-high, three-ribbed shoe, which he called a crow's foot. On it rests the shaft, or stem, nine inches wide at the bottom and widening two and a half degrees from the vertical axis. The taller columns are mostly hollow, the walls being only three and a half inches thick. Capping is a wider hollow, ringed band, which Wright referred to as a calyx.

On the calyx sits a twelve-and-a-half-inch-thick hollow pad Wright called a petal. Two radial concrete rings and continuous concrete struts run through it. Both stem and calyx are reinforced with expanded steel mesh, and the petal is reinforced with both mesh and bars.[67]

Each of the aforementioned petals had a diameter of nineteen feet and was prevented from overturning by being linked on axis through tangent connections to adjacent lily pads on all four sides. The entire system was, in effect, a continuous, multisupport two-way frame, and the corresponding absence of a bending moment in the columns permitted the installation of a hinged, momentless bearing at the foot of each support.[68] Once again Wright and his engineers Peters and Glickman were on the cutting edge, since the casting of columns of such intricate form entailed the use of early-strength concrete and the application of internal vibration together with the pumped delivery of freshly mixed concrete to where it was needed. This unprecedented construction method discouraged the aggregate from settling and facilitated a close monitoring of each concrete batch. The precise shape resulted from casting the columns in welded steel forms, while the concrete itself was reinforced in its narrower sections through the application of expanded metal mesh (figure 16). Needless to say, none of this was achieved without extensive, troublesome, on-site field tests of prototypical columns cast in situ (figure 17).

However, this was not the only pioneering innovation to be broached in the realization of the Johnson Administration Building, for its more dramatic and in some respects most foolhardy feature was Wright's audacious application of Pyrex glass tubing in the construction of the clerestory around the perimeter of the so-called Great

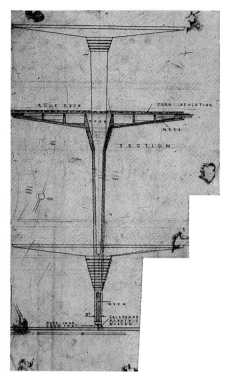

Figure 16: Frank Lloyd Wright. S. C. Johnson & Son, Inc. Administration Building, Racine. 1936–39. Section, columns; pencil on tracing paper. The Frank Lloyd Wright Foundation

Figure 17: Frank Lloyd Wright. S. C. Johnson & Son, Inc. Administration Building, Racine. 1936–39. Column load test, with Frank Lloyd Wright at right

Workroom, a space that was otherwise windowless on all four sides. It is clear that Wright first thought of using two layers of interlocking hollow glass blocks, which were then, surprisingly enough, already being produced as a standard line by Libby-Owens-Ford.[69] In this early study, later rejected out of hand, Wright proposed running a single reinforcing rod through the air space between the glass-block walls in order to provide a lateral tie between the upper and lower brick walls. This composite solution, however sound from a technical standpoint, did not meet with the *streamlined* look Wright desired, and no visually satisfying solution could be found until he happened upon the standard chemical glass tubing, patented under the name Pyrex, that was then being produced by the Corning Glass Company. Because this tubing was produced in curved segments, the material could be carried smoothly around the streamlined corners of the building, which may have been the main reason Wright decided against the use of hollow glass blocks. The Pyrex tubes were eventually supported on specially designed, cast-aluminum scalloped racks, to which they were secured with wires before being mastic-jointed along the entire length of the building (figure 18). The same tubes were used on the flat to form the herringbone matrix of the lower skylight filling the interstices between the lily pads (plate 258). Needless to say, this translucent infill had to be covered with a raised, fully glazed skylight, gently sloped so as to drain water into the circular, saucerlike roofs situated over each dendriform column. Of an equally woven character were the brick walls themselves made out of inner and outer leaves of fair-faced brickwork separated by three inches of cork insulation, with reinforcement inserted into the interstitial spaces on either side and the whole filled

up with concrete to render the entire fabric monolithic (figure 19). As per Wright's habitual practice, the horizontal brick joints were deeply raked and the corresponding vertical joints were flush-pointed with matching mortar. Of this overall interwoven horizontality he wrote: "Glass tubing laid up like bricks in a wall composes all the lighting surfaces. Light enters the building where the cornice used to be. In the interior the box-like structure vanished completely. The walls carrying the glass ribbing are of hard red brick and red Kasota sandstone. The entire fabric is reinforced concrete, cold-drawn mesh being used for the reinforcement."[70] He also wrote: "Laid out upon a horizontal unit system twenty feet on centers both ways, rising into the air on a vertical unity system of three and a half inches: one especially large brick course. Glass was not used as bricks in this structure. Bricks were bricks. The building itself became—by way of long glass tubing laid like bricks—crystal where crystal either transparent or translucent was felt to be most appropriate. In order to make the structure monolithic, the exterior enclosing wall material appeared inside wherever it was sensible."[71]

Here the concept of a woven fabric is metaphorically reinforced by hollow glass tubing that can be seen as the material antithesis of the steel reinforcing rods. As realized, the tubular glass anti-cornice, artificially lit at night, effects a magical dematerialization in which solid material becomes void, and vice versa. The building is illuminated at night by sweeping, streamlined bands of glowing glass and by equally light-diffusing, radiant laylights woven from the same material.

Wright's inverted ziggurat, the Solomon R. Guggenheim Museum in New York, for which Wright was finally commissioned by the

Baroness Hilla Rebay in 1943,[72] ended up pushing the state of reinforced concrete technology to its limits, not only in terms of calculability and the sheer capacity of the material to resist the stresses induced by excessively long cantilevers but also with respect to its actual buildability (plates 301–310). To this end, the ingenious contractor George M. Cohen faced a formidable task: how to construct within a reasonable budget a cast-concrete, expanding helicoidal ramp, which at each turn of the spiral would theoretically acquire its resistance from the upstand stiffness of the spiral itself.[73] The project was unrealizable in this form largely because unlike short-rise helicoidal stairs in reinforced concrete, the feasibility of which had been demonstrated by L. G. Mouchel at the Franco-British Exhibition at Shepherd's Bush, London, in 1908, the Guggenheim ramp imposed a rather large, unsupported span, which at each turn required a great deal of intermediate support. Wright proposed to carry this load through diminutive columns and struts and later through struts alone, bracing against the cumulative weight of the structure across the gap separating one turn of the ramp from the next. However, once fireproofing codes had been met, these members proved altogether too bulky to sustain the desired effect of a self-supporting spiral, and Wright and his engineers, among them Jaroslav Polivka, finally opted for eleven evenly spaced radial walls to carry the giant helicoid, the twelfth support being provided by the elevator and utility core. Adding to the spatial complexity of the work, Wright's spiral ramp expanded in width as it rose both inward and outward, aligning its curved sides with two virtual cones with centers 270 feet above and 180 feet below the structure.[74] This unorthodox geometry initially presented an all but insoluble problem

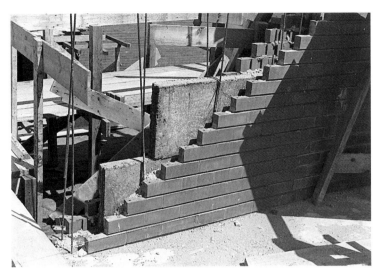

Figure 19: Frank Lloyd Wright. S. C. Johnson & Son, Inc. Administration Building, Racine. 1936–39. Exterior wall under construction

from the point of view of construction method. Cohen finally opted for casting the ramps as flat-slab segments, together with their downward tapering radial walls, while fabricating the outer drum of the spiral over a cylindrical basket of steel reinforcement. This last was cast into the concrete by blowing cement into the reinforcement against curved plywood "climbing" formwork hung off the ramp as it rose. As in the cantilevers of Fallingwater, the balustrades on the inner perimeter of the spiral offered insufficient structural resistance. They were finally dispensed with as an integral structure and simply hung off the inner lip of the spiraling ramp, together with an annular soffit made of falsework that provided for a continuous service duct around the inner rim (figure 20).

The fact that Wright had originally envisioned casting this intricate matrix in one continuous pour, rising progressively upward, represents the point in his late career when his imagination began to outstrip his command of the building process. First conceived in 1943, the Guggenheim stands at the watershed in this regard, as the last truly potent work, prior to Wright's precipitous descent into the kitsch of his last years. His public pronouncement in 1957 that the Midwest would have been a more deserving recipient of his museum; his frustrated desire to move the site into Central Park; and his subsequent dispute with the museum's first director, James Johnson Sweeney, who chose to render the interior in white (an unacceptable non-color for Wright), all pointed to the total alienation of Wright's Usonia from the European utopia of the International Style, as it was then being promoted on the East Coast. By this time Wright was totally transfixed before a mythical Atlantis that did not exist and had never existed, not even in the lost continent of America![75]

REALITY AND DELUSION

Wright's Broadacre City, first publicly exhibited as a twelve-foot-square model in Rockefeller Center in New York in 1935, can be divided more categorically than any of his other visionary projections into its real

Figure 18: Frank Lloyd Wright. S. C. Johnson & Son, Inc. Administration Building, Racine. 1936–39. Pyrex tubes in upper clerestory

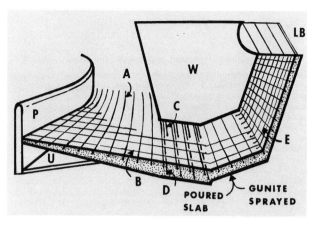

Figure 20: Schematic structural diagram of ramp, Solomon R. Guggenheim Museum: A–D, reinforcing rods; E, lightweight welded metal fabric; W, web; LB, light band; P, parapet; U, utilities duct

and delusional aspects (plates 403–404). It was real in the sense that he correctly anticipated the exponential expansion of the suburb along with the demise of the railroad and the decline of the great metropolises of the nineteenth century. It was delusional in that he envisioned a miraculous neocapitalist future in which rent and interest would be replaced by the principles of social credit, as advocated by C. H. Douglas.[76] And while Wright was correct in predicting that the automobile, as the new "machine in the garden,"[77] would effectively eliminate the time-honored split between town and country in ways that neither Karl Marx[78] nor Ebenezer Howard[79] could have foreseen, he was wrong in believing that this could be spontaneously achieved without the intervention of the state. As far as America is concerned, we need only remark on the symbiosis that was patently engineered after World War II between the massive freeway-building program, totally subsidized at both state and federal levels, and the FHA mortgage regulations that clearly favored suburban subdivision over any other form of development, not to mention the way in which this symbiosis served the interests of the automobile and oil industries, and vice versa.[80] Prescient in predicating his regional urbanization thesis on the electrical grid, the automobile, and modular machine-production, he felt— rather inconsistently—that Broadacre City would come into being spontaneously.

Wright was equally deluded as to the ideal agrarian form that this megalopolitan expansion would eventually take, even if the subsequent destruction of the traditional main street by the suburban supermarket was somehow implied in the importance that he gave to the Roadside Market in his various accounts of Broadacre City, as published in *The Disappearing City* of 1932 and *The Living City* of 1958. Neotechnological urbanization, of course, did not lend itself to the regeneration of agriculture, which Wright the agrarian so urgently desired. Moreover, for all the popularity of the Depression-driven "back-to-the-land"[81] movements of the 1930s, the net migration of the population from the farm belt to the urbanized regions continued unabated, as it had done for the previous four decades. Equally delusional was Wright's presupposition that "deurbanization"[82] would depend on the universal ownership of land, to be somehow arrived at through the inevitable and

natural workings of Jeffersonian democracy, aided where necessary by the draconian application of Henry George's single land tax, as set forth in his *Progress and Poverty* of 1879. In some laissez-faire future of gradual expropriation, Wright imagined, every American would be accorded an acre of land at birth, although the conservative farmer-architect in Wright never once advocated violent revolution as a means to this end.[83]

At the same time, for all his constant harping about democracy, Wright hadn't a parliamentary bone in his body. Patriarchal in his landed strongholds to the point of feudal parody, Wright, as Robert Fishman has remarked, displayed no interest whatsoever in participatory modes of government.[84] While Wright's twin encampments—his Taliesins East and West—may have been collectivized according to the codes of the Wrightian clan, they were in no way socialist. They were communes without being communal in any political sense, so that when it came to the form of government that Wright imagined for Broadacre City it was an invisible administration of things, to be presided over by an elect philosopher-king-architect who rather predictably resembled himself.[85] Aside from Wright's perennial megalomania, there were evident difficulties with the overall conceptualization of Broadacre City at a theoretical level. As Fishman has put it: "Wright's conception left him with one great difficulty. He was so concerned to establish Broadacre City as an ideal city that he could offer no plausible path to reach so exalted a goal. In this respect he was the opposite of Ebenezer Howard, who, as Lewis Mumford has pointed out, often seemed more concerned with the process of creating the Garden City than with its design."[86]

Although in the early 1930s at the rate of an acre a head the entire population of the United States could have been easily accommodated in the state of Texas, it was already clear that any family so settled could not have survived solely from the cultivation of the land, and this arrangement presupposed, as Meyer Schapiro was prompt to recognize, the wholesale creation of a small-holding underclass, to be sustained through part-time work in relatively small-scale industrial plants scattered through the urbanized region. Thus Schapiro wrote in 1938: "The economic conditions that determine freedom and a decent living are largely ignored by Wright. He foresees, in fact, the poverty of these new feudal settlements when he provides that the worker set up his own factory-made house, part by part, according to his means, beginning with a toilet and kitchen, and adding other rooms as he earns the means by his labor in the factory. His indifference to property relations and the state, his admission of private industry and second-hand Fords in this idyllic world of amphibian labor, betray its reactionary character."[87]

It is one of the paradoxes of Wright's radicalism that his assessment of neotechnology, as this would have an impact on future land settlement, carried within itself a latent conservative streak, having its ultimate origin in the flowering of the industrial Northeast in the aftermath of the American Civil War. Convinced throughout his life of the benevolent ethics of Emersonian natural law, Wright, after his excommunication from the arcadia of Oak Park, harbored a resentment

Figure 21: Frank Lloyd Wright. The Living City. Project, 1958. Perspective; sepia ink, pencil, and color pencil on tracing paper. The Frank Lloyd Wright Foundation

against the cosmopolitan city of mercantile-industrial power and exploitation, together with its multicultural émigré populations, which he contemptuously dismissed as a "mobocracy" in *Genius and the Mobocracy*, his 1949 appraisal of Sullivan's ornament.[88] Far from being alone in his isolationism, which bordered on racial prejudice, Wright was able to relate his agrarian retreat of 1911 to the "back-to-the-land" impulses of the succeeding period, which had covered a wide range of proposals, from Henry Ford's government-backed Muscle Shoals regional project of 1921[89] to Ralph Borsodi's self-sufficient diminutive community established in Suffern, New York, in the late 1920s.[90]

Forever hostile to the hegemony of the metropolis and above all to that of New York, Wright began to side increasingly with the resistance of the impoverished agricultural South, as it set itself against the fiscal and technological domination of the Northeast.[91] This is the anarchic mind-set that reinforced his habitual pacifism during World War II, so that in 1941, as America entered the conflict, he wrote with characteristic myopia: "I can look with perfect confidence upon a world entirely undemocratic provided I and my friendly neighbors, if I happen to have any such, are not directly molested."[92] It was a similar reactionary spirit that brought him to propose the subdivision of the United States into three federated nations: Usonia proper, comprising the Midwest and the West, with its capital in Denver; Usonia South, governed from Atlanta; and what for Wright were the Eurocentric states of the Northeast as they already existed, to be disassociated by this new form of federation from the manifest destiny of America in its purest sense.[93] Thus, as Giorgio Ciucci has written:

Broadacres was an attempt to bring together an entire life experience in a single general vision, to overcome the contradiction between the world of the clan and the reality of the clan, between human relationships and what is hidden behind them. Broadacres overcame the essentially urban arcadian myth and proposed the return to the life of the farmer, where life and culture are not yet separate, to the world of the frontier conceived as an autonomous culture, to a prebourgeois world and thus one not corrupted by capitalist development. Whitman had lucidly cried, "Do I contradict myself? / Very well then I contradict myself / (I am large, I contain multitudes)." Wright, while he recognized Whitman as a precedent, wished to propose nothing other than the absence of contradiction. In this sense, Broadacres was neither utopian nor real but simply outside time.[94]

Although it appeared to be deceptively like the Midwest, Broadacre City was totally removed from the reality of the Prairie in an operational sense, as is evident from the aerial perspectives[95] that illustrate its last incarnation—*The Living City* of 1958 (figure 21; plate 411). Here, at the very end of Wright's life, we are confronted with quixotic, "oriental" versions of the helicopter and the car, redesigned so as to accord with the formal tropes of Wright's last *Gesamtkunstwerk*. That all of this was totally removed from the technological potential of the future was unconsciously confirmed by the shocks of wheat that stood, anachronistically, stacked in the fields of the vital city. Wright's ideal city seemed caught in a time warp in which, while all the most advanced technologies evidently prevailed, the combine harvester had yet to be invented.

1. Walter Benjamin, "Louis Philippe, or the Interior, from Paris Capital of the Nineteenth Century." This exceptionally perceptive text, written in 1936, was but a draft for a larger work that was never completed. It was first published in German in 1956 by Theodor Adorno. See Walter Benjamin, *Reflections: Essays, Aphorisms, Autobiographical Writings*, trans. Edmund Jephcott (1978; reprint ed., New York: Shocken Books, 1986), pp. 154–55.

2. Although the invention of the mechanical reaper had no direct impact on Wright's architecture, the fortune that it created led indirectly to one of the great disappointments of Wright's life. Harold McCormick, heir to the farm-machinery fortune, approached Wright in 1907 for the design of a house to be built in Lake Forest. Wright made very elaborate designs, but the commission fell through.

3. See Frederick Baumann, *The Art of Repairing Foundations for All Kinds of Buildings* (Chicago: J. M. Wing, 1873); Joseph Kendall Freitag, *Architectural Engineering, With Especial Reference to High Building Construction* (New York: John Wiley, 1909), p. 7; and Frank A. Randall, *History of the Development of Building Construction in Chicago* (Urbana: University of Illinois Press, 1949), p. 18.

4. Dankmar Adler, "The Chicago Auditorium," *Architectural Record* 1, no. 4 (April–June 1892), p. 429.

5. Cecil D. Elliott, *Technics and Architecture: The Development of Materials and Systems for Buildings* (Cambridge, Mass.: MIT Press, 1992), pp. 419–21.

6. Radial reinforcement came into being around the turn of the century through the pioneering work of L. G. Halberg and the Boston engineer Orlando W. Norcross who patented such a system in 1902. Claude Allen Turner combined radial and diagonal reinforcing in the development of his beamless mushroom-column system. See Carl W. Condit, *American Building Art: The Twentieth Century* (New York: Oxford University Press, 1961), pp. 167–69.

7. The exponential expansion of these devices into the growing white-collar world of tertiary industry is revealed by the following statistics: in 1879 Remington sold 146 machines; a decade later, by 1890, this figure had risen to about 65,000. Two years after Alexander Graham Bell's first patent in 1876, there was a single line telephone operating between Boston and Cambridge; by the turn of the century, there were over a million telephones in use in the United States. See H. A. Rhee, *Office Automation in Social Perspective* (Oxford: Basil Blackwell, 1968).

8. See Larry A. Viskochil, ed., *Chicago at the Turn of the Century* (New York: Dover, 1984), pl. 80, photograph by Barnes Crosby. See also Carl W. Condit, *The Rise of the Skyscraper* (Chicago: University of Chicago Press, 1952), p. 205: "Aside from the ornament and the contraction of the central bay, the facade is a great open area of glass crossed by the thin lines of the molded piers and the narrow bands of the spandrels."

9. According to Grant Carpenter Manson, sometime between 1909 and 1911 Henry Ford went to Wright's studio with the aim of having him design a house on the family land near Dearborn; see Manson, *Frank Lloyd Wright to 1910: The First Golden Age* (New York: Van Nostrand Reinhold, 1958), p. 213.

10. Catherine Beecher and Harriet Beecher Stowe, *The American Woman's Home: or, Principles of Domestic Science* (New York: J. B. Ford; Boston: H. A. Brown, 1869). See also Gwendolyn Wright, *Moralism and The Model Home: Domestic Architecture and Cultural Conflict in Chicago, 1873–1913* (Chicago: University of Chicago Press, 1980), p. 11.

11. Charles Horten Cooley, *Social Organization: A Study of the Larger Mind* (New York: Charles Scribner's Sons, 1924).

12. Wright's professional brochure of 1898 reads: "At 1119 Rookery from twelve to two, P.M. . . . At corner of Forest and Chicago Avenues, Oak Park: Eight to eleven, A.M. Seven to nine, P.M."

13. See H. Allen Brooks, *The Prairie School: Frank Lloyd Wright and his Midwest Contemporaries* (Toronto and Buffalo: University of Toronto Press, 1972), p. 17. The author makes it clear that there was a great deal of contact with England at this time, with Walter Crane lecturing in Chicago in 1891 and C. R. Ashbee visiting the United States in 1900 and 1901.

14. Tiffany bricks: "This was a term commonly used between 1890 and 1910 to designate Roman bricks of tan hue with small, dark vitreous spots and cavities where silicon had fused during firing. Presumably it gave an antique appearance recalling that of Tiffany glass." Manson, *Frank Lloyd Wright to 1910*, p. 175, n. 1.

15. Frank Lloyd Wright, "The Art and Craft of the Machine," in Bruce Brooks Pfeiffer, ed., *Frank Lloyd Wright: Collected Writings*, vol. 1 (New York: Rizzoli, 1992), pp. 63–65.

16. See Vincent Scully, Jr., *Frank Lloyd Wright* (New York: Braziller, 1960), p. 24.

17. Frank Lloyd Wright, "A Fireproof House for $5000," in Pfeiffer, *Collected Writings*, vol. 1, pp. 63–65.

18. See Leonard Eaton's 1964 interview with the clients of this house, wherein Mrs. Greene remarks on Wright's hot-air system: "Breaks in the ducts retarded the flow. Of course, at that time they didn't have forced air heating. It was all gravity flow." Leonard Eaton, *Two Chicago Architects and Their Clients: Frank Lloyd Wright and Howard Van Doren Shaw* (Cambridge, Mass.: MIT Press, 1969), p. 106.

19. Reyner Banham, *Architecture of the Well-Tempered Environment* (London: The Architectural Press; Chicago: University of Chicago Press, 1969), pp. 115–20.

20. Frank Lloyd Wright, "Introduction," in *Ausgeführte Bauten und Entwürfe von Frank Lloyd Wright* (Berlin: Ernst Wasmuth, 1910).

21. "A U.S. patent for Carrier's 'Apparatus for Treating Air' was issued in 1906. The first installation was made at the LaCross National Bank in Wisconsin, but there the system was used only to wash air in the ventilation system." Elliott, *Technics and Architecture*, pp. 319–22. By the late 1920s Carrier had succeeded in putting freestanding man-sized air-conditioning units into production. Spaced about, these were capable of controlling the temperature and humidity of a room without the installation of ductwork. The truly small-scale window air-conditioners did not go into full production until after World War II.

22. Eaton, *Two Chicago Architects*, p. 61. See also David Riesman, *The Lonely Crowd: A Study of the Changing American Character* (New Haven: Yale University Press, 1950).

23. Eaton, *Two Chicago Architects*, p. 31.

24. Ibid., p. 38.

25. Ibid., pp. 39, 43–45.

26. The Wallers were Wright's potential clients throughout the early Prairie period, as Grant Carpenter Manson testifies: "The Wallers, father and son, were forever entertaining thoughts of further subdivision of their family property in River Forest. . . . For these proposed Waller Estates Wright designed three houses with variants to be built speculatively." Manson, *Frank Lloyd Wright to 1910*, p. 204.

27. Eaton, *Two Chicago Architects*, p. 70.

28. See Dietrich Neumann, "Prismatic Glass," *Building Renovation* (March–April 1993), pp. 57–60. According to Neumann: "In 1892 the US government sponsored a competition for innovative energy efficient ways to light office spaces and warehouses. Henry Crew, a physics professor at Northwestern University and his assistant Olin H. Basquin, won the competition and exhibited their so-called prismatic glass at the Chicago World's Fair in 1893, where it gained immediate success. Crew and Basquin decided to use their invention commercially. They developed a whole range of products and founded the Luxfer Prism Company with the help of Chicago businessmen in 1896. Luxfer refers to the latin *lux* (light) and *ferre* to carry. Their product was basically a refinement of factory ribbed glass, but took the direct inspiration from Augustin Fresnel's mathematically precise system of prismatic lenses. . . . After only a year on the market, the company had equipped 296 buildings throughout the US."

For the spread of Luxfer Prism glass see Arthur Louis Duthie, *Decorative Glass Processes* (London: A. Constable, 1908). Duthie makes a specific allusion to the British Luxfer Prism Syndicate, Ltd., and to the approval of the product by the relevant British building authorities. In all this I am indebted to a number of individuals, first to Patrick Pinnell of Yale University, who drew my attention to the existence of this remarkable material, and then to Peter Reed of The Museum of Modern Art, who put me on to Julie L. Sloan, of the stained-glass consultants McKernan Satterlee Associates, Inc., and Tim Samuelson, of the Commission on Chicago Landmarks, all of whom provided me with invaluable information.

29. Augustin-Jean Fresnel (1788–1827) was a French physicist who pioneered the field of optics during the Napoleonic period. With Francois Arago he studied the laws of polarized light and employed such effects in the development of lenses for lighthouses. See *Encyclopaedia Britannica: Micropaedia*, vol. 5, p. 4. Similar phenomena had, in fact, been discovered in the late seventeenth century in England, when Edward Wyndur developed conically shaped lenses for the distribution of light into the interior of ship's decks. The device may have been the origin of Thadeus Hyatt's pavement lights of 1873, known by the trade name Hyatt Lights.

30. Text drawn from *Specification of Patents*, January 5, 1897, William H. Winslow, Chicago, Illinois. Filed November 2, 1896. Serial No. 610,818.

31. See Gwendolyn Wright, *Moralism and the Model Home: Domestic Architecture and Conflict in Chicago* (Chicago: University of Chicago Press, 1980), p. 282. I am indebted to Professor Wright for her seminal and, unfortunately, insufficiently known study of the period. As she points out on p. 281: "The program drew from the best of the English garden city concepts of community, using centralized social institutions to make up for the loss of space in smaller dwellings and to bring the residents together for a unified, well-organized social life."

32. The period of so-called progressivism in the United States occurred roughly between the 1890s and the end of World War I, and included within its trajectory Theodore Roosevelt's abortive attempt to form the Progressive Party as a third political party. While the social and intellectual core of the progressive movement was centered on the University of Chicago, particularly in the work of John Dewey, Robert Park, and others, the overall reformist drive had a wider base and achieved major governmental reform in the United States. See Richard Hofstadter, *The Age of Reform: From Bryan to F.D.R.* (New York: Vintage, 1955).

33. Roger Cranshawe, "Frank Lloyd Wright's Progressive Utopia," *Architectural Association Quarterly* 10, no. 1 (1978), pp. 1–9.

34. H. Th. Wijdeveld, ed., *The Life-Work of the American Architect Frank Lloyd Wright* (Santpoort, Netherlands: C. A. Mees, 1925), pp. 63–64.

35. Louis Sullivan, "The Tall Office Building Artistically Considered," in *Kindergarten Chats and Other Writings* (1901; reprint ed. New York: Dover, 1979), pp. 202–13.

36. Jack Quinan, *Frank Lloyd Wright's Larkin Building: Myth and Fact* (New York: Architectural History Foundation; Cambridge, Mass.: MIT Press, 1987), p. 137.

37. Herbert Johnson also at one time envisioned installing an organ in his new administration complex, Wright's S. C. Johnson & Son, Inc. Administration Building in Racine, Wisconsin, of 1936–39.

38. Ibid., p. 142.

39. Anatole Kopp, *Town and Revolution: Soviet Architecture and City Planning 1917–1935* (New York: Braziller, 1970).

40. Quinan, *Larkin Building*, p. 146.

41. Frank Duffy, "Office Buildings and Organizational Change," in Anthony King, ed., *Buildings and Society* (London: Routledge & Kegan Paul, 1980), p. 266. Duffy also observed: "It is no accident that the Larkin Building was used to illustrate an exemplary, 'modern office building' in one of the many hand-

books for office managers published in the United States at the beginning of the century. In a sense, both the building and these handbooks are products of the same movement, the application of 'scientific management' principles developed in industry to the growing clerical force. . . . Just as it is one building externally, so internally, it [the Larkin] is one space proclaiming unity of organization. Slogans on the walls affirmed corporate values. Within this organization, everyone takes his place. This is apparent . . . from the tight and rigid planning of the desks."

42. See Patrick J. Meehan, *Truth Against the World: Frank Lloyd Wright Speaks for an Organic Architecture* (Washington, D.C.: The Preservation Press, 1992), p. 110.

43. As Edward Ford has written: "In the Willits house the windows, although narrowly spaced at 39' 2", are wider than the 16-inch spacing of the studs. In the Ready-cut system the windows are narrowed and the stud spacing is increased to 24 inches so that the studs continue uninterrupted from foundation to roof. A carpenter cutting studs for the Willits house would have to plan his work carefully, cutting many studs of varying lengths to accommodate the unique openings in the walls. The studs of a Ready-cut house were nearly identical and were to be cut beforehand to uniform length, since they had no relationship to the pattern of openings." Edward R. Ford, *The Details of Modern Architecture* (Cambridge, Mass.: MIT Press, 1990), p. 325.

44. Frank Lloyd Wright, ibid., p. 119.

45. Frank Lloyd Wright, "On Building Unity Temple," in Edgar Kaufmann and Ben Raeburn, eds., *Frank Lloyd Wright: Writings and Buildings* (New York: Meridian Books, 1960), p. 76.

46. Frank Lloyd Wright, "In the Cause of Architecture, VII: The Meaning of Materials—Concrete," *Architectural Record* 64, no. 2 (August 1928), p. 99.

47. Frank Lloyd Wright, *An Autobiography* (London, New York, and Toronto: Longmans, Green, and Co., 1932), p. 235.

48. Wright, "The Meaning of Materials," in Kaufmann and Raeburn, *Writings and Buildings*, p. 225.

49. Wright, "La Miniatura," ibid., p. 216.

50. Charles Calvo, "The Concrete Block Designs of Frank Lloyd Wright," *Forum voor Architectur en Daarmee Verbonden Kunsten* 30, no. 4 (1985–86), p. 168.

51. See Jeffrey M. Chusid, "The American Discovery of Reinforced Concrete," *Rassegna* 49 (March 1992), p. 72.

52. Calvo, "Concrete Block Designs," p. 168.

53. Chusid, "American Discovery of Reinforced Concrete," p. 71.

54. Frank Lloyd Wright, "In the Cause of Architecture, VIII: Sheet Metal and a Modern Instance," *Architectural Record* 64 (October 1928), pp. 334–42; reprinted in Frederick Gutheim, ed., *In the Cause of Architecture: Essays by Frank Lloyd Wright for Architectural Record 1908–1952* (New York: Architectural Record, 1975), pp. 217–19.

55. M. F. Hearn, "A Japanese Inspiration for Frank Lloyd Wright's Rigid-Core High-Rise Structures," *Journal of the Society of Architectural Historians* 50, no. 1 (March 1991), p. 70.

56. Frank Lloyd Wright, *An American Architecture*, ed. Edgar Kaufmann, Jr. (New York: Horizon Press, 1955), pp. 217–18.

57. Frank Lloyd Wright, "Usonian House for Herbert Jacobs," in "Frank Lloyd Wright," Special Issue, *Architectural Forum* 68, no. 1 (January 1938), p. 79.

58. John Sergeant, *Frank Lloyd Wright's Usonian Houses: The Case for Organic Architecture* (New York: Whitney Library of Design, 1976), p. 19.

59. Ibid., p. 11.

60. See Gottfried Semper, *The Four Elements of Architecture and Other Writings*, trans. Harry Francis Mallgrave and Wolfgang Herrmann (Cambridge: Cambridge University Press, 1989).

61. Donald Hoffmann, *Frank Lloyd Wright's Fallingwater: The House and Its History* (New York: Dover, 1978), p. 17.

62. The author received the following information concerning Mendel Glickman in a letter dated June 15, 1993, from a former Wright apprentice, Mark Hayman: "I worked closely with him on several projects, including Marin County, for which I laid out the basic plans from the preliminaries. Mendel was both a brilliant structural and mechanical engineer, and he was, first, Wes' mentor, and later—when I was there—his partner. The most self-effacing person I ever met, Mendel's important contributions over thirty years are—so far—lost to history. When Fallingwater and JWax were built, Wes was in his early twenties, and Mendel must have been the senior engineer. He left Taliesin for Oklahoma, because his wife, Babette, didn't like the Fellowship style of life."

63. Hoffmann, *Fallingwater*, p. 34.

64. Ibid., p. 48.

65. Ibid., pp. 52–53.

66. Jonathan Lipman, *Frank Lloyd Wright and the Johnson Wax Buildings* (New York: Rizzoli, 1986), pp. 8–12.

67. Ibid., p. 51.

68. Condit, *American Building Art*, p 172.

69. Lipman, *Johnson Wax Buildings*, p. 65.

70. Frank Lloyd Wright, quoted in Kenneth Frampton, *Modern Architecture: A Critical Study* (New York and Toronto: Oxford University Press, 1980), p. 188.

71. Frank Lloyd Wright, *An Autobiography* (1932; rev. ed., New York: Duell, Sloan and Pearce, 1943), p. 472.

72. See Joan M. Lukach, *Hilla Rebay: In Search of the Spirit in Art* (New York: Braziller, 1983), pp. 182–210.

73. William H. Jordy, *American Buildings and Their Architects: The Impact of European Modernism in the Mid–Twentieth Century*, vol. 4 (Garden City, N.Y.: Doubleday, 1972), pp. 318–19.

74. Ibid., pp. 291, 294.

75. Ibid., pp. 335–37.

76. See C. H. Douglas, *Social Credit* (London: C. Palmer, 1924).

77. Leo Marx, *The Machine in the Garden: Technology and the Pastoral Ideal in America* (New York: Oxford University Press, 1964).

78. Karl Marx, *The Communist Manifesto* (reprint ed., Harmondsworth: Penguin Books, 1967).

79. Sir Ebenezer Howard, *To-morrow: A Peaceful Path to Real Reform* (London: Swan Sonnenschein, 1898).

80. "Veterans, with their World War II savings, were encouraged by a national policy promoting home ownership in suburban areas to participate in the transformation of the American city and the American economy. The central city was abandoned by many younger workers and their families in favor of the suburban ring. Young people left their parents and kin in the ethnic neighborhoods of the old central cities and, whistling the tune 'I'll Buy That Dream,' bought new cars and went to live in new tract houses, with nothing down and low FHA monthly payments." Dolores Hayden, *Redesigning the American Dream: The Future of Housing, Work, and Family Life* (New York: W. W. Norton, 1984), pp. 35–36. As Hayden shows, the popularity and success of Levittown was directly related to these governmental provisions and policies. She writes: "Levitt made his fortune on the potato farms that he subdivided with the help of both federal financing programs for FHA and VA mortgages and federal highway programs to get people to remote suburbs." Ibid. p. 8. That this was a global policy is confirmed by the massively subsidized postwar road building programs, sponsored, of course, by the oil and automobile lobbies. "Subsidies [after the 1949 Housing Act] were greatest for the FHA/VA homeowner (suburban mortgage supports, tax deductions, and highways, rather than direct housing construction and public transportation subsidies), while the public housing that was built was often cheap, nasty, and badly thought-out." Ibid., p. 122.

81. Robert Fishman, *Urban Utopias in the Twentieth Century: Ebenezer Howard, Frank Lloyd Wright, and Le Corbusier* (Cambridge, Mass.: MIT Press, 1982), p. 147.

82. See Kopp, *Town and Revolution*.

83. Fishman, *Urban Utopias*, pp. 127, 132.

84. Ibid., p. 136.

85. Ibid., pp. 142–43.

86. Ibid., pp. 145–46.

87. Meyer Schapiro, "Architect's Utopia," *Partisan Review* 4, no. 4 (March 1938), p. 43.

88. Frank Lloyd Wright, *Genius and the Mobocracy* (New York: Duell, Sloan and Pearce, 1949).

89. Giorgio Ciucci, "The City in Agrarian Ideology and Frank Lloyd Wright: Origins and Development of Broadacres," in Ciucci, *The American City: From the Civil War to the New Deal* (Cambridge, Mass.: MIT Press, 1979), p. 362.

90. Ibid., p. 341.

91. Ibid., pp. 341–43.

92. Fishman, *Urban Utopias*, p. 149.

93. Ibid., p. 150.

94. Ciucci, "The City in Agrarian Ideology," p. 309.

95. Frank Lloyd Wright, *The Living City* (New York: Horizon Press, 1958), pp. 127, 181.

FRANK LLOYD WRIGHT AND THE DOMESTIC LANDSCAPE

Of the few modern dwellings that resonate as iconic images for both architects and the general public, two are surely Frank Lloyd Wright's Frederick C. Robie House of 1908–10 and Fallingwater, for Edgar J. Kaufmann, of 1934–37 (plates 100–106, 234–240). They seem at once inspiring and familiar, unique yet widely influential, especially in the United States. *House and Home* christened the Robie House "the house of the century" when it was threatened with demolition in 1958 (figure 1).[1] Less than a year earlier the same magazine called Fallingwater "the most famous modern house in the world today, and the house that most powerfully stirred the public's imagination (figure 2)."[2] Architectural critics and fellow designers, both American and European, have expressed similar sentiments, especially about Fallingwater, which architect Kevin Roche called a "dream realized."[3]

At the heart of this response is the sense that both structures respond perfectly to the natural landscape, nestling comfortably into the particular contours of their sites, even as they assert a strong architectural statement that heightens the effect of the surroundings. This ability to enunciate natural settings suggests only one dimension of Wright's complex enterprise. His houses also were part of a broad cultural landscape, a domain of far-reaching formal patterns and social expectations that engaged the architect throughout his career. This expanded landscape can be seen in three distinct ways, each contiguous with the others. First, the interior of the dwelling provides a stage for an envisioned scenario of family life; second, individual residences often represent pieces within a larger whole, at once a social community and a formal configuration of urban or suburban design; and third, Wright always projected his work into a media landscape of potent images, hoping to affect what was yet to be imagined and built by himself and others.

The term *landscape* is problematic, however, for it evokes a romantic notion of timeless constancy and harmony, resistant to the specificity of history or culture.[4] Whereas *home* seems to represent a universal ideal, we have become sensitized to the shifts, variations, and conflicts once subsumed and masked within this word. We must therefore recognize historically contingent, multiple, and overlapping boundaries for Wright's domestic landscapes, situating them within the contexts of historical change and cultural manipulation.

Wright himself sought a transcendent quality in his architecture, a poetic concept he called "essential pattern significant of purpose."[5] At a fundamental level, the "essential pattern" of Wright's architecture did remain consistent. The seventy-two years of a prodigious career continuously affirmed certain design principles he called *organic*. These

principles—the plan as the generating force of a design, the appropriate siting of the building in its particular environs, and the honest, eloquent expression of materials—were themes he reiterated throughout his life.

Wright's significant purpose remained the desire to distill the most basic feelings of well-being and protection that reside in the Germanic *Heim*, source of the English word *home*.[6] His ideas were rooted in nineteenth-century notions of family and community, nature and creativity, which he, like so much of America, carried into the next century.

Acknowledging Americans' deep-seated anxieties about independence and intimacy, Wright offered a comforting "sense of shelter."[7] He celebrated the simple routines of daily life with an artistry that elevated the familiar in startling ways. In 1957 *House Beautiful* extolled the "poetry [he] makes of the ordinary prose of existence."[8] This empathy eschewed avant-garde efforts to remake society in a radically new mold. Wright's landscapes, like his architecture, did not seek to defamiliarize, but rather to embrace established national ideals, such as harmony with nature, individual self-expression, and the autonomy of the nuclear family, rendering them more striking and compelling.

This is not to say that Wright was uncritical of American society, or its effect on the landscape. His antipathy to urban congestion with its "harsh haphazard masses" of novelty-seeking architecture is well known; likewise, he condemned the ravenous sprawl and "crooked sentimentality" of the nation's suburban terrain.[9] As an antidote to these forces of development, Wright described a triumphal narrative of invention in the cause of restoration. From the smallest details through a grandiose plan for the entire nation, he envisioned nothing less than perfect harmony, where nature would flourish and individuals thrive.

A fundamental key to the success of Wright's architectural vision is the conventionality of his social vision. His designs stood in a familiar "Middle Landscape" of separate houses, self-sufficient families, and bucolic nature. This allowed the daring innovations of his forms to attain renown. A popular magazine like *House Beautiful* could proclaim that "now, at last, America has found a framework equal to the greatness of its concept . . . of the dignity and worth of the individual," fully confident that the premises of Wright's work would appeal to their middle-class readers.[10]

Like Walt Whitman, the poet of democracy whom he much admired, Wright sustained his reputation through carefully orchestrated media coverage and the purposeful fabrication of a heroic myth. His skill as a publicist matched his remarkable talent as a designer.

Voluminous writings, frequent speeches, even radio and television appearances later in life, all conveyed images for public consumption. His charismatic self-portrait as an iconoclastic original resonates throughout American popular culture. His autobiography consciously emulated that of Benjamin Franklin, the archetypical self-made, self-promoting American.[11] Wright's composite was, at least in part, a willful construction, a product of his own creative use of images, human as well as architectural, and a calculated manipulation of the modern media, which he understood so well.

Yet the mythic figure of idealistic constancy does not hold up to scrutiny. Within the basic parameters of Wright's life and work there are significant variations, as well as distortions and alterations, some driven by internal inconsistencies or personal difficulties, others by political and cultural circumstances. Wright himself never denied this complexity. Three editions of his autobiography acknowledge "innumerable . . . collaterals, diagonals and opposites that went into place."[12] Readers were repeatedly admonished to read "between the lines."[13]

Wright completed over three hundred designs for residences and drew up hundreds more that were never built. This portfolio chronicles his evolution as both designer and cultural interpreter. The path does not always follow a clear and purposeful trajectory. A succession of distinct phases marks the work, though earlier themes continue to reappear. Each architectural phase parallels new formal concerns, different milieus, and subtle shifts in his concepts of nature and family life—though neither side of this equation can be said to cause or explain the other.

Architects, scholars, and the general public are most familiar with Wright's Prairie houses from the first two decades of the twentieth century. The vast majority were designed for the Midwest, most for Chicago suburbs like Oak Park, where Wright lived with his wife and children until 1909. These environs provided a compelling generic landscape: vast, low-lying fields, an open terrain where each dwelling could benefit from a spacious site and bucolic vista. Even smaller suburban tracts could evoke a connection to this expanse at a time when many adjacent lots still remained vacant.

Figure 2: Robert Day. Cartoon based on Fallingwater. From *The New Yorker*, May 3, 1952

The Prairie houses accentuate the horizontal extension of the region's terrain and the unique, soft undulations of each location. Responding as much to the symbolism of an open frontier as to that of a stable homestead—as well as the physical qualities of the land—they hug the ground and open outward along its contours. "The horizontal line is the line of domesticity," Wright declared; it enables the house to "lie serene beneath a wonderful sweep of sky."[14]

High, narrow ribbons of casement windows and the spread of a deep, overhanging roof seemed to press the structures into the soil. A continuous sweep of materials—usually brick or stucco in these early designs—reinforced the lines that lodged the dwelling into the earth, while the weight of "the *integral* fireplace" at the center added to the gravitational pull.[15] The houses seem reassuringly permanent, their solid blocklike forms resolutely settled in place, dispelling the mutability implicit in any evocation of nature. Each dwelling is "'married' to the ground," the architect told the poet Harriet Monroe.[16]

Facades, especially those turning away from the street, reverberate with the remarkable plasticity of the complex, free-flowing interior volumes. The ground floor opened up into one "big room," so that "all came together as enclosed space—so divided that light, air and vista permeated the whole with a sense of unity."[17] Within the continuous flow of space only a few walls remained as screens, partitioning off certain household functions and framing views as a person moved through the space. In contrast, Wright likened more typical parlors and dining rooms of the era to the "cells of penal institutions."[18]

Although Wright designed in plan, he projected a third dimension of intricate volumes in each scheme. A favorite metaphor for this design process invoked the weaver, aware of texture and size, pattern and weight, details and entirety: "The architect weaves into it all his sense of the whole. He articulates—emphasizes what he loves."[19] The image seems fitting, for Wright's houses, indeed, wove together plan and section, indoors and out, the voluminous space of the center and the minute particulars of the edges. However, the quiet, feminine associations of the word *weaver* tend to de-emphasize the power of these compositions. Like a detonation of fireworks, the space seems at first to

'House of the century' gets a reprieve from demolition

Figure 1: Frank Lloyd Wright. Frederick C. Robie House, Chicago. 1908–10. From *House and Home*, February 1958

focus on the central core of the massive, low hearth, then explodes outward in a multitude of smaller bursts of visual excitement. One can say, as Henry-Russell Hitchcock and Philip Johnson did in 1932, that Wright's spatial complexity "dynamited" the boxlike forms of conventional homes.[20]

Even so, some critics, including Hitchcock and Johnson, have not been certain that Wright fully moved out of the nineteenth century. They are partly right. Wright worked both within and beyond the culture of late Victorian America. His Prairie houses certainly represent a rupture, breaking resolutely with the architectural fashions of the era. One can also read them in terms of that lexicon. As a young architect he had studied the lessons and probed the cultural resonance of the styles he displaced. We can see the close analysis of classical symmetry and refined public facades, so characteristic of more dignified Beaux-Arts architecture, especially in the James Charnley, William H. Winslow, and Orrin Goan residences of the last decade of the nineteenth century (plates 8–13, 16). The axial plan and stately elevation continued to find a place in many of Wright's Prairie houses. As late as 1905, the Thomas P. Hardy House in Racine, Wisconsin, maintained a dignified, flat elevation with two symmetrical entryways onto the street (plates 96–97). This contrasted sharply with the liberated play of volumes pulsating on the rear facade, which faced Lake Michigan.

Similarly, while Wright deplored the "butchery and botchwork" of the Queen Anne style,[21] which festooned facades with a mix of rough-hewn textures and earth-tone colors, protruding porches and bay windows, some of his earliest commissions incorporated naturalistic imagery into their facades. One can certainly recognize his grasp of the simplified American version of the Queen Anne, now called the Shingle style. Even his own house of 1889–90 echoes that smooth flow of interior space, intricately chiseled around the periphery.

Just as Wright assimilated the architectonic lessons of late Victorian styles, he grasped the underlying cultural motives—especially the desire for harmony with nature and a distinctive haven for family life. But he radically transformed the means for their representation. Wright found new and more emphatic ways to represent old domestic values.

Thus the Prairie house designs accentuated the ideal of a sanctuary for familial intimacy. They provided insulation from prying neighbors with a low roof and a recessed front entrance, almost hidden from view. Windows, while abundant, were located under deep overhanging eaves, while the intricate lead detailing on each pane made it virtually impossible to look inside. The raised platform of the Robie House, like many others of the period, elevated the living area to a piano nobile. This allowed the client to "look out and down the street to my neighbors without having them invade my privacy."[22] Such architectural gestures showed a keen awareness of paradoxes in middle-class American family life: the yearning for stability and excitement, comfort and elegance, visibility and seclusion.

These efforts to give strong visual expression to domestic ideals drew directly from nineteenth-century associationist theories, notably those of John Ruskin. Wright was equally familiar with popular Amer-

Figure 3: Frank Lloyd Wright. A Home in a Prairie Town. Project, 1900. Page from *Ladies' Home Journal*, February 1901

ican literature on what is now called the cult of domesticity, proclaiming the critical importance of the domestic sphere. Ideally, under the woman's guidance, the home was supposed to foster a sense of mutual harmony and personal growth, safe from the frenzied dangers of the city.

The reclusive passivity of this feminine ideal came under attack at the turn of the century. In discursive and design terms Wright adhered to progressive-era feminism, which also espoused his goal "to make the whole world Homelike."[23] Indeed, some called his designs "dress reform houses" to emphasize the parallels.[24] The crusading modernist metaphors of domestic scientists echo in his description of the kitchen as "a chemist's laboratory" or "the working department."[25] The idea that women should spend less time and bother cleaning house provided additional justification for Wright's aesthetic of smooth surfaces and built-in furnishings. In his translation of Ellen Key's feminist tract, *Love and Ethics*, undertaken with Mamah Borthwick Cheney during their sojourn abroad, Wright extolled modern women's rights to work and productivity outside the home—so long as women did not renege on their duties to make homes "biographies and poems" for their families.[26]

In turn, the feminist movement provided an eager audience for Wright's design ideas. He first elaborated the basic tenets of the Prairie style before such a group, speaking on "Art in the Home" to the annual congress of Chicago's Central Art Association in 1898, when he joined the organization's board of directors. "A process of elimination is the necessity now," he explained to his audience, "to get rid of the load of meaningless things that choke the modern home; to get rid of them by teaching the teachable that many things considered necessities now are really not so." Wright's lecture then went on to describe "a set of golden rules for house building," based on his principles of organic design: simplicity, horizontality, the open plan, natural materials, and integral (or built-in) furnishings. These points were not portrayed as revolutionary; quite the contrary, they had become "well-established principles" for such an audience.[27]

Nowhere in America did progressive reform find such support as in Chicago's civic clubs, schools, universities, and settlement houses—all places Wright frequented at the time. The groups who met there recommended simplified houses, believing they would be more healthy and economical, reduce competition among neighbors, and lessen the household demands on women. On an urbanistic level they advocated lower densities, coordinated design of dwellings, the use of modern industrial technology, and neighborhood facilities to encourage civic participation. In other words, the nascent Prairie house, like the burgeoning suburbs, embodied a pervasive ideal, rather than a lonely and iconoclastic assault on popular taste.

Major advocates of reform in New York, as in Chicago, soon lauded Wright's houses as exemplars of their goals. Herbert Croly, the editor of *Architectural Record*, and Helen Campbell, an economist who specialized in domestic issues, praised his work as the embodiment of their ambitions for "American democracy at its best," which encompassed women's freedom from household drudgery.[28] Wright reiterated the popular progressive contention that important public reforms, including a strengthened sense of civic unity, would be enhanced through good domestic architecture. Taking up a pervasive progressive goal, he sought "to translate the better thought and feeling of this time to the terms of environment that make the modern home."[29]

Soon after the Central Art Association speech, Edward Bok, the editor of *Ladies' Home Journal*, commissioned the first of three model houses from Wright. Bok had decided to publish a series called "Model Suburban Homes Which Can Be Built at Moderate Cost," hoping these prototypes would improve the quality of the suburban environment. To facilitate dissemination the full plans and specifications of each model dwelling were available by mail-order for the nominal fee of five dollars. The editor did not espouse a particular stylistic bent, stipulating only modest requirements: a less formal "living room" should replace the parlor and all servants' quarters should have adequate space and cross ventilation. Although Bok hoped many professional architects would lend their talents to this worthy cause, Wright was one of only a few to recognize the value of this opportunity: the chance to present one's ideas and one's name to a large and diverse audience, unencumbered by the vagaries of a particular client.

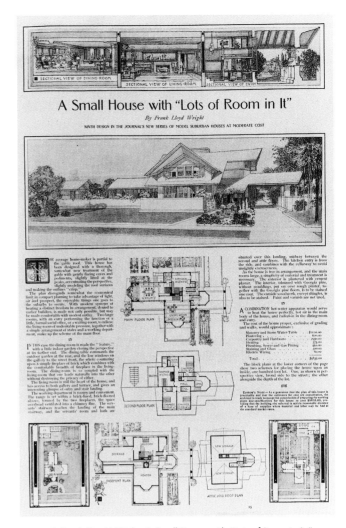

Figure 4: Frank Lloyd Wright. A Small House with "Lots of Room in It." Project, 1900. Page from *Ladies' Home Journal*, July 1901

Wright's first *Ladies' Home Journal* house, of February 1901, remains one of the touchstones of his career. The title, "A Home in a Prairie Town," initiated the use of the prairie slogan to evoke the environmental and cultural context for his early residential work (figure 3; plate 42).[30] The design itself embodies virtually all of the revolutionary themes that would define the next decade of his practice. Space in the cruciform plan is loose, flowing around the centrifugal core; interior walls on the ground floor are reduced to a minimum and often replaced with high screens. A charming drawing accentuates the expansive volume created by a balcony that overlooks the hearth; Wright praised "the happy sense of variety and depth it lends to the composition."[31] All the same, he allowed for alternatives, including a plan that substituted additional bedrooms for the two-story space. The second model house, which appeared a few months later, provided a more conventional gabled roof, greater separation between living and dining rooms, and "Lots of Room in It," as if in deference to his readers' conservative preferences (figure 4; plate 43).

Six years later Wright published "A Fireproof House for $5000" in the *Ladies' Home Journal*. Here a trellised terrace softened and extended a simple cubic block, identical on every side and made of fire-retardant, reinforced concrete. This compact and moderately inexpensive model, "the result of a process of elimination," condensed the principles of the Prairie house.[32] The early decision to use concrete allowed this design to be recycled fifty years later as Wright's Usonian B, a prototype intended for mass production.

The adaptability of the scheme had come to light at the time of initial publication. Builders in various parts of the country produced small houses that show a visible resemblance (though most used stucco rather than concrete). The Stephen Hunt residence in La Grange, Illinois, of 1907 allowed Wright himself to interpret the model. This commission was part of a series of small, compact dwellings in which Wright sought to concentrate the Prairie house, adapting it to a restricted site and budget. He had discovered how to achieve plasticity and continuity within minimalist expression. This process highlights his interest in two modernist agendas: the reduction of design to essential patterns and a progression by which simplified architectural forms would facilitate the production of well-designed mass housing.

The relative homogeneity of Wright's work since 1900 came to an end after 1909. A few adaptations of the Prairie house appeared during the next decade, but his attention turned elsewhere, first to the European publications of Ernst Wasmuth in 1910–11, then to public and commercial buildings, hundreds of drawings for partially prefabricated residences, and his own great house, Taliesin.

Having resolved the first residential paradigm of his career with the quintessentially suburban Prairie house, Wright felt himself at the end of a "closed road"; he had completed one "phase of [his] experience as an architect."[33] At Taliesin, on the family land outside Spring Green, Wisconsin, he began to chart another course. Broad expanses of weathered wood and rough-hewn local stone now seemed to grow directly from the hillside, signaling a turn toward more expressionistic materials and forms. This first *natural* house no longer evoked associations

of domestic repose, but a more transcendent union, such as the kind he had with his companion, Mamah Borthwick.[34] Just as the people who resided there challenged the conventional definitions of a family, so Taliesin, too, was more than a residence—including a studio, farm, and eventually a school for apprentices (plates 122–132).

Relocating to Los Angeles in 1917, between trips to Japan where he oversaw construction of the Imperial Hotel in Tokyo of 1912–23 (plates 151–163), Wright discovered the joyous sense of opportunity that characterized Southern California during the early decades of the movie industry. A desire for radical experimentation extended to every aspect of his life, from personal relations to technical prowess. A succession of concrete-block houses transmuted a lowly building material, bringing out new potential for dramatic effect. "Why not see what could be done with that gutter-rat?" he later asked. "Concrete is a plastic material—susceptible to the impress of imagination."[35]

In his response to the region Wright emphatically rejected naturalistic metaphors of fitting in with a landscape. (Indeed, Wright continued to disdain naturalism throughout his life.) Here on the Pacific Rim—the domain of earthquakes, mud slides, and brushfires—Wright confronted and embraced more disruptive forces of nature. He searched out steep hillsides and craggy ravines that accentuated the "true property of . . . character."[36] Free interpretations of Mayan and Amerindian myths inspired flights of fancy about symbolic ornament and massing. Wright aptly compared his West Coast architecture with a free-form musical romanza or, alternatively, "a holiday adventure in Romanza."[37]

After moving to Arizona in 1927 to help design the Arizona Biltmore Hotel, Wright discovered yet another challenge to his ingenuity. In the parched heat of an arid landscape, "Nature, driven to economize in materials by hard conditions," generated bare, spartan forms.[38] By analogy, these constraints conjured up an abstract and "space-

Figure 5: Frank Lloyd Wright, Olgivanna (beside him), Svetlana, and Iovanna Wright at Ocotillo Desert Camp, Chandler, Arizona, 1929, with boxboard wall in background

loving architecture . . . as nobly simple in outline as the region itself is sculpted."[39] He turned again to unprecedented raw materials that seemed "indigenous" or representative of this region and its culture: thin wood frame, unbleached canvas, and natural rock formations.[40]

Ocotillo was to be the temporary base of operations for Wright and his apprentices as they designed the sumptuous Arizona resort oasis of San Marcos-in-the-Desert of 1928–29 (plates 200–201). Existing boulders and giant saguaro cacti largely determined the site plan. A thin wall of boxboard zigzagged around the compound to keep it safe (figure 5). The architect had by now abandoned all symmetry, seeking to embrace and replicate the intrinsic pattern in nature's placement of elements in the landscape. Accepting what was given, he hoped to tap into a hidden order of natural forces.

Wright had also learned to accept chance and mutability as part of nature's cycle; no longer did architecture or its materials need to seek the illusion of permanence. Ocotillo was begun in January 1929, completed within a few weeks, then abandoned in May when the heat became overbearing. Such "ephemera" seemed appropriate in a modern world characterized by rapid social change, especially in the desert with its comparable ecological fluctuations. Furthermore, Ocotillo reminded the architect of his social conscience, attuned "to making slight buildings beautiful."[41]

The several projects for resort complexes of the 1920s also revealed a delight in playful unpredictability amidst invigorating natural surroundings. Concrete residences at the Doheny Ranch Resort of 1923 were terraced into the Sierra Madre mountains outside Los Angeles (plates 198–199); cabins and houseboats at the Lake Tahoe Summer Colony of 1922–24 nestled into wood and water in upstate California (plates 172–173); a luxurious hotel complex stretched out across a great expanse for San Marcos-in-the Desert near Chandler, Arizona; smaller cabins provided a modicum of fantasy for inexpensive motel accommodations at the nearby San Marcos Water Gardens of 1929 (plate 204). The separate, individualized units were combined into elaborate, magical compositions of crystalline beauty. The effect relied on "symmetry occult, graceful, rhythm throughout."[42] Each group created a carefree, yet magisterial, equilibrium that heightened the distinctive splendor of its setting. Unfortunately, financial scandals and the onset of the Depression foreclosed all of these grand resort projects. This relegated a remarkable phase of Wright's career to an apparition of joyful communality that would never develop beyond the stage of artfully arranged site plans.

The social landscape for Wright's houses similarly metamorphosized during these years. Clients included a "kaleidoscopic" variety of types: apprentices at Ocotillo, developers of vacation communities, independent single women and solitary males, as well as stable families.[43] For Aline Barnsdall, a wealthy Los Angeles socialite and theater patron, Wright built the majestic Hollyhock House of 1916–21 (plates 165–169); for Mrs. George Madison (Alice) Millard, the smaller, elegant dwelling he called La Miniatura in Pasadena of 1923 (plates 178–181), promising "a new Architecture for a new Life."[44] A. M. Johnson commissioned an aerielike retreat on the rim of a canyon at Death

Valley, California, in 1922–25 (plate 196), seeking to provide a vacation spot for himself and a permanent home for his friend, Death Valley Scotty, a reclusive hermit.

Residences for more conventional clients showed only slight modifications in Wright's thoughts about gender roles in family life. Women still bore the full burden of household labor, though their job was made somewhat more tolerable by integrating it into the life and space of the house. The first proposal for the Malcolm Willey House in 1932 (plate 229) had isolated the kitchen in a separate wing, but budgetary constraints helped generate a major change the next year. Now the kitchen, soon to be designated the "work-space," opened directly into the dining area, minimally screened on one side by a wall of glazed shelves.

"I think a cultured American housewife will look well in it," Wright explained chivalrously.[45] His ideal of the patriarch never faded but, rather, intensified after his marriage in 1928 to Olgivanna Hinzenberg. Several houses of the late 1930s added a male "sanctum" alongside the female "work-space," where the "lord of it all" could retreat, removed from the everyday turmoil of domestic life.[46]

"Nothing is trivial because it is not 'big,'" Wright had assured Nancy Willey when she first wrote to him.[47] In fact, this small commission had to sustain Wright and his entourage through the early years of the Depression. Nor did he eschew grandeur and wealth. Working on his own in 1931, Wright imagined a spacious, sumptuous dwelling in Denver he called the House on the Mesa (plates 226–228). A model for this "good time place" took a place of honor in the 1932 International Style exhibition at The Museum of Modern Art, *Modern Architecture: International Exhibition*, where, like the masters of the European modern movement, Wright could suggest "machine age luxury at its best."[48]

That fantasy materialized in 1934 with the commission for the Kaufmann family's grand vacation home at Mill Run, Pennsylvania, which saved Wright from financial disaster and brought him instant celebrity. Even before it was finished, photographs of Fallingwater appeared in magazines and newspapers throughout the world. A drawing of it hangs behind the photograph of Wright that appeared on the cover of *Time* magazine in January 1938 (figure 6). A new paradigm had materialized. Fallingwater exploited the startling dramatic potential of a precarious slash of rock that extended over a waterfall, epitomizing the interplay of daring technologies and theatrical gestures, which had been evolving through the 1920s.

All the same, Wright was not oblivious to the painful realities of the Depression years, which affected every part of the country, from urban Hoovervilles to the midwestern Dust Bowl. His attention turned again to the need for high-quality, affordable housing for all Americans—housing he called Usonian.

In the enthusiasm for experiments and neologisms of the late 1920s, Wright had begun to use the term *Usonian* to describe his version of the nation's architectural and social purpose.[49] Despite claims that the word originated with the novelist Samuel Butler, Usonia was his own fabrication: it alluded, if cryptically, to the USA, with over-

FIFTEEN CENTS January 17, 1938

TIME

The Weekly Newsmagazine

Volume XXXI   **FRANK LLOYD WRIGHT**   Number 3
His city would be everywhere and nowhere.
(See Art)

Figure 6: Frank Lloyd Wright on the cover of *Time*,
January 17, 1938

tones of technological acronyms like New Deal agencies and his friend R. Buckminster Fuller's Dymaxion schemes. In the process Wright fabricated a new ideal client, a national leader determined to transform the entire political and physical landscape: "the architect of an organic social order."[50] Usonian City would lead directly into Broadacre City, signaling yet another stage in the architect's development. A renewed commitment to the social problem of affordable housing and the architectural challenge of minimalism now envisioned a vast scale that encompassed the whole of the United States.

One of the most forceful statements of Wright's Usonian concerns appeared in the January 1938 issue of *Architectural Forum*, devoted entirely to his recent work. Without referring directly to the Depression, Wright's text acknowledged shortages and inequities, as well as the architectural profession's general reluctance to address these matters. The American "small house" problem is a "pressing, needy, hungry, confused issue," he intoned, then boldly promised that his new prototype would resolve the nation's economic, social, and moral problems.[51]

The Herbert Jacobs House in Madison, Wisconsin, of 1936–37 (plates 241–245), served, here as elsewhere, to illustrate Wright's concept of the Usonian dwelling. Herbert and Katherine Jacobs were the "common sense," mobile young professionals whom Wright now had in mind as generic clients.[52] They eagerly embraced modernity, which is to say they wanted a house that maximized economy and flexibility without sacrificing familiarity or comfort.

"What are the essentials in their case, a typical case?" Wright asked the readers of *Architectural Forum*.[53] Essentials included a shelter for

the automobile, though a simple carport saved the expense of a separate, enclosed garage. (The meaning of this frugal choice extended into the cultural domain, for the car and carport now became an integral part of the dwelling.) Nor could nature be discarded; a transparent wall of glass with French doors opened onto a small enclosed garden, which replaced the expansive homestead of the Prairie houses. Brick or horizontally lapped wood replaced stucco and masonry as the basic building materials. The compact kitchen—now always called the work-space—stood back-to-back with the bathroom, creating an economical service core that replaced the hearth as the nucleus of the scheme.

The Usonian dwelling sought to reduce, condense, and consolidate. Wright focused on two domains: technological innovations in the construction system, including the use of radiant heating in the concrete floor slab; together with radical reductions in square footage (1,500 square feet in the case of the Jacobs House). Since the basic prototype was a one-story house, all activities had to be grouped horizontally into multipurpose zones.[54] A third technique—the use of unpaid labor—sometimes helped him stay within the budget but could not be considered an inherent principle. Not only did Herbert Jacobs do much of the woodworking himself, but apprentices in the Taliesin Fellowship acted as a construction crew.

Wright's approach differed substantively from that of the *Neue Sachlichkeit* aesthetic of the European modern movement in the 1920s. This New Objectivity renounced idealism in the arts, calling instead for straightforward designs derived from the conditions of machine production. Architecturally this translated into the *Existenzminimum*: unornamented, compact living units, completely standardized, and grouped in uniform rows of *Zeilenbau* apartment buildings.

Wright denounced European modernism as "a childish attempt to make buildings resemble steamships, flying machines or locomotives," asking, "Why should Architecture or objects of Art in the Machine Age, because they are made by Machines . . . resemble Machinery?"[55] He could respond avidly to the challenge of an apartment tower but, like most Americans, Wright still wanted a landscape of single-family homes, each one redolent with the symbolic expression of autonomy and individuality. Wright challenged the priorities of the modern movement, insisting that machine technology should not disdain "organic simplicity . . . [in] the harmonious order we call Nature."[56] He accepted standardization, but there is no triumphant endorsement of the mass-produced prototype in his rhetoric.

Inquiries flooded into Wright's office following the considerable publicity given the Jacobs House and the immediate prestige of Fallingwater. He built Usonian dwellings in fourteen states, reinforcing the claim to national stature. Twenty-six examples were completed before the war, although thirty-one others remained unbuilt, victims of cautious mortgage bankers, financial pressures, or client frustrations.[57]

As singular objects these Usonian houses perpetuated Wright's ideal of freedom and diversity within the confines of a modular system or the "self-imposed discipline of space: the unit system."[58] Plans explored various simple geometrical shapes as the basic module from which to generate a design. Most of the dwellings concentrated the space in a large rectilinear core with a diminished diagonal extending outward.[59] The Jacobs House is a prime example of this plan type, comprising an L with the small, efficient kitchen work-space as the joint between living area and bedrooms. Seeming to belie the constraints of budget and space, other house plans eschewed all use of right angles. The Ralph Jester House, a project first proposed for Palos Verdes, California, in 1938–39 (plate 269), consisted of interlocking circles, as if a diagram had been transposed into a floor plan. A second house, Solar Hemicycle in Middleton, Wisconsin, of 1943–48 (plates 311–314), for the Jacobs family, which had grown too large for the first Usonian home, used a smooth arc to derive its plan.

Another series explored clusters of hexagons, a shape Wright asserted to be more natural than squares and right angles. The Paul R. and Jean S. Hanna House in Palo Alto, California, of 1935–37, called Honeycomb House (plates 270–274), was the first, the largest, and the most elegantly resolved of these. This hexagonal module was soon revised into a moderate-cost Usonian dwelling, the Sidney Bazett House in nearby Hillsborough of 1939. Here, too, one finds "the essential Joy"[60] in small but radiant spaces defined by ingenious details: the nautical precision of the tiny bedrooms; light filtered through perforated woodwork; a high ceiling with a skylight in the diminutive kitchen; glass doors that look out on the enclosed garden, bringing a sense of expansiveness to the compact living area.

The rapport between landscape and architecture again metamorphosized during the 1940s, as Wright sought to improve climatic conditions and maximize visual continuity with the outdoors. In the process he again recast and softened notable tropes of the European modern movement, such as transparency and orientation to sunlight. The 1945 Lowell Walter House in Quasqueton, Iowa, adapted Wright's Glass House, published in a 1945 *Ladies' Home Journal*, in which the living-dining area was contained within a transparent sun room, glazed from floor to ceiling on three sides, with additional light pouring in from skylights.[61] The Jacobses' Solar Hemicycle had countered the cold midwestern plains with berms of rammed earth piled high against the northern wall, reaching almost to the roof; excavation for that soil produced a concave garden facing south, visible through a sweeping expanse of glass whose arc followed the elliptical path of the sun.

The conviction that he could successfully wrestle with nature and triumph over the landscape dominated the last, highly prolific phase of Wright's life after World War II. The most celebrated architect in the country was now free to explore the limits of his own imagination in form and symbolism throughout the country and the world, unbound by conventions. Each building will "have a grammar of its own," he announced boldly.[62] Yet in casting aside the constraints of his earlier lexicon, Wright sometimes lost the bearings that had anchored his work: empathy with the site and the demands of climate, systematic explorations of a type, and a commitment to simplification as an aesthetic and a cultural ideal.

There are still calm, low-lying residences set in lush greenery, such as the Isadore J. and Lucille Zimmerman House in Manchester, New Hampshire, built in 1950, though even here the asymmetrical roof and larger expanses of glass attest to a major shift in idiom. Yet most of the residential work is startling, a jolt to come upon. Parts of the roof suddenly veer up at acute angles. "You can do with a roof almost anything you like," Wright asserted. "But the type of roof you choose must not only deal with elements in your region but be appropriate to the circumstances, according to your personal preference—perhaps."[63] In these testimonials to uniqueness, nothing tempered Wright's individuality or that of the clients.

Within the house asymmetrical rooms jut out and up, lit by floor-to-ceiling expanses of windows and clerestories under the irregular roofline. Ceilings undulate or zigzag, their surfaces turning in complex syncopation. Thick partitions of stone, brick, or concrete block command a powerful sculptural presence, rising and falling in height with the changes in ceiling level.

Surfaces are intense with a constant play of light and shadow, hue and texture—at once inherent in the materials and wrested from them. Colors provide vibrant contrasts: sheet-metal roofs of bright turquoise blue offset the warm browns of wood and stone, the putty gray of concrete block. Vivid assertion had become "*the reality of the whole performance.*"[64] With their theatrical flair as a backdrop to rather conventional scenarios, these houses highlight American domesticity of the 1950s, in which consumer pleasures and stereotyped gender roles simulated more complex possibilities for individual expression.

Playful gestures responded to the private fantasies of wealthy clients and, in turn, delighted the public. The Kaufmann family's project for Boulder House, a new dwelling at Palm Springs, California, of 1951 (plate 351), featured an undulating moat around the periphery, crossed by bridges, to enliven a daily swim. A large model of the project for the Pergola House for Gerald Loeb in Redding, Connecticut, of 1944, on display at The Museum of Modern Art, New York, in 1946, showed a special vertical window, making it possible to watch smoke rise inside the chimney. The success of Wright's architecture seemed to validate the national dream that "free choice [had generated] a greater range of Freedom."[65] As in other domains of postwar American culture, Wright's energetic discourse—and, by implication, his architecture—celebrated the quality of life in the "Free World."[66]

Rather similar residences for two of Wright's sons, David (1950–52) and Robert Llewellyn (1953–57), for Phoenix, Arizona, and Bethesda, Maryland, respectively (plates 348–350, 352–354), exemplify the bravado of this late period—and its limits. In both cases Wright used a synthetic material, concrete block, juxtaposing its rough texture with the sensuous allure of mahogany. In both, a virtuoso spiral form rises up off the land along a gentle ramp. Again, there is the image of a perfect fit between design and the biological generation of a family, between the house and its environs. Yet the children remain enclosed within their father's vision for them, a father whose ideas about the environment could be equally egotistical. While in theory David Wright's house in Phoenix described "How to Live in the Southwest," lifting the residents above the desert's heat, the fact remains that heat rises off the ground.

Throughout his life, even in his later success, Wright continued to take risks with materials, finances, and clients. Records of correspondence always moved between grand theory, details of daily life, and importunate protests. The usually obsequious Hannas had wired, "*IMPOSSIBLE LIVING CONDITIONS*," insisting that their children deserved separate bedrooms and an adequate hallway to reach them.[67] (The architect had proposed a width of one foot, seven inches.) His son David begged plaintively to see a set of plans for the contractor, then timidly suggested that "90% Frank Lloyd Wright, but 10% Gladys and David Wright, would be about the right proportion, don't you think?"[68] In response to all such entreaties Wright flattered, cajoled, and intimidated, sometimes adjusting minor details but never the principle of his scheme.

This recalcitrance may seem surprising, given that the architect proclaimed individuality to be the very heart of his personal and design philosophy. But of course Wright had his own definitions. He rejected the Victorian idea that the private dwelling should reflect the husband's personality and wealth and the wife's distinctive taste. Domestic architecture should reveal the powerful originality of *his own* individual creativity, rather than a cacophony of personal expressions.

Nonetheless, Wright was not averse to evoking this cherished American value whenever its cadence suited his purpose. "Individuality is a national ideal," he declared in the introduction to the Wasmuth portfolio in 1910, then clarified the choice of words. "Where this degenerates into petty individualism, it is but a manifestation of weakness."[69] True individuals were those with sufficient independence of mind to commission a genius. Wright would "idealize" such clients so that each house represented a type or class of person "with unspoiled instincts and untainted ideals," not the "mere personal idiosyncrasy" of that client.[70] He compared the process to a portrait by John Singer Sargent that bore the unmistakable imprint of the artist.[71]

Wright then expanded on the possibilities for individuality through a multiplicity of designs generated from a basic type. Herein lay a distinct interpretation of modern construction systems. Every modern architect confronted the benefits and constraints of mass production; most alternated between the unique and the uniform, designing exquisite dwellings for wealthy clients and devising—or at least extolling—factory-built housing for the masses. Wright took another approach, using the machine to make every design distinctive. "Standardization is a mere, but indispensable, tool," he wrote in 1928. Embraced without reserve, it risked becoming "a prison house for the creative soul and mind."[72]

Instead, by a process Wright called "conventionalization," nature's "organic" patterns would "crystallize" into geometric abstractions. Since these forms could be manufactured, modern technology could generate an infinite number of permutations, without losing touch with the underlying principles of natural order. "A richer variety in unity is, therefore, a rational hope," he explained, professing his belief that Americans should embrace the machine, without giving up its inherent promise of diversity, which he felt to be their birthright.[73]

Wright's first experiment with mass production had affirmed this

Figure 7: Frank Lloyd Wright. American System-Built Houses for the Richards Company. 1915–17. Interior perspective, model C3; lithoprint. The Museum of Modern Art, New York. David Rockefeller, Jr. Fund, Ira Howard Levy Fund, and Jeffrey P. Klein Fund

approach early in his career. In 1915 he had joined forces with Arthur L. Richards of Milwaukee to design American System-Built Houses (see plate 176). That affiliation lasted for several years, during which time Wright produced over nine hundred drawings. Richards's American Ready-Cut system was based on factory production of precut framing units and interior details in wood; these parts were then assembled and reassembled in the multiplicity of configurations Wright created. Recognizing that the publication and dissemination of images was an important part of the process, Richards made sure that Wright's illustrations circulated widely in brochures, magazine inserts, and newspaper advertisements (figures 7 and 8).

The themes of this early design experiment reverberated in later efforts Wright carried out on his own, using a range of materials. The 1920s saw the City Block House as a first prototype in concrete, and numerous proposals for the All-Steel Houses in Los Angeles (see plate 251). Thirty years later Wright introduced the Usonian Automatic, a more advanced concrete-block house, and built several examples in different parts of the country. He soon assembled over one hundred drawings, intending to publish them as a book to emphasize the multiple versions.

In the last years of his life, Wright continued to explore prefabrication techniques in an effort to reduce the expense of housebuilding. He designed prototypes using wood panels, synthetic fiber, and concrete block. *House and Home* insisted that these designs made industrialized houses acceptable, breaking old stereotypes, for they showed "integrity, character, individuality in a house as you know it in a man."[74] Despite these hopes, like the government's Operation Breakthrough of the next decade, final costs far exceeded initial estimates.

From the American Ready-Cut system to the Usonian Automatic we recognize a unified approach. Wright condensed the house to a simple cubic or rectangular block, then reduced the applied ornament to a minimum—without eliminating the ornamental possibilities of materials and massing—in order to facilitate multiple production. Construction technology relied on advanced, even daring, ideas and materials. Yet most of the assembly still took place on site, where the architect could oversee production and modify each design. Self-build methods for the "assembled house" fulfilled both a belief in systems and an enthusiasm for practical experience, yet Wright did not want to be "castrated by a factory-aesthetic."[75] He remained ambivalent about the anonymity that full-scale industrialization would impose on the designer as well as the resident.

Wright balanced reservations about factory production with enthusiasm for the media, another phenomenon closely associated with modernism. A striking number of clients were involved in publishing, especially editors and reporters for midwestern newspapers, including William Allen White, Henry J. Allen, Lloyd Lewis, Herbert Jacobs, Loren Pope, and his cousin, Richard Lloyd Jones. More than any architect since Palladio, Wright used all types of publications, not only to win fame, but also to disseminate his ideas. "Any *design* has far-reaching effect, today," he proclaimed, "because our machine so easily gives it, as a design, to the mind's eye of all [through the] ubiquity of publicity."[76]

Wright insisted on close collaboration and often full control over articles about his work, determining layout and graphics as well as the content of images and text. Eloquence as a goal went hand in hand with legibility. Laypeople found his drawings immediately comprehensible, for Wright refused axonometrics and other devices that were difficult for nonarchitects to grasp. (A notable exception is the 1938 model house for *Life* magazine, which specified a cutaway axonometric.[77]) Luxuriant landscaping, dazzling precision, and rich colors—especially rose, carmine, bronze, and periwinkle, delicately applied in pencil—lifted his magazine images from the realm of mass-produced plans into that of fantasy. Articles in popular women's magazines and specialized journals for builders often treated Wright's work as a paradigm for general advances in American residential design. In the early 1900s *House Beautiful*, *Ladies' Home Journal*, and *National Builder* had used Wright's drawings of Prairie houses to illustrate how one might resolve problems such as a difficult site or the need for an economical plan.[78] Sometimes this was done without even mentioning the architect's name, for the issue at hand involved a generic problem in residential design, not one man's place in the canon.

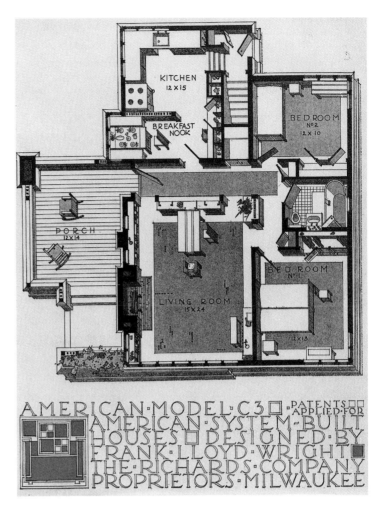

Figure 8: Frank Lloyd Wright. American System-Built Houses for the Richards Company. 1915–17. Axonometric plan, model C3; lithoprint. The Museum of Modern Art, New York. David Rockefeller, Jr. Fund, Ira Howard Levy Fund, and Jeffrey P. Klein Fund

Widespread public acceptance culminated in a hymn of praise during the 1950s. *House Beautiful* devoted an entire issue to Wright in 1955, again analyzing the lessons illustrated by his houses, now in terms of Wright's signature techniques and his "greater principles." *House and Home* focused on the Zimmerman House in one issue, annotating its techniques to make a small house "look bigger" and "work better," inside and out. Another article, "Frank Lloyd Wright and 1,000,000 Houses a Year," highlighted his use of the open plan, compact kitchen, broad central fireplace, floor-to-ceiling windows, butterfly roof, and natural materials. As countless builders incorporated these elements into their repertoires, Wright "made an intensely practical contribution to better housing for millions of families."[79]

Wright was by no means oblivious to this appropriation. In many ways he sought to orchestrate the message and emphasize particular themes. John DeKoven Hill, a longtime associate at Taliesin, joined the staff of *House Beautiful* in part to oversee their campaign in his behalf. In one note to Elizabeth Gordon, a senior editor at the magazine, Wright confided, "It is no longer necessary for any architect to know construction. He must know journalism."[80]

Wright thus accepted a difficult truth for modern architects: if their work is widely published and admired, others will inevitably draw from it, often without understanding the larger philosophy. At times the creolization could become frustrating, sometimes because he could not countenance someone else's design, at other times because he wanted to see more daring creativity among his compatriots. In a 1953 interview Wright described his greatest disappointment: "Instead of emulation I have seen chiefly imitation."[81] Yet, by and large, the belief in a missionary role prevailed. Both his design philosophy and the abundant publicity about his work affirmed a crusade to "make Beauty of the Environment come alive for our own people."[82]

Wright made a different sort of niche for himself in the professional media, where he won praise but also had to put up with disdainful commentaries from some early critics. In 1900 the *Architectural Review* of Boston published a laudatory article by his friend and associate Robert C. Spencer, Jr. Within a few years a long article—and then an entire issue—appeared in *Architectural Record*.[83] After a long lull (during which time Wright oversaw major German and Dutch publications about his work), *Architectural Forum* profiled him with an entire issue—in 1938, again ten years later, and once more in 1951.

This coverage refined a different set of conventions: a sequence of buildings and projects, classified in terms of type, both programmatic and formal, using consummate graphic skill to clarify an individual imprimatur. Quotations from Whitman and Thoreau, together with his own aphoristic statements, contrasted Wright's ideal of architecture with his unveiled contempt for the mundane, self-serving tendencies of most practitioners.[84] Thus, after 1938, the professional press lionized a persona and an oeuvre that seemed to rise above commercialism. Wright had won a place in the architectural canon—that is, his work transcended time and place; it was no longer situated in terms of particular landscapes but, rather, in a media environment (see figure 9).

Under Wright's supervision, the architectural press consigned considerable space to his proposals for residential neighborhoods and resorts. Not surprisingly, the large detailed drawings highlighted the skillful geometric patterns of the compositions. Wright also assumed a social covenant as the basis for each design. From houses to yards, playgrounds to shopping districts, the separate strands were intertwined, at once an element in a formal pattern and a thread in a social fabric. Wright noted in pencil at the side of one early sketch, "This plan is arranged on the assumption that the community interests are of greater value to the whole."[85]

All the same, the underlying notion of a community remained celebratory and comfortable rather than participatory and transformative. The collectivity represented an amalgam of individuals. For each one Wright proposed "a new Freedom [that] would consist largely in this fresh opportunity to have and to hold his own shelter . . . free to go and come conveniently."[86] The values of abundance and independence took precedence over any other conception of public or private goals.

None of Wright's residential settings materialized as he imagined them, even during his last years of fame. A desire to affect the larger

Figure 9: Automobile advertisement, c. 1948, featuring Gregor Affleck House. Legend at top reads: "This home designed by Frank Lloyd Wright represents the finest of contemporary architecture. Just as the Futuramic Oldsmobile represents the farthest advancement in automotive design."

landscape had motivated these proposals, but the boundlessness of that desire led him to insist upon an absolute and unattainable control, hoping thereby to achieve perfection everywhere. Orderly form became an all-powerful metonym for social order, leading Wright to believe that where "only good design is available," there would never be a problem of disharmony.[87]

In addition, these landscapes of the mind became increasingly placeless, neglecting the keen response to particular sites that still resonated in most individual house designs. Yet the very anonymity of the settings—principally the frayed edges of American cities, from the suburbs outward toward the highway's edge—engaged a vast and problematic domain, largely ignored, even today, by professional architects.

From the start of Wright's independent career, one can chronicle his concern for the design of suburban enclaves. The first *Ladies' Home Journal* article of 1901 presented a modest proposal to group four Prairie houses into a "Quadruple Block Plan." Each house represented a slight variation of a common plan and elevation. Together the four dwellings formed a cohesive compound on a square parcel of land, sharing a lush garden with garages for each residence at the center of the composition. The size of the parcel, four hundred feet to a side, suggested abundant land and autonomy for each household, even within the collective enterprise. A peripheral brick wall reinforced the unity of the group, isolating it from the mundane world beyond those boundaries.

This Quadruple Block Plan was one of a scheme for twenty-four houses commissioned by C. E. Roberts of Oak Park. Wright began work on the project in the late 1890s. Over the next several years he proposed numerous arrangements of house plans, outbuildings, and lot formations, exploring various rhythms and scales (plates 394–395). Nonetheless, the local community continued to reject the idea. A smaller group of five houses—each using the same precut frame and detailing, subtly individualized in plan, elevation, and roofline—was built in Glencoe, Illinois, in 1915. Again and again, the architect returned to this format for equilibrium in and through design.[88]

In 1909 Wright addressed a larger, more autonomous scale with master plans for two projects in the Bitter Root Valley in western Montana: University Heights (later renamed Como Orchards Summer Colony), intended as a summer resort for university families, and the nearby Village of Bitter Root (plates 396–399).[89] The resort incorporated his early experiments in prefabrication with a projected total of fifty-nine dwellings, each to be derived from one of three prototypes, though all that came to fruition was a clubhouse and twelve cabins. These early schemes reveal an avid enthusiasm for urban design and a certain youthful awkwardness. Both were unduly grand, with all activities coerced into a rigid axial scheme. Nor had Wright found a way to fit his preference for rectilinear design into the contours of the site or his desire for conviviality. He boldly asserted the need for architectural order, even in an informal setting.

The progressive milieu of Chicago likewise believed that strict design guidelines could promote social harmony. In 1913, hoping to codify these principles, the Chicago City Club sponsored a competition for a model suburb southwest of the city, a quarter-section in size.[90] Wright's entry, the Noncompetitive Plan for City Residential Land Development (plate 400), at once visionary and realizable, can be considered his most accomplished and complex domestic landscape.

Like Le Corbusier's Contemporary City for Three Million People of 1922, Wright's model suburb segregated socioeconomic classes through the various kinds of dwellings.[91] Not surprisingly, the "Residence Park" specified an ample density of four houses to the block. Two adjacent districts grouped progressively smaller dwellings on denser lots, while blocks of low-rise apartment buildings housed single men to the north and single women to the south. However, Wright's various districts were all set within a single neighborhood, accessible by walking. In addition, by concentrating generous public spaces at the intersections, he hoped to encourage social mixing. Residents were invited to congregate in parks and playing fields, at a "moving picture building" or a model kindergarten. The periphery was zoned for small shops and offices, forming subordinate "business centers" that would draw people together. This intricately woven landscape by no means ostracized a complex public realm.

To be sure, the arrangement of structures, streets, and spaces involved formal choices and cultural referents. The continuation of Chicago's grid underscored a connection to the larger city with a distinctly urban syncopation.[92] It also affirmed a respect for Thomas Jefferson's visionary National Survey, meant to encourage mobility and unity for the new nation through a standardized, rectilinear pattern of land use.

Wright projected that single people living in apartments would comprise over a thousand people, or half the population of his model suburb. This social vision went far beyond the competition's program. Following the lead of contemporary zoning reformers, the sponsors had not included multiple dwellings or stores in the residential area. While Wright certainly favored single-family houses, he recognized the need for apartments and commerce, asking how design could help incorporate them into a suburban neighborhood.

A major break occurred when Wright returned to urban design after the failed resort projects of the late 1920s.[93] The intricate matrix of various elements—not only shapes, but also people and activities—was now subsumed into a rigid configuration of repeated patterns and homogeneous residents. Such rigidity was not simply a disoriented reaction to the lack of work during the Depression. Despite drastically curtailed investment in private building, governmental agencies and local cooperatives offered opportunities for large-scale residential design, and Wright eagerly took part in several such ventures. Unlike most projects of the 1930s and 1940s, which sought to convey a sense of cohesiveness and adaptation to the site, he emphasized the autonomy of each unit and de-emphasized the exigencies of the site. He deemed a commitment to organic architecture sufficient to guarantee both harmony and variety.[94]

Despite Wright's instantaneous fame after 1936, the government's home-mortgaging agency would not tolerate what looked unconventional, fearing social deviance and a decline in the value of property. For years the Federal Housing Authority rejected mortgages for Wright's houses and residential groups, citing a criterion it called "Adjustment for Conformity."[95] Yet Wright's proposals, in fact, anticipated postwar patterns of land use that the government chose to underwrite: insular suburbs with protected natural amenities, majestic civic centers, industrialized building technologies, and an extensive network of high-speed freeways with concentrated nuclei of shopping facilities. His words and designs continued to embody "the here and now of *our own* life in its Time and Place."[96]

Wright's proposals continued to focus on ideal suburban enclaves. Whatever the scale of development, he stressed the absolute sovereignty of each private dwelling. The trend is first evident in 1938–39 with Suntop Homes in Ardmore, Pennsylvania (figure 10). The site originally encompassed four clusters, each comprising four row houses arranged in a pinwheel configuration around the intersection of two brick walls. (Whereas a wall had surrounded the early Quadruple Block Plan, it now separated the houses from one another.) The dwellings were arranged vertically, with split levels to increase spaciousness and visibility, culminating in rooftop sundecks that gave the project its name.

Figure 10: Frank Lloyd Wright. Typical house, Suntop Homes, Ardmore, Pennsylvania. 1938–39

Wright again considered numerous arrangements, treating the architecture like interlocking pieces in a puzzle. Each one concentrated all activities within the individual units, including a laundry and carport, hoping to do away with "the general untidiness characteristic of the usual low-cost housing."[97] In the end, only one of the four units was built, yet it is the progenitor of countless postwar condominiums.

That same year a more asymmetrical and differentiated scheme pertained with Usonia I in Lansing, Michigan (plate 405). In this case the client was a cooperative of seven households, all affiliated with nearby Michigan State University. On a roughly triangular site Wright spun out triangular lots, encompassing seven separate houses with gardens and a larger farm unit at the center. The Federal Housing Authority refused to approve a mortgage, claiming that the construction system was unfeasible and the unusual design would impair possible resale of the houses. That decision aborted the project just as construction was about to begin.[98]

A few years later, a group in the Detroit area asked Wright to help them develop a scheme for inexpensive houses they could build themselves, to be called Cooperative Homesteads of 1941–45 (plate 407). Wright adapted the bermed Usonian dwelling that was soon to become the second Jacobs House. He also insisted on collective farming, in keeping with his belief in self-sufficiency and ties to the land. Prospective residents, all of whom had jobs as teachers or auto workers, resisted this pressure, then fell into bickering, such that the project "was abandoned for lack of cooperation"—Wright's as well as theirs.[99]

Visually and pragmatically, the Cloverleaf Housing Project for the federal government, planned for Pittsfield, Massachusetts, in 1942 (plate 406), seemed the most promising of the wartime efforts. "Usonian Houses for the USA" encompassed one hundred residences and a factory for defense workers. Circular lots with four houses at the center formed the basic geometric pattern, elaborating on the pinwheel configuration used at Ardmore. Some of the housing groups were turned askew to break the monotony of the repetition. Within the

dwellings a split-level system maintained maximum privacy, between and within family groups. Yet, once again, unforeseen problems stopped construction just as it was about to begin. Conflicts over the requisite documents for the government bureaucracy were compounded by protests from local architects, who complained that someone from out of state had received such a large commission.

Just after the war, Wright embarked on several larger subdivisions that proved somewhat more fruitful—and even more restricted. Parkwyn and Galesburg (plate 408) were nonprofit cooperatives near Kalamazoo, Michigan, as was Usonia II in Pleasantville, New York, which was the largest Wrightian cooperative. For all three Wright proposed a template of one-acre circular plots, providing protective membranes like the walls of a cell around each dwelling. Triangular wedges between the discs contained serpentine roads and shared natural amenities but no longer any public facilities. House plans were based on triangular, rectilinear, and circular schemes, highlighting the varieties of his Usonian prototype. Diversity was now a matter of house design, no longer of social mix. These same techniques characterize the popular Planned Unit Developments of the 1970s, which endeavored to foster an idyllic image of a like-minded community ensconced in a protected natural landscape.

A grand axial site plan then reappeared in a surprising setting: Paradise on Wheels, a Trailer Park for Lee Ackerman and Associates in Paradise Valley, Arizona (plate 410). Conceived in 1952, this setting shows Wright's ability to unite the themes of mobility and stability that pervaded his own imagination and that of the larger culture. Paradise on Wheels was designed to catch the attention of passing motorists with landscaped kiosks on all four corners, for the heart of the development, surrounded by parking, consisted of a small shopping center and recreational area—the stymied modern definition of public space. Around this core were spaces for 390 trailers; "A Veritable City of Trailers" proclaimed an early brochure.[100] In reality, even though this project was unrealized, neither the formal conception nor the social program can be considered cosmopolitan.

During all this time, of course, Wright continued to devote considerable attention to Broadacre City (plates 403–404). This was a utopia in the sense that it occupied a vague and idealized site: an expanse of flat, open land, crossed with major highways, potentially anywhere and everywhere. Yet Wright felt sure it was a historical necessity, destined to replace the urban congestion, suburban sprawl, and rural disarray that were decimating the country. He imagined the pattern he called Broadacres taking root around the edges of existing American cities, then "organically" spreading until it encompassed the entire nation. On one occasion Wright even suggested that the wartime bombing of London provided an auspicious opportunity to implement his scheme in Europe.[101]

For several years Taliesin apprentices worked on a representative portion of Broadacre City encompassing four square miles (figure 11). An immense and detailed model of this microcosm went on display in 1935 at the Industrial Arts Exposition in New York's Rockefeller Center, afterward traveling to other cities. For the rest of his life Wright relentlessly promoted his proposal, insisting it was not just a metaphor for order but a feasible, even an imperative, reality.

Broadacre City sought to introduce a measured variety of form and use into a dense rectilinear fabric. As with all of Wright's designs, the grid determined the symmetrical arrangement of parts and linkages.[102] It also defined the internal street system and the great highways leading outward. Automobiles for every resident provided access to this expansive domain, representing the means and ends of individual freedom.

In keeping with the agrarian myth of self-sufficiency, Broadacre revolved around home and family. "The true center (the only centralization allowable) in Usonian democracy, is the individual in his true Usonian home," Wright explained.[103] All housing stood independently on ample plots of land—a minimum of one acre per person, from whence derived the name. Wright thus represented his society as a pyramid with its "broad base in the ground."[104] Hierarchy did not disappear, however; position and need ranked dwellings according to the number of cars, from the "minimal" one-car house to the five-car "luxurious" model that had generated the House on the Mesa in 1932.

The domain for public interaction was, in contrast, sparse and uniform, even if Wright's prose described joyous unity. Roadside markets at major highway junctions anticipated postwar shopping malls, fusing consumerism with conviviality. People would also congregate at service stations and community centers, which provided sports facilities and other entertainment, including art galleries and museums.

Broadacre City provided both an affirmation of and an antidote to the prevailing American patterns of land use. It represented a cohesive plan of suburban dispersal, regulating the patterns of expansion and the points of concentration to prevent monotonous sprawl. An extensive article in *Architectural Record* described "a general decen-

tralization and architectural reintegration of all units into one fabric."[105] To assure that all parts adhered to organic principles, a single architect functioned as the agent of the state. Extending over every aspect of the environment, his dominion allowed no possibility of chaos or confusion.

Presciently, Wright outlined three modern systems that already provided the underpinnings of his vision: the automobile, which assured mobility for each individual; telecommunications, which prevented isolation; and industrial production, which provided modern goods for a mass clientele. As he saw it, these unharnessed forces threatened to undermine the American landscape and the national character. The time had come to apply them to Usonian purposes, promoting social and economic independence for every individual, as well as ecological interdependence with nature. In his enthusiasm, Wright refused to engage the more pernicious aspects of these technologies, convinced that good design would nullify all potential problems.

Broadacre City could easily be dismissed as an autobiographical fantasy. It became a repository for Wright's own unrealized projects, including the Gordon Strong Automobile Objective and Planetarium of 1924–25, the New Theatre for Woodstock, New York, of 1931, and the skyscraper for St. Mark's-in-the-Bouwerie of 1927–31 (plates 209–214). While its anarchism disdained a role for local government, the state architect—obviously intended to be Wright himself—wielded absolute authority.

Yet Broadacre City should not be passed over as a purely subjective reverie. This vast terrain captured the rhythms and forms that revolutionized the country after World War II: suburban expansion, landscaped highways, shopping malls, entertainment complexes, and national recreational areas. It cannot be said to have caused these phenomena or even to have directly validated them. Rather, it shows the extent to which Wright felt the pulse of American life and looked across the full extent of the national landscape.

Certain aspects of the proposal are unquestionably regressive: the rigid class hierarchy, wasteful overreliance on the automobile and electricity, and the substitution of consumerism and leisure activities for a true public sphere. There is also a commendable effort to come to terms with contemporary reality. Wright accepted the social trends of American culture, then tried to fit them into a different pattern of land use, one that celebrated individual autonomy and protected ecological balance, encompassing both within a controlled system. That system had no boundaries, for Wright recognized that one could not bracket or segregate problems in a complex, interconnected world.

Even if we might question his proposed solutions, Wright addressed difficult problems and amorphous sites that need the attention of talented designers. Here and elsewhere, he felt that architecture implied a larger perspective, well beyond that of the isolated, fetishized object. One cannot but be struck by his lifelong commitment to the idea of an architectural landscape as a public realm. That landscape was transposed into a formal pattern. Yet it always remained a world of natural beauty and human interaction for which Wright, as an architect and an individual, felt full responsibility.

Figure 11: Frank Lloyd Wright. Broadacre City. Project, 1934–35. Model

1. "'House of the Century' Gets a Reprieve from Demolition," *House and Home* 13 (February 1958), p. 68.

2. "100 Years of the American House," *House and Home* 11 (May 1957), p. 120.

3. Cited in Neil Levine, "The Temporal Dimension of Fallingwater," Fiftieth Anniversary Symposium on Fallingwater, Buell Center for the Study of American Architecture, Columbia University, November 7, 1986, p. 1.

4. See Raymond Williams, *The Country and the City* (New York: Oxford University Press, 1973). [Rosalyn Deutsch], "Expertise: Rosalyn Deutsch on Men in Space," *Artforum* 28 (February 1990), pp. 21–23, provides a thoughtful critique of similar problems with the word *space*.

5. Frank Lloyd Wright, "Chicago Culture," Lecture to the Chicago Women's Aid, 1918, p. 9. Wright Papers, Library of Congress, Washington, D.C. The phrase is later repeated in Frank Lloyd Wright and Baker Brownell, *Architecture and Modern Life* (New York and London: Harper & Brothers, 1937), p. 45.

6. See Gwendolyn Wright, "Prescribing the Model Home," *Social Research* 58 (Spring 1991), pp. 213–26.

7. Frank Lloyd Wright, *Modern Architecture, Being the Kahn Lectures for 1930* (Princeton: Princeton University Press, 1931), p. 70.

8. "Our Strongest Influence for Enrichment," *House Beautiful* 99 (January 1957), p. 45.

9. Frank Lloyd Wright, *The Living City* (New York: Horizon Press, 1958; reprint ed., New York: New American Library, 1963), pp. 55, 84.

10. "The Dramatic Story of Frank Lloyd Wright," *House Beautiful*, Special Issue 98 (November 1955), p. 235.

11. Thomas Bender, "A Great American Life," *Grand Street* 7 (Spring 1988), pp. 186–93.

12. Frank Lloyd Wright, *An Autobiography*, 2nd ed. (New York: Duell, Sloan and Pearce, 1943), p. 561.

13. Frank Lloyd Wright, *An Autobiography* (New York: Longmans, Green, and Co., 1932), p. 363. (Unless otherwise noted, all references to the *Autobiography* are to the first edition of 1932.)

14. Frank Lloyd Wright, "Introduction," *Ausgeführte Bauten und Entwürfe von Frank Lloyd Wright* (Berlin: Ernst Wasmuth, 1910); reprinted in Bruce Brooks Pfeiffer, ed., *Frank Lloyd Wright: Collected Writings*, vol. 1 (New York: Rizzoli, 1992), p. 113. The occasional "Forest houses" of this decade, located in wooded suburbs or lakefront sites, are somewhat more rustic in plan and elevation, with a counterthrust in their vertical lines. Yet they, too, represent variations on a single theme.

15. Wright, *Kahn Lectures*, p. 70.

16. Letter to Harriet Monroe, April 18, 1907, cited in Joseph Connors, *The Robie House of Frank Lloyd Wright* (Chicago: University of Chicago Press, 1984), p. 69.

17. Wright, *Kahn Lectures*, pp. 72, 73.

18. Ibid., p. 72.

19. Frank Lloyd Wright, "In the Cause of Architecture, I: The Logic of the Plan," *Architectural Record* 63 (January 1928), p. 57.

20. Henry-Russell Hitchcock and Philip Johnson, *The International Style: Architecture since 1922* (1932; reprint ed., New York: W. W. Norton, 1966), p. 26.

21. Frank Lloyd Wright, "In the Cause of Architecture, IV: The Meaning of Materials—Wood," *Architectural Record* 63 (May 1928), p. 482.

22. Fred C. Robie and Fred C. Robie, Sr., "Mr. Robie Knew What He Wanted," *Architectural Forum* 109 (October 1958), p. 126.

23. Frances Willard, *How to Win: A Book for Girls* (New York: Funk & Wagnalls, 1886), p. 54; cited in Gwendolyn Wright, *Moralism and the Model Home: Domestic Architecture and Cultural Conflict in Chicago, 1883–1913* (Chicago: University of Chicago Press, 1980), p. 105.

24. Frank Lloyd Wright, "In the Cause of Architecture," *Architectural Record* 23 (March 1908), p. 160.

25. Wright used such phrases in "A Small House with 'Lots of Room in It,'" *Ladies' Home Journal* 18 (July 1901), p. 15; and in "Architect, Architecture and the Client," Lecture to the University Guild, Evanston, Illinois, 1896, p. 11; and a revised version, "The Modern Home as a Work of Art," lecture to the Chicago Woman's Club, 1902, p. 12. Both lectures are in the Wright Papers, Library of Congress, Washington, D.C.

26. See Ellen Key, *Love and Ethics*, trans. Mamah Bouton Borthwick and Frank Lloyd Wright (Chicago: Ralph Fletcher Seymour, 1912), pp. 43–44; and Wright, "The Modern Home as a Work of Art," p. 5. Mamah Borthwick also translated *The Morality of Women and Other Essays* (1911) and *The Woman Movement* (1912) from Key's original Swedish texts after she left her husband and Wright's client, Edwin Cheney, and resumed her maiden name.

27. Frank Lloyd Wright, "Art in the Home," paper read before the Home Decorating and Furnishing Department of the Central Art Association's Third Annual Congress, Chicago, May 1898; reprinted in *Arts for America* 7 (June 1898), p. 581.

28. Herbert Croly, "New York as the American Metropolis," *Architectural Record* 13 (March 1903), p. 199. See also idem, "Architecture of Ideas," *Architectural Record* 15 (April 1904), p. 363; Helen Campbell, *Household Economics: A Course of Lectures in the School of Economics of the University of Wisconsin* (New York: G. P. Putnam's Sons, 1896), pp. 98–105; and idem, "Household Furnishings," *Architectural Record* 6 (October–December 1896), pp. 97–104. These refer specifically to Wright.

29. Wright, "The Modern Home as a Work of Art," p. 5.

30. Wright referred to the "New School of the Middle West" in "In the Cause of Architecture" (1908), p. 39; Thomas E. Tallmadge used the term *Chicago School* in "The 'Chicago School,'" *Architectural Review* 15 (1908), pp. 69–74; and Wilhelm Miller first spoke of the "Prairie Style" in *The Prairie Spirit in Landscape Gardening* (Urbana: University of Illinois Press, 1915), p. 5. See H. Allen Brooks, *The Prairie School: Frank Lloyd Wright and His Midwest Contemporaries* (Toronto and Buffalo: University of Toronto Press, 1972), pp. 8–13.

31. Frank Lloyd Wright, "A Home in a Prairie Town," *Ladies' Home Journal* 18 (February 1901), p. 17. Bok proudly quoted Theodore Roosevelt, who called him "the only man I ever heard of who changed, for the better, the architecture of an entire nation, and he did it so quickly and yet so effectively that we didn't know it was begun before it was finished." Bok, *The Americanization of Edward Bok* (New York: Charles Scribner's Sons, 1924), pp. 249–50. Other model houses by William L. Price, Ralph Adams Cram, Arthur Little, Bruce Price, and Joy Wheeler Dow adapted the Shingle style or colonial revival.

32. Frank Lloyd Wright, "A Fireproof House for $5000," *Ladies' Home Journal* 24 (April 1907), p. 24.

33. Wright, *Autobiography*, p. 165.

34. Ibid., p. 171.

35. Ibid., p. 235.

36. Ibid., p. 232; see also Wright, "In the Cause of Architecture, II: What 'Styles' Mean to the Architect," *Architectural Record* 63 (February 1928), p. 151, for a discussion of "genuine character."

37. Wright, *Autobiography*, pp. 227–28. He was referring to the Hollyhock House in particular.

38. Frank Lloyd Wright, "To Arizona," *Arizona Highways* 16 (May 1940), p. 15; reprinted in Raymond Carlson, "Frank Lloyd Wright and Taliesin West," *Arizona Highways* 25 (October 1949), pp. 10–11.

39. Ibid.

40. Wright, *Autobiography*, p. 309. The same materials and design approach prevailed in Wright's 1927 demountable, prefabricated beach cottages at Dumyât, Egypt.

41. Ibid., p. 305.

42. Frank Lloyd Wright, *An Organic Architecture: The Architecture of Democracy* (London: Lund, Humphries, 1939), p. 9.

43. Wright, *Autobiography*, p. 251.

44. Ibid., p. 245.

45. Frank Lloyd Wright, "Frank Lloyd Wright," *Architectural Forum* 68 (January 1938), p. 83.

46. Frank Lloyd Wright, "Frank Lloyd Wright," *Architectural Forum* 83 (January 1948), p. 80. Male "sanctums" appear in the floor plans of the Lusk House project (1936), the Hanna House (1936), the Lewis House (1939), the Baird House and Pope House (both 1940), though not in smaller Usonian dwellings. This seems to represent a more gender-defined variation of the study (or quiet zone) and kitchen (or active zone) in the Two-Zoned House project of 1934–35. To be sure, such gender stereotypes were quite common during these years.

47. Letter to Nancy Willey, July 5, 1932. The Frank Lloyd Wright Foundation.

48. Frank Lloyd Wright, "1932: The House on the Mesa," in Frederick Gutheim, ed., *Frank Lloyd Wright on Architecture: Selected Writings* (New York: Duell, Sloan and Pearce, 1941), p. 166; and Wright in *Architectural Forum* (1938), p. 76.

49. Wright's first published use of the word occurred in the Dutch magazine *Wendingen* in 1925; see H. Th. Wijdeveld, ed., *The Life-Work of the American Architect Frank Lloyd Wright* (Santpoort, Netherlands: C. A. Mees, 1925), p. 51; reprint ed., *Frank Lloyd Wright: The Complete 1925 'Wendingen' Series* (New York: Dover, 1992).

50. Frank Lloyd Wright, *The Disappearing City* (New York: William Farquhar Payson, 1932), p. 89.

51. Wright in *Architectural Forum* (1938), p. 78.

52. Ibid. For their account, see Herbert Jacobs with Katherine Jacobs, *Building with Frank Lloyd Wright* (Carbondale: Southern Illinois University Press, 1975).

53. Wright in *Architectural Forum* (1938), p. 78.

54. The idea for the Two-Zoned House of 1934–35 had been suggested in a letter from a mother/housewife, Dorothy Johnson Field. Both this letter and Wright's response to the idea appear in *Taliesin* 1 (1934), pp. 13–20. Field later amplified her proposal in *The Human House* (Boston: Houghton Mifflin, 1939), which featured illustrations of Wright's Malcolm Willey House.

55. Wright, *Kahn Lectures*, p. 66; idem, "The Logic of Contemporary Architecture as an Expression of This Age," *Architectural Forum* 52 (May 1930), p. 638.

56. Frank Lloyd Wright, "In The Realm of Ideas," in *Two Lectures on Architecture* (Chicago: Art Institute of Chicago, 1931), p. 13.

57. For a thorough discussion of the Usonian houses, see John Sergeant, *Frank Lloyd Wright's Usonian Houses: The Case for Organic Architecture* (New York: Whitney Library of Design, 1984).

58. Frank Lloyd Wright, "A Four-Color Portfolio of the Recent Work of the Dean of Contemporary Architects, with His Own Commentary on Each Building," *Architectural Forum* 94 (January 1951), p. 91.

59. Wright called this shape a "polliwog," attesting once again to his ability to capture the popular imagination with vivid images, both verbal and architectural. See *The Natural House* (New York: Horizon Press, 1954), p. 167.

60. Wright, "Logic of Contemporary Architecture," p. 638.

61. The Glass House appeared in Richard Pratt, "Opus 497," *Ladies' Home Journal* 62 (June 1945), pp. 138–41.

62. Wright, *The Natural House*, p. 181.

63. Ibid., p. 157.

64. Frank Lloyd Wright, "Organic Architect Looks at Modern Architecture," *Architectural Record* 111 (May 1952), p. 150. Wright's unrealized house of 1957 for Marilyn Monroe and Arthur Miller embodies this theme of stylized performance.

65. Frank Lloyd Wright, *When Democracy Builds* (Chicago: University of Chicago Press, 1945), p. 122. The Loeb model is described in "Wright Makes It Right," *Time* 48 (July 1, 1946), p. 73.

66. See Serge Guilbaut, *How New York Stole the Idea of Modern Art*, trans. Arthur Goldhammer (Chicago: University of Chicago Press, 1983); and Thomas Bender, *New York Intellect: A History of Intellectual Life in New York City from 1750 to the Beginnings of Our Own Time* (New York: Alfred A. Knopf, 1987), p. 339.

67. Telegram from Paul Hanna to Frank Lloyd Wright, January 29, 1936. The Frank Lloyd Wright Foundation. Paul and Jean Hanna discuss their house in "Our Love Affair with Our House," *House Beautiful*, Special Issue 105 (January 1963), pp. 54–63; and *Frank Lloyd Wright's Hanna House: The Client's Report* (New York: The Architectural History Foundation, 1981).

68. Letter from David Wright, September 14, 1950. Collection Frank Lloyd Wright Memorial Foundation.

69. Wright, "Introduction," *Ausgeführte Bauten und Entwürfe*, p. 107.

70. Frank Lloyd Wright, "In the Cause of Architecture" (1908), p. 158; idem, *Disappearing City*, p. 82.

71. Wright, "In the Cause of Architecture" (1908), p. 158.

72. Wright, "What 'Styles' Mean to the Architect," p. 145.

73. Ibid. Wright first spelled out his idea of "conventionalization" in the 1896 speech, "Architect, Architecture, and the Client."

74. "Frank Lloyd Wright and 1,000,000 Houses a Year," *House and Home* 3 (March 1953), p. 105.

75. Frank Lloyd Wright, "The House of the Future," *National Real Estate Journal* 33 (July 1932), pp. 25–26; idem, "Logic of Contemporary Architecture," p. 638.

76. Wright, *Autobiography*, p. 306.

77. "A Little Private Club," in "*Life* Presents in Collaboration with the *Architectural Forum* Eight Houses for Modern Living, Especially Designed by Famous American Architects for Four Representative Families Earning $2,000 to $10,000 a Year," *Life* 5 (September 26, 1938), pp. 45–65; reprinted as "Frank Lloyd Wright, Architect: House for $5,000–$6,000 Income," *Architectural Forum* 69 (November 1938), pp. 331–40.

78. Notable examples are C. E. Percival, "House on a Bluff," *House Beautiful* 20 (June 1906), pp. 11–13; idem, "Solving a Difficult Problem: A House at South Bend, Indiana, Frank Lloyd Wright, Architect," *House Beautiful* 20 (July 1906), pp. 20–21; and idem, "A House without a Servant," *House Beautiful* 20 (August 1906), pp. 13–14.

79. "This Rich and Rhythmic House Expresses 32 Simple and Basic Design Ideas," *House and Home* 10 (September 1956), pp. 136–41; "1,000,000 Houses a Year," p. 105.

80. Frank Lloyd Wright to Elizabeth Gordon, May 9, 1953. The Frank Lloyd Wright Foundation. He reported having heard this opinion from Auguste Perret.

81. "A Conversation," with Hugh Downs, from an NBC telecast of May 17, 1953; reprinted in Frank Lloyd Wright, *The Future of Architecture* (New York: Horizon Press, 1953), p. 38.

82. Wright, *An Organic Architecture*, p. 6; Wright, "A Four-Color Portfolio of Recent Work," p. 89.

83. Robert C. Spencer, Jr., "The Work of Frank Lloyd Wright," *Architectural Review* 7 (June 1900), pp. 61–72. See also idem, "Brick Architecture in and about Chicago," *The Brickbuilder* 12 (September 1903), pp. 178–87. While Wright was preparing material for the 1908 issue of *Architectural Record* that became "In the Cause of Architecture," the magazine ran a shorter article, "Work of Frank Lloyd Wright, Its Influence," *Architectural Record* 17 (July 1905), pp. 60–65.

84. Characteristic examples of Wright's criticism include "The Architect," *The Brickbuilder* 9 (June 1900), pp. 124–28; "Architecture as a Profession Is All Wrong," *American Architect* 138 (December 1930), pp. 22–23, 84–88 (which calls the AIA the "Arbitrary Institute of Appearances"); and *A Testament* (New York: Horizon Press, 1957), pp. 249–50.

85. Note on the side of a 1903 sketch of the Quadruple Block Plan for C. E. Roberts.

86. Wright, *When Democracy Builds*, p. 124.

87. Wright, *The Living City*, p. 171.

88. Wright continued to incorporate variations into later work, up through the 1957 proposal for black families in Whiteville, North Carolina.

89. After Wright left for Italy, construction was completed under the supervision of Marion Mahoney, Hermann von Holst, and Walter Burley Griffin. For the most extensive coverage, see Donald Leslie Johnson, "Frank Lloyd Wright's Architectural Projects in the Bitterroot Valley, 1909–10," *Montana: The Magazine of Western History* 37 (Summer 1987), pp. 12–25.

90. The competition entries, including extensive coverage of Wright's proposal, were published in Alfred B. Yeomans, ed., *City Residential Land Development: Studies in Planning, Competitive Plans for Subdividing a Typical Quarter Section of Land in the Outskirts of Chicago* (Chicago: University of Chicago Press,

1916). See also G. Wright, *Moralism and the Model Home*, pp. 281–91; and idem, "Architectural Practice and Social Vision," in Carol R. Bolon, Robert S. Nelson, and Linda Seidel, eds., *The Nature of Frank Lloyd Wright* (Chicago: University of Chicago Press, 1988), pp. 105–08.

91. See the excellent article by Paul and Percival Goodman, "Frank Lloyd Wright on Architecture," *Kenyon Review* 4 (Winter 1942), pp. 7–28.

92. Robert Craik McLean quotes Wright to this effect in "City Residential Land Development," *Western Architect* 25 (January 1917), p. 6.

93. See also Wright's urban residential projects of the 1920s–1940s: the Elizabeth Noble Apartments for Los Angeles, St. Mark's-in-the-Bouwerie in New York, Grouped Towers for Chicago, Crystal Heights in Washington, D.C., and the Rogers Lacy Hotel for Dallas. There are also important projects for civic groups and cultural institutions such as the Solomon R. Guggenheim Museum. This essay concentrates on Wright's suburban residential schemes.

94. "All individual Free City features naturally harmonize with those of immediate nature environment. . . . Endless unity-in-variety thus becomes inevitable. Indigenous character is as inevitable." Wright, *When Democracy Builds*, p. 58.

95. "Usonia Homes," *Journal of Housing* 10 (October 1953), pp. 319–20, 344; cited in Gwendolyn Wright, *Building the Dream: A Social History of Housing in America* (Cambridge, Mass.: MIT Press, 1983), p. 251.

96. Wright, *A Testament*, p. 23.

97. Memo to Otto Mallery, January 1, 1938. The Frank Lloyd Wright Foundation.

98. Only one of the proposed houses, the Goetsch-Winckler residence, was built later that year at nearby Okemos.

99. Frank Lloyd Wright, "Frank Lloyd Wright," *Architectural Forum* 88 (1948), p. 83; letter from Jim Smith, a member of the proposed cooperative, December 4, 1941. Collection Frank Lloyd Wright Foundation.

100. Brochure proof. The Frank Lloyd Wright Foundation.

101. "A City for the Future," *Time* 36 (November 25, 1940), p. 58.

102. Wright acknowledged that in Broadacre City "all is symmetrical but it is seldom obviously and never academically so. . . . Rhythm is the substitute for such repetitions." Frank Lloyd Wright, "Broadacre City: A New Community Plan," *Architectural Record* 77 (April 1935), p. 244.

103. Wright, *The Living City*, p. 231.

104. Wright, *When Democracy Builds*, p. 128.

105. Wright, "Broadacre City," p. 243.

TERENCE RILEY

THE LANDSCAPES OF FRANK LLOYD WRIGHT: A PATTERN OF WORK

In attempting to characterize American culture for a European audience, Frank Lloyd Wright combined his broad speculation regarding democracy and the individual with specific geographic references: "The real American spirit . . . lies in the West and Middle West."[1] His belief that architecture, culture, and the landscape were bound in a common course of development was not, in itself, singular. However, in Wright's work the relationship between architecture, landscape, and culture was a complex one, particularly as his definition of culture rejected the universal values of classicism and embraced the virtuousness of daily life. This stance can be seen in his description of the paradigmatic qualities of indigenous architecture: "Its virtue is intimately related with environment and the habits of the life of the people."[2]

The relationship was further complicated by the fact that the landscape was intensely familiar to Wright and because the prevailing culture was undergoing dramatic changes. And these changes, around the turn of the century, were matched by equally voluble transformations in Wright's own orientation toward the signal compass points of American culture: a strong sense of common destiny and an equally passionate exaltation of individual liberty. It is the intention of this essay to explore Wright's changing interpretations of an architecture that reflected the environment and the patterns of daily life in America over a seventy-two-year career.

A half-century after he left his uncle James Lloyd Jones's farm to attend the state university in Madison, Wisconsin, Wright's recollection of his youth retained a fresh familiarity with the particular and inescapable rhythms of farm life: "After one thousand two hundred and sixty todays and tomorrows like those yesterdays the boy was coming sixteen. Farmdays for him were over."[3] Although Wright spent a fraction of his early years actually working his uncle's land, his entire childhood, like that of approximately eighty percent of the generation born in the years immediately following the Civil War,[4] was spent in agricultural communities. Even during the years he lived in Weymouth, Massachusetts, his minister father was often paid by the congregation in farm products.[5] Nonetheless, his accounts of his years of hard work on the farm are often seen as the architect's fashioning of a Horatio Alger–like childhood myth and little else. But his architectural production suggests the opposite, and also suggests that Frank Lloyd Wright's farm days were not over even as he left for Madison and the world beyond.

In considering his first, intimate experience of the interrelationship between landscape and culture, it is important to note that Wright's years in southern Wisconsin were profoundly framed by the physical environment: the fertile rolling hills on the cusp of the broad midwestern prairie and the predominant activity, farming. Although mid-nineteenth-century life on the farm was full of hardships, farming was widely perceived as a virtuous activity. The writings of Thomas Jefferson and of Wright's own uncle the Reverend Jenkin Lloyd Jones amply confirm this. A highly respected Unitarian minister and author of *The Gospel of the Farm*, Jones wrote: "The miracle of the harvest field is beyond distrust; here is no place for skepticism. Nowhere do the laws above more clearly establish their kinship with the laws below than upon the farm."[6]

The affinities between Jefferson and Wright with regard to their attitudes toward the landscape are notable. Both were self-taught as architects and rejected the city in favor of rural living. Jefferson's home, Monticello, in Virginia and Wright's Wisconsin residence, Taliesin (figures 1 and 2), each interwove the rhythms of farming with intellectual pursuits centered in the library and studio. Ideally, the term *cultivated* applies to both Monticello and Taliesin, as well as their respective owners. It is a word that shares the roots of, and bridges the contemporary distinctions between, *culture* and *agriculture*. Despite these affinities, Jefferson and Wright had fundamentally different inspirations. Jefferson's Monticello, with its sweeping lawns and Palladian architecture, sought to evoke the Virgilian serenity of preindustrial classicism, while Wright's design for Taliesin, with its rough-cut local limestone and informal siting, was responsive to the more immediate patterns of the "environment and the habits of the life of the people." During the forty-one years between Jefferson's death and Wright's birth these patterns had begun to change at a rapid pace.

By 1880, when Wright was working on his uncle's farm, southern Wisconsin was increasingly bound into a web of connections with the regional capital, Chicago. The character of the Midwest is captured in Jenkin Lloyd Jones's words: "The mighty mills of Minneapolis, the thousand elevators on lakeshore and railroad siding, transcontinental trains and mighty grain ships of the ocean are all indispensable parts of the great feeding machinery of the world."[7] Yet even as the Midwest became a vast market for commodities and products, agrarian life retained its moral advantage in its association with physical labor and nature. An example of this nineteenth-century attitude can be seen in an early project for a planned community in Darby, Montana, called University Heights, Como Orchards Summer Colony of 1909–10 (plate 399) for which the Bitter Root Valley Irrigation Company "developed the land and then attempted to induce a group—without farming experience and from an urban background—to engage

Figure 1: Thomas Jefferson. General view, Monticello, Charlottesville. 1768–1809

Figure 2: Frank Lloyd Wright. General view, Taliesin III, Spring Green. 1925

in orcharding. The companies appealed to an intellectual, elite class, composed mostly of university professors."[8] The implication of the program was quite specific: Bitter Root could provide a working "vacation" out-of-doors and the academics could then "return to their scholastic duties with freshened interest."[9] The residents' orchards would not only provide them with an income but would give the entire settlement a character based in the belief that physical activity in the out-of-doors was both spiritually and physically healing.[10] As the historian David Strauss has noted, this type of retreat was seen as morally superior to the "idleness and indulgence" of spas such as Saratoga Springs, and it specifically addressed the spiritual and physical needs of the city-dweller. [11]

The high-mindedness of this midwestern culture of work was foretold earlier in the nineteenth century by Ralph Waldo Emerson: "Beauty must come back to the useful arts, and the distinction between the fine arts and the useful art be forgotten. If history were truly told, if life were nobly spent, it would no longer be easy or possible to distinguish the one from the other. In nature all is useful, all is beautiful."[12] Despite the benefits of agrarian life, derived from its relationship with both work and nature, the role of machinery in post–Civil War agriculture and particularly in Wright's early years should not be underestimated. Indeed, the machine itself was seen in a benign, if not virtuous, light by its association with the farm. In his series of sermons on farming Jenkin Lloyd Jones repeatedly referred to John Deere and Cyrus McCormick, whose mechanized agricultural implements revolutionized farming: "Here again, the gospel of the farm parallels the Gospel of the New Testament. These inventors and manufacturers were profound evangelists of the better life."[13] Jones's influence on his nephew is evident; in describing the benefits of the machine Wright declared: "Every age has done its work, produced its art with the best tools or contrivances it knew, the tools most successful in saving the most precious thing in the world—human effort."[14]

The first machine Wright ever operated was, no doubt, a farm machine. His uncle's horse-drawn mechanical reaper, invented by Cyrus McCormick in 1831 was, in Wright's words, "a bright-red affair with a varnished wood grain-platform on to which bright blue, green, yellow and red reels knocked the yellow grain as it was cut by the busy to and fro of the gleaming sickle."[15] The reaper was not the only machine that determined this new dimension of farming. Harrows, seeders, markers, plankers, cultivators, turntables, threshing machines, saws, hayracks, and hay rakes, all horse-drawn, were cited by Wright as the tools that marked the rhythms of life on the farm and transformed its landscape: "Pitching hay, hoeing, dropping corn with a 'checker'. Cultivating corn as the green hills passed regularly four feet between the shovels, planted four feet apart each way."[16]

The four-by-four-foot grid Wright perceived underlying the fields of corn was directly related to the regularizing effect of the machine's work on the landscape. Wright's subsequent use of the grid as an architectural device was not, of course, his own invention, nor can his widespread use of it in his architecture throughout the 1920s and frequently thereafter be attributed to the specific influence of the agrarian landscape. It would be more correct to say that Wright perceived the grid as the common denominator of the machine's work and that this provided him with a way of understanding not only the work of farming and building but also the commonalities among all activities transformed by the machine.

Wright's notation of the four-foot-square module of the underlying grid, determined by the work itself, has a fundamental relevance to the character and course of his architecture. The distance between farm rows was determined by how closely a team of horses could be hitched to pull the machinery through the fields. The module was determined by the need to optimize the work and then reflected in such variables as the spacing of the blades of the tiller, which were, in turn, limited in number by the turning radius of a hitched team.

As such, the grid was seen by Wright as a way of reflecting the process of the work rather than as an abstraction. Similarly, the module of La Miniatura, the Mrs. George Madison Millard House in Pasadena of 1923 (plates 178–181), Wright's first realized concrete-block house, was determined by the maximum size of a block that could be handled efficiently by a mason. The standardized components of the American System-Built Houses for the Richards Company of 1915–17 (plate 176) and the two-by-four-foot module of the Herbert Jacobs House in Madison of 1936–37, (plates 241–245) conformed to the standard dimensions of readily available plywood and lumber, themselves reflecting the work of their own manufacture.

While the grid and objectively derived module constituted a static model, Wright portrayed the dynamic nature of the work itself: "Any monotonous task involving repetition of movement has its rhythm. If you can find it the task can soon be made interesting in that sense. The 'job' may be syncopated by changing the accent or making an accent. Binding grain and shocking it, or pitching bundles to the wagons and the racks."[17] The syncopation and repetition of movement could be noted in manual tasks, but the machine refined and regularized its effect: "The gaily painted reaper, pulled by three white horses, cuts its way around, round after round. . . . The stubble is interlined by the big wheel of the reaper as it is also patterned by grain shocks. . . . The entire field is becoming a linear pattern of Work."[18]

Thus, added to the basic grid are various counterpoints: the grid is made directional by the path of the machine, then striated by the alternating rows, and further delineated by the wheel of the reaper. An overlaying pattern is made by shocks cast off by the passing of the blade. A larger pattern is superimposed by the regular intervals at which the bales are dropped. This image of a pattern of work is particularly evident in Wright's community proposals, such as the Noncompetitive Plan for City Residential Land Development of 1913–16: the grid as an organizer, the module determined by the requirements of the various land uses, the basic pattern being overlaid with additional rhythms and syncopations (plate 400). The metaphor is even more evident in his later proposals for the Cloverleaf Housing Project of 1942 and the Cooperative Homesteads development of 1941–45, both of which, from an aerial perspective, have unmistakable references to the cultivated landscape (plates 406–407). Even so, it is perhaps more important to note Wright's ability to discern the pattern of work as a principle that affects not only the landscape but the architecture as well. Wright's remarks describing his work in 1910 confirmed this attitude: "So I submit that the buildings and drawings here illustrated have for the greatest part been conceived and worked . . . in respect to the tools that produced them, the methods of work behind them, and, finally in their organic nature."[19]

The work Wright described in 1910 was the increasingly rationalized production of the Prairie period. Most of the better-known work was commissioned for sites in the garden suburbs of Chicago. Despite Wright's frequent literary references to nature, this particular landscape, like the agrarian landscape and the landscapes of Japan, which he visited in 1905, was a highly stylized form of nature, and increasingly so after the turn of the century. In this sense, Wright's use of the word *organic* in association with the tools and methods of working is critical

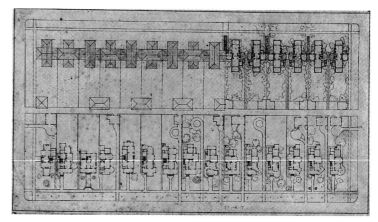

Figure 3: Frank Lloyd Wright. Quadruple Block Plan for C. E. Roberts, Oak Park. Project, c. 1900–03. Plan; ink, pencil, and color pencil on linen. The Frank Lloyd Wright Foundation

in understanding his conception of the relationship between architecture and the landscape. The organic quality he sought in his work rejected not only the forms of classical architecture, which would "detach the beautiful from the useful,"[20] but embraced the productive landscape over an idealized vision of nature. In this sense, the regularity of the suburban landscape could be seen as its potential virtue. In a demonstration drawing attributed to the project known as the Quadruple Block Plan for C. E. Roberts of 1900–03 (figure 3), Wright seemed to be making an argument for even greater regularization by contrasting the disorderliness of a typical suburban block with a tight-knit row of Wright-designed houses, each with a repetitive ground plan, side-by-side entryways, adjoining stables, and alternating rooflines. The paradox Wright appears to be illustrating is the tension between the ethos of the garden suburb, which promoted the single family home as the symbol of the individual, and the logic of work involved in its production.

From this point of view, another drawing of great interest is the perspective rendering of the Isidore Heller House in Chicago of 1897 (plate 30). The project is a brilliant example of Wright's late-nineteenth-century work: handcrafted detail, custom-designed furniture, and stained glass all emphasize the unique character of the house and, by implication, its client. The living spaces were raised up a half-story from the street, with the entry off to the side, and screened by bands of narrow windows. This arrangement removed them from the public realm and defined the family unit. Curiously, Wright drew an exact replica of the "unique" Heller House on the adjoining lot as if to represent the paradox of the unique aesthetic object and the utilitarian aspects of production. The first structure represents the requisite individual unit, the second the logic of the work: replication rather than individuality complements the rationale of mechanized production. Of course, only one Heller House was built. Nevertheless, Wright further explored this paradox in other drawings for C. E. Roberts (plates 394–395) wherein he attempted to regularize the suburban landscape by adjusting the balance between the individual and communal: while the identity of each unit is retained through the singular relationship of each house to a specific plot of land with clearly marked property lines, the landscape itself becomes a pattern of work.

Wright's attempts to rationalize the already stylized landscape of the garden suburb are also evident in his architectural work of the period. The influence of Sullivan, in terms of his floral and vegetal motifs and his judicious balance of decorated and planar surfaces, was still apparent, but after 1900 Wright's work became simpler and more abstract in conception. Ironically, it may have been the actual work of architectural design that began to transform his production. Relying increasingly on drafting tools rather than freehand drawing, Wright gave greater emphasis to the underlying geometries of his work. In this regard the mechanically drawn, stylized butterflies depicted in the glazed opening over the arched entry to the Susan Lawrence Dana House in Springfield, Illinois, of 1902–04 (plate 37) contrast sharply with the frieze on the Heller House (plate 31), sketched freehand and then cast in a hand-made mold. The decorative schemes for the mosaic-tile frieze of the Avery Coonley House in Riverside, Illinois, of 1906–08 (plates 91, 93) subsequently pushed the level of abstraction even further. Rejecting the initial design of highly stylized, but recognizable, floral motifs, Wright rendered the final design as a pattern, emphasizing nature's rhythms rather than its forms. So, too, did his architecture begin to acquire a rhythm of work. Colleagues described him as drafting various aspects of a design simultaneously, skipping from plan to elevation to section and back again, achieving the quality of "weaving" evident in his design drawings throughout his career and used as his own metaphor for architecture.[21] The Frederick C. Robie House in Chicago of 1908–10 (plates 100–106) was described as machinelike not because it resembled a machine but, rather, because, like the cultivated fields of the midwestern prairie, it was itself machined.

The textile metaphor is apparent in Wright's description of the linear pattern of work. His observation of the stubble being interlined by the reaper's wheel points to one of his lifelong architectonic fascinations: the field as a fabric, possessing a slight, but critical, spatial quality that distinguished it from a two-dimensional abstract surface. This delight in shallow depths can be found throughout Wright's career in the raked joints of the Prairie period brickwork, the fissures in the *oya* stone ornament of the Imperial Hotel, the impressions in the California concrete-block projects, and the cavities and voids in the desert-rubble walls of Taliesin West in Scottsdale, Arizona, of 1937–38 (plate 280). This sensibility is also expressed in the way Wright's buildings met the ground. Beginning with the William H. Winslow House in River Forest, Illinois, of 1893–94 (plates 9–13), his first independent residential commission, the sites for his houses do not seem to have been excavated but, rather, the foundations appear to have been pressed into the soil. The floor slabs for the Herbert Jacobs House and the many single-story houses patterned after it appear to be planted in the soil, like a farmer's boots, at a depth no greater than necessary to assure stability.

Ultimately, the success of Wright's synthesis of landscape, architecture, and the general culture in his Prairie period work depended

Figure 4: Frank Lloyd Wright. View from hilltop, Taliesin III, Spring Green. 1925

on his intimacy with all three. Initially, this synthesis was emblematic of a particular moment in history directly related to a pattern of work: the specific rhythms of agrarian activity and the general rhythms of the machine in the Midwest at the turn of the century. As seen in Wright's projects of later years, the synthesis of the Prairie period was not confined to that stylistic mode but represented a way of working and an achievement that reached beyond the geographic and historical moment in which it was developed.

The construction of Taliesin represents a turning point in Wright's formulation of the relationship between architecture and landscape and their role in American culture, particularly with regard to the machine and the balance between individual and collective values. Taliesin differs from the work that preceded it to the extent that it is less machined and more responsive to the natural aspects of the landscape. Sited in a supremely subtle manner, the main mass of the house is broken into smaller elements that rise and fall, like a collar, with the slope of the hill. From the interior court, the mastery of the siting is most evident: protected by a retaining wall, the crown of the hilltop has been preserved and, indeed, acts as a fourth wall to enclose the court. Despite its protective sense of enclosure, various lines of sight open up from the court into the landscape beyond, crowning the landscape with space itself (figure 4).

While in his previous work Wright displayed a willingness to modify the landscape to conform to a pattern of work, in designing the landscape of Taliesin he was exceedingly cautious about interrupting the natural patterns of the site. While Wright's change in attitude could be a result of his tiring of the mechanical process of designing that he had developed and sustained over two decades, it is equally plausible that his experience in Italy just prior to building the first phase of Taliesin had considerable effect. The year Wright spent living outside Florence in Fiesole proved to be a powerful stimulus to his romantic nature. In addition to the familiar activities of the Tuscan landscape (like southern Wisconsin, the area around Fiesole was characterized by farming and stonecutting), certain physical elements appear to have strongly affected Wright. The scores of small quarries around Fiesole provided Florence and its surrounding towns with a seemingly endless supply of *pietra serena*, the gray sandstone cut into thin slabs as an architectural finish, thick slabs for paving, small blocks for cobbles, and large blocks as raw building material for foundations. If the *pietra serena* gave much of Florence and its environs a consistent coloration, the more rustic buildings in the countryside had similar qualities. Local sand was the most available admixture for stucco, which was, in turn, the cheapest material for finishing the exterior of a building. The stucco took its coloration from the sand and other locally available earth pigments, resulting in entire villages that appeared as if they had grown out of the surrounding fields. If Wright's conception of organic architecture had implied the effect of the work on nature, in Fiesole he would have seen demonstrations of the opposite: the effect of nature on the work.

Wright appears to have found the physical relationship between the buildings and landscape in Tuscany exceptionally sympathetic. At Taliesin he employed limestone from nearby quarries and in later projects actually sought the building material from the site itself. The pattern of work became an imitation of nature's work: the raked brickwork of the Prairie house is replaced by an irregular pattern of cleft-faced stone that mimics its own sedimentary formation. Wright's use of local materials was repeated in the construction of Taliesin West (plates 278–283) and numerous other projects throughout his career, such as the Rose Pauson House in Phoenix of 1938–41 (plates 291–292), Eaglefeather, the Arch Oboler House, a project for Malibu of 1940–41 (plate 289), and Meteor Crater Inn for Sunset Crater National Monument, Arizona, of 1947–48 (plate 315). In the technique developed at Taliesin West, rubble boulders were not only culled from the desert site but wrapped in newspaper during construction so that the color and texture of the stone would not be affected by the mason's work. The Memorial to the Soil, a Chapel for the Newmann Family of 1934 (plate 268), raises Wright's intermingling of the architecture and the landscape to a near sacramental level. In this project, the construction material is the landscape itself, the four sides of the structure being embraced by sculpted berms of compacted soil.

Despite the inherently romantic aspects of these projects and their intimate relationship with the site, more pragmatic motivations can also be seen, particularly economic ones. Without denying the substantial differences between contemporary attitudes toward the environment and Wright's attitude, it is clear that the Solar Hemicycle, a second house for Herbert Jacobs in Middleton, Wisconsin, of 1943–48 (plates 311–314) and the Cooperative Homesteads project for Detroit of 1941–45 (plate 300) are related to the Memorial to the Soil both physically and conceptually: all of them have earth berms, although what is symbolic in the Memorial to the Soil is explicitly practical in the later projects, which rely on the berms for energy efficiency. Furthermore, the second Jacobs House was sited to maximize the sun's passive heating effect. Despite our familiarity with the frugal use of

resources implied in these projects, Wright's motivations should be distinguished from present attitudes toward the environment. Inasmuch as all of these projects were proposed decades before the current consciousness about energy consumption, it would be more correct to ascribe Wright's protoenvironmentalism to the judicious use of land and other natural resources, which, in the early twentieth century, was known as "conservation."

The building of Taliesin was intimately involved with dramatic changes in Wright's personal life. His decision to relocate was due in part to his decision to leave his wife and family to live with Mamah Borthwick Cheney, the wife of a client. The ensuing scandal, played out in the Chicago press, was a clear censure of Wright's behavior by the society whose values he had sought to portray in his Prairie period. Wright's rejection of this criticism established the scenario for a quintessentially American morality play, in which the individual was pitted against the community in determining national values. At the time he began living with Mrs. Cheney, Wright attempted to formulate this balance: "America . . . places a life premium upon individuality—the highest possible development of the individual consistent with a harmonious whole . . . the whole, to be worthy as a whole, must consist of individual units, great and strong in themselves. . . . It means lives lived in greater independence and seclusion."[22]

Despite the assertiveness of Wright's statement, its true implications are not obvious. If the logic of Wright's work of the Prairie period led him steadily to the conclusions that allowed him to replicate the Heller House, his statement could be read as placing a greater emphasis on the creation of the harmonious whole. However, considering the nature of the personal crisis that surrounded the decision to build Taliesin, Wright's statement is more clearly an endorsement of the individual. It is clearly linked both to a long romantic tradition, which glorified and intertwined the individual and nature, and to the American political tradition, which related suffrage, and hence identity, to land ownership. In this regard, Wright was not far removed from the pioneer ethos; it was, after all, not until he turned twenty-three that the American frontier was declared closed. Furthermore, the government policy that allowed free men to settle open lands continued well into the twentieth century, with ten million acres of public land transferred to private ownership during the year Wright built Taliesin.[23]

Not surprisingly, Wright conceived of Taliesin as a working farm. However, the changes that characterized his reformulation of the relationship between architecture, landscape, and the individual are also evident in his conception of the nature of agrarian activity. While earlier in his life the interrelationship of farming, particularly mechanized farming, and a larger pattern of activity in the Midwest indicated an inescapable interdependence of the environment and "the habits of the life of the people," Wright's vision of Taliesin as a farm was motivated by a desire to be "self-sustaining, if not self-sufficient."[24] Given Wright's perceptiveness with regard to the regional connections of Chicago and its suburbs, the pastoral farmlands across several states, and the wilderness hinterlands beyond, his idealization of self-sufficiency was less than realistic. Ultimately it was an instance of personal determination rather than universal vision. The gap between the two can be seen in the scale of Wright's farming enterprise: Taliesin was built on two parcels of land totaling sixty-one acres.[25] The reality of farming in the twentieth century can be seen at its outset, when an average farm in the Corn Belt was between 125 and 150 acres.[26] While throughout his early career and beyond, Wright had synthesized the logic of the work of the agrarian landscape, Taliesin enshrined the *image* of farming, and all its references, more in a romantic than a pragmatic way.

The romantic aspects of Taliesin were not unprecedented in Wright's work. We need only cite such early works on picturesque sites as the Thomas P. Hardy House in Racine, Wisconsin, of 1905 (plates 96–97) or the Lake Delavan Cottage project of 1907 (plate 99). Nevertheless, it is interesting to compare the Harold McCormick House in Lake Forest, Illinois, of 1907 (plate 98) designed for the bluffs overlooking Lake Michigan, with the design for the Sherman M. Booth House in Glencoe, Illinois, of 1911–12 (plates 118–121). In the former, the fabric of the house completely replaces the natural landscape—the bluffs rendered as sheer escarpments and the water's edge transformed by seawalls and jetties. In the latter, designed after Wright returned from Italy, the house is sited so it hardly disturbs the existing topography, the masses rising and falling with the sloping contours and bridging over the adjacent ravines.

Given Wright's personal attachment to Taliesin and the circumstances that caused him to build it, there are few subsequent projects that express the interrelationship of individual, architecture, and landscape as forcefully. However, to the extent that Wright's emphasis on the individual is related to an increased focus on the romantic, particularly the natural landscape, the changes in his perspective represented by Taliesin can be seen broadly in his California projects. Their collective designation, Romanzas—borrowing a term from music— also reflects Wright's romantic attitude.

In the Los Angeles houses for Charles E. Ennis and Samuel Freeman (plates 187–195) and the Hollywood house for John Storer (plates 182–186), all of 1923–24, as well as the 1923 Millard House in Pasadena, Wright employed a concrete-block system that recalls the efforts of the Prairie period in its rationalized method of production (figure 5). Even so, Wright tried to localize the concrete: small amounts of soil from the building site were added to the concrete batches for these houses; as a flexible building system they allowed Wright to respond to the canyons and hillsides overlooking Los Angeles. Whereas Taliesin, even at its most romantic, maintained the orderly appearance of a cultivated landscape, the renderings for the California projects are overgrown with a lushness that recalls the jungle-covered Mayan ruins with which Wright was familiar through photographs. The perspective of the Millard House, particularly, shows the architecture as nearly obscured by tropical growth (plate 178), in stark contrast to his earlier vision of nature presented by the neat lawns and gardens of the highly stylized landscape of suburb and farm. The perspectives of the Doheny Ranch Resort, also designed for Los Angeles in 1923, evoke this image on a grander scale, the myriad structures blending into the densely covered

Figure 5: Frank Lloyd Wright. Exterior detail, Charles E. Ennis House, Los Angeles. 1923–24

canyon landscape (plates 198–199, 402). Suggesting a relationship between the Doheny Ranch Resort and the Southern California landscape, Wright described the project as "becoming a terraced garden similar to the region."[27]

While Wright was completing the designs for the Doheny Ranch Resort he made his first visit to the desert with A. M. Johnson to see the Death Valley site on which Johnson intended to build a residence. The austerity of the desert presented Wright with yet another landscape and a vision of possibilities for architectural expression. The importance of this experience can be seen in the dramatic changes in his work. For over forty years all of Wright's important works were regulated by his devotion to the orthogonal grid. As the historian Neil Levine has noted,[28] diagonal composition, or at least diagonal movement, frequently underlay Wright's planning, even in early projects such as the Henry N. Cooper House in La Grange, Illinois, of 1890–95. Even so, the abrupt appearance in Wright's work after 1923 of numerous projects with diagonal compositions and various grids derived from nonrectilinear geometries is not easily explained without reference to the landscape, in this instance the desert: "Out here in the great spaces obvious symmetry claims too much, I find, wearies the eye too soon and stultifies the imagination. Obvious symmetry usually closes the episode before it begins. So for me there could be no obvious symmetry in any building in this great desert."[29]

The design for the A. M. Johnson Desert Compound and Shrine of 1922–25 (plate 196) incorporated both existing and new structures into a complex site plan, with multiple axes based on the rectilinear ninety-degree angle and thirty- and sixty-degree angles. The axes con-

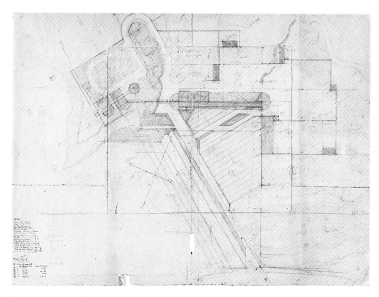

Figure 6: Frank Lloyd Wright. A. M. Johnson Desert Compound and Shrine, Death Valley. Project, c. 1922–25. Site plan; pencil and color pencil on paper. The Frank Lloyd Wright Foundation

verge and form a stepped court in the shape of an isosceles triangle, evident in the center of the site plan (figure 6). In addition to the angles in the plan, the walls of the structures themselves are slightly canted, as in the Ennis and Hollyhock houses. However, in the Johnson Compound the terraces and abutments surrounding it are also angled, suggesting, as Levine has noted, the quality of an "earthwork." While the canted profiles of the California projects have been attributed to the influence of Mayan architecture, Wright noted the formal relationship between his diagonal planning and massing in his desert projects: the sloping "streamlines of these endless mountain ranges coming gently down to the mesa."[30]

Six years after Wright began the designs for the Johnson Compound he received the commission for a sprawling resort, San Marcos-in-the-Desert, which was to have been built on a rugged site outside Chandler, Arizona (plates 200–201). To prepare the drawings for this project, Wright relocated his staff to Arizona for the winter, where they assisted in building a temporary camp on the site of the resort project. Named after a desert cactus, the Ocotillo Desert Camp was arranged around the crest of a hillock and consisted of a dozen rough board-and-batten cabins connected by a palisade enclosure of the same construction. In the center of the encampment stood a concrete-block "model," a full-scale rendition of a corner of the proposed structure (figure 7). Like the Johnson Compound, the site plan of the Ocotillo Camp was composed of both rectilinear and diagonal elements, deployed to intimately reflect the changes in the site's contours (figure 8). However, when designing the structures Wright extended the diagonal vocabulary more literally to the facades of the cabins. Rather than being slightly canted, as in the Johnson Compound, the canvas-covered cabins all had profiles of thirty and sixty degrees.

Wright's encampment in the desert allowed him to know the site for the San Marcos-in-the-Desert Resort intimately. The design comprises a central pavilion with two extensions containing living quarters

for the guests. The extensions cant backward at an angle as if to wrap the desert slope on which they sit, a landscape gesture that Wright would repeat in the Cottage Group Hotel in Hollywood for Huntington Hartford of 1946–48 (figure 9; plate 316), among other projects. Each of the extensions had three levels, each stepped back to allow for terraces overlooking the desert landscape. The entry pavilion is also asymmetrical, sited over an arroyo that serves as the main approach, and defined by a tower placed off-center that rises from the flat desert like a rock formation. Even the texture of the concrete blocks, serrated on the surface, imitates the vertical ridges of the saguaro cactus.

Taliesin West was built in the winter of 1937–38 (figure 10). Reminiscent of the Ocotillo Desert Camp in its free diagonal composition—in plan, elevation, and the direct relationship of buildings to environment—Taliesin West was Wright's most eloquent statement of the lessons of the desert. Like the camp, the main structures were covered by canvas roofs and had large unobstructed openings to the landscape that could be shuttered at night. Thus the main drafting room, as originally designed, was more of an open pavilion in the arid landscape than a traditional enclosure. The hand-selected desert rubble incorporated into the masonry ensured an explicit chromatic relationship between the structures and the landscape, which from a distance are almost indistinguishable from each other. While the Ocotillo Camp was, in Wright's words, "ephemera,"[31] Taliesin West appears to have an almost eternal presence. The extent to which Wright achieved this quality without losing the spontaneity and intimacy of the desert camp is remarkable.

The reasons for Wright's strong attachment to the landscape of the Southwest are worth considering. Like the Midwest prairie, the desert had a discernible formal character. In citing the angled profiles of the mountain ranges and the asymmetrical nature of the rugged terrain as the sources for his canted structures and diagonal planning, Wright recalled his own formal rationalization of the Prairie house: "The exterior recognizes the influence of the prairie, is firmly broadly associated with the site, and makes a feature of its quiet level."[32] While neither Wright's desert projects nor his work of the Prairie period

Figure 7: Frank Lloyd Wright. View of San Marcos-in-the-Desert model and studio, Ocotillo Desert Camp, Chandler, Arizona. 1929

should be seen as a purely formal response to the landscape, in both instances the dominant landscape was such that broad, general characteristics could be discerned. That is, both the prairie and the desert suggested the possibility of a broadly based response to the landscape that transcended the specific site.

Considering that Taliesin represented Wright's romantic advocacy of lives lived in greater independence and seclusion, the desert environment—a searing wilderness of biblical proportions and associations—could be seen as an extension of his exaltation of the individual. As with the construction and design of Taliesin in Spring Green, Wright's adoption of the desert as a second home in the late 1920s must also be viewed in a biographical light. In 1914 a deranged servant killed Mrs. Cheney, two of her children, and four other people, then set fire to Taliesin. Although this tragedy garnered Wright a tremendous amount of sympathy, his estrangement from Chicago society caused by his desertion of his family continued. Soon after Mrs. Cheney's death, although he was still married to Catherine Tobin Wright, he began a relationship with Miriam Noel. Wright eventually married Noel, but his relationship with her was increasingly unstable. Despite the successful completion of the Imperial Hotel in 1923 and its withstanding a severe earthquake soon after, other commissions were scarce and Wright was beset with constant financial problems as well as other personal losses: the death of his mother and of Louis Sullivan, and a second disastrous fire at Taliesin.

The construction of the Ocotillo Desert Camp marked a point in Wright's life when, at sixty years of age, the problems that had beset him for a decade or more seemed to have been resolved. Before obtaining a divorce from Noel in 1927, Wright had begun a relationship with Olgivanna Hinzenberg, with whom he had a child and, in 1928, married. Though the stock market crash of 1929 would cause ongoing financial problems, Wright's personal life was increasingly stable. The

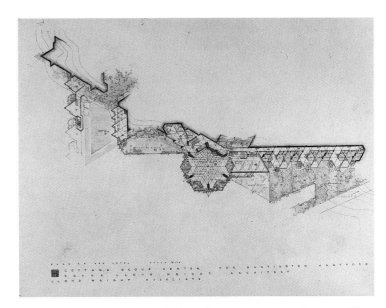

Figure 9: Frank Lloyd Wright and Lloyd Wright, Associate. Cottage Group Hotel for Huntington Hartford, Hollywood. Project, 1946–48. Plan; pencil and ink on tracing paper. The Frank Lloyd Wright Foundation

publication of his charismatic autobiography in 1932 presented a compelling image to a younger generation of architects and students born long after Wright's famous Prairie period. The establishment of the Taliesin Fellowship in 1932 brought an additional degree of stability to his professional life. Wright was bolstered by the efforts of a group of devoted young apprentices who, in addition to paying tuition, provided him with the labor to revive his practice in the midst of the Depression, to maintain Taliesin, and subsequently to build Taliesin West. In its various aspects, from architectural enterprise to social experiment, the Fellowship was a unique institution among other models of professional practice (figure 11).

The emergence of a way of responding to a new landscape can thus be seen as occurring at a time when Wright was seeking new personal and professional beginnings. In this connection, it is interesting to note how the historian Frances Fitzgerald described the motivations of the founders of America's utopian experiments: "Uncomfortable with, or simply careless of, their own personal histories and their family traditions, they thought they could shuck them off and make new lives, new families, even new societies. They aimed to reinvent themselves."[33]

While there were important similarities between Wright's responses to the agrarian and desert landscapes, there also were significant differences. The desert had no relation to the usefulness or fertility that Emerson had described as the counterpart of nature's beauty: "In nature, all is useful, all is beautiful. It is therefore beautiful, because it is alive, moving and reproductive; it is therefore useful, because it is symmetrical and fair."[34] The desert contradicted Emerson's definition in almost every sense. While it was beautiful and natural, there was no obvious usefulness in the "unmitigated wilderness"; nature was not moving but "rock-bound-earth prostrate to the sun." Nor was the desert reproductive but "all life there dies a sun-death."[35] Moreover,

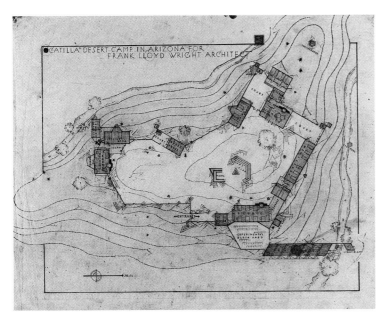

Figure 8: Frank Lloyd Wright. Ocotillo Desert Camp, Chandler, Arizona. 1929. Site plan; pencil on tracing paper. The Frank Lloyd Wright Foundation

nature's symmetry and fairness were not in evidence. The desert's lack of a discernible pattern, as seen in the stylized landscapes of the garden suburb, no doubt further contributed to Wright's abandonment of symmetry and rectilinear planning. Unlike the productive landscapes of the Midwest, the desert displayed no particular pattern of work, no to-and-fro of the weaver (figure 12).

In this regard, Wright's use of the diagonal also became a more universal language for the architecture and landscapes of the less developed areas of the country, which, like the desert, were often characterized by a relative openness and lack of established pattern of activity. Many of these places seemed to contain, on a smaller scale, the qualities he found throughout the West: "virgin" landscapes, unfettered by the constraints of history and immune to the encroachment of the metropolis. A good example was Florida Southern College in Lakeland, a new master plan commissioned by Dr. Ludd Spivey in 1938. Built over a number of years according to Wright's plan (plate 284), the campus, like the Johnson Compound, included a number of structures organized by rectilinear geometries as well as thirty- and sixty-degree angles. Connecting the various buildings were covered walkways that, according to the original design, were to pass on the diagonal through groves of orange trees planted throughout the campus. And in the Auldbrass Plantation in Yemassee, South Carolina, of 1938–42 (plates 293–297) the walls of the structures themselves are canted, from the foundations to the eaves, resembling the bases of the live oak and cypress trees that cover the site. Even the rain leaders suspended from the buildings' eaves are given a topical aspect: their cast-copper forms mimic the hanging moss of the swamp environment.

Wright's attraction to the desert landscape and the new work he

Figure 11: Frank Lloyd Wright. Taliesin Fellowship Complex, Spring Green. 1933. Aerial perspective; pencil and color pencil on tracing paper. The Frank Lloyd Wright Foundation

derived from it did not imply a repudiation of the lessons of the prairie. Rather, the course of his work is mirrored in his new personal circumstances wherein he migrated annually between Wisconsin in the summer and Arizona in the winter, embracing both landscapes and their respective cultures. In this regard, any understanding of Wright's complex thinking must take into account his ability to expand and multiply his frames of reference. Furthermore, his inclination to transform a particular theme or idea, rather than discard it, best characterizes his fundamental pragmatism in a century in which ideology often held sway. The increasingly polyphonous nature of Wright's attitudes toward the landscape and architecture are mirrored in his work through the 1930s and later: while much of it followed the broad patterns suggested by his archetypal landscapes, other projects appeared as exceptional counterpoints, particularly when the characteristics of the site suggested a singular rather than generalized attitude. No doubt, the most notable example in this regard is Fallingwater, Wright's house for Edgar J. Kaufmann of 1934–37 (plates 234–240), built on a remote wooded site in Mill Run, Pennsylvania. The house's concrete cantilevers dramatically hover over an equally dramatic waterfall without disturbing it. Exploiting fully the unique characteristics of the site, an open staircase descends from the main living area to the surface of the stream's shallows just above the falls. Built with local stone and designed so that the fireplace was positioned over natural rock formations, which appear through the building's fabric, Fallingwater evokes the romantic splendor of Wright's vision of the independent and isolated life of the individualist.

The extensive use of reinforced concrete in the formation of the cantilevered terraces appears to be a response to the machine imagery of Le Corbusier and an attempt to address the paradox of individualism and mechanical culture Wright found in his own earlier work in

Figure 10: Frank Lloyd Wright. Taliesin West, Scottsdale. 1937–38. Under construction

the Prairie period: a fusion of the most machinelike of images and an almost hypernatural landscape. As a rebuke to Le Corbusier's dictum that a house was a "machine for living in,"[36] Fallingwater appears to embody Emerson's fear, expressed a century earlier, that the injudicious use of the machine by "mercenary impulses" would deny "our great mechanical works" the potential to be "continuations of the material creation."[37]

Wright's distaste for the machine aesthetic, that is, for the idea that architecture should look like a machine, is rooted in his earlier experiences in which the benefit and the virtue of the machine were determined by its use: its aesthetic qualities were related to its effect rather than its image. Despite these differences, Wright's enthusiasm for one particular machine, the automobile, was shared by many Europeans, Le Corbusier included. Wright's experiences throughout the West can be characterized in part by its intimate relationship with the automobile.[38]

Wright's use of the automobile was certainly a matter of preference and one that ignored questions of comfort. Indeed, the Santa Fe Railroad, which ran from Chicago to Arizona, was a much more secure way of traveling at a time when roadside facilities were scarce. Nevertheless, Wright's advocacy of the automobile in the 1920s was more ideological than practical. If the railroads created the axis that connected Chicago to the garden suburbs, the pastoral landscape of southern Wisconsin, and the wilderness beyond, the highway for Wright was the critical piece of infrastructure that made the vast western hinterlands accessible.

Wright's auspicious prediction that the automobile would change American life—"Complete mobilization of our American people is one natural asset of the machine, fast approaching"[39]—was both accurate and fundamental to his own migration to the Southwest. If he was a man of his time before the turn of the century in realizing the regional interrelationships of the urban-suburban-exurban axis, he was well ahead of his time in the 1930s in projecting those interrelationships onto a national scale. These changes, wrought principally by advances in communication and transportation, would have profound effects on the postwar American landscape and create heretofore unknown cultural phenomena; there would be new cities built principally by real-estate speculators, whole communities comprising retired people, and entire regions devoted to specific activities such as tourism. All of these considerations were behind Wright's conception of Broadacre City of 1934–35 (plates 403–404), a theoretical proposal, conceived as an alternative to the traditional development pattern of the metropolis. Elements here are recognizable from his previous work; in fact, a number of his projects (including Taliesin) are literally inserted into the landscape. The overall grid is modulated by an infrastructure providing power, water, and transportation. The patchwork construction of the landscape as a linear pattern of work, manipulated to create distinctions among various programmatic elements and social groups is much like his Noncompetitive Plan for City Residential Land Development of 1913–16 (plate 400). The dispersal of traditional urban activities within an overall pattern of farm activity confirmed the romantic

Figure 12: Frank Lloyd Wright. Taliesin West, Scottsdale. 1937–38. View with desert landscape

ethos of Taliesin, expanded to a vision of a deurbanized, automotive America set out in an agrarian mode. Wright also included the possibility of the unique and the exceptional: opposed to the predominant horizontal landscape of the archetypal prairie, a corner of the Broadacre model rose as a picturesque mountaintop, crowned with its own castle, the Gordon Strong Automobile Objective and Planetarium, originally designed in 1924–25 (plates 209–210).

As the historian Donald Leslie Johnson has shown, Broadacre City combined a number of influences, such as Frederick Law Olmsted's landscape theories, and its antiurban position was widely shared—from Ebenezer Howard's Garden City to Henry Ford's proposals to revitalize rural life by dispersing industry throughout sparsely populated areas.[40] Even so, its political and economic structures were extremely vague. Like Taliesin, Broadacre City promoted the image and virtue of agrarian living rather than a clear, viable economic model. It was envisioned within a continuous fabric of orchards, vineyards, and "small farms" based on a design by Wright for a Prefabricated Farm Unit for Walter V. Davidson of 1932 (plate 230). The plan for the farm unit called for prefabricated steel construction and included a "shipping room." While these features implied certain practical economies, their limitations were obvious: one farm of thirty acres would have been vastly more efficient than ten smaller units.

Wright's promotion of the agrarian landscape in Broadacre City was rooted in personal and moral issues rather than in practical concerns that defined agrarian activity in the 1930s. As in the Quadruple Block Plan for C. E. Roberts of 1900–03, Broadacre City regularized expression while preserving the identity of the individual: house types and plot sizes, representing a range of incomes and distinguished principally by patterning strategies, each maintained their identifiable boundaries. Even so, the balance between individualism and regulation was quite different in these proposals. While the Quadruple Block Plan was conceived within the sociability of the garden suburb, the romantic aloofness of Taliesin was implied in Broadacre's minimum plot size of one acre. Consistent with contemporary attitudes toward the individual, Broadacre City represented yet another reformulation of Wright's call for "the highest, possible development of the individual consistent with a harmonious whole."

Ironically, the viability of Broadacre City is not most questionable in its economics or in its antiurban, anticapital position but, rather, in the character of the citizenry it implies. Broadacre City was imagined to spread across the flat countryside with no government higher than the county level; this suggested a citizenry of uncommonly uniform political values as well as negligible economic, social, and religious differences. The ideal citizens of Broadacre, not surprisingly, appear to be people like Wright's family, the Lloyd Jones clan, and the people he grew up with in southern Wisconsin: European immigrants with common historical and linguistic roots, determined to take their place in an American dream, church-going but free-thinking Unitarians, industrious, prosperous, and devoted to the virtues of agrarian culture. Whether there were enough such Americans to fill Broadacre City from coast to coast in 1930 is doubtful. In an 1878 novel Henry James described characteristics similar to those attributed to the fictional inhabitants of Broadacre City. In describing one of the Emerson-reading Wentworths, he noted: "Our hero was an American of the earlier and simpler type—the type of which it is doubtless premature to say that it has wholly passed away, but of which it may be at least said that the circumstances that produced it have been greatly modified."[41]

The contradictory individual and communal visions of Broadacre City might be considered an American national characteristic, for surely the cultural development of the nation has been guided by these often incompatible forces. That Broadacre City, despite its indefensible economic and political positions, continues to captivate us indicates that the issues it raises are still part of the national dialogue.

Despite the irresolvable practical problems in Wright's conception of Broadacre City, his observation that it would build itself proved to be partially accurate, particularly with regard to the single-family home. Coining a word to represent the new middle-class culture, Wright declared: "There is spaciousness for all in Usonia. The great highway is becoming, and rapidly, the new horizontal line of Freedom extending from ocean to ocean."[42] He further stated: "There are millions of individual building sites, large and small, now easy of access and available owing to our great continually developing road-systems."[43]

The relationship between the automobile and cheap land was not limited to the West. Wright's middle-class clients of the 1930s were vastly different from their counterparts of the Prairie period. They were less likely to have servants and more likely to build smaller houses, if they could afford to build at all, and in less developed locations than the garden suburbs. The stable and garage of the Prairie period, separate structures located discreetly behind the house, gave way to the carport—prominently integrated with the entry to the house and symbolic of mobility.

If Wright was optimistic about automobile-oriented residential programs, he also anticipated a new architecture of the highway landscape: "The roadside service station may be—in embryo—the future city-service-distribution. Each station may well grow into a well-designed convenient neighborhood distribution center naturally developing as meeting place, restaurant, restroom, or whatever else will be needed as decentralization processes and integration succeeds."[44]

A generation later, the boundless enthusiasm for the automobile and high hopes for a new roadside architecture with "beautiful countryside features" seem hopelessly naive. Given Wright's mistrust of commercial interests, it is even questionable whether his optimism was warranted. Nevertheless, his sincerity is evident; the Daniel Wieland Motor Hotel and the Lindholm Oil Company Service Station of 1955–57 (plates 366–367) both presented the roadside landscape as having what might be called a dignified populism in which commercial interests were balanced with aesthetic concerns. The image of the highway, seamlessly flowing across the landscape, was first explored by Wright in the Gordon Strong Automobile Objective and Planetarium, a spiral ziggurat enclosing a domed structure. In the streamlined administration building for S. C. Johnson & Son, Inc., the roadway is continuous under and through the building. Even the structure reflects the versatility of concrete, wherein the circular columns flare, joining with the ceiling in one continuous unit. In its relationship to the horizontal line of freedom, the Johnson Administration Building prefigures the Adelman Laundry of 1945 (plate 365), which was also designed as a drive-through building. The spiraling ramps of the Roy Wetmore Automobile Showroom in Detroit of 1947–48, the V. C. Morris Gift Shop in San Francisco of 1948–49, and the Solomon R. Guggenheim Museum in New York of 1943–59 reflect not only the boundless mobility of the idealized automotive landscape but the essential characteristic of its predominant material—poured concrete (plates 301–310, 345–347, 364). Throughout his career Wright had tried to give some meaning to the material, either symbolically, by adding local soil to it, or representationally, by associating it with an indigenous architecture. The spiral can be seen as Wright's successful attempt to discipline an essentially formless material, to create of it a pattern of work and relate it to the lifestyles of his clients of the 1940s and 1950s.

Wright's experience in the desert led him to predict that the Southwest would become "the playground for these United States,"[45] a prediction as astute as that regarding the automobile's proliferation. The change in Americans' attitudes toward the landscape and its relationship to leisure is evident in Wright's resort projects. If the Village of Bitter Root retreat was emblematic of a culture of work (plates 396–398), Wright's postwar resorts certainly embody a pattern of leisure. The Cottage Group Hotel and Sports Club for Huntington Hartford in Hollywood of 1946–48 (plates 316–318) best represents this transformation. The ethos of work, which was so much a part of the Bitter Root scheme, is nowhere to be found in the cascading pools of water, tennis courts, and restaurants of the later scheme. Architecturally, the transformation is also complete: the rustic unpainted board-and-batten construction of Bitter Root is replaced by sensuously molded, sun-drenched concrete forms.

The horizontal line of freedom not only transformed the West into a national recreational region, but brought a vast migration of new inhabitants to the southwestern states, attracted by its fair weather and the prospect of informal living. Numerous houses were designed for the hillsides overlooking Los Angeles and featured cantilevered decks, open to the sun and sky, and distant views. The Ralph Jester House, designed for a site in Palos Verdes, California, of 1938–39, the Boulder House in Palm Springs for Liliane and Edgar J. Kaufmann of 1951, and Crownfield, the Robert F. Windfohr House, in Fort Worth of 1948–50, with their sensuously curving and circular forms, suggest leisure culture on a grand scale: sybaritic swimming pools, sun terraces, and flowing spaces for "home entertainment" (plates 269, 343–344, 351).

The proliferation of a leisure culture in the postwar period affected every aspect of American culture as well as the course of architecture, Wright's as much as anyone else's. The rigors of prewar modernism, fueled by an avant-garde critical position, dissipated in the postwar years and were integrated into mainstream culture. If Wright's work never fit completely into the modern movement, he achieved in the 1950s a level of acceptance unparalleled since his popularity of the Prairie period. His early success was linked to the degree

to which he internalized the pattern of work, and his late success was equally linked to the degree to which he appropriated the leisure ethic. While development never took precisely the form he had envisioned, those areas of the country that did expand became a kind of ad hoc Broadacre City, particularly in the Southwest. As he had predicted, roadside development eventually replaced the traditional public realm of the city, and a concomitant expansion in the private realm had, indeed, made for many "lives lived in greater independence and seclusion."

A generation after Wright's death, in the wake of successive energy crises, suburban congestion that rivals that of any crowded city, and the alienation resulting from the diminishment of the public realm, it is vital to reconsider Wright's work in the light of our present, contemporary culture. The values reflected in his work must be reformulated yet again if they are to have any impact on the current needs of American society. The themes he developed over his seventy-two-year career are still relevant: the analysis of the landscape, with regard to its broad formal and cultural characteristics; the design of an architecture that in its materials and methods of construction is related to its specific site and to a generalized vision of the landscape; and the relationship among architecture, landscape, and the patterns of activity of its inhabitants, both communally and individually.

NOTES

1. Frank Lloyd Wright, "Introduction," *Ausgeführte Bauten und Entwürfe von Frank Lloyd Wright* (Berlin: Ernst Wasmuth, 1910); reprinted in Bruce Brooks Pfeiffer, ed., *Frank Lloyd Wright: Collected Writings*, vol. 1 (New York: Rizzoli, 1992), p. 108.

2. Ibid., p. 103.

3. Frank Lloyd Wright, *An Autobiography*, 2nd ed. (New York: Duell, Sloan and Pearce, 1943), p. 48.

4. Adna Ferrin Weber, *The Growth of Cities in the Nineteenth Century* (Ithaca: Cornell University Press, 1899), table 2, p. 22.

5. Wright, *Autobiography*, p. 11.

6. Jenkin Lloyd Jones, "Concerning Soil: Plowing," *The Agricultural Social Gospel in America: The Gospel of the Farm*, edited with an introduction by Thomas E. Graham (Lewiston, N. Y., and Queenston, Ont.: The Edwin Mellen Press, 1986), p. 41.

7. Jenkin Lloyd Jones, "The Harvest Field: Reaping," ibid., p. 100.

8. Dorothy J. Zeisler, "The History of Irrigation and the Orchard Industry in the Bitter Root Valley" (master's thesis, University of Montana, Missoula, 1982), pp. 74–75. See also Donald Leslie Johnson, "Frank Lloyd Wright's Architectural Projects in the Bitterroot Valley, 1909–1910," *Montana: The Magazine of Western History* (Summer 1987), p. 14.

9. Ibid.

10. See William Henry Harrison Murray, *Adventures in the Wilderness or Camp Life in the Adirondacks* (1869; reprint ed., Syracuse, N.Y.: Syracuse University Press, 1970).

11. David Strauss, "Toward a Consumer Culture: 'Adirondack Murray' and the Wilderness Vacation," *American Quarterly* 39, no. 2 (Summer 1987), p. 277.

12. Ralph Waldo Emerson, "Essay XII: Art," *Essays, First and Second Series* (New York: First Vintage Books/The Library of America Edition, 1990), p. 210.

13. Jenkin Lloyd Jones, "The Harvest Field: Reaping," p. 98.

14. Frank Lloyd Wright, "The Art and Craft of the Machine," reprinted in Pfeiffer, *Collected Writings*, vol. 1, p. 61.

15. Wright, *Autobiography*, p. 39.

16. Ibid., p. 40.

17. Ibid.

18. Ibid., p. 121.

19. Wright, "Introduction," *Ausgeführte Bauten und Entwürfe*, p. 108.

20. Emerson, "Essay XII," p. 209.

21. Wright, *Autobiography*, p. 168.

22. Wright, "Introduction," *Ausgeführte Bauten und Entwürfe*, p. 106.

23. Thomas A. Bailey and David M. Kennedy, *The American Pageant: A History of the Republic*, 8th ed. (Toronto: D.C. Heath & Company, 1987), p. 569.

24. Wright, *Autobiography*, p. 171.

25. Anthony Alofsin, "Taliesin 1: A Catalogue of Drawings and Photographs," in Narciso Menocal, ed., *Wright Studies: Taliesin 1911–1914*, vol. 1 (Carbondale: Southern Illinois University Press, 1992), p. 98.

26. Allan G. Bogue, *From Prairie to Corn Belt: Farming on the Illinois and Iowa Prairies in the Nineteenth Century* (Chicago: University of Chicago Press, 1963), p. 286, table 29.

27. Erving and Joyce Wolf Collection. See plate 198.

28. Neil Levine, "Frank Lloyd Wright's Diagonal Planning," in Helen Searing, ed., *In Search of Modern Architecture: A Tribute to Henry-Russell Hitchcock* (New York: The Architectural History Foundation; Cambridge, Mass.: MIT Press, 1982), pp. 245–77.

29. Wright, *Autobiography*, p. 309.

30. Ibid., p. 313.

31. Ibid., p. 331.

32. Frank Lloyd Wright, "A Home in a Prairie Town," *Ladies' Home Journal* 18 (February 1901), p. 15.

33. Frances Fitzgerald, *Cities on the Hill: A Journey Through Contemporary American Cultures* (New York: Simon & Schuster, 1981), p. 23.

34. Emerson, "Essay XII," p. 210.

35. Wright, *Autobiography*, p. 310.

36. Le Corbusier, *Towards a New Architecture*, trans. Frederick Etchells (1927; reprint ed., New York: Holt, Rinehart, & Winston, 1960), p. 222.

37. Emerson, "Essay XII," p. 210.

38. Although Wright was born into a time dominated by the railroads, he was an early advocate of the automobile, having purchased a Stoddard Dayton while living in Oak Park. His preference for driving was such that he brought a Country Club Overland with him from Chicago to Tokyo while working on the Imperial Hotel. In the late 1920s he and his staff and family all drove from Wisconsin to Phoenix for the winter, to work on the San Marcos-in-the-Desert Resort, returning to Taliesin in the summer.

39. Wright, *Autobiography*, p. 329.

40. Donald Leslie Johnson, *Frank Lloyd Wright Versus America* (Cambridge, Mass.: MIT Press, 1990), pp. 108–40.

41. Henry James, *The Europeans: A Sketch* (London: Penguin Books, 1984), p. 14.

42. Wright, *Autobiography*, p. 326.

43. Ibid., p. 327.

44. Ibid., p. 328.

45. Ibid., p. 308.

PLATES

The following plates present a selection of Frank Lloyd Wright's most important designs and buildings, organized thematically within a general chronology of seventy-two years. Brief texts serve as guides to nine thematic sections; the last of these is devoted to community plans developed throughout Wright's long professional career.

All works are by Wright unless otherwise designated. In the captions the name of a work is followed by its location and date. If a design is unexecuted, the word *project* appears before the date. Works are dated from the beginning of the commission or the design phase through completion of the building or design process if unbuilt. Occasionally a publication date is also given. A built work no longer extant is noted as such.

The illustrations of the works are of three types: original drawings, photographs, and redrawn plans or sections. Each illustration has its own plate number, which is followed by a description.

For original drawings the following may be given in parentheses after the description: the initials of the delineator to whom the drawing is attributed, the date of the drawing if known, and the date inscribed on the drawing (following the abbreviation *insc.*). Both dates are given where necessary to indicate that an inscription is known to be incorrect. (A list of delineators appears at the end of this note.) This information is followed by the medium and full dimensions of the drawing; if only a portion of the drawing is shown, the word *detail* will have appeared in parentheses following the description. Dimensions are given in feet (if above six feet) and inches, height before width. The name of the collection to which the drawing belongs follows the dimensions. Archive numbers for works in The Frank Lloyd Wright Foundation appear with the Photograph Credits.

For photographs of built works the view is given after the plate number. For redrawn plans a legend identifying rooms or areas is given in the caption; a graphic scale totaling twenty-five or fifty feet—in increments of one to twenty-five feet—is given on each plan. Sources, photographers, and credits for redrawn plans and sections are found in the Photograph Credits. Original drawings are attributed to the following delineators: AD: Allen Davison, AGG: Aaron G. Green, ALW: A. Louis Wiehle, AR: Antonin Raymond, BBL: Birch Burdette Long, BD: Blaine Drake, EB: Emil Brodelle, FLLW: Frank Lloyd Wright, GC: George Cronin, HF: Herbert Fritz, Jr., HK: Heinrich Klumb, HR: Harry Robinson, JHH: John H. Howe, JR: John Rattenbury, JT: James Thomson, KT: Kameki Tsuchiura, MM: Marion Mahoney, PB: Peter Berndtson, RM: Robert Mosher, RMS: Rudolph M. Schindler, TO: Takehiko Okami, VK: Vladimir Karfik, WD: William Drummond.

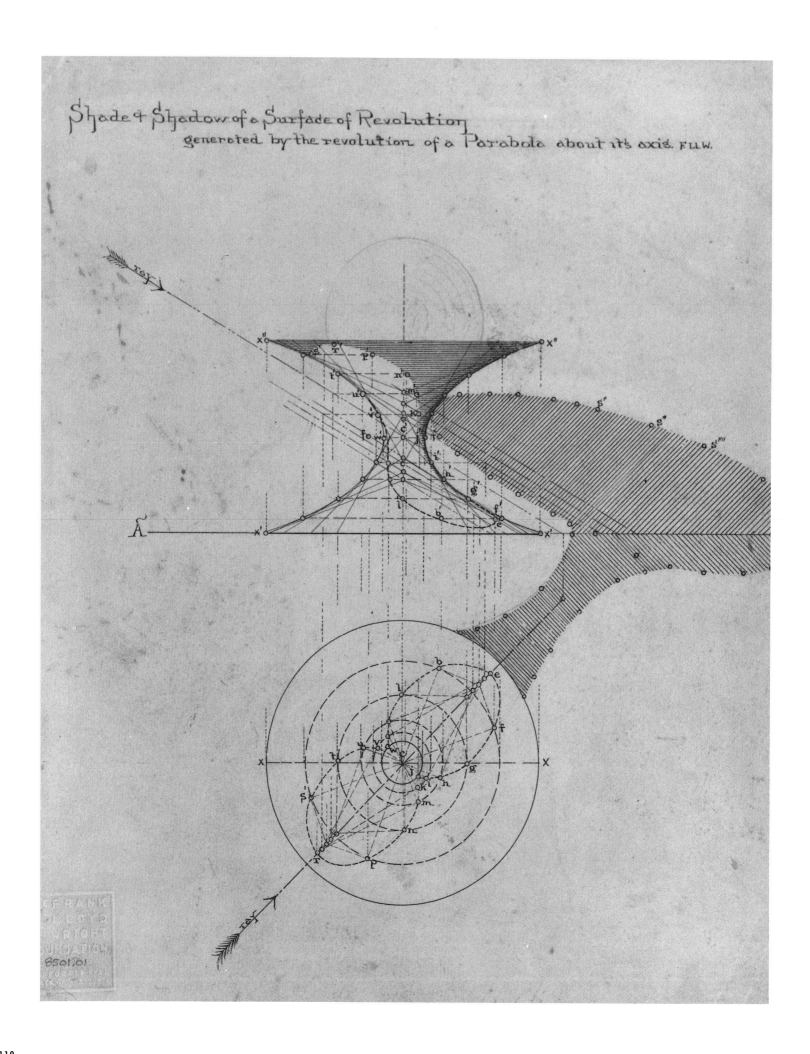

Shade & Shadow of a Surface of Revolution
generated by the revolution of a Parabola about it's axis. F.LL.W.

Opposite

ENGINEERING DRAWING   1885

1.   Surface parabola (FLLW). Pencil and ink on paper, 13 x 10⅝". The Frank Lloyd Wright Foundation

Below
Adler and Sullivan

ORNAMENTAL DRAWING   c. 1890

2.   Design for carved wainscot (FLLW). Pencil on tracing paper, 9⅜ x 4". Frank Lloyd Wright Collection, Avery Architectural and Fine Arts Library, Columbia University, New York

Adler and Sullivan

AUDITORIUM BUILDING
Chicago, Illinois. 1886–90

3.   Ornamental design for newel post, upper fragment (FLLW; c. 1888–89). Pencil on tracing paper, 9¾ x 9¼". Frank Lloyd Wright Collection, Avery Architectural and Fine Arts Library, Columbia University, New York

4.   Ornamental design for newel post, lower fragment (FLLW; c. 1888–89). Pencil on tracing paper, 9⅝ x 9⅝". The Frank Lloyd Wright Foundation

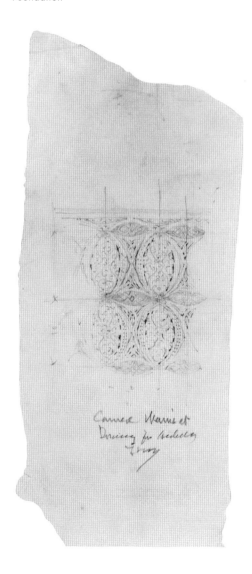

5. Front facade

FRANK LLOYD WRIGHT HOUSE
Oak Park, Illinois. 1889–90

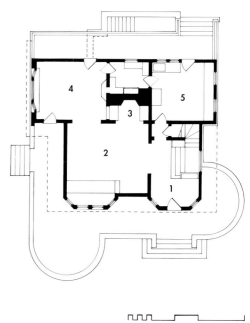

6. Inglenook

7. First-floor plan: 1 entrance, 2 living room, 3 inglenook, 4 dining room, 5 kitchen

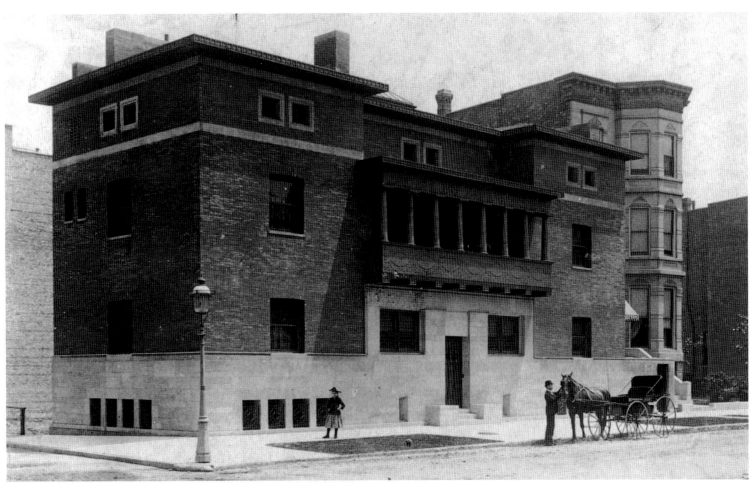

Adler and Sullivan **JAMES CHARNLEY HOUSE** Chicago, Illinois. 1891–92

8. Exterior

In 1887 Frank Lloyd Wright left his native southern Wisconsin to seek work and opportunity in Chicago, the rapidly growing metropolis of the Midwest. A year later, at the age of twenty, he was hired as an apprentice architect by Dankmar Adler and Louis Henri Sullivan, whose Chicago office had recently begun work on the celebrated Auditorium Building, one of the most aesthetically and technologically advanced structures of its time. Wright's talent was quickly recognized despite his lack of formal training and less than a year's experience in an architectural office. He soon became Sullivan's assistant, developing sketches for decorative details, and ultimately designed several of the firm's smaller commissions, the James Charnley House (above) among them.

The following year, Wright married Catherine Tobin and built a house in the Chicago suburb of Oak Park (opposite). Four years later, at the age of twenty-six, he estab-

lished his own practice with a small office in Chicago, and subsequently built a studio adjoining his Oak Park home (plates 21–26). Wright's early independent projects, such as the Lake Mendota Boathouse, the Wolf Lake Amusement Park, the Luxfer Prism Office Building, and the cast-concrete Monolithic Bank project (plates 14–15, 19–20, 27–29), reflect Adler's enthusiasm for technological innovation and Sullivan's formal strategies: variations on Beaux-Arts planning, devices such as the arched entryway, and elaborate floral and vegetal ornamentation. Wright also shared Sullivan's idealistic belief that the architect should create a new and quintessentially American architecture in the Midwest.

Wright's sympathy for the aesthetic and social ethos of the garden suburb made him a sensitive interpreter of late-nineteenth-century, upper-middle-class values, as reflected in the delicate hand-cast friezes, polychromatic murals, and custom-designed furniture

and window glass of the William H. Winslow and Orrin Goan houses (plates 9–13, 16) as well as other residential commissions of the period. His early work, immediately recognized as progressive, shared a number of concerns with his contemporaries: the aesthetic and moral consciousness of the Arts and Crafts movement, H. H. Richardson's informal interior planning, and the equally informal massing of the Shingle style. Not only did Wright avoid the Victorian preference for historical styles, but his lavish ornamentation, inspired by nature, became more inventive, simplified, and rationally integrated into the whole. This can be seen in the Susan Lawrence Dana House (plates 34–41). Increasingly enamored of the regularity of the machine's effect, particularly in the production of ornament, Wright began to move away from freehand drawing toward the geometrical rigor of mechanical drafting.

9.   Elevation. Pencil on paper, 15½ x 20½". Oak Park Public Library, Oak Park, Illinois

WILLIAM H. WINSLOW HOUSE
River Forest, Illinois. 1893–94

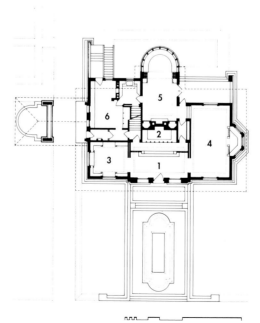

10.   First-floor plan: 1 entrance, 2 inglenook, 3 library, 4 living room, 5 dining room, 6 kitchen

11. Front facade

12. Rear facade

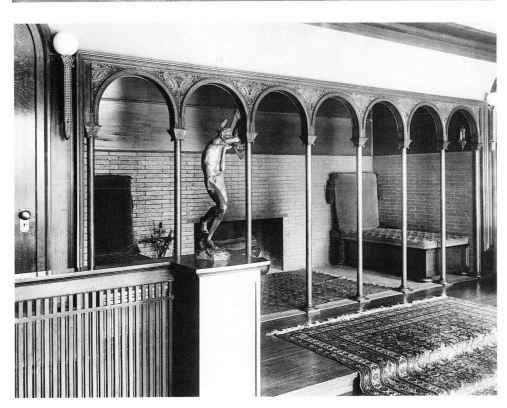

13. Inglenook

LAKE MENDOTA BOATHOUSE

Madison, Wisconsin. 1893 (demolished 1926)

15. Plan (FLLW). Ink and ink wash on tracing paper, 23¾ x 11⅛". The Frank Lloyd Wright Foundation

14. View from lake

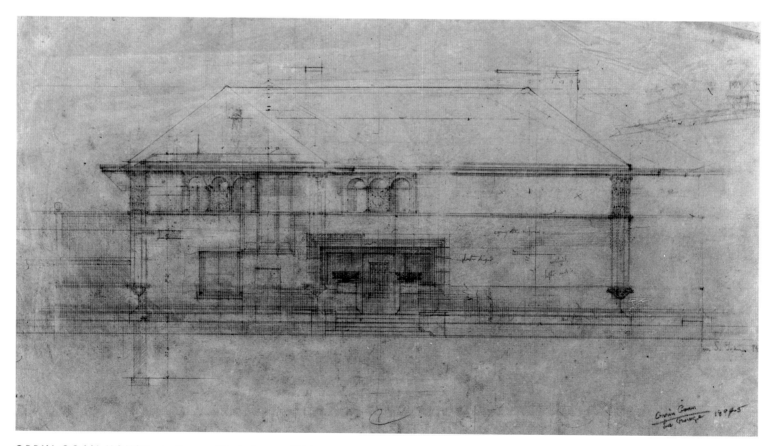

ORRIN GOAN HOUSE   La Grange, Illinois. Project, 1894

16. Elevation (FLLW). Pencil on tracing paper, 15¼ x 24". The Frank Lloyd Wright Foundation

17.   Perspective. Ink on tracing paper, 14³⁄₈ x 24¹⁄₈". The Frank Lloyd Wright Foundation

FRANCIS APARTMENTS
Chicago, Illinois. 1895 (demolished 1971)

18.   Perspective: entrance court. Sepia ink and pencil on paper, 6⁷⁄₈ x 16¹⁄₂". The Frank Lloyd Wright Foundation

WOLF LAKE AMUSEMENT PARK
Wolf Lake, Illinois. Project, 1895

19. Aerial perspective. Watercolor, white gouache, ink, and gold ink on paper mounted on canvas, 20 x 48¾". Erving and Joyce Wolf Collection

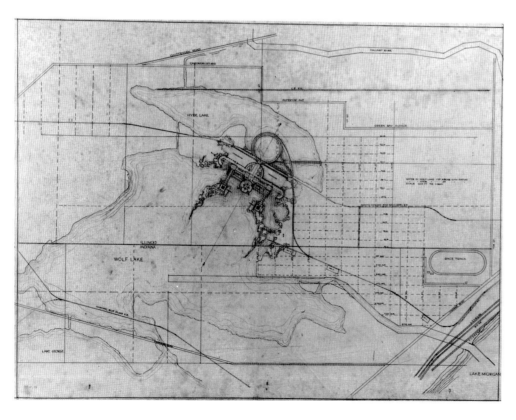

20. Site plan. Ink on linen, 24 x 31¾". The Frank Lloyd Wright Foundation

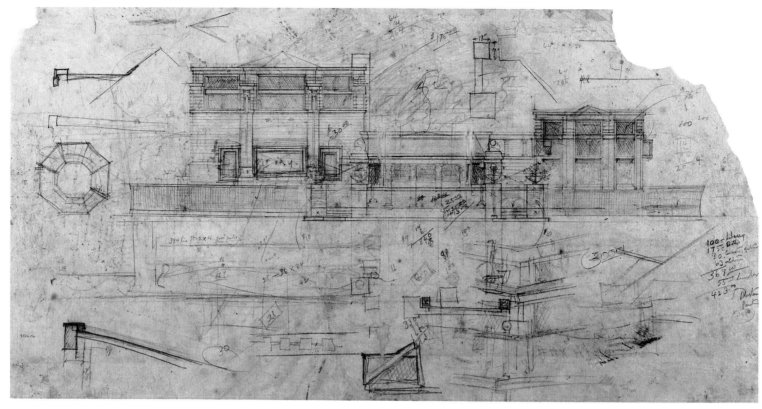

21. Elevation and details: studio (FLLW; c. 1897).
Pencil on tracing paper, 15⅝ x 30". The Frank
Lloyd Wright Foundation

FRANK LLOYD WRIGHT HOUSE AND STUDIO
Oak Park, Illinois. 1889–98

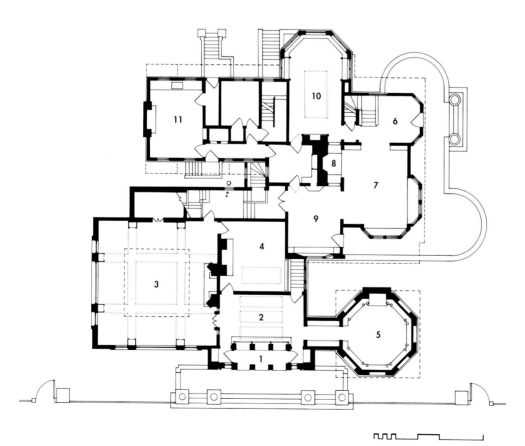

22. First-floor plan: 1 studio entrance, 2 reception, 3 drafting room, 4 office, 5 library, 6 house
entrance, 7 living room, 8 inglenook, 9 study, 10
dining room, 11 kitchen

23. Drafting room

24. Exterior

25. Studio entrance

26. Library

**LUXFER PRISM
OFFICE BUILDING**
Chicago, Illinois.
Project, c. 1896–97

27.   Elevation (FLLW; insc.
1894–95). Pencil on tracing paper,
28¾ x 17⅝". The Frank Lloyd
Wright Foundation

28. Perspective (WD; insc. 1894). Ink and watercolor on art paper, 10⅞ x 18⅛". The Frank Lloyd Wright Foundation

MONOLITHIC BANK
Project, c. 1901

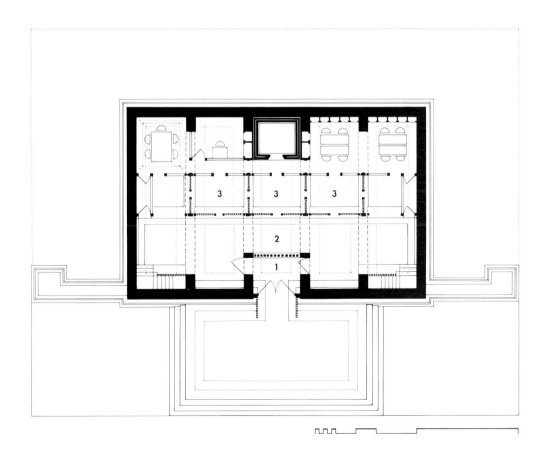

29. Plan: 1 entrance, 2 hall, 3 tellers' stations

EXTERIOR WALLS FACED WITH VITRIFIED BUFF ROMAN BRICK + BETWEEN SECOND AND THIRD STORY + ILE COURSE GREY BRICK ALTERNATE WITH BUFF + ATTIC STORY TREATED IN HIGH RELIEF + SOFFITS PANELLED WITH PERFORATED APRON DROPPED INSIDE OUTER BAND + TRIMMINGS GREY STONE + ROOF COVERING OF FLAT RED TILES + ALL HORIZONTAL JOINTS WHITE + VERTICAL JOINTS COLOR OF BRICK + + + + + + + + +

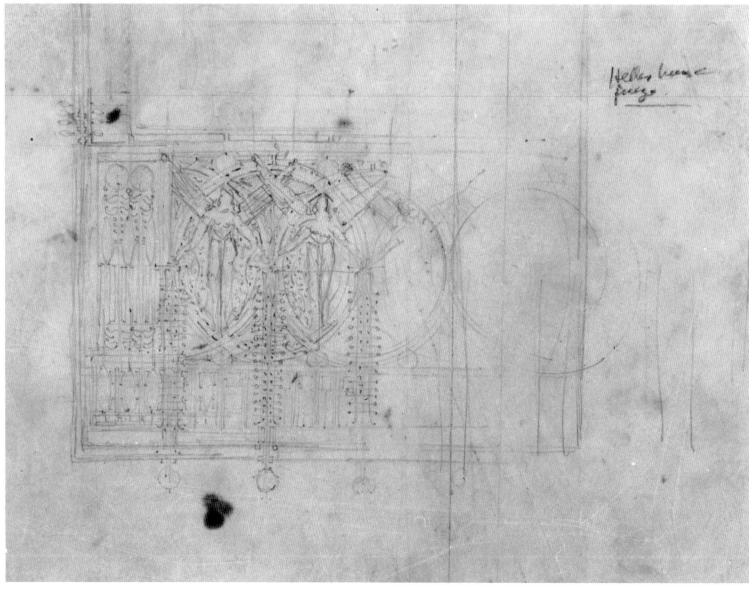

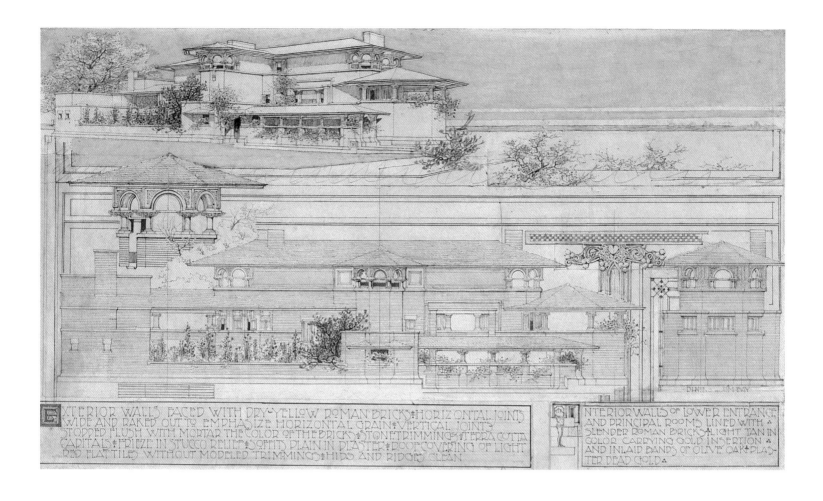

Opposite

ISIDORE HELLER HOUSE
Chicago, Illinois. 1897

30. Perspective. Pencil, ink, and ink wash on paper, 9 x 20¼". The Frank Lloyd Wright Foundation

31. Study of frieze detail (FLLW). Pencil on tracing paper, 8 x 12". The Frank Lloyd Wright Foundation

JOSEPH HUSSER HOUSE
Chicago, Illinois. 1899 (demolished c. 1923–24)

32. Perspective and elevation. Ink and ink wash on paper, 17 x 23". Erving and Joyce Wolf Collection

33. Fireplace elevation with Wisteria mural. Pencil, ink wash, and photograph on paper, 13⅜ x 19⅞". The Frank Lloyd Wright Foundation

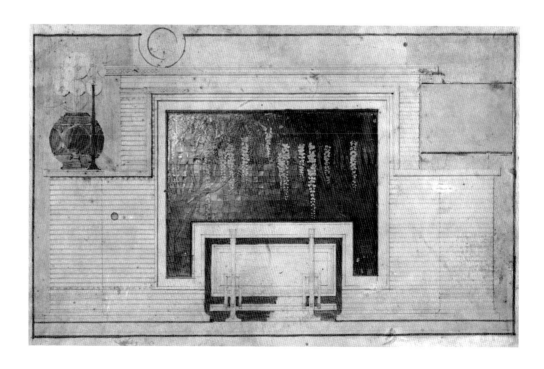

34. Exterior

35. Entrance

SUSAN LAWRENCE DANA HOUSE
Springfield, Illinois. 1902–04

36. East facade

37. Butterfly Wreath glass design for foyer (FLLW). Pencil on tracing paper, 14½ x 23¾". The Frank Lloyd Wright Foundation

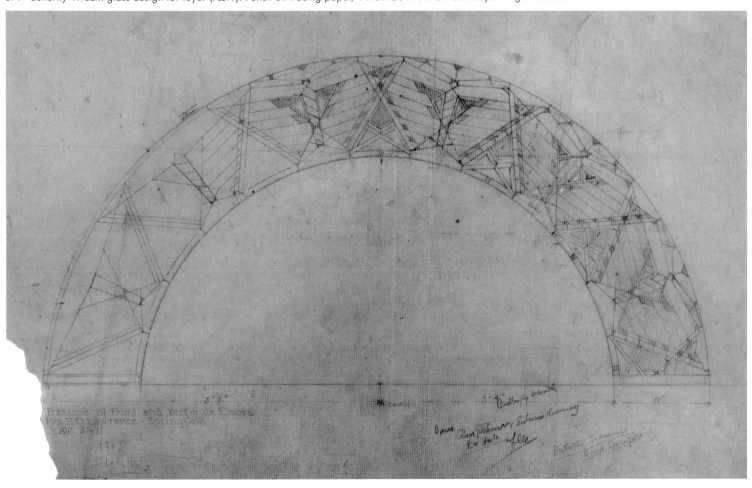

38. Reception hall and foyer

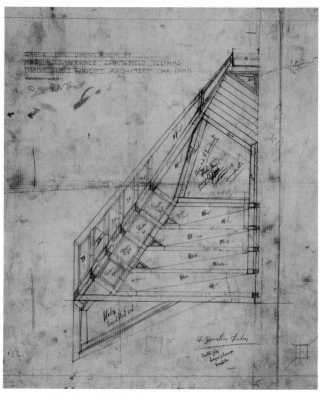

39. Study for lampshade (detail; FLLW). Pencil on tracing paper, 25½ x 32". The Frank Lloyd Wright Foundation

SUSAN LAWRENCE DANA HOUSE Springfield, Illinois. 1902–04

40. Interior perspective: reception hall. Pencil on tracing paper, 11⅝ x 19¾". The Frank Lloyd Wright Foundation

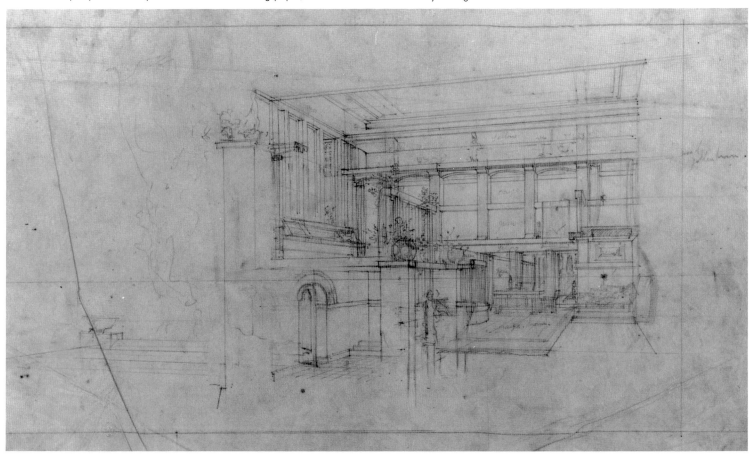

41.   Interior perspective: dining room. Pencil and watercolor on paper, 25 x 20⅜". Frank Lloyd Wright Collection, Avery Architectural and Fine Arts Library, Columbia University, New York

A HOME IN A PRAIRIE TOWN FOR *LADIES' HOME JOURNAL*   Project, 1900 (published February 1901)

42.   Elevation (FLLW). Pencil and color pencil on art paper, 7⅝ x 20⅛". The Frank Lloyd Wright Foundation

Wright's prolific output in the first decade of the twentieth century was accompanied by a growing practice and a concomitant expansiveness in his architectural conception. His design for a prototypical Home in a Prairie Town, published in the *Ladies' Home Journal* (above), crystallized many of the issues that had characterized his work to date and provided a strong direction for his work of this decade. The horizontal composition of the typical Prairie house, with low overhanging eaves, organized around a central vertical element—the fireplace—became the formal program of numerous residential projects, beginning with the Ward W. Willits House (plates 46–48) and culminating in the Frederick C. Robie House (plates 100–106). Whereas the Winslow House had been compact in character, the plans of these houses were fluid and extended into the landscape, as in the Darwin D. Martin and Avery Coonley houses (plates 55–59, 87–95).

Conceived for the pocketbooks of an expanding middle class, the first Prairie houses were decidedly more simple than Wright's work of the previous decade: interiors were generally less elaborate and rendered in flat planes of tinted plaster with simple wood trim. Similarly, Wright's delicate leaded glass and custom-designed furniture became increasingly rationalized, reflecting the linear conception of the Prairie house. Even in grander projects, such as the Coonley House, the ornamental program is greatly simplified. Relying more and more on linear composition, the detailing there reflects the geometric precision of drafting tools, and the decorative frieze is composed of machine-cut tiles rather than hand-cast elements. The sense of ab-

straction in Wright's work was also stimulated by Japanese art, with which he had become increasingly enamored. It is significant that his first trip abroad was not to the Continent but to Japan.

The fluidity of the Prairie house floor plan is matched by the expansion of the vertical dimension in such projects as the Hillside Home School (plates 50–52) and the Thomas P. Hardy House (plates 96–97), where the space flows upward through a series of interlocking double- and single-height spaces. But it was in the Larkin Company Administration Building (plates 65–73) that Wright fully exploited the practical and aesthetic possibilities of the free-flowing plan and section by combining the uninterrupted space of open-office floors with a five-story Light Court, achieving a remarkable sense of spatial depth and continuity. Wright extended this sensibility to the building fabric itself by separating the corner stair towers from the main building mass, thus prefiguring the highly articulated interweaving of space and form in Unity Temple, where a seamless plasticity and a new spatial awareness were achieved (plates 74–82). In both structures ornamental devices were minimalized and characterized by the planar abstraction of their broad flat surfaces. Wright described his work as organic, suggesting a relationship of part to whole and the integration of buildings with their sites, while taking full advantage of the machine processes in the making and functioning of buildings.

A SMALL HOUSE WITH "LOTS OF ROOM IN IT" FOR *LADIES' HOME JOURNAL*
Project, 1900 (published June 1901)

43. Perspective. Pencil and ink on paper, 10⁹⁄₁₆ x 30". The Frank Lloyd Wright Foundation

B. HARLEY BRADLEY HOUSE
Kankakee, Illinois. 1900

44. Elevation. Ink and color pencil on linen, 19 x 38¾". The Frank Lloyd Wright Foundation

45. First-floor plan: 1 entrance, 2 reception, 3 living room, 4 dining room, 5 porch, 6 kitchen, 7 stables

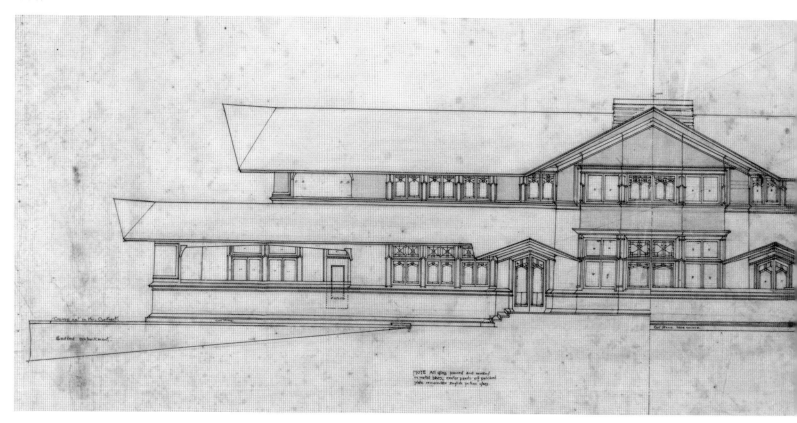

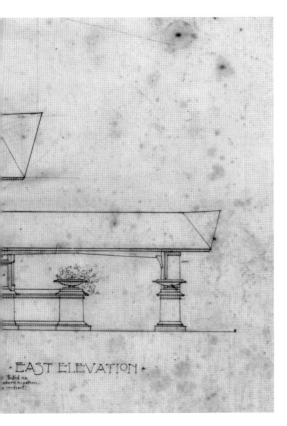

· EAST ELEVATION ·

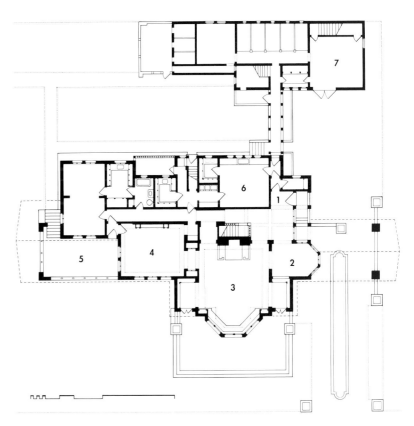

WARD W. WILLITS HOUSE

Highland Park, Illinois. 1902–03

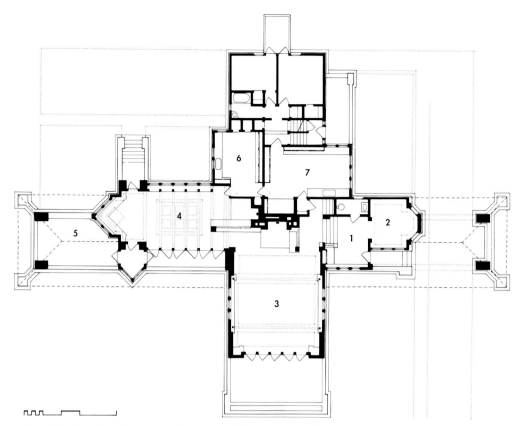

46.   First-floor plan: 1 entrance, 2 reception, 3 living room, 4 dining room, 5 porch, 6 pantry, 7 kitchen

47.   Perspective (MM). Crayon, gouache, ink, and ink wash on paper, 8½ x 32".
Erving and Joyce Wolf Collection

48. Dining room

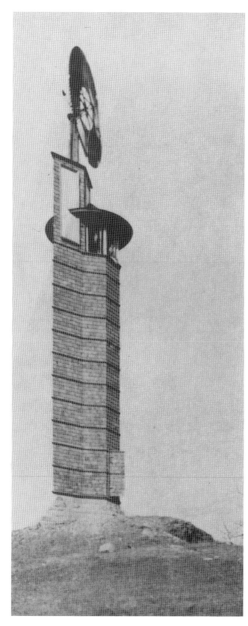

ROMEO AND JULIET WINDMILL
Spring Green, Wisconsin. 1896

49. Exterior

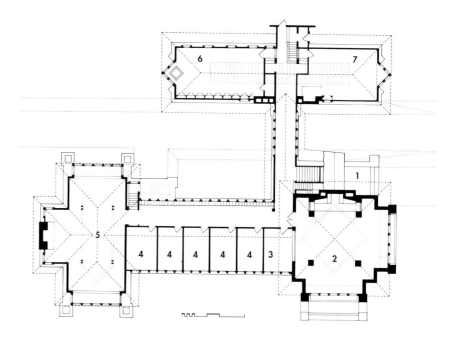

HILLSIDE HOME SCHOOL
Spring Green, Wisconsin. 1901–03

50. Exterior

51. Assembly room

52. Plan: 1 entrance, 2 assembly room, 3 principal's office, 4 classroom, 5 gymnasium, 6 physics laboratory, 7 art school

W. A. GLASNER HOUSE   Glencoe, Illinois. 1905

53.   Perspective. Pencil and sepia ink on tracing paper, 16¼ x 20¼". The Frank Lloyd Wright Foundation

RIVER FOREST GOLF CLUB
River Forest, Illinois. 1898 (demolished)

54.   Exterior

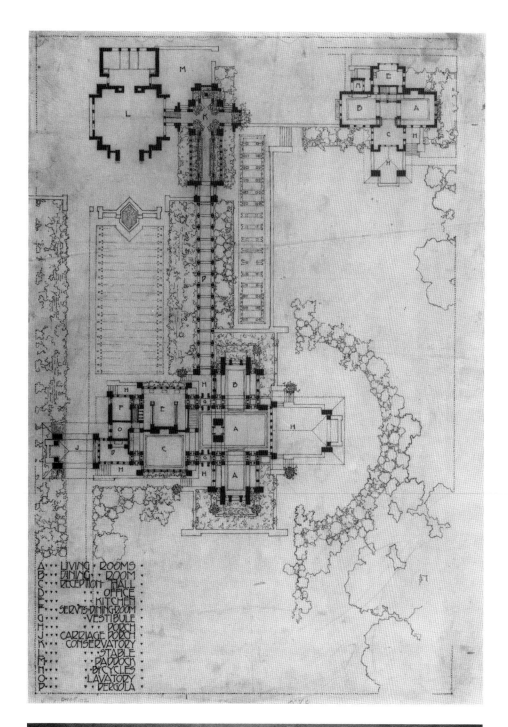

A··· LIVING·ROOMS
B··· DINING·ROOM
C··· RECEPTION·HALL
D··· ·OFFICE
E··· ·KITCHEN
F··· SERVTS·DINING·ROOM
G··· ·VESTIBULE
H··· ·PORCH
J··· CARRIAGE·PORCH
K··· CONSERVATORY
L··· ·STABLE
M··· ·PADDOCK
N··· ·BICYCLES
O··· ·LAVATORY
P··· ·PERGOLA

DARWIN D. MARTIN HOUSE
Buffalo, New York. 1902–04

Left
55. Site plan. Ink on tracing paper mounted on board, 21¾ x 15½". The Frank Lloyd Wright Foundation

56. Living room

Above
57. Exterior

Opposite
58. Interior detail

59. View of pergola from vestibule

60. Aerial perspective (c. 1909; insc. 1898). Watercolor, ink, and pencil on art paper, 16⅜ x 32¾". The Frank Lloyd Wright Foundation

LEXINGTON TERRACE APARTMENTS   Chicago, Illinois. Project, c. 1901–09

61. Perspective: entrance (c. 1901). Pencil, ink, and gouache on paper, 14¾ x 8½". The Frank Lloyd Wright Foundation

62. Section

Opposite
Frank Lloyd Wright and Dwight Heald Perkins
ABRAHAM LINCOLN CENTER
Chicago, Illinois. 1898–1905

63. Elevation (1903). Ink and pencil on linen, 30¾ x 37⅛". The Frank Lloyd Wright Foundation

64. Interior perspective (BBL). Pencil, ink, and watercolor on paper, 11⅜ x 29⁹⁄₁₆". The Frank Lloyd Wright Foundation

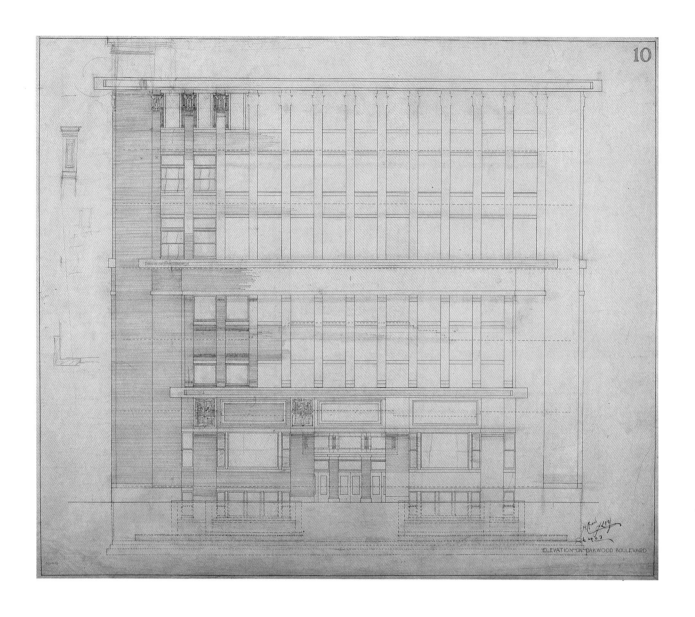

ELEVATION ON OAKWOOD BOULEVARD

65.   Perspective (detail). Pencil and color pencil on tracing paper, 20½ x 24¼". The Frank Lloyd Wright Foundation

LARKIN COMPANY ADMINISTRATION BUILDING
Buffalo, New York. 1902–06 (demolished 1950)

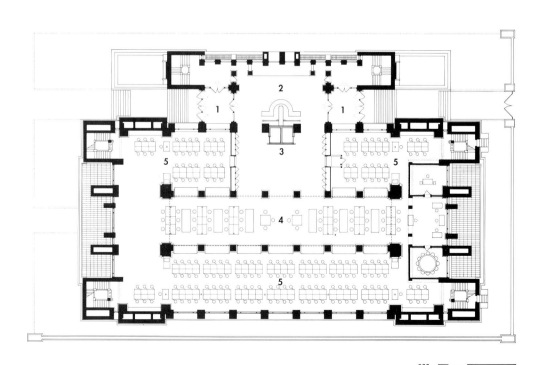

66.   First-floor plan: 1 entrance, 2 reception, 3
elevators, 4 Light Court, 5 office area

67.   Exterior

68.   Perspective: pier capitals (FLLW).
Pencil on tracing paper, 13¾ x 7½".
The Frank Lloyd Wright Foundation

69.   Perspective: pier capitals (FLLW).
Pencil on tracing paper, 9⅝ x 6⅞".
The Frank Lloyd Wright Foundation

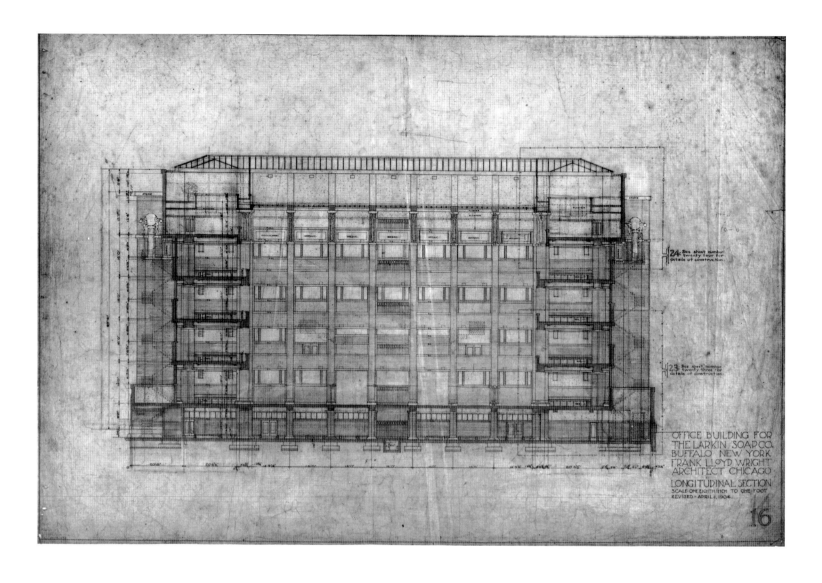

LARKIN COMPANY ADMINISTRATION BUILDING
Buffalo, New York. 1902–06 (demolished 1950)

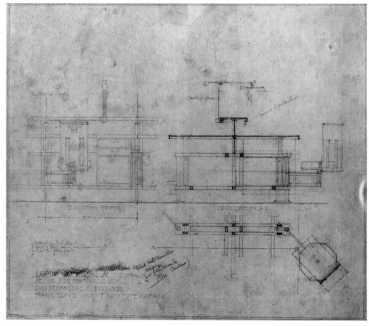

Opposite
70.   Longitudinal section. Ink, ink wash, and pencil on linen, 24¼ x 36¾". The Frank Lloyd Wright Foundation

71.   Work area

72.   Elevation, section, and plan: desk. Pencil on tracing paper, 19 x 21½". The Frank Lloyd Wright Foundation

73.   Light Court

74.   Perspective. Sepia ink and watercolor wash on paper, 11½ x 25". The Frank Lloyd Wright Foundation

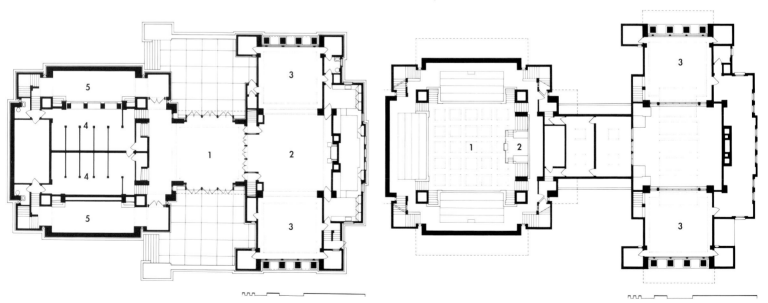

75.   First-floor plan: 1 entrance, 2 parish house, 3 classroom, 4 coat room, 5 corridor to stairs

76.   Second-floor plan: 1 sanctuary, 2 altar, 3 classroom

UNITY TEMPLE
Oak Park, Illinois. 1905–08

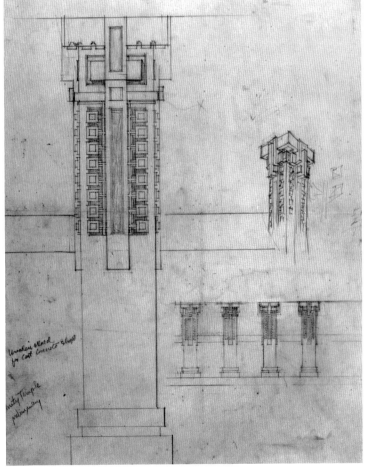

77.   Studies for columns (FLLW). Pencil and color pencil on tracing paper, 21 x 16". The Frank Lloyd Wright Foundation

UNITY TEMPLE
Oak Park, Illinois. 1905–08

78. Skylight

79. Interior detail

80. Ceiling plans and section (1906). Ink, ink wash, and pencil on linen, 28¾ x 42⅝". The Frank Lloyd Wright Foundation

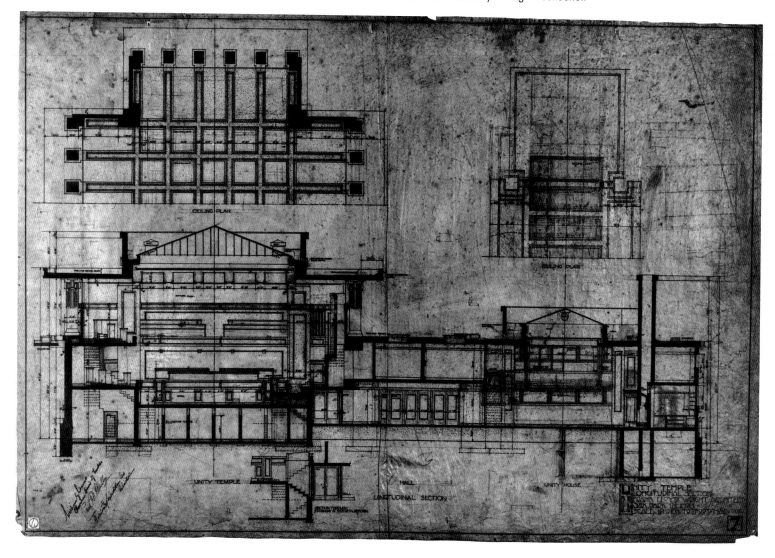

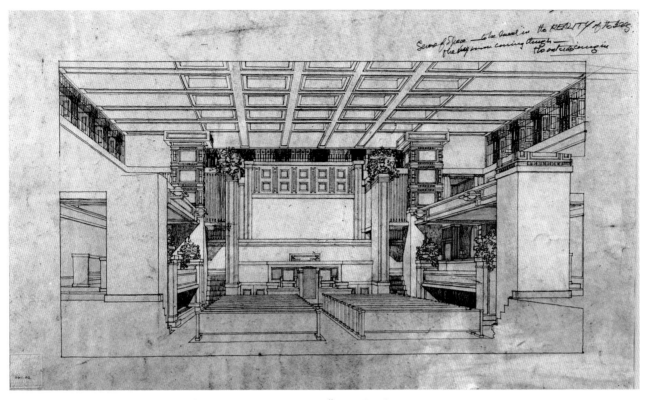

81. Interior perspective. Ink and pencil on paper, 15¼ x 25⅜". Collection Der Scutt

82. Interior

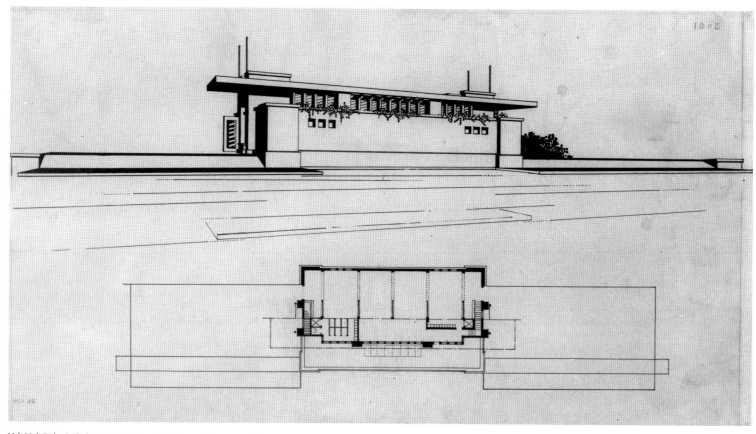

YAHARA BOATHOUSE   Madison, Wisconsin. Project, 1905

83.   Perspective and plan (HK and TO; c. 1930). Ink on tracing paper, 10⅛ x 17⅞". The Frank Lloyd Wright Foundation

RICHARD W. BOCK HOUSE AND STUDIO   Maywood, Illinois. Project, 1906

84.   Perspective (HR). Color pencil on tracing paper, 11¾ x 22¼". The Frank Lloyd Wright Foundation

LARKIN COMPANY EXPOSITION PAVILION   Jamestown, Virginia. 1907 (demolished)

85.   Perspective. Watercolor and pencil on paper, 7⅞ x 23⅝". The Frank Lloyd Wright Foundation

MRS. THOMAS GALE HOUSE   Oak Park, Illinois. 1909

86.   Perspective (insc. 1904, 1911 on verso). Ink, pencil, and watercolor wash on paper, 12¾ x 16⅛". The Frank Lloyd Wright Foundation

87. Site plan. Ink, pencil, and watercolor on linen, 21⅜ x 25¼". The Frank Lloyd Wright Foundation

AVERY COONLEY HOUSE
Riverside, Illinois. 1906–08

88. Exterior

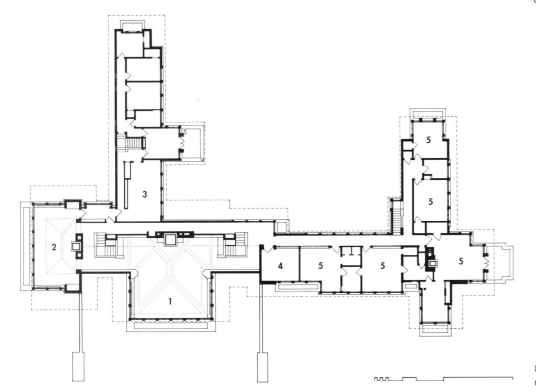

89. Second-floor plan: 1 living room, 2 dining room, 3 kitchen, 4 study, 5 bedroom

AVERY COONLEY HOUSE
Riverside, Illinois. 1906–08

91. Exterior detail: tile frieze

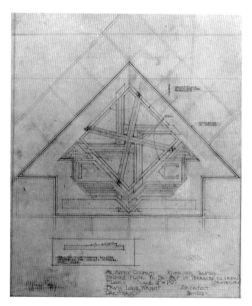

90. Plan of compass for terrace. Pencil on tracing paper, 18 x 15¼". The Frank Lloyd Wright Foundation

92. Living room

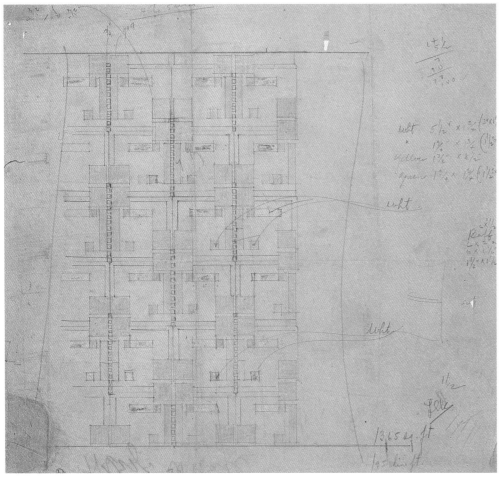

93.   Exterior tile elevation detail (FLLW). Pencil and color pencil on tracing paper, 14¾ x 14½".
The Frank Lloyd Wright Foundation

94.   Interior perspective: living room. Pencil on tracing paper, 14⅝ x 18¼". The Frank Lloyd Wright
Foundation

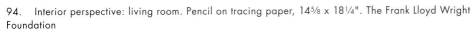

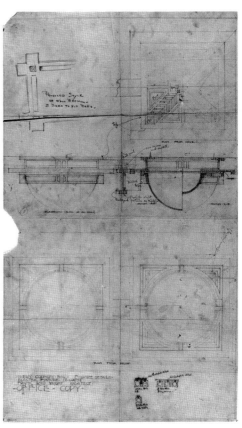

95.   Plan, section, and elevation: light fixture.
Pencil and ink on tracing paper, 34⅝ x 20¾".
The Frank Lloyd Wright Foundation

THOMAS P. HARDY HOUSE
Racine, Wisconsin. 1905

96.   Perspective (MM). Watercolor on paper,
18⅞ x 5½". The Frank Lloyd Wright Foundation

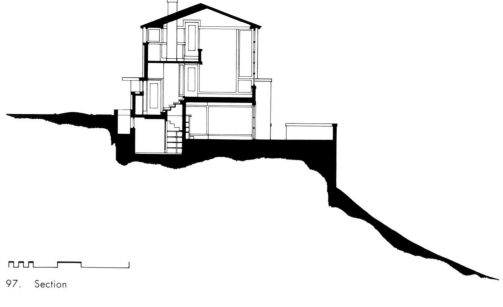

97.   Section

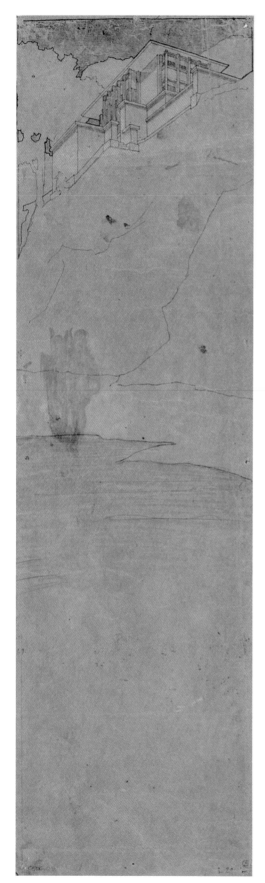

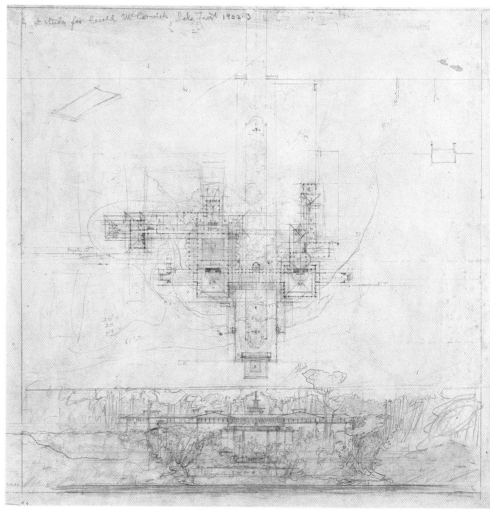

HAROLD McCORMICK HOUSE   Lake Forest, Illinois. Project, 1907

98.   Plan and elevation (FLLW; insc. 1902–03). Pencil and color pencil on tracing paper, 18⅛ x 18⁵⁄₁₆".
The Frank Lloyd Wright Foundation

LAKE DELAVAN COTTAGE   Lake Delavan, Wisconsin. Project, 1907

99.   Perspective and plan (FLLW). Pencil on tracing paper, 21½ x 14⅜". The Frank Lloyd Wright Foundation

FREDERICK C. ROBIE HOUSE
Chicago, Illinois. 1908–10

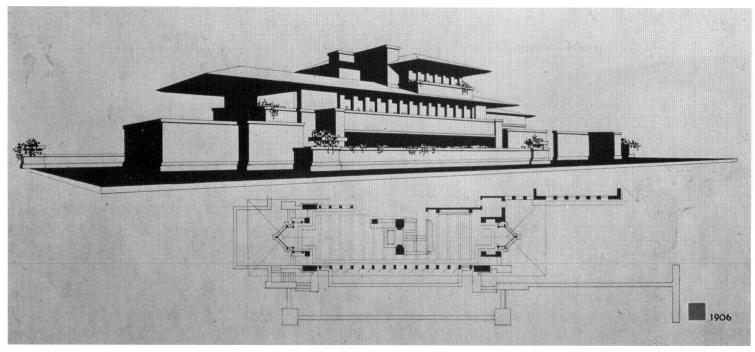

100.   Perspective and second-floor plan (HK; c. 1930; insc. 1906). Ink on paper, 21½ x 37½". Erving and Joyce Wolf Collection

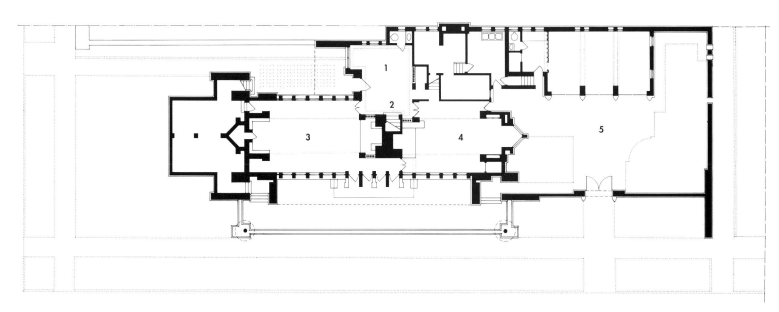

101.   First-floor plan: 1 entrance, 2 stairs to second floor, 3 billiard room, 4 playroom, 5 service court

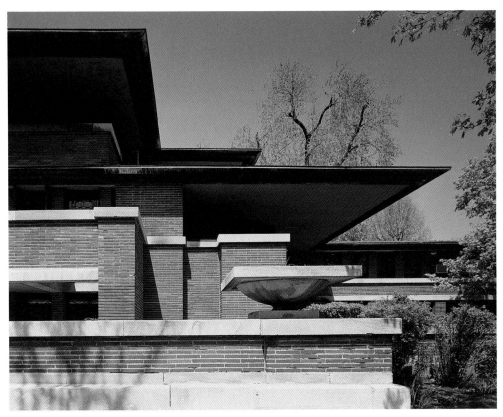

102. Exterior detail

103. Exterior

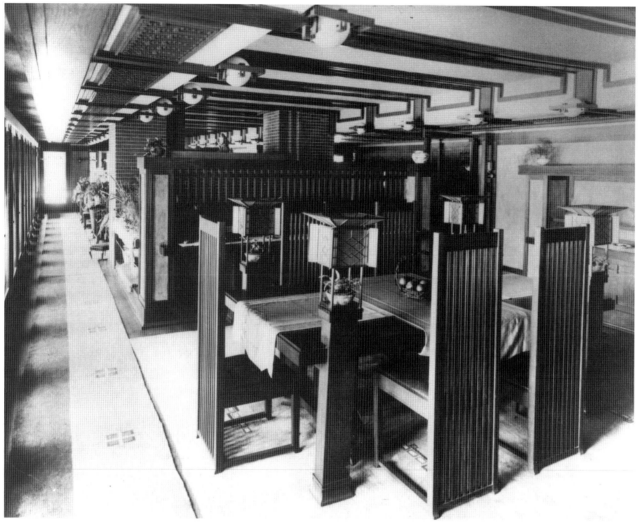

104. Dining room

Opposite
106. Interior detail

FREDERICK C. ROBIE HOUSE
Chicago, Illinois. 1908–10

105. Elevation: garage gate. Pencil on tracing paper, 18½ x 21⅛".
The Frank Lloyd Wright Foundation

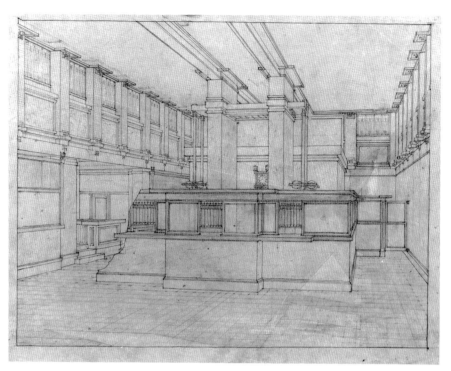

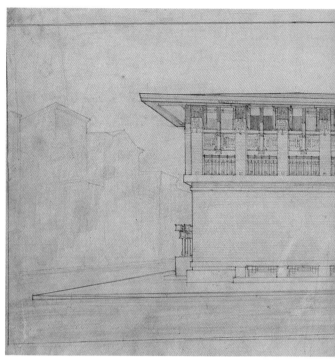

107. Interior perspective. Pencil, color pencil, and ink on tracing paper, 15¼ x 19½". The Frank Lloyd Wright Foundation

108. Perspective. Ink, pencil, and color pencil on tracing paper, 10½ x 35⅝". The Frank Lloyd Wright Foundation

CITY NATIONAL BANK AND HOTEL
Mason City, Iowa. 1909–11

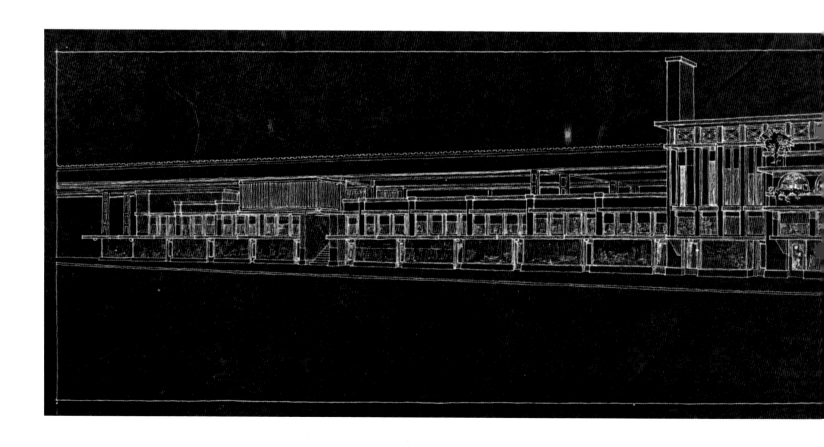

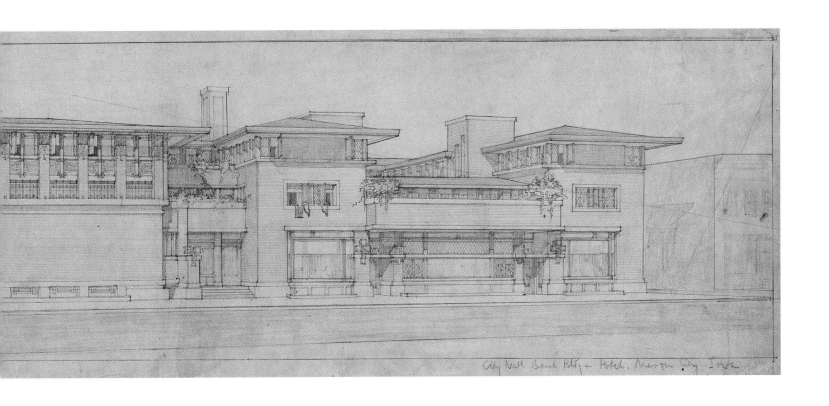

City Nat. Bank Bldg & Hotel, Mason City, Iowa

PETER C. STOHR ARCADE BUILDING
Chicago, Illinois. 1909 (demolished c. 1921)

109. Perspective. Print on paper (reversed),
18⅜ x 31⅛". The Frank Lloyd Wright Foundation

110. Exterior detail with elevated train station in background

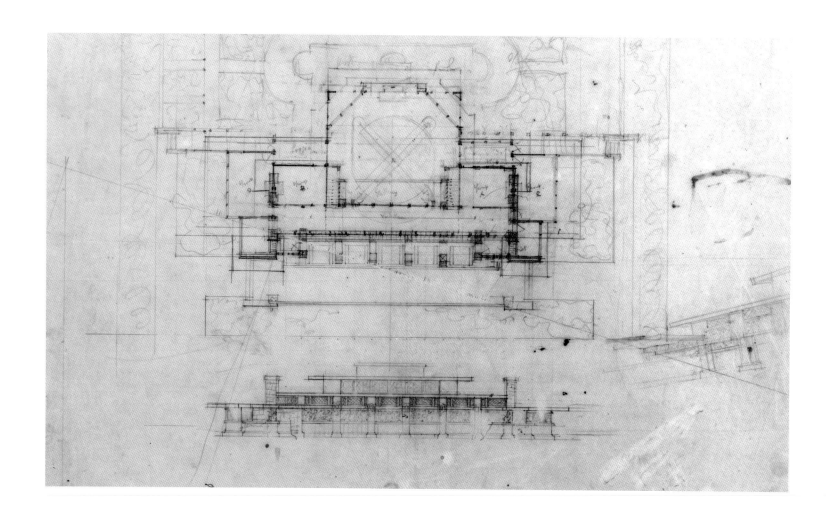

AVERY COONLEY KINDERGARTEN
Riverside, Illinois. Project, 1911

111.　Plan, elevation, and perspective (FLLW).
Pencil and color pencil on tracing paper, 17⅝ x
26¾". The Frank Lloyd Wright Foundation

AVERY COONLEY PLAYHOUSE
Riverside, Illinois. 1912

Opposite below
112.　Perspective. Pencil and color pencil on
paper, 10 x 16½". The Library of Congress

113.　Interior detail

114.　Interior

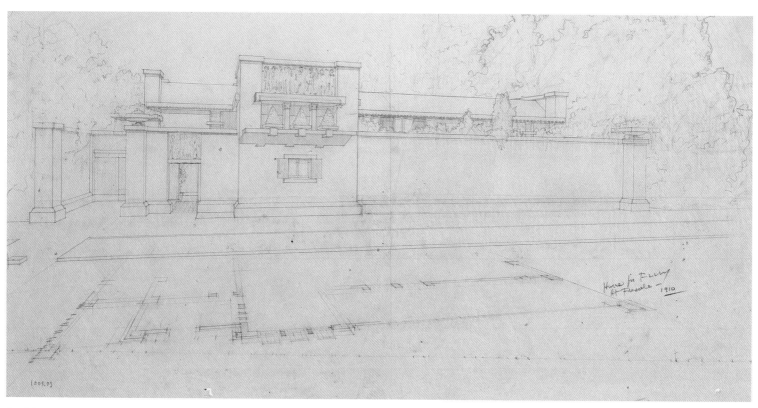

FRANK LLOYD WRIGHT HOUSE AND STUDIO   Fiesole, Italy. Project, 1910

115.   Perspective and plan (FLLW). Pencil and color pencil on tracing paper, 13¼ x 25⅝". The Frank Lloyd Wright Foundation

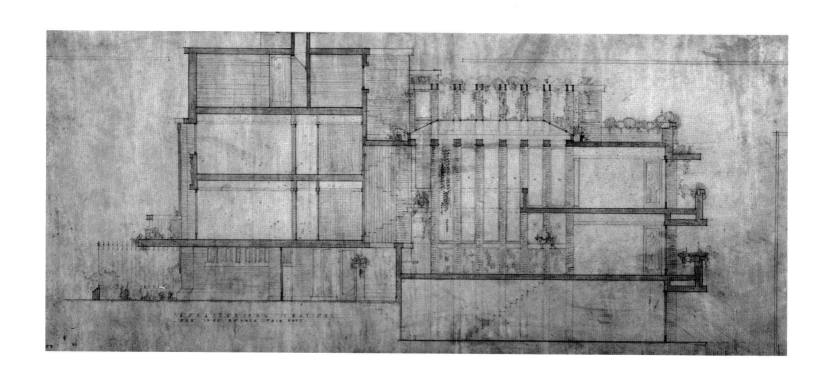

In 1909 Wright scandalized Chicago society when, at the age of forty-two, he left his wife and six children and sailed for Europe with Mamah Borthwick Cheney, the wife of his client and friend Edwin Cheney. There he visited Germany, Austria, France, and Italy, and prepared two editions of his works with the Berlin publisher Ernst Wasmuth.

Soon Wright made drawings for several dwellings for himself and Mrs. Cheney: a villa in Fiesole (opposite above), a townhouse in Chicago (right and opposite below), and a country house in southern Wisconsin, which he named Taliesin (plates 122–124). Built and rebuilt over a period of many years (plates 125–132), Taliesin was sited masterfully around the crest of a hill overlooking the land on which his Welsh immigrant grandparents had established themselves in the mid-nineteenth century. Different from the plastic, abstract compositions and linear precision of earlier projects, the design of Taliesin responded directly to the landscape: its masonry walls were made with rough-cut, local limestone, laid up in irregular courses to reflect its natural character. While the design for Taliesin was intertwined with the unique circumstances of its site and Wright's personal history, the work produced there is related to a more general theme: the revival of his interest in ornament, its production, complexity, underlying geometries, and relationship to specific types of buildings as well as to the culture at large.

Midway Gardens, an entertainment and restaurant complex (plates 133–144), was emblematic of the revitalization of Wright's interest in ornament, spurred in part by his trip to Vienna and the vigor of its Secessionist artists and architects. It is noteworthy, too, for its extensive geometric complexity, which ranged from quasi-Cubist figural designs to highly articulated abstract patterning. Other works included more literal ornamental references, such as the frieze of Amerindian chieftains in the Frederick C. Bogk House (plates 148–150) and the so-called Mayan influences of the Hollyhock House for Aline Barnsdall (plates 165–169).

The apogee of Wright's interest in ornament of this time can be seen in the Imperial Hotel in Tokyo (plates 151–163). He took full advantage of the money available for this grand project, the plentiful supply of lightweight, easily carved volcanic stone, and highly skilled, inexpensive labor in executing the lavishly detailed surfaces. The complex was designed as a series of interlocking building masses and open courts, which subordinated a Beaux-Arts plan to the spatial character of traditional Japanese temple precincts. Amalgamating specific local cultural references, such as the canted roof profiles of Buddhist temples and the battered walls of monumental castle architecture, with inventive references to classical European architecture, such as the projecting entablature of the cornice rendered in stone and copper, Wright addressed both his own and his clients' concerns: that the hotel be perceived as a modern Western facility and as specifically Japanese.

FRANK LLOYD WRIGHT HOUSE AND STUDIO   Goethe Street, Chicago, Illinois. Project, 1911

Opposite
116.   Longitudinal section (detail; FLLW). Pencil and color pencil on tracing paper, 10½ x 38⅞". The Frank Lloyd Wright Foundation

Right
117.   Perspective (FLLW). Pencil, ink, and watercolor on tracing paper, 25 x 8⅜". The Frank Lloyd Wright Foundation

118.   Perspective (FLLW; insc. 1913). Pencil, color pencil, and ink on art paper, 26¼ x 38". The Frank Lloyd Wright Foundation

SHERMAN M. BOOTH HOUSE
Glencoe, Illinois. Project, 1911–12

119.   Plan: 1 entrance, 2 living room, 3 pergola, 4 bedroom, 5 service court

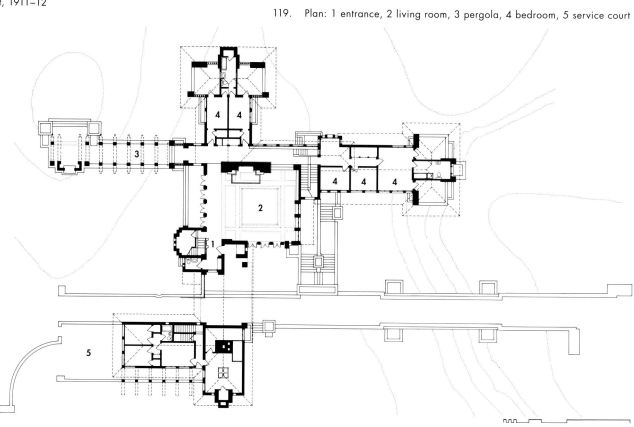

120. Section. Pencil and color pencil on tracing paper, 17⅛ x 33⅞". The Frank Lloyd Wright Foundation

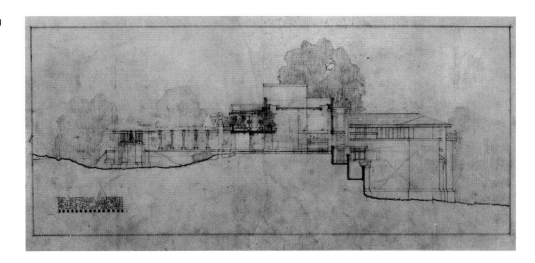

121. Landscape plan (Jens Jensen). Print on paper, 35⅞ x 39¼". The Frank Lloyd Wright Foundation

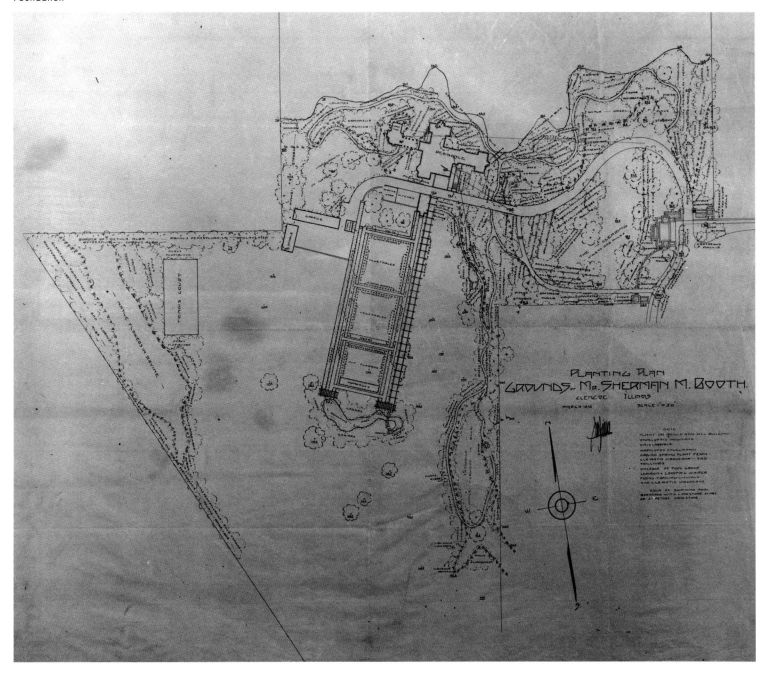

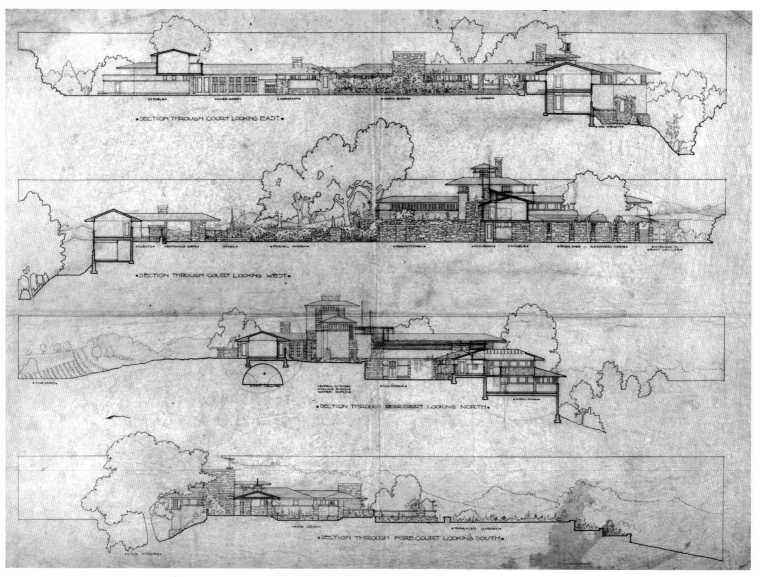

122. Sections through court (c. 1913). Ink and pencil on linen, 30⅝ x 43⅝". The Frank Lloyd Wright Foundation

Taliesin I
FRANK LLOYD WRIGHT HOUSE AND STUDIO
Spring Green, Wisconsin. 1911 (partially destroyed)

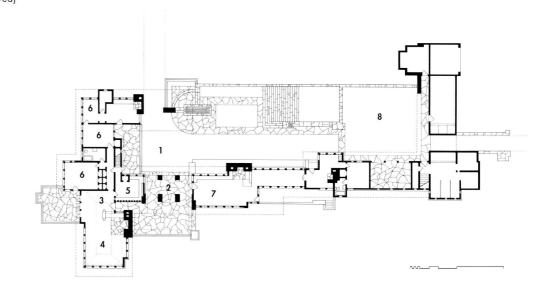

123. Plan: 1 court, 2 loggia, 3 entrance, 4 living room, 5 kitchen, 6 bedroom, 7 drafting room, 8 service court

Opposite above
124. Court

Below

Taliesin II
FRANK LLOYD WRIGHT HOUSE AND STUDIO
Spring Green, Wisconsin. 1914
(partially destroyed)

125.   Aerial perspective, partially executed (EB).
Ink and ink wash on linen, 32 x 38⅝". The Frank
Lloyd Wright Foundation

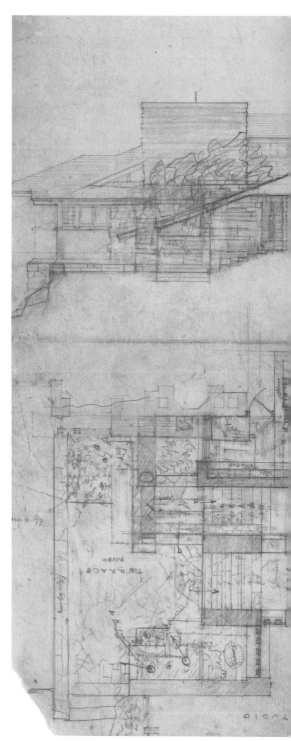

Taliesin II
**FRANK LLOYD WRIGHT HOUSE
AND STUDIO**
Spring Green, Wisconsin. 1914
(partially destroyed)

Left
126. Workroom

Taliesin III
FRANK LLOYD WRIGHT HOUSE AND STUDIO
Spring Green, Wisconsin. 1925

Opposite below
127.   Exterior detail

128.   Elevation and plan (FLLW). Pencil and color pencil on tracing paper, 22⅝ x 35¹³⁄₁₆". The Frank Lloyd Wright Foundation

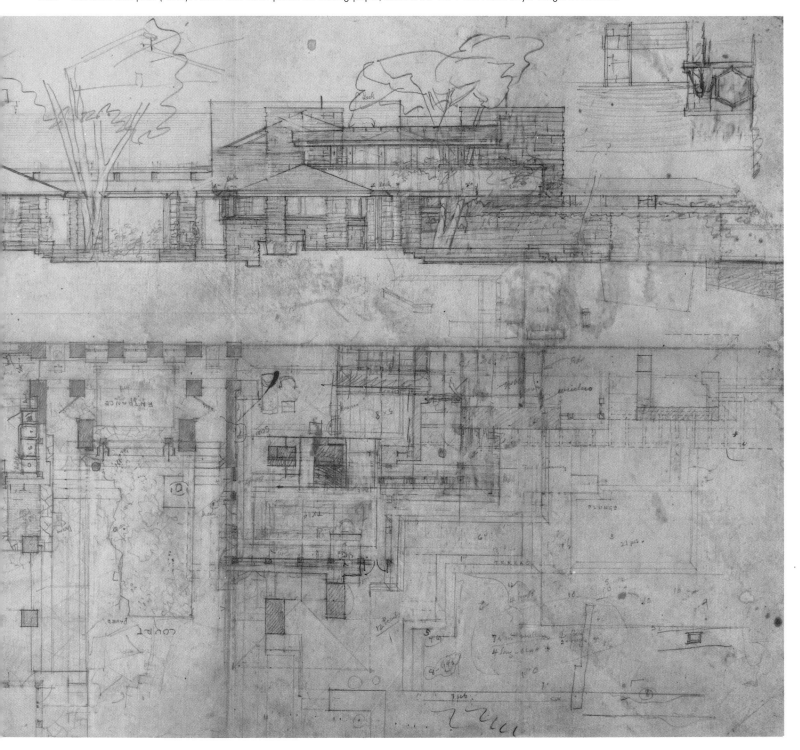

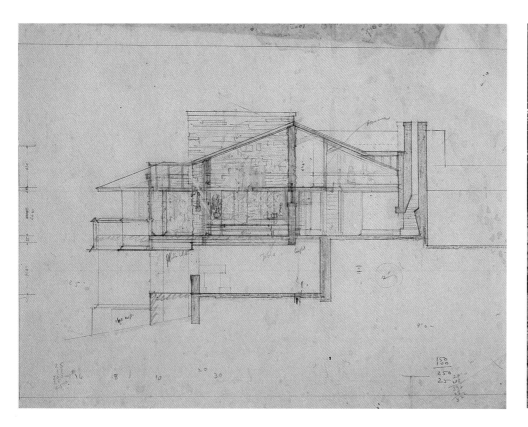

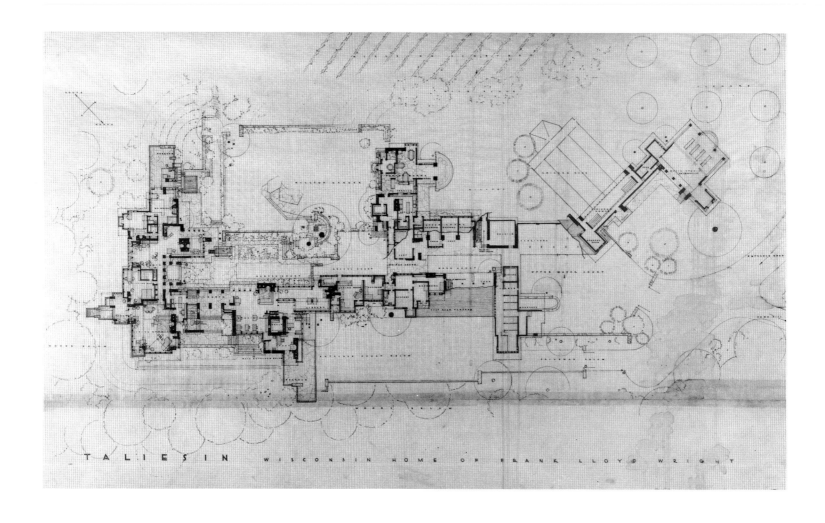

TALIESIN WISCONSIN HOME OF FRANK LLOYD WRIGHT

Taliesin III
FRANK LLOYD WRIGHT HOUSE AND STUDIO
Spring Green, Wisconsin. 1925

Opposite
129.   Section through living room (FLLW). Pencil
and color pencil on tracing paper, 15⅞ x 20⅞".
The Frank Lloyd Wright Foundation

130.   Plan. Pencil, color pencil, and ink on
tracing paper, 35 x 57⅝". The Frank Lloyd Wright
Foundation

Above
131.   General view

Right
132.   Living room

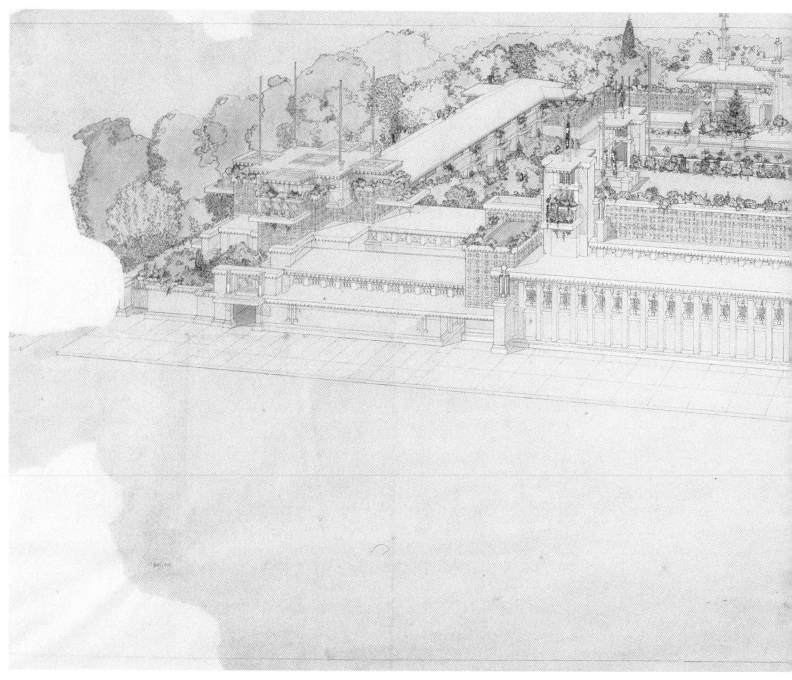

133. Aerial perspective. Color pencil, ink, and watercolor on tracing paper mounted on linen, 21 x 48". Erving and Joyce Wolf Collection

MIDWAY GARDENS
Chicago, Illinois. 1913–14 (demolished 1929)

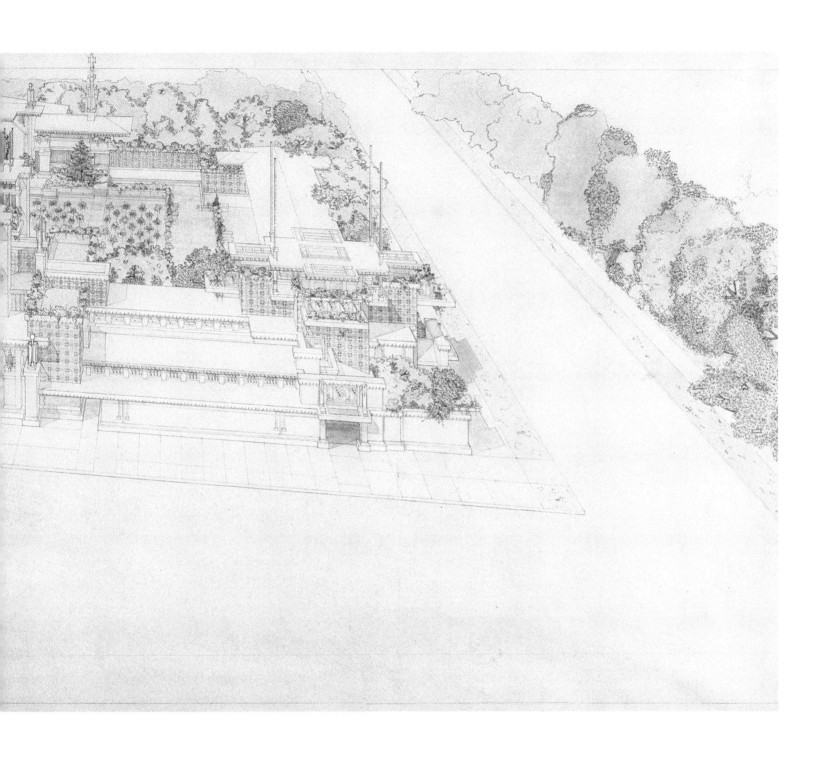

MIDWAY GARDENS
Chicago, Illinois. 1913–14 (demolished 1929)

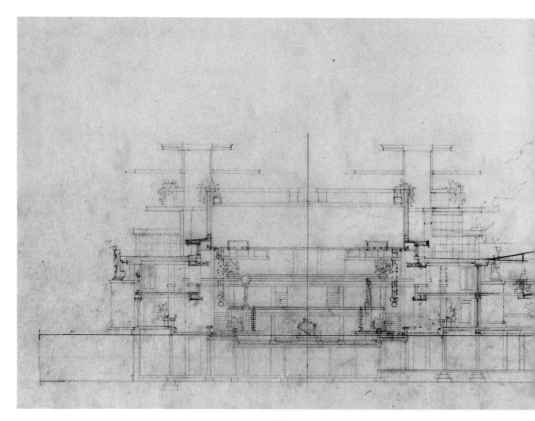

134. Section (FLLW). Pencil, color pencil, and ink on tracing paper, 12½ x 42⅞". The Frank Lloyd Wright Foundation

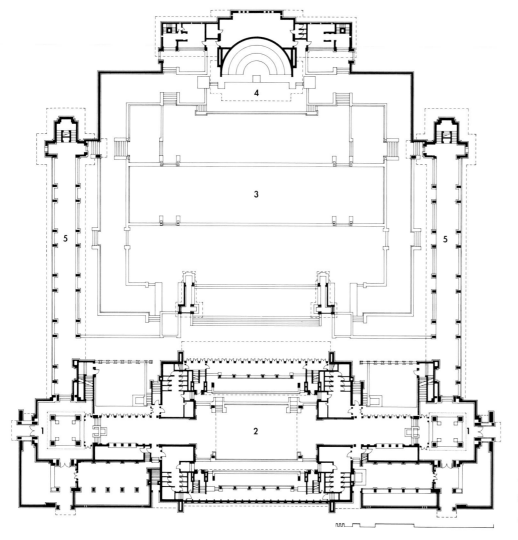

135. Plan: 1 entrance, 2 winter garden, 3 summer garden, 4 band shell, 5 arcade

136. Summer garden and band shell

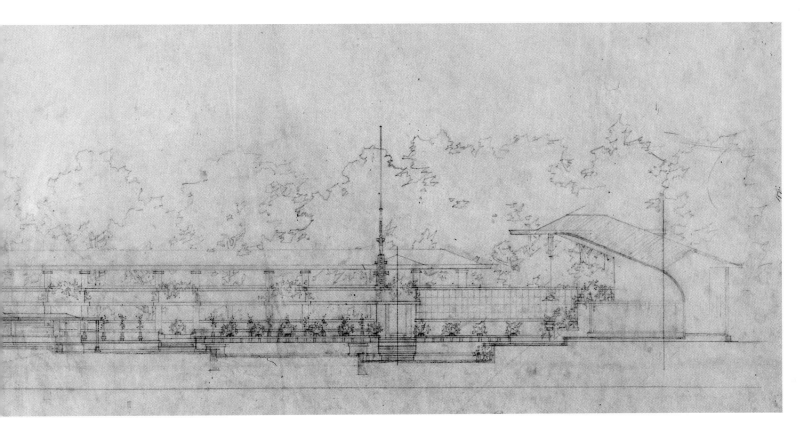

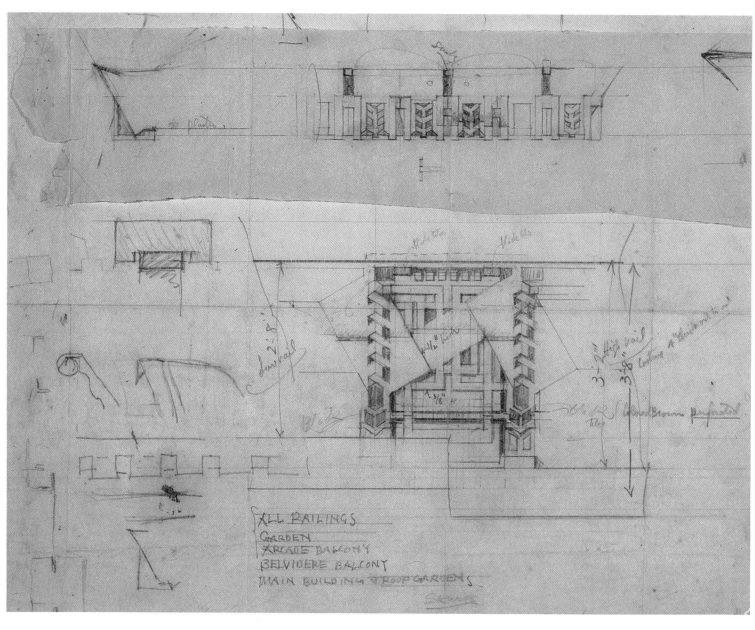

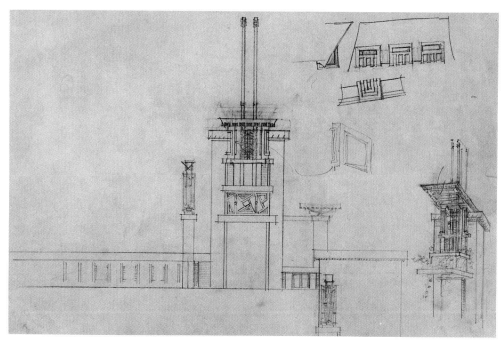

MIDWAY GARDENS
Chicago, Illinois. 1913–14 (demolished 1929)

137. Studies of railings (FLLW). Pencil and color pencil on tracing paper, 15 x 19". The Frank Lloyd Wright Foundation

138. Studies of ornament (FLLW). Pencil on tracing paper, 14 x 19". The Frank Lloyd Wright Foundation

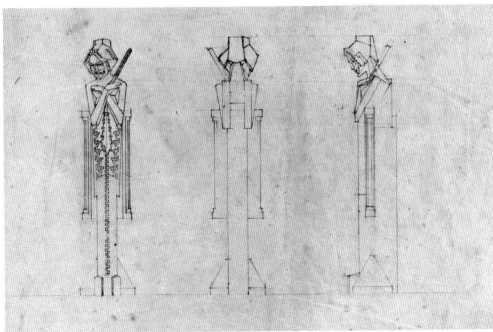

139.   Lantern and ornamental pier

140.   Entrance

141.   Studies of Sprite sculpture (detail). Pencil on tracing paper, 21 x 16½". The Frank Lloyd Wright Foundation

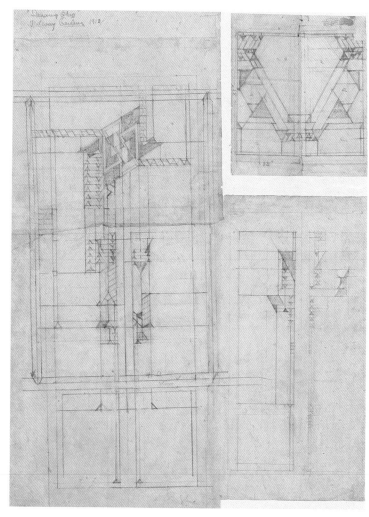

MIDWAY GARDENS
Chicago, Illinois. 1913–14 (demolished 1929)

142.   Winter garden

143.   Dancing Glass window design (FLLW).
Pencil and color pencil on tracing paper, 16¾ x
12¼". The Frank Lloyd Wright Foundation

144.   City by the Sea mural design (FLLW).
Pencil, color pencil, gold ink, watercolor, and
crayon on tracing paper, 32½ x 30⅞".
The Frank Lloyd Wright Foundation

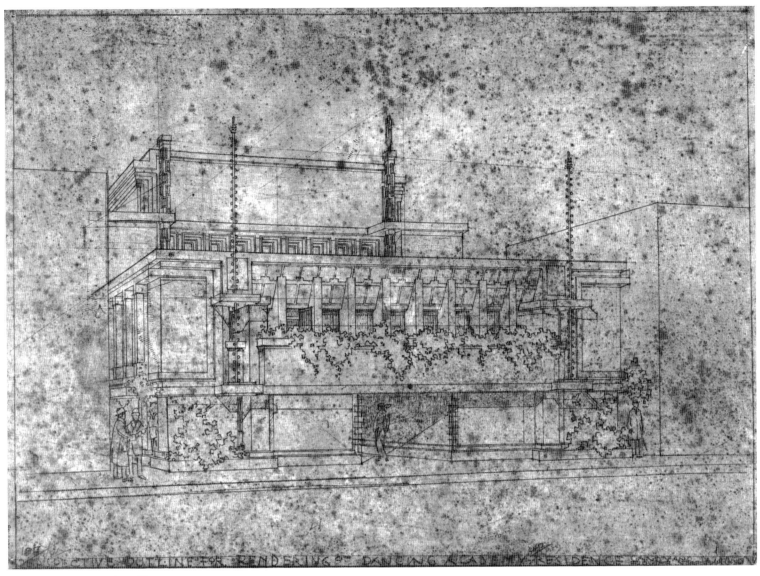

KEHL DANCE ACADEMY   Madison, Wisconsin. Project, c. 1914

145.   Perspective (insc. 1911). Pencil on linen, 14¼ x 19¾". The Frank Lloyd Wright Foundation

146. Perspective. Pencil, pastel, and gouache on paper and linen, 21½ x 24⅜". Erving and Joyce Wolf Collection

147. Exterior detail

A. D. GERMAN WAREHOUSE
Richland Center, Wisconsin. 1915–20

FREDERICK C. BOGK HOUSE
Milwaukee, Wisconsin. 1916–17

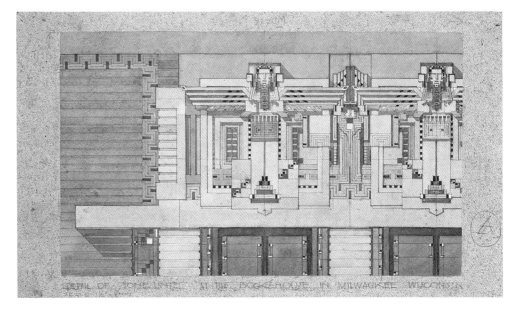

148. Detail of stone lintel. Pencil, watercolor, and gold ink on paper, 11⅞ x 17¾". The Library of Congress

149. Detail of exterior frieze

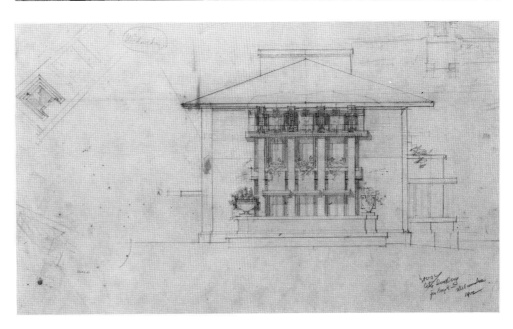

150. Elevation (FLLW; insc. 1912). Pencil on tracing paper, 13¾ x 24⅛". The Frank Lloyd Wright Foundation

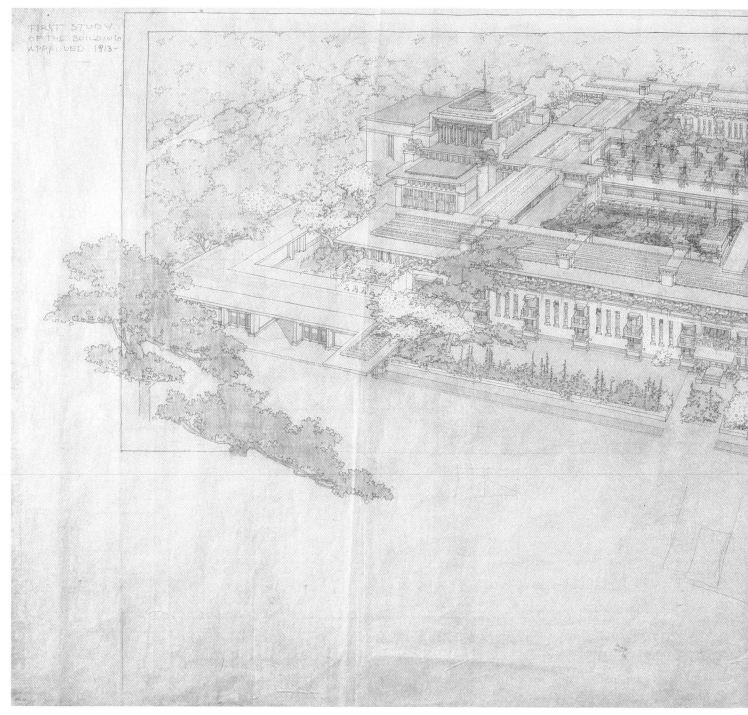

151.   Aerial perspective, first scheme (EB; c. 1913–14). Pencil, color pencil, and ink on linen, 33½" x 6'2½". Erving and Joyce Wolf Collection

IMPERIAL HOTEL
Tokyo, Japan. c. 1912–23 (demolished 1968)

IMPERIAL HOTEL TOKIO JAPAN
GENERAL VIEW "
FRANK LLYD WRIGHT
ARCHITECT "
CHICAGO ILLINOIS "

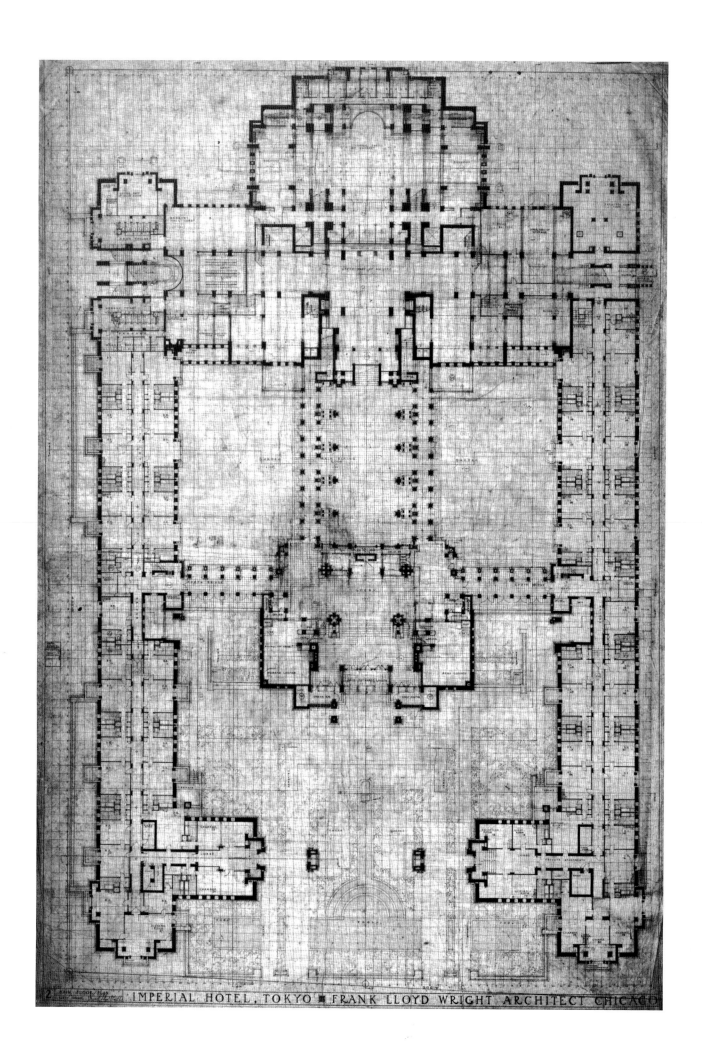

2 MAIN FLOOR PLAN   IMPERIAL HOTEL, TOKYO — FRANK LLOYD WRIGHT ARCHITECT CHICAGO

IMPERIAL HOTEL
Tokyo, Japan. c. 1912–23 (demolished 1968)

152.   Plan of first floor (c. 1921). Ink and pencil on linen, 58½ x 40½". The Frank Lloyd Wright Foundation

153.   Exterior detail

154.   Court

155.   Exterior

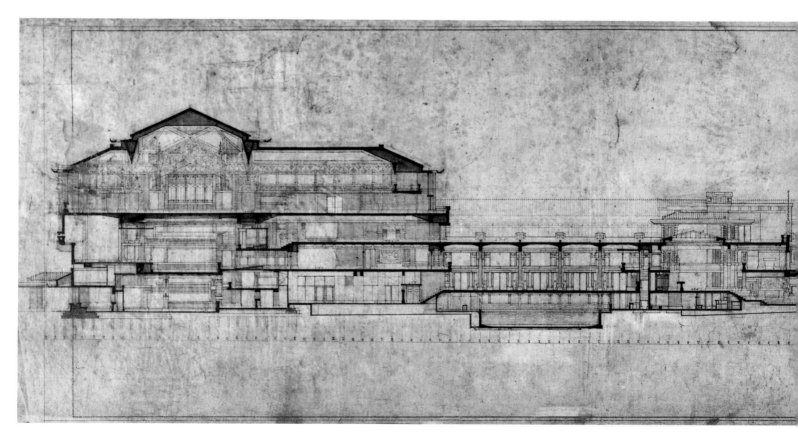

IMPERIAL HOTEL

Tokyo, Japan. c. 1912–23 (demolished 1968)

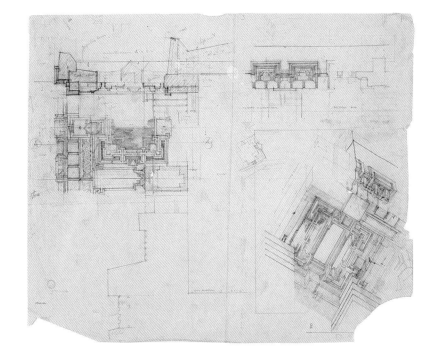

Opposite
156.   Exterior detail

Below
157.   Longitudinal section. Ink, ink wash, and pencil on linen, 20⅛ x
60⅝". The Frank Lloyd Wright Foundation

Right
158.   Studies of cornice details (c. 1921). Pencil and color pencil on
tracing paper, 18⅞ x 23". Centre Canadien d'Architecture/Canadian
Centre for Architecture, Montreal

159.   Partial section of cabaret, auditorium, and banquet hall
(c. 1921). Ink, pencil, and color pencil on linen, 58 x 40¾".
The Frank Lloyd Wright Foundation

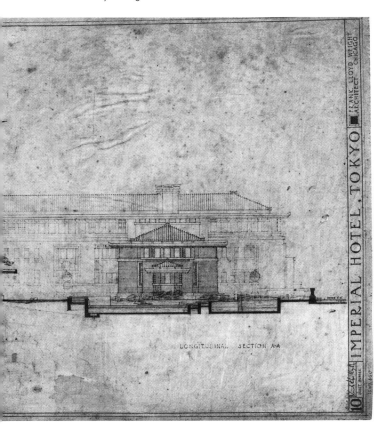

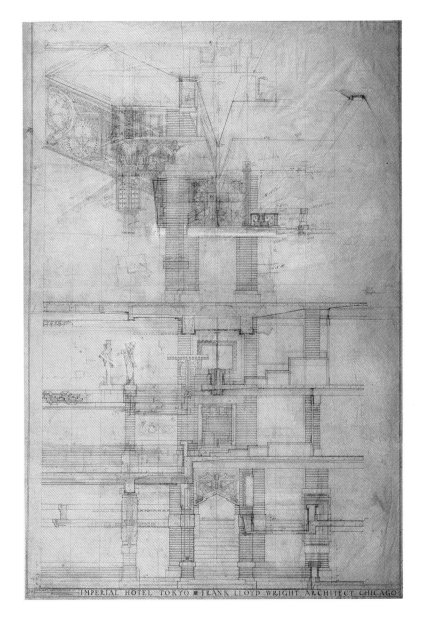

160.   Promenade

161.   Peacock Room

ALINE BARNSDALL THEATER   Los Angeles, California. Project, c. 1915–20

170.   Perspective (FLLW; 1919; insc. 1913). Pencil and color pencil on tracing paper, 6½ x 22¾". The Frank Lloyd Wright Foundation

Little Dipper   **KINDERGARTEN AND PLAYHOUSE FOR ALINE BARNSDALL**   Los Angeles, California. Project, 1923

171.   Perspective. Pencil and color pencil on tracing paper, 15½ x 26¾". The Frank Lloyd Wright Foundation

LAKE TAHOE SUMMER COLONY
Lake Tahoe, California. Project, c. 1922–24

172.   Perspective: cabin (KT). Pencil and color pencil on tracing paper.
21¾ x 15". The Frank Lloyd Wright Foundation

173.   Perspective: cabin barge (FLLW). Pencil
and color pencil on tracing paper, 9¾ x 14⅜".
The Frank Lloyd Wright Foundation

174.   Perspective. Pencil and color pencil on tracing paper, 13¼ x 27⅝". The Library of Congress

NAKOMA COUNTRY CLUB
Madison, Wisconsin. Project, 1923–24

175.   Interior perspective. Color pencil on print,
18 x 20". Collection Alden Franz Aust

AMERICAN·MODEL·C3 □ ·PATENTS □□ ·APPLIED·FOR
AMERICAN·SYSTEM-BUILT
HOUSES □ DESIGNED·BY
FRANK·LLOYD·WRIGHT ■
THE·RICHARDS·COMPANY
PROPRIETORS·MILWAUKEE

In the years during which Wright developed the Imperial Hotel in Tokyo, he devoted himself to a continuing investigation into systems of low-cost construction such as the American System-Built Houses (opposite), known as the Ready-Cut system, and a series of concrete-block houses, including The Monolith Homes for Thomas P. Hardy (right), which were compact and relatively abstract in character.

Following the tragedy at Taliesin in 1914 in which Mrs. Cheney and six others were killed and the homestead burned, Wright passed through Los Angeles several times during the design and construction of the Imperial Hotel and Hollyhock House with his new companion Miriam Noel (whom he later married). He briefly established an office there and designed a series of houses in southern California known as the Textile Block houses in which he attempted to integrate his interest in efficient, low-cost construction and ornament. The Millard, Storer, Freeman, and Ennis houses (plates 178–195) were constructed—on the interior and exterior—of a combination of plain-faced and ornamental concrete blocks, cast on the site from molds designed by Wright. The relatively small scale of the blocks allowed for designs that closely followed the contours of the landscape, as in the Samuel Freeman House, which had a stepped section. This can also be seen in various dwellings in the design for the Doheny Ranch Resort (plates 198–199, 402), a romantically evocative project where the structures were interwoven with the hills above Los Angeles.

The flexibility of concrete-block construction provided Wright with the opportunity to explore compositions based on the diagonal, which seemed particularly appropriate to the rugged landscapes of the Southwest. The design for the San Marcos-in-the-Desert Resort in Arizona (plates 200–203) was particularly representative of the picturesque effect Wright created with the diagonal plan and terraced elevations. Not only was the plan oblique, but the concrete blocks themselves had diagonally split faces that imitated the serrated ridges of the native saguaro cactus.

Opposite

AMERICAN SYSTEM-BUILT HOUSES FOR THE RICHARDS COMPANY   1915–17

176.   Perspective of model C3 (AR). Lithoprint, 11 x 8½". The Museum of Modern Art, New York. David Rockefeller, Jr. Fund, Ira Howard Levy Fund, and Jeffrey P. Klein Fund

THE MONOLITH HOMES FOR THOMAS P. HARDY   Racine, Wisconsin. Project, 1919–20

177.   Elevations (RMS). Ink and pencil on linen, 28⅝ x 18⅛". The Frank Lloyd Wright Foundation

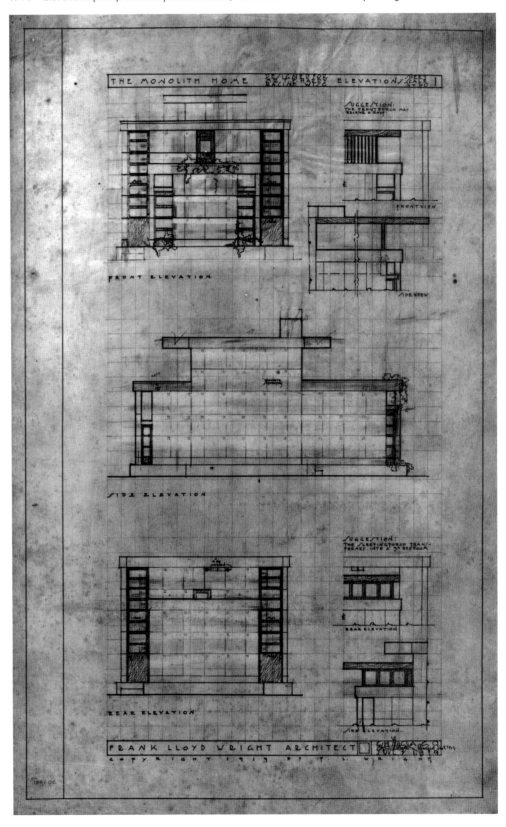

178.   Perspective. Color pencil and pencil on paper, 20⁹/₁₆ x 19¹¹/₁₆". The Museum of Modern Art, New York. Gift of Mr. and Mrs. Walter Hochschild

La Miniatura
MRS. GEORGE MADISON MILLARD HOUSE
Pasadena, California. 1923

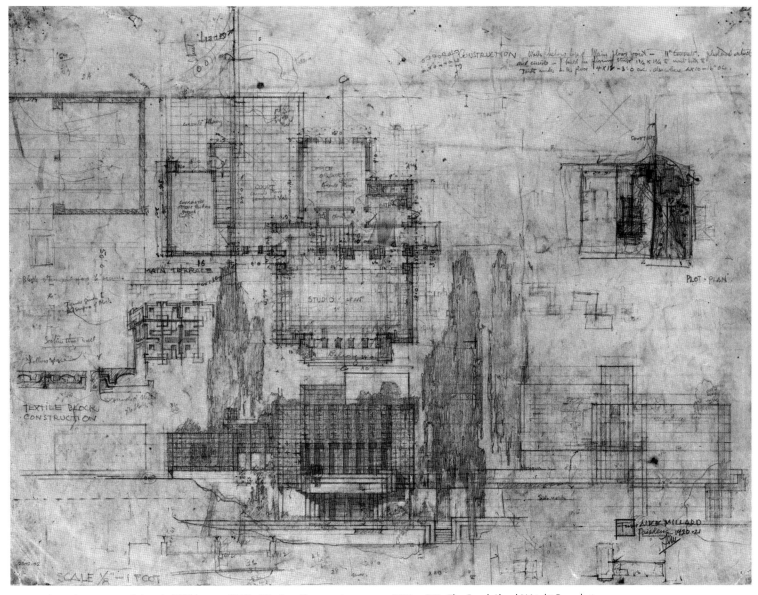

179. Plan, elevation, and details (FLLW; insc. 1920–21). Pencil on tracing paper, 15½ x 21". The Frank Lloyd Wright Foundation

180. Exterior detail

181. Living room

JOHN STORER HOUSE
Hollywood, California. 1923–24

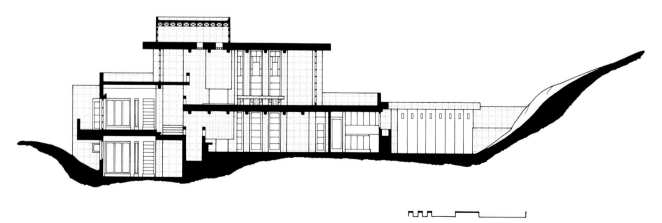

183. Section

184. Exterior detail

185. Living room

186. Perspective (FLLW). Pencil and color pencil on tracing paper, 11⅛ x 21¼". The Frank Lloyd Wright Foundation

187.   Aerial perspective (FLLW). Pencil and color pencil on tracing paper, 10¾ x 21⅜". The Frank Lloyd Wright Foundation

SAMUEL FREEMAN HOUSE
Los Angeles, California. 1923–24

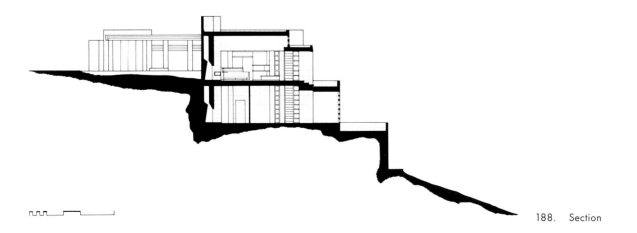

188.   Section

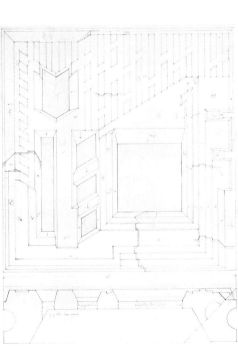

Left
189.   Full-size drawing of concrete block (detail). Pencil and color pencil on tracing paper, 22⁷/₁₆ x 27⁷/₈". The Library of Congress

190.   Exterior detail

191.   Interior detail

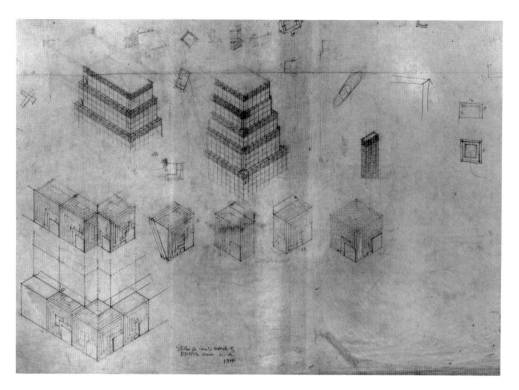

CHARLES E. ENNIS HOUSE
Los Angeles, California. 1923–24

192.   Perspective studies of concrete blocks
(insc. 1914). Pencil on tracing paper, 24¾ x 35".
The Frank Lloyd Wright Foundation

193.   Interior detail

194. Perspective and partial plan. Pencil, color
pencil, and ink on tracing paper, 20¼ x 39".
The Frank Lloyd Wright Foundation

195. Exterior detail

ALINE BARNSDALL HOUSE
Beverly Hills, California. Project, 1923

197.   Elevation (FLLW). Pencil and color pencil
on paper, 12⅛ x 27". The Library of Congress

A. M. JOHNSON DESERT COMPOUND AND SHRINE

Death Valley, California. Project, c. 1922–25

196.   Aerial perspective (FLLW). Pencil and color pencil on tracing paper,
12 x 33⅜". The Frank Lloyd Wright Foundation

198. Perspective (FLLW; insc. 1921). Pencil, color pencil, and crayon on tracing paper lined with Japanese tissue, 18½ x 36⅝".
Erving and Joyce Wolf Collection

DOHENY RANCH RESORT
Los Angeles, California. Project, 1923

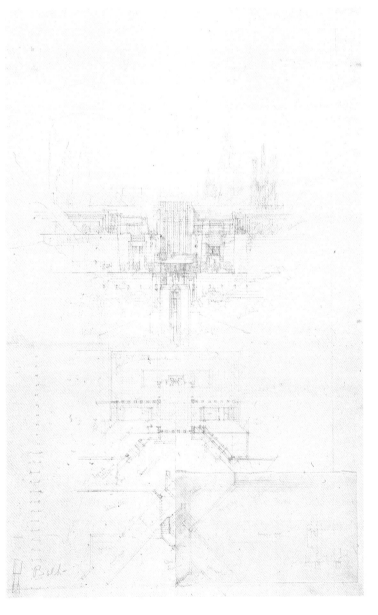

199.   Elevation and plan: House C. Pencil and color pencil on tracing paper,
30¾ x 19⅞". The Library of Congress

200. Perspective (VK). Pencil and color pencil on tracing paper, 16 x 54¾". The Frank Lloyd Wright Foundation

201. Plan of upper level (FLLW). Pencil and color pencil on tracing paper, 22 x 51¾". The Frank Lloyd Wright Foundation

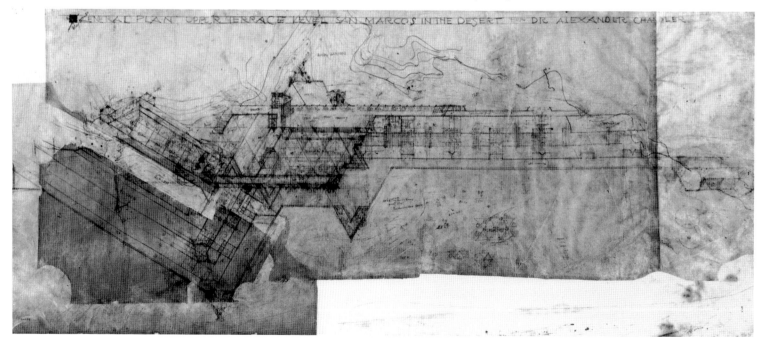

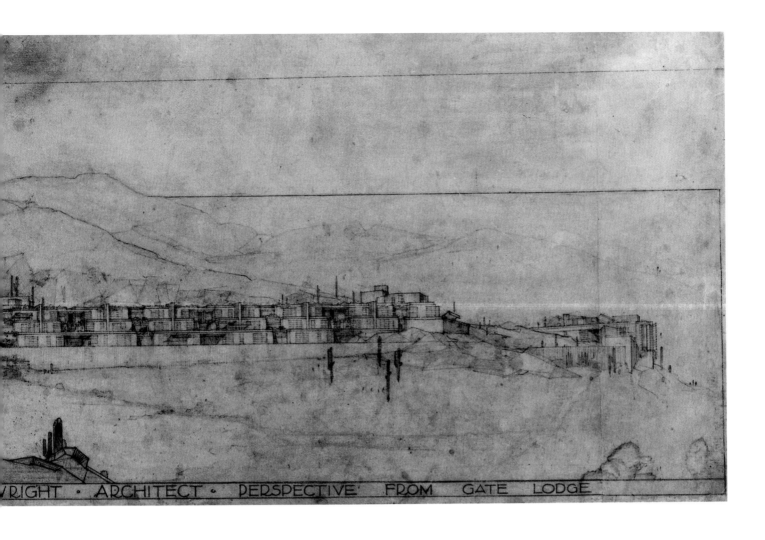

RIGHT · ARCHITECT · PERSPECTIVE FROM GATE LODGE

SAN MARCOS-IN-THE-DESERT RESORT
Chandler, Arizona. Project, 1928–29

202. Perspective (insc. June 1927). Pencil and color pencil on tracing paper, 13¾ x 21¼". The Frank Lloyd Wright Foundation

Ralph and Wellington Cudney House
SAN MARCOS-IN-THE-DESERT RESORT
Chandler, Arizona. Project, 1929

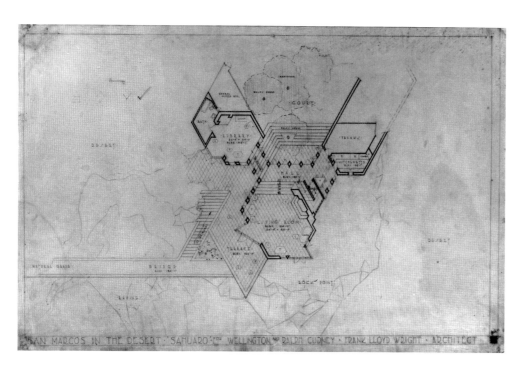

203. Plan of upper level. Pencil and color pencil on tracing paper, 21¾ x 32¾". The Frank Lloyd Wright Foundation

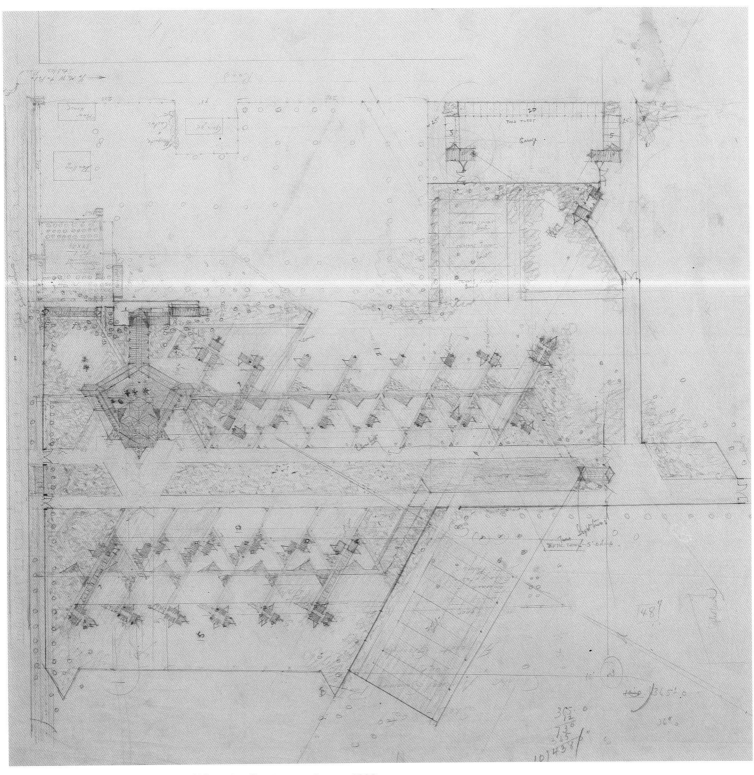

SAN MARCOS WATER GARDENS   Chandler, Arizona. Project, 1929

204.   Plan (FLLW). Pencil and color pencil on tracing paper, 28⅞ x 23⅝". The Frank Lloyd Wright Foundation

OFFICE BUILDING FOR NATIONAL LIFE INSURANCE CO. OF U.S.A. CHICAGO.· A.M.JOHNSON PRESIDENT.   FRANK LLOYD WRIGHT ARCHITECT 1925

Opposite
NATIONAL LIFE INSURANCE COMPANY BUILDING
Chicago, Illinois. Project, 1924–25

205.   Perspective. Pencil, color pencil, and ink on paper, 49½ x 41½".
Collection Seymour H. Persky

SKYSCRAPER REGULATION   Project, 1926

206.   Elevation (detail; FLLW). Pencil on tracing paper, 20⅜ x 30¼".
The Frank Lloyd Wright Foundation

In the mid-1920s Wright was approaching sixty years of age. Despite the publicity he received when the newly completed Imperial Hotel withstood a serious earthquake in 1923, critical reaction to the project was mixed. In addition, continuing turmoil in his personal life, financial instability, and long absences from the United States diverted Wright's energies and ultimately led to fewer commissions.

Much of his work of this period can be seen as a response to his growing professional isolation and to the architectural status quo, particularly in the design of skyscrapers. The National Life Insurance Company Building (opposite), with its floor slabs cantilevered from interior columns and lightweight metal-and-glass skin, was a rebuke to the masonry-clad, historicist designs of the period. His project for St. Mark's-in-the-Bouwerie Towers (plates 211–214) further developed this concept, creating a central core from which the entire edifice was cantilevered. This became known as the tap-root structural system, after the basic structure of a tree. The study called Skyscraper Regulation (above), specifically criticized the density of high-rise development.

Wright's activity in these speculative projects coincided with an increasingly stable personal situation after his marriage to Olgivanna Hinzenberg in 1928 and the establishment of the Taliesin Fellowship in 1932. This allowed him to pursue literary and theoretical projects, such as his autobiography and Broadacre City (plates 403–404). Wright's vision of a deurbanized, automotive American landscape was also a critique of American cities, central to which was his development of the Usonian house for the new middle class. Best represented by the Herbert Jacobs House (plates 241–245), this suburban house was less likely to have servants' quarters and more likely to be smaller; also, the stable and garage of the Prairie house gave way to the carport.

Although Wright had some sympathy for contemporary European developments, he rejected the machine aesthetic and the emphasis on mass-produced, collective housing. Wright's residential masterpiece, Fallingwater, the Edgar J. Kaufmann House (plates 234–240), was a tour de force in planar abstraction pointedly balanced by romantic imagery and the use of natural materials. Immediately and widely celebrated, it reestablished Wright's career.

As important as Fallingwater, in this regard, was the S. C. Johnson & Son, Inc. Administration Building (plates 254–260, 264–267), a large office structure that recalled the openness and dignified monumentality of the Larkin Building. With its streamlined massing and flaring dendriform columns, Wright achieved an unmatched spatial and tectonic fluidity. Several years later the addition of a Research Laboratory Tower (plates 261–267) provided the first opportunity to realize his conception of a centrally supported, cantilevered multistory structure.

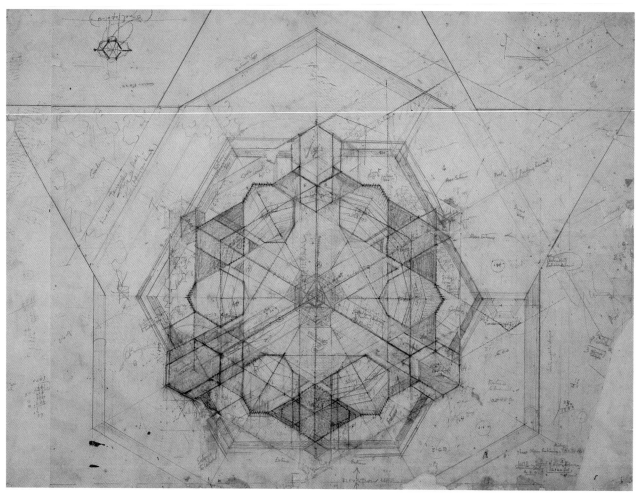

STEEL CATHEDRAL   New York, New York. Project, 1926

207.   Elevation (FLLW; insc. 1932). Pencil and color pencil on tracing paper, 22⅝ x 30¾". The Frank Lloyd Wright Foundation

208.   Plan (FLLW). Pencil and color pencil on tracing paper, 23⅜ x 31". The Frank Lloyd Wright Foundation

GORDON STRONG AUTOMOBILE OBJECTIVE AND PLANETARIUM
Sugarloaf Mountain, Maryland. Project, 1924–25

209.   Aerial perspective (FLLW). Pencil on tracing paper, 10¾ x 8⅜". The Frank Lloyd Wright Foundation

210.   Section (detail). Pencil and color pencil on tracing paper, 26¾ x 34⅛". The Frank Lloyd Wright Foundation

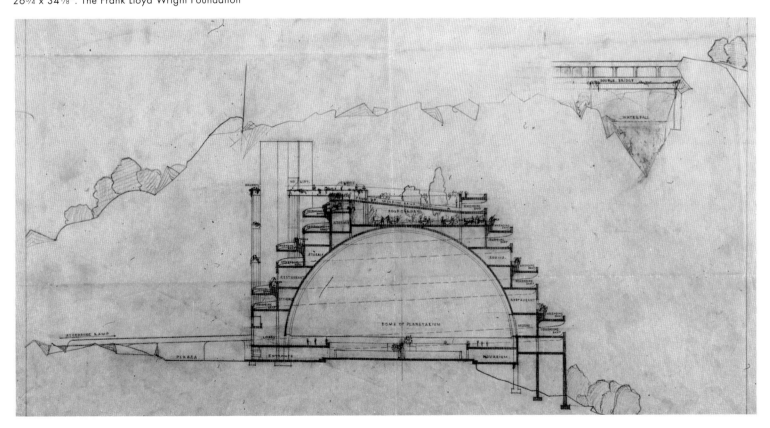

211. Perspective (FLLW; 1928). Pencil and color pencil on tracing paper, 28¼ x 10⅛". The Frank Lloyd Wright Foundation

ST. MARK'S-IN-THE-BOUWERIE TOWERS
New York, New York. Project, 1927–31

212. Plans: typical apartment. Pencil and color pencil on tracing paper, 34¼ x 24¼". The Frank Lloyd Wright Foundation

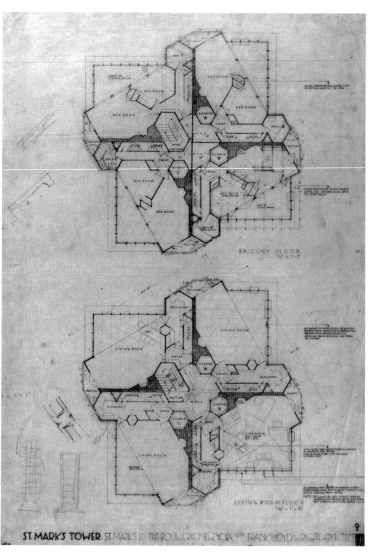

213.   Perspective. Pencil on tracing paper,
8⅜ x 15⅜". The Frank Lloyd Wright Foundation

214.   Interior perspective: typical apartment
(1930). Pencil and color pencil on tracing paper,
26⅜ x 25⅜". The Frank Lloyd Wright Foundation

215.   Perspective. Pencil on tracing paper, 19 x 28¼". The Frank Lloyd Wright Foundation

GROUPED TOWERS   Chicago, Illinois. Project, 1930

216.   Plan. Pencil on tracing paper, 13¾ x 35⅜". The Frank Lloyd Wright Foundation

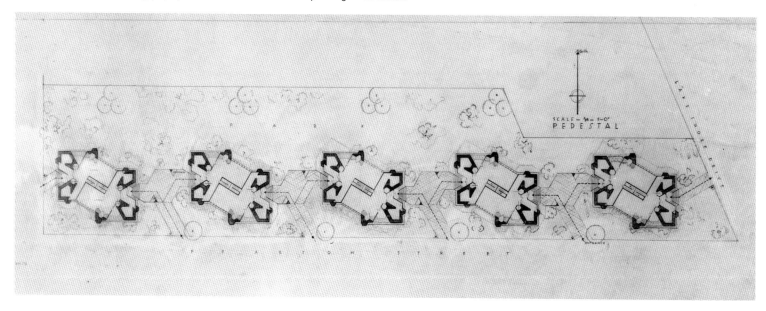

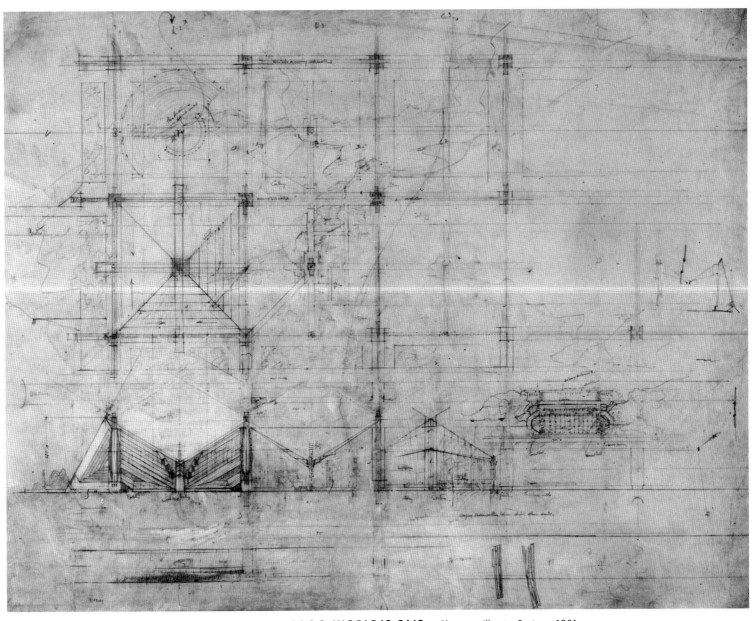

PAVILION FOR CENTURY OF PROGRESS, CHICAGO WORLD'S FAIR Chicago, Illinois. Project, 1931

217. Plan and elevation (FLLW). Pencil and color pencil on tracing paper, 27¾ x 35". The Frank Lloyd Wright Foundation

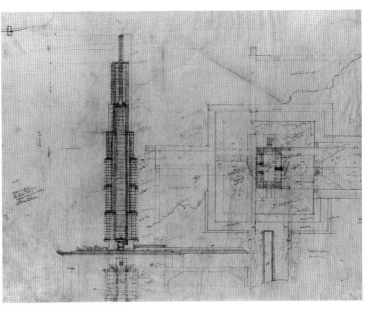

SKYSCRAPER FOR CENTURY OF PROGRESS, CHICAGO WORLD'S FAIR

Chicago, Illinois. Project, 1931

218. Plan and elevation (FLLW). Pencil and color pencil on tracing paper, 27¾ x 35¾". The Frank Lloyd Wright Foundation

219.   Aerial perspective (FLLW and GC). Pencil and color pencil on tracing paper, 10 x 19¼". The Frank Lloyd Wright Foundation

220.   Isometric plan (GC). Pencil on tracing paper, 27 x 40⅜". The Frank Lloyd Wright Foundation

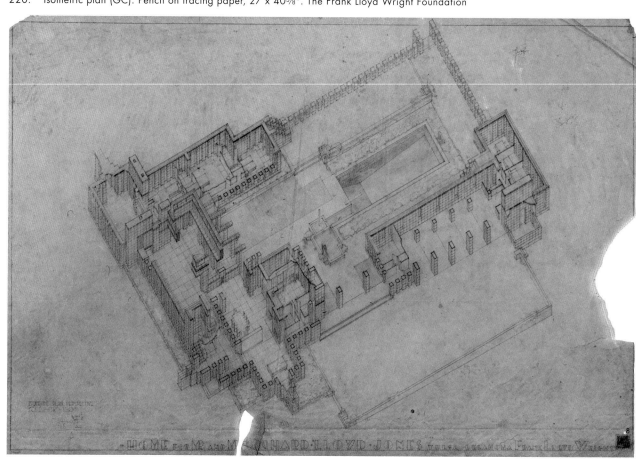

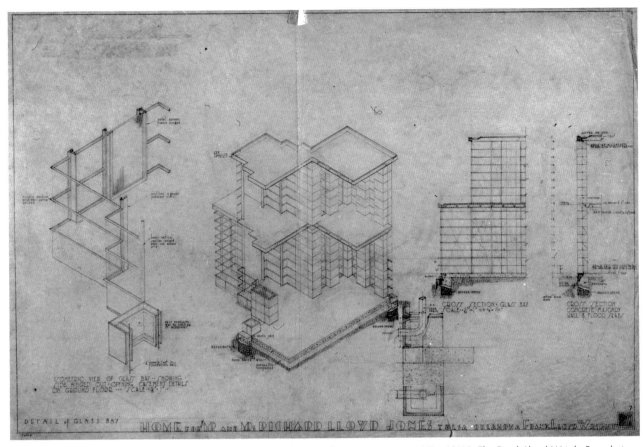

221. Isometrics and sections: glass bay (GC). Pencil and color pencil on tracing paper, 27 x 40⅝". The Frank Lloyd Wright Foundation

Westhope RICHARD LLOYD JONES HOUSE Tulsa, Oklahoma. 1928–31

222. Exterior detail

223. Interior detail

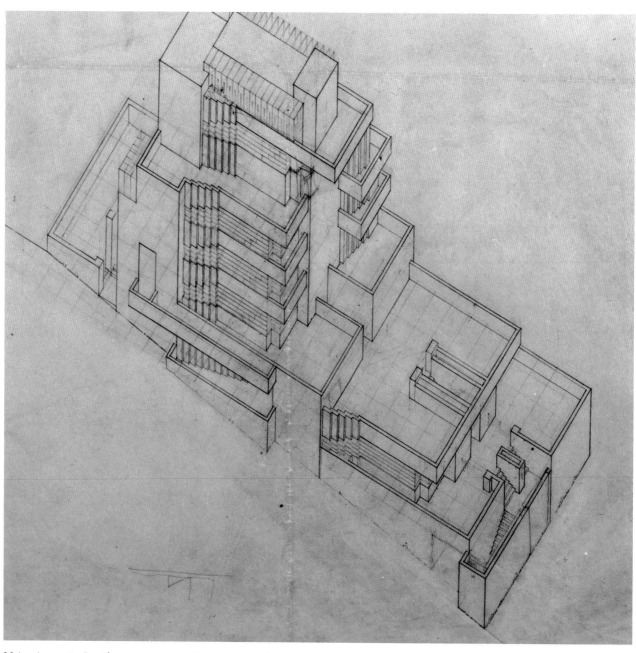

224.   Isometric. Pencil on tracing paper, 20½ x 29¾". The Frank Lloyd Wright Foundation

ELIZABETH NOBLE APARTMENTS
Los Angeles, California. Project, 1929–30

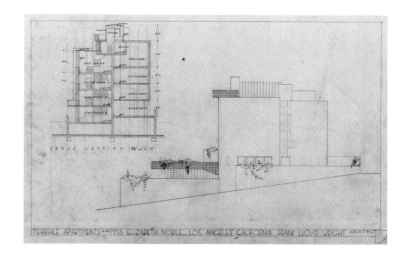

225.   Section and elevation. Pencil on tracing paper, 21¾ x 31¼".
The Frank Lloyd Wright Foundation

226.   Perspective. Pencil on tracing paper, 10¼ x 36". The Frank Lloyd Wright Foundation

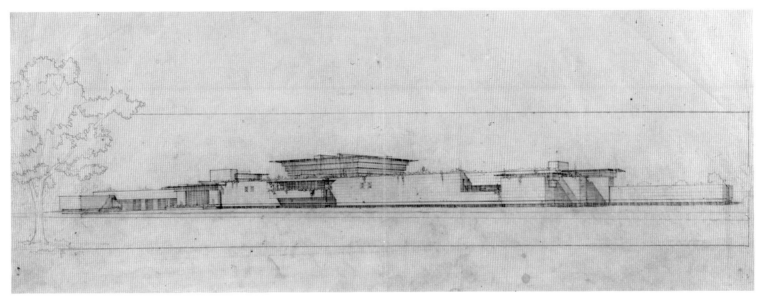

227.   Perspective. Pencil on tracing paper, 15¾ x 36". The Frank Lloyd Wright Foundation

228.   First-floor plan: 1 entrance, 2 dining room, 3 bedroom, 4 billiard room, 5 pool, 6 lake, 7 service court

HOUSE ON THE MESA
Denver, Colorado. Project, 1931

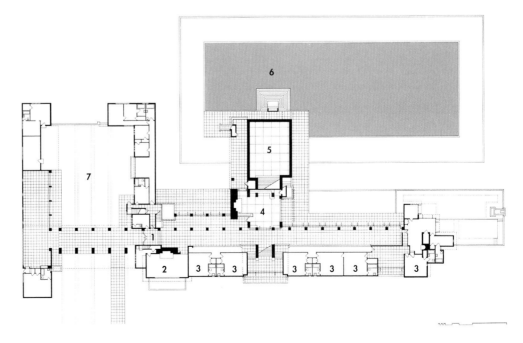

MALCOLM WILLEY HOUSE   Minneapolis, Minnesota. 1932–34

229.   Perspective, first scheme (1932). Pencil and color pencil on tracing paper, 15¾ x 32⅜". The Frank Lloyd Wright Foundation

PREFABRICATED FARM UNIT FOR WALTER V. DAVIDSON   Project, 1932

230.   Aerial perspective. Pencil and color pencil on tracing paper, 11⅝ x 22⅞". The Frank Lloyd Wright Foundation

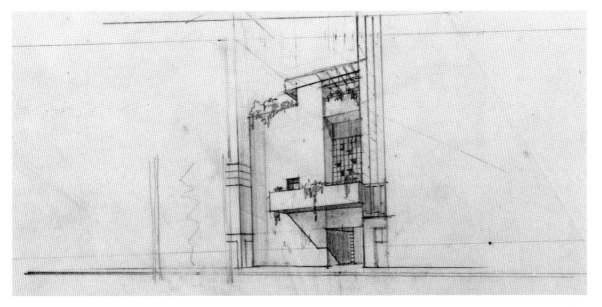

**THE TWO-ZONE HOUSE
FOR CITY**
Project, 1935

231.   Perspective. Pencil on
tracing paper, 8 x 12½". The
Frank Lloyd Wright Foundation

**THE TWO-ZONE HOUSE
FOR SUBURB**
Project, 1935

232.   Perspective. Pencil on
tracing paper, 10⅛ x 10¼". The
Frank Lloyd Wright Foundation

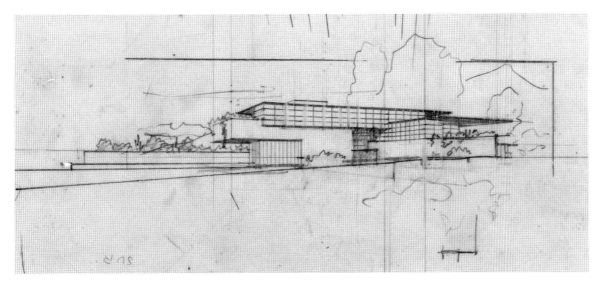

**THE TWO-ZONE HOUSE
FOR COUNTRY**
Project, 1935

233.   Perspective. Pencil on
tracing paper, 5⅜ x 14". The
Frank Lloyd Wright Foundation

234.   Perspective (FLLW and JHH; insc. 1936). Pencil and color pencil on tracing paper, 15⅜ x 27¼".
The Frank Lloyd Wright Foundation

Fallingwater
EDGAR J. KAUFMANN HOUSE
Mill Run, Pennsylvania. 1934–37

235. View from below

Fallingwater
EDGAR J. KAUFMANN HOUSE
Mill Run, Pennsylvania. 1934–37

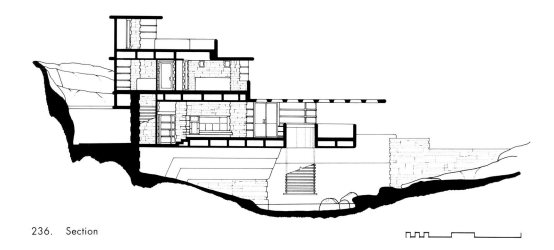

236. Section

237. View from bridge

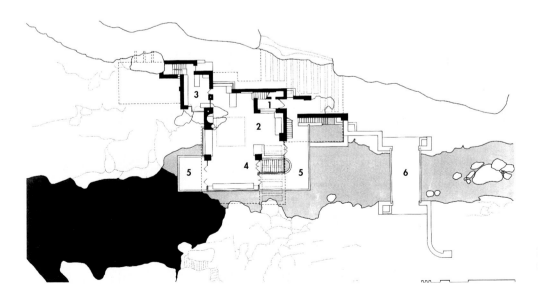

238. First-floor plan: 1 entrance, 2 living room, 3 kitchen, 4 stairs to pool, 5 terrace, 6 bridge

239. Exterior detail

240. Living room

Fallingwater
EDGAR J. KAUFMANN HOUSE
Mill Run, Pennsylvania. 1934–37

241.   Perspective and aerial perspective (FLLW and JHH; insc. 1938). Pencil, color pencil, and ink on tracing paper, 21 x 31¾". The Frank Lloyd Wright Foundation

HERBERT JACOBS HOUSE
Madison, Wisconsin. 1936–37

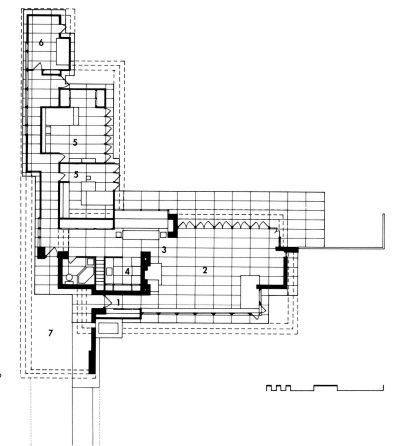

242.   Plan: 1 entrance, 2 living room, 3 dining area, 4 kitchen, 5 bedroom, 6 study, 7 carport

243. Entrance

244. Fireplace
and dining area

245. Living room

246. Aerial perspective (FLLW and JHH). Pencil and color pencil on tracing paper, 23 x 35⅞". The Frank Lloyd Wright Foundation

LLOYD LEWIS HOUSE   Libertyville, Illinois. 1939–41

247.   Exterior

248.   Living room

249.   Dining area

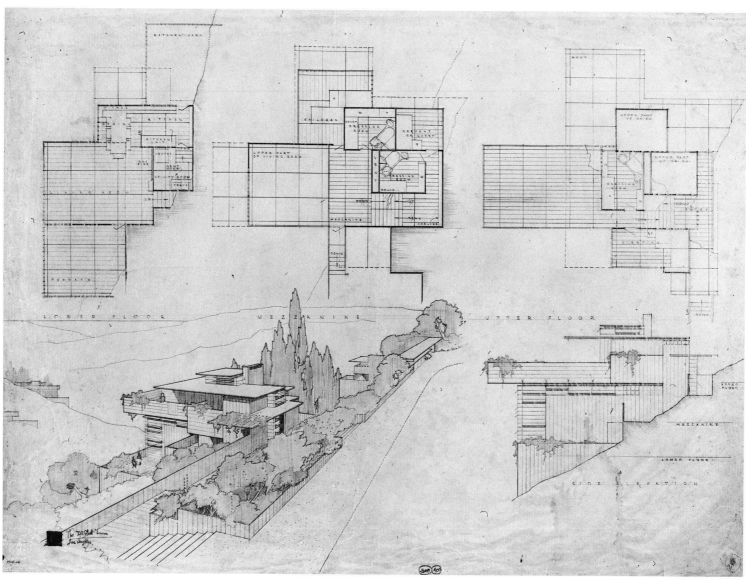

Opposite

JOHN C. PEW HOUSE
Madison, Wisconsin. 1938–40

250.   Perspective (FLLW and HF). Pencil
and color pencil on tracing paper, 22 x 36".
The Frank Lloyd Wright Foundation

ALL-STEEL HOUSES
Los Angeles, California. Project, 1937

251.   Plans, perspective, and elevation (JHH).
Pencil, color pencil, and ink on tracing paper,
28¼ x 36". The Frank Lloyd Wright Foundation

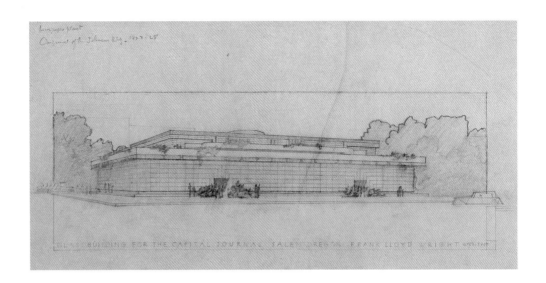

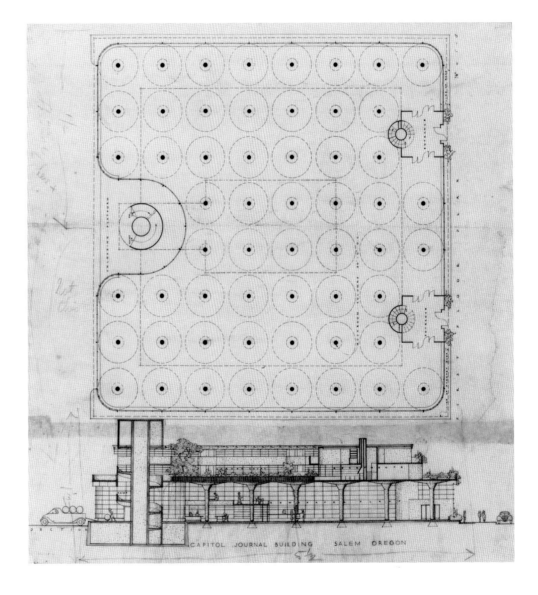

CAPITAL JOURNAL BUILDING   Salem, Oregon. Project, 1931–32

252.   Perspective (insc. 1927–28). Pencil and color pencil on tracing paper, 14 x 29½".
The Frank Lloyd Wright Foundation

253.   Plan and section. Ink and pencil on tracing paper, 30¼ x 28½".
The Frank Lloyd Wright Foundation

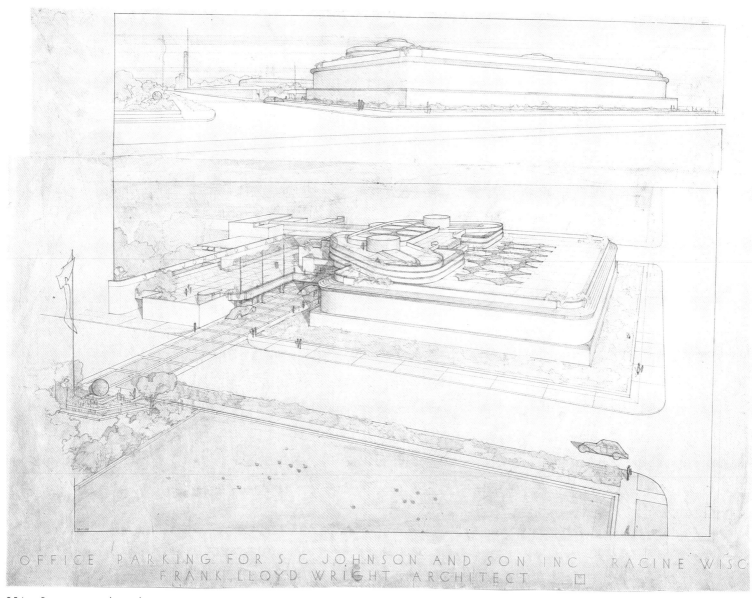

OFFICE PARKING FOR S C JOHNSON AND SON INC RACINE WISC
FRANK LLOYD WRIGHT ARCHITECT

254.   Perspective and aerial perspective (JHH). Pencil, color pencil, and ink on tracing paper, 28¾ x 38⅝". The Frank Lloyd Wright Foundation

S. C. JOHNSON & SON, INC. ADMINISTRATION BUILDING
Racine, Wisconsin. 1936–39

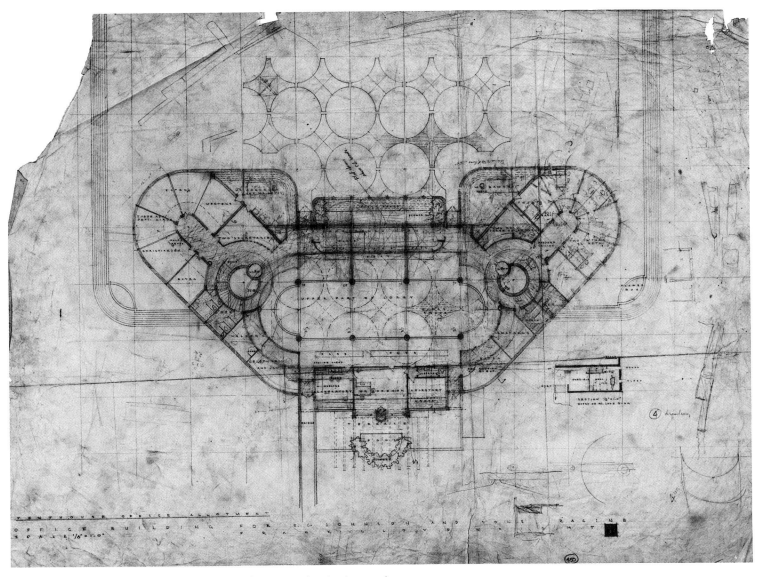

255. Plan and section: penthouse offices (FLLW and JHH). Pencil and color pencil on tracing paper, 25 x 34¼". The Frank Lloyd Wright Foundation

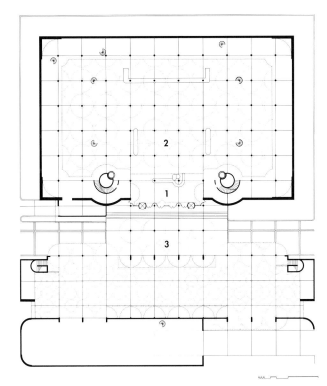

256. First-floor plan: 1 entrance, 2 Great Workroom, 3 carport

257. Entrance

258. Ceiling detail

S. C. JOHNSON & SON, INC. ADMINISTRATION BUILDING
Racine, Wisconsin. 1936–39

259. Great Workroom

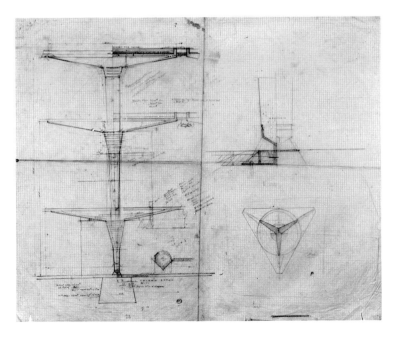

260. Elevation, section, and plan: columns. Pencil and color pencil on tracing paper, 34 x 41⅞". The Frank Lloyd Wright Foundation

S. C. JOHNSON & SON, INC.
RESEARCH LABORATORY TOWER
Racine, Wisconsin. 1943–50

261.   Interior detail: laboratory

262.   Section and plan: third floor (1946). Pencil, ink, and color pencil on tracing paper, 36 x 46¼". The Frank Lloyd Wright Foundation

Opposite
263.   Exterior

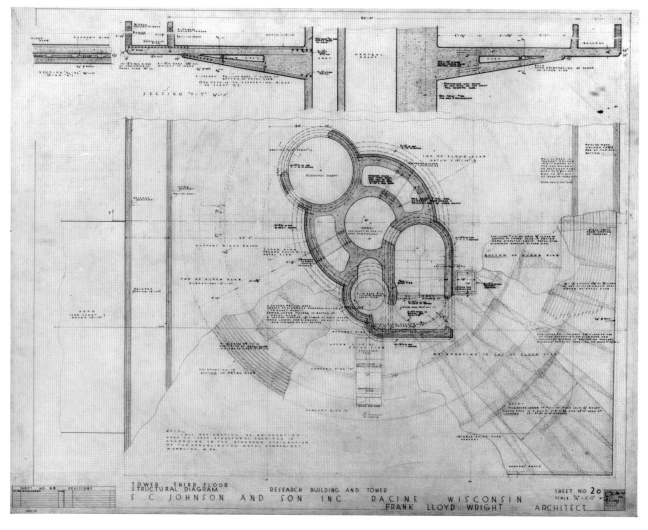

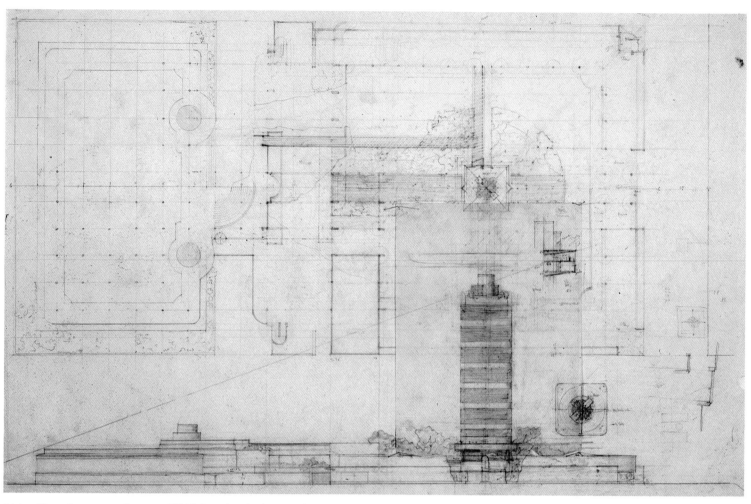

264.   Plan, elevation, and section (FLLW). Pencil and color pencil on tracing paper, 24 x 36". The Frank Lloyd Wright Foundation

S. C. JOHNSON & SON, INC. ADMINISTRATION BUILDING AND RESEARCH LABORATORY TOWER
Racine, Wisconsin. 1936–50

265.   Section

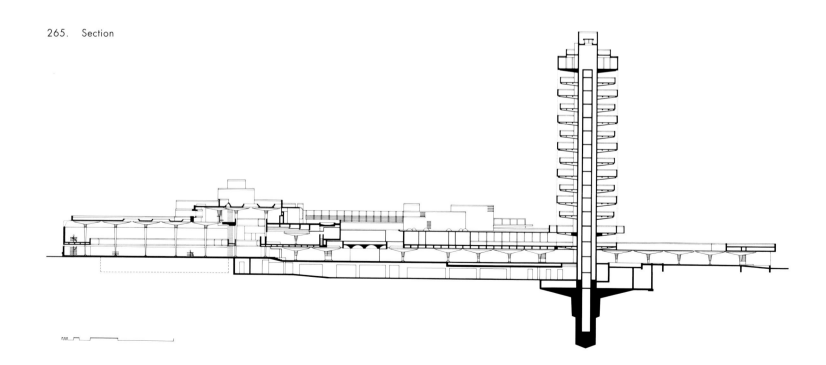

266. Exterior

267. Entrance

251

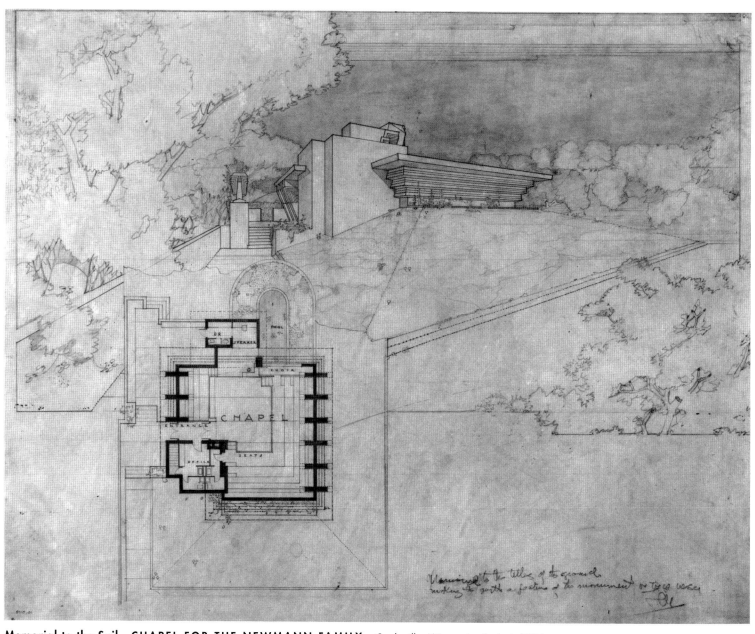

Memorial to the Soil CHAPEL FOR THE NEWMANN FAMILY Cooksville, Wisconsin. Project, 1934

268.   Perspective and plan (FLLW and BD). Pencil on tracing paper, 22 x 25". The Frank Lloyd Wright Foundation

Ten years after his first exposure to the desert landscape, Wright, at seventy, began the construction of winter quarters for himself and his expanding Fellowship. Taliesin West (plates 278–283), as it would be called, had a freely composed diagonal plan that reflected the rugged contours of the site, as had his project for the A. M. Johnson Desert Compound and Shrine. At Taliesin West, however, Wright extended the diagonal geometries from the plan to the vertical dimension, angling the profiles of the structures.

At this time in his career he freely employed nonorthogonal compositions for numerous projects, from Auldbrass Plantation (plates 293–297) to Florida Southern College (plate 284). He also experimented with a hexagonal grid for such projects as the Honeycomb House for Paul R. and Jean S. Hanna (plates 270–274). Wright then further expanded his repertoire of planning devices by introducing circular elements, as in the Ralph Jester House, which he called a "true abstraction" (opposite) and the Cottage Group Hotel and Sports Club for Huntington Hartford (plates 316–318).

Until the late 1930s these configurations had remained rare in his work. The spiral, which had defined the Gordon Strong Automobile Objective and Planetarium (plates 209–210) as exceptional in the 1920s, was used repeatedly by Wright in the years around World War II but nowhere more spectacularly than in the Solomon R. Guggenheim Museum (plates 301–310). A museum dedicated to nonobjective art, Wright's sculptural abstraction, with underlying natural metaphors, was the structure with which he was most successful in his search for an ex-

RALPH JESTER HOUSE Palos Verdes, California. Project, 1938–39

269. Plan and elevation (FLLW). Pencil and color pencil on tracing paper, 13¾ x 21". The Frank Lloyd Wright Foundation

pression of the seamless, flowing potential of poured concrete. A continuous spiral ramp cantilevered from the gallery walls offered the visitor an uninterrupted experience in one of the most astonishing interior spaces constructed in this century.

Wright's development of these varied geometries coincided with his publication of *An Organic Architecture.* Although he and others had used the term *organic* since the nineteenth century, the emergence in Wright's work of forms derived from nature reflects his expansion of the term. Included in this re-

definition is what might be considered a protoenvironmentalism often coupled with low-cost materials and construction methods. Particularly striking in this regard are the Solar Hemicycle, the second Herbert Jacobs House, designed to maximize passive solar heating (plates 311–314), and the Cooperative Homesteads of rammed-earth construction (plate 300), which, like the Memorial to the Soil, a Chapel for the Newmann Family (opposite), were insulated by earth berms.

Wright often favored construction methods that used rubble walls for projects such as

Taliesin West and the Rose Pauson House (plates 291–292). Made of rough stone gathered from the desert floor, the buildings were united—in terms of form, color, and material—with their surroundings. Other projects were perched daringly on the edge of a crater or a hillside in order to take advantage of stunning views of the landscape.

270. Aerial perspective (FLLW and JHH). Pencil and ink on tracing paper, 21½ x 36". The Frank Lloyd Wright Foundation

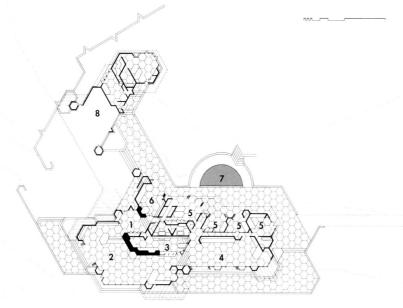

Honeycomb House
PAUL R. AND JEAN S. HANNA HOUSE
Palo Alto, California. 1935–37

271. Plan: 1 entrance, 2 living/dining room, 3 kitchen, 4 playroom, 5 bedroom, 6 study, 7 pool, 8 carport

272.   Exterior

273.   Aerial view

274.   Living room

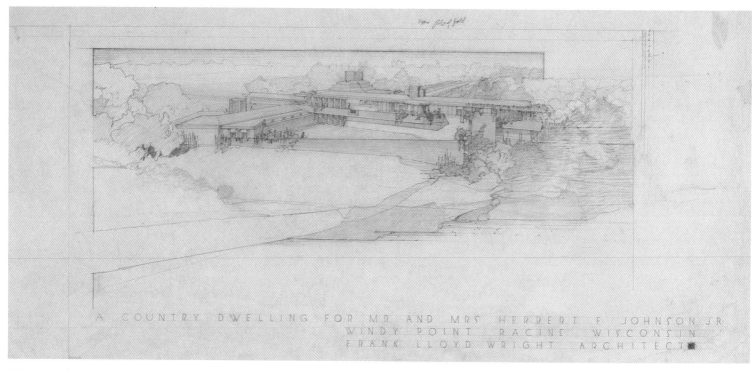

A COUNTRY DWELLING FOR MR AND MRS HERBERT F JOHNSON JR
WINDY POINT RACINE WISCONSIN
FRANK LLOYD WRIGHT ARCHITECT

275.   Aerial perspective (FLLW and JHH). Pencil and color pencil on tracing paper, 18⅝ x 41⅛". The Frank Lloyd Wright Foundation

276.   Plan. Ink and pencil on tracing paper, 29 x 38". The Frank Lloyd Wright Foundation

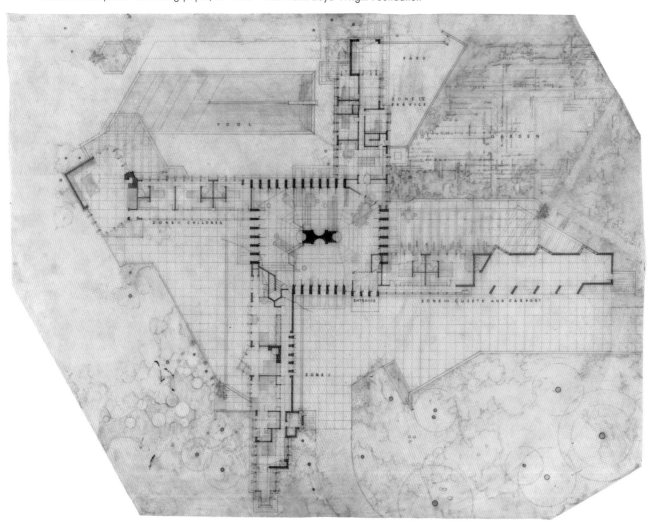

277. Living room

Wingspread
HERBERT F. JOHNSON HOUSE
Racine, Wisconsin. 1937–39

278. Aerial perspective (FLLW). Pencil, color pencil, and ink on tracing paper, 24" x 8'10⅛". The Frank Lloyd Wright Foundation

Taliesin West
FRANK LLOYD WRIGHT HOUSE AND STUDIO
Scottsdale, Arizona. 1937–38

279. Entrance court

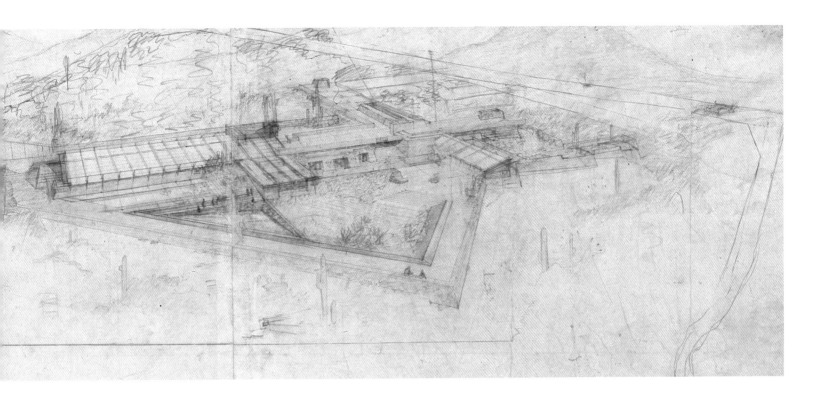

280.   Bell tower and pergola

281. Drafting room

282. Living room

283. General view

Taliesin West
FRANK LLOYD WRIGHT HOUSE AND STUDIO
Scottsdale, Arizona. 1937–38

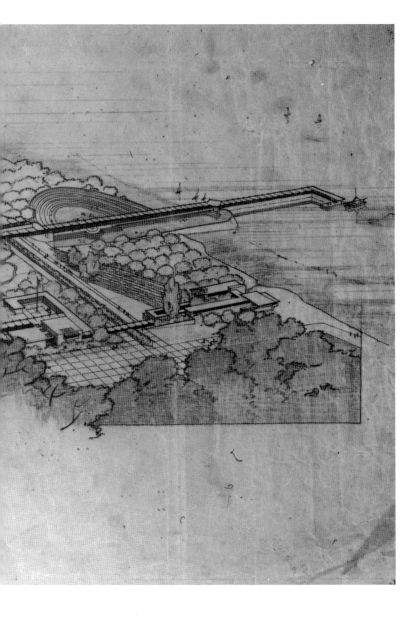

FLORIDA SOUTHERN COLLEGE

Lakeland, Florida. Partially realized, begun 1938

284.   Aerial perspective (JHH). Pencil, color pencil, and ink on tracing paper, 22¼ x 46⅞". The Frank Lloyd Wright Foundation

Opposite below

ROUX LIBRARY, FLORIDA SOUTHERN COLLEGE

Lakeland, Florida. 1941–42

285.   Exterior

286.   Interior

Below

PFEIFFER CHAPEL, FLORIDA SOUTHERN COLLEGE

Lakeland, Florida. 1938–41

287.   Exterior

288.   Interior

Eaglefeather
ARCH OBOLER HOUSE
Malibu, California. Project, 1940–41

289. Perspective. Pencil and color pencil on tracing paper, 22 x 35¾".
Max Protetch Gallery, New York

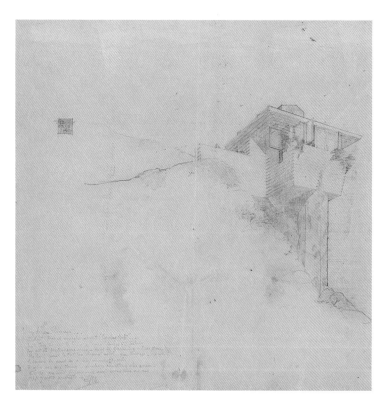

Eleanor's Retreat
ARCH OBOLER GUEST HOUSE
Malibu, California. 1941

290. Perspective. Pencil and color pencil on tracing paper, 17 x 19½".
The Museum of Modern Art, New York. Arthur Drexler Fund

291.   Perspective (FLLW and JT). Pencil and color pencil on tracing paper, 14¼ x 28¼". The Frank Lloyd Wright Foundation

292.   Exterior

ROSE PAUSON HOUSE
Phoenix, Arizona. 1938–41 (destroyed 1943)

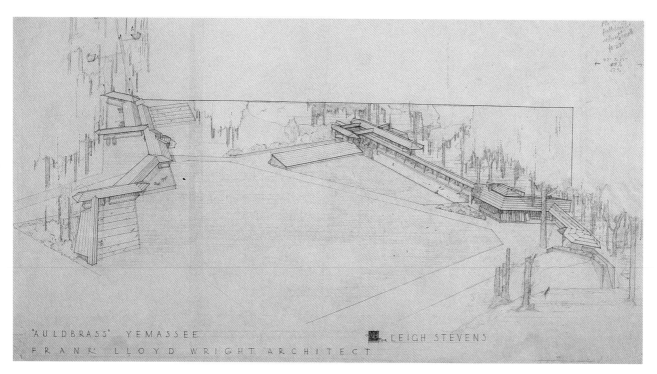

'AULDBRASS' YEMASSEE   LEIGH STEVENS
FRANK LLOYD WRIGHT ARCHITECT

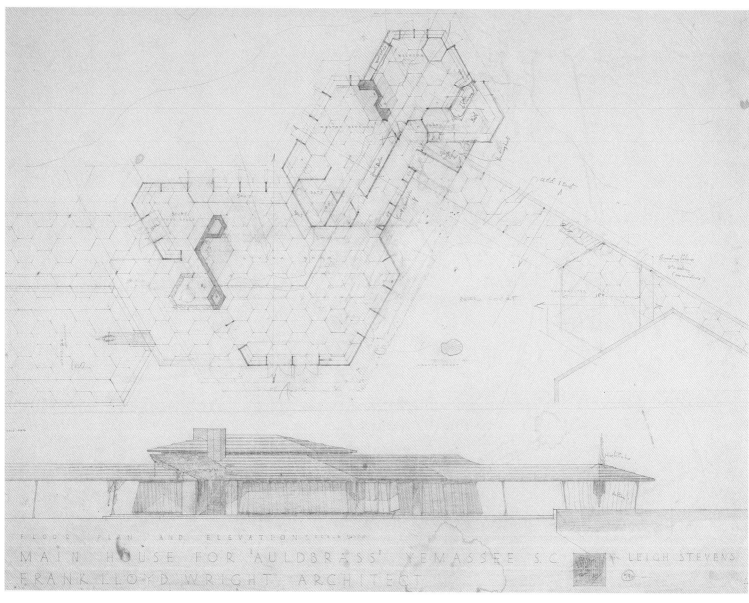

FLOOR PLAN AND ELEVATION SCALE 1/8"
MAIN HOUSE FOR 'AULDBRASS' YEMASSEE S.C.   LEIGH STEVENS
FRANK LLOYD WRIGHT ARCHITECT

AULDBRASS PLANTATION FOR C. LEIGH STEVENS

Yemassee, South Carolina. 1938–42

Opposite

293.   Perspective (FLLW and JHH; 1940). Pencil, color pencil, and ink on tracing paper, 26 x 47¼". The Frank Lloyd Wright Foundation

294.   Plan and elevation (1940). Pencil, color pencil, and ink on tracing paper, 31⅜ x 35¾". The Frank Lloyd Wright Foundation

295.   Exterior

296.   Exterior detail

297.   Living room

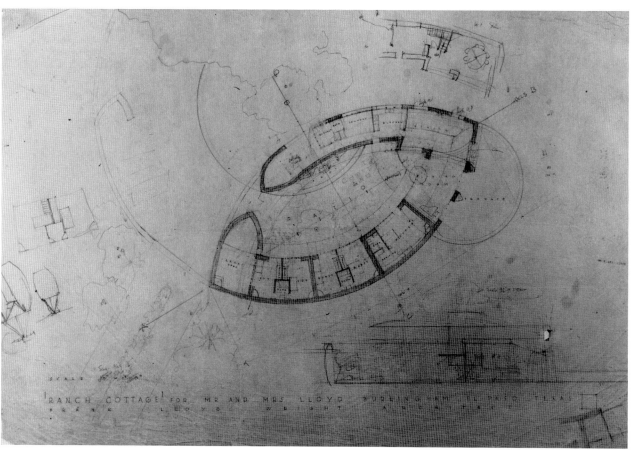

RANCH COTTAGE FOR MR AND MRS LLOYD BURLINGHAM EL PASO TEXAS
FRANK LLOYD WRIGHT ARCHITECT

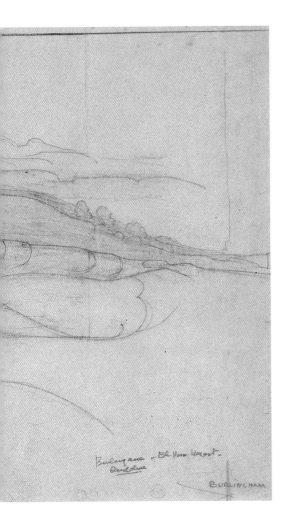

Opposite

LLOYD BURLINGHAM HOUSE   El Paso, Texas. Project, 1941–43

298.   Aerial perspective (FLLW and RM). Pencil, color pencil, and ink on tracing paper, 18⅛ x 41¼". The Frank Lloyd Wright Foundation

299.   Plan and section (FLLW). Pencil and color pencil on tracing paper, 27 x 40⅞". The Frank Lloyd Wright Foundation

COOPERATIVE HOMESTEADS
Detroit, Michigan. Project, 1941–45

300.   Perspective of bermed house (1942). Color pencil and ink on tracing paper, 26 x 34". Collection Gil and Lila Silverman, Detroit, Michigan, and Max Protetch Gallery, New York

SOLOMON R. GUGGENHEIM MUSEUM
New York, New York. 1943–59

301.   Perspective (PB; 1944). Gouache and ink on paper, 20 x 24".
Erving and Joyce Wolf Collection

302.   Elevation (c. 1944). Pencil and color pencil on paper, 20 x 24⅜".
The Frank Lloyd Wright Foundation

Opposite
303.   Sketch on photograph of model (c. 1955). The Frank Lloyd Wright
Foundation

304.   Elevation, section, and sketches (FLLW; c. 1943). Pencil and color
pencil on tracing paper, 26¼ x 30⅜". The Frank Lloyd Wright Foundation

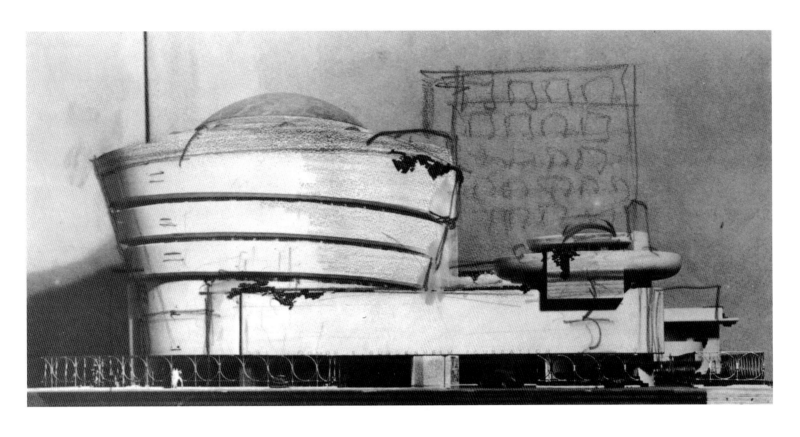

ZIGGURAT

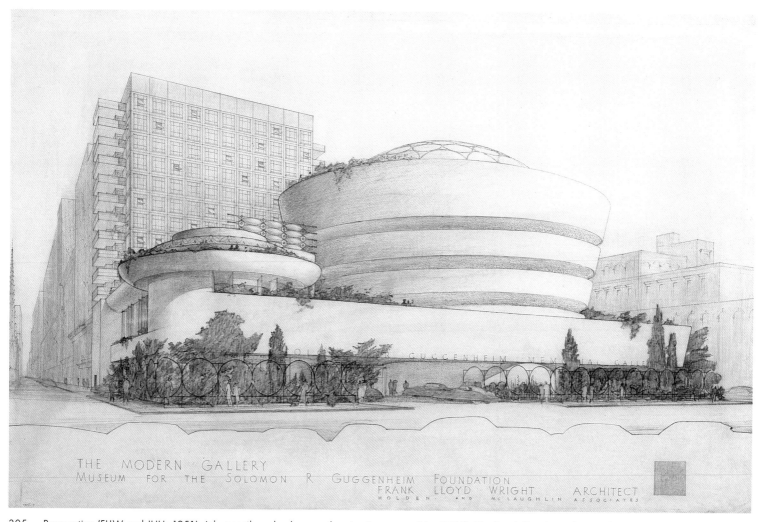

305.   Perspective (FLLW and JHH; 1951). Ink, pencil, and color pencil on tracing paper, 26 x 39½". The Frank Lloyd Wright Foundation

SOLOMON R. GUGGENHEIM MUSEUM
New York, New York. 1943–59

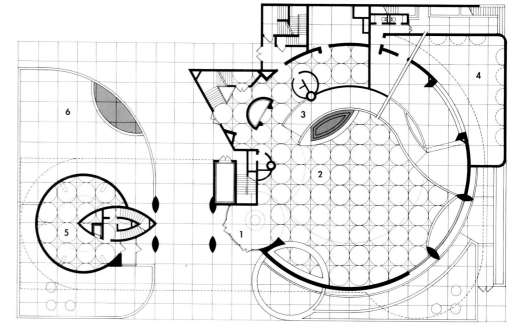

306.   First-floor plan: 1 entrance, 2 main gallery, 3 ramp, 4 gallery, 5 offices, 6 sculpture garden

Opposite
307.   Entrance

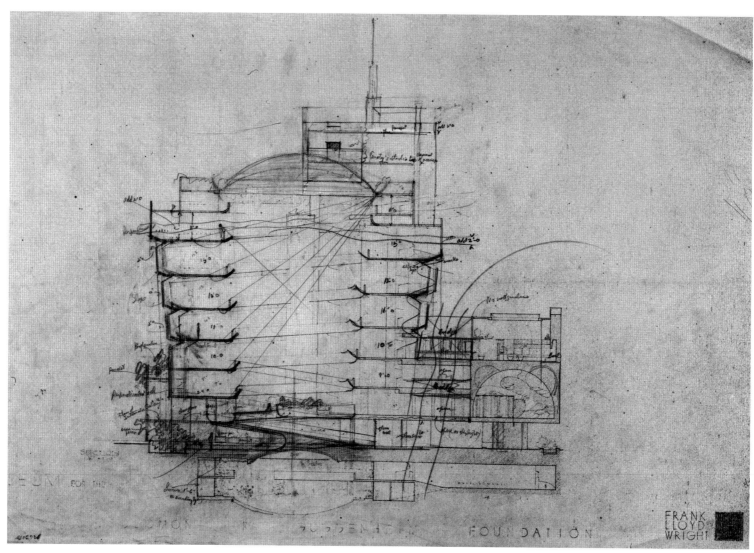

308. Section (FLLW; c. 1945). Pencil and color
pencil on print, 23½ x 36". The Frank Lloyd
Wright Foundation

SOLOMON R. GUGGENHEIM MUSEUM
New York, New York. 1943–59

309. Interior view from above

310.   Interior view from below

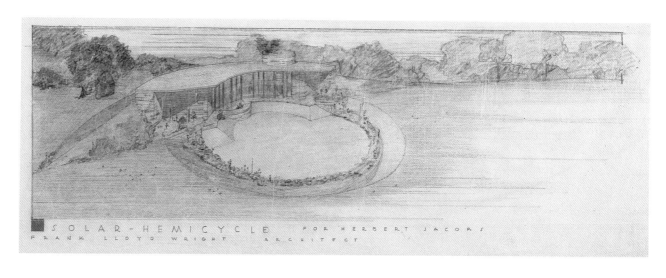

SOLAR-HEMICYCLE   FOR HERBERT JACOBS
FRANK LLOYD WRIGHT   ARCHITECT

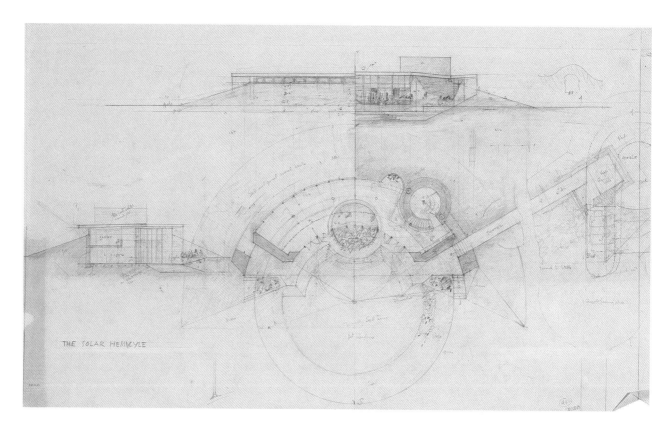

THE SOLAR HEMICYLE

Solar Hemicycle
HERBERT JACOBS HOUSE
Middleton, Wisconsin. 1943–48

Opposite
311.   Aerial perspective (FLLW). Pencil and color pencil on paper, 12⅝ x 31". The Frank Lloyd Wright Foundation

312.   Exterior

313.   Plan, elevation, and section (FLLW). Pencil and color pencil on tracing paper, 19⅞ x 34¼". The Frank Lloyd Wright Foundation

Left
314.   Living room

METEOR CRATER INN   Sunset Crater National Monument, Arizona. Project, 1947–48

315.   Aerial perspective (FLLW and JHH). Pencil, color pencil, and ink on tracing paper, 21 x 35⅝". The Frank Lloyd Wright Foundation

Frank Lloyd Wright and Lloyd Wright, Associate

COTTAGE GROUP HOTEL AND SPORTS CLUB FOR HUNTINGTON HARTFORD

Hollywood, California. Project, 1946–48

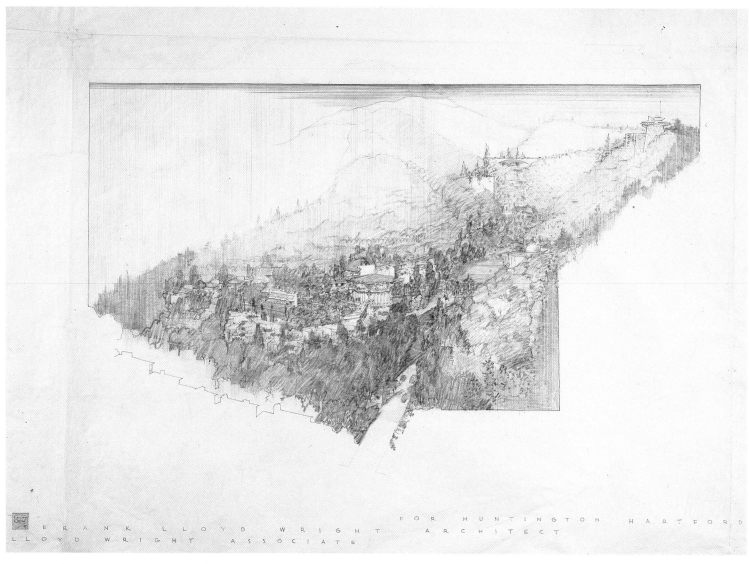

316.   Aerial perspective (JHH). Crayon and ink on tracing paper, 35¼ x 47⅞". Erving and Joyce Wolf Collection

Opposite
317.   Perspective: sports club (JHH). Ink
and color pencil on tracing paper, 35½ x 52".
The Frank Lloyd Wright Foundation

318.   Plan and elevation: sports club (FLLW).
Pencil, color pencil, and ink on tracing paper,
45⅝" x 6'2". The Frank Lloyd Wright Foundation

COUNTRY CLUB FOR HUNTINGTON HARTFORD HOLLYWOOD
FRANK LLOYD WRIGHT ARCHITECT

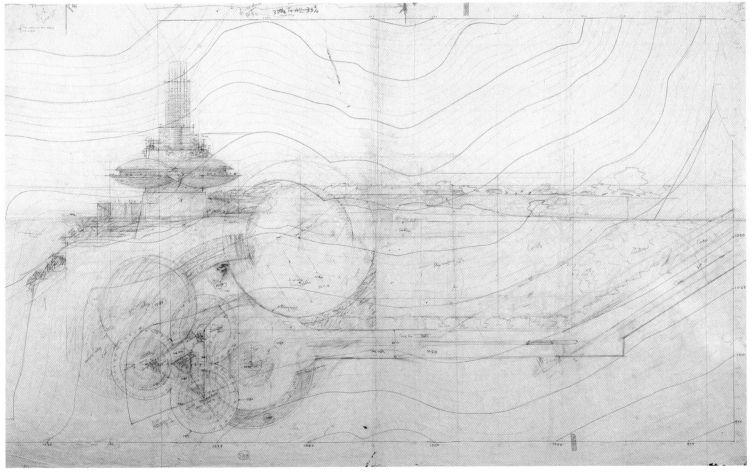

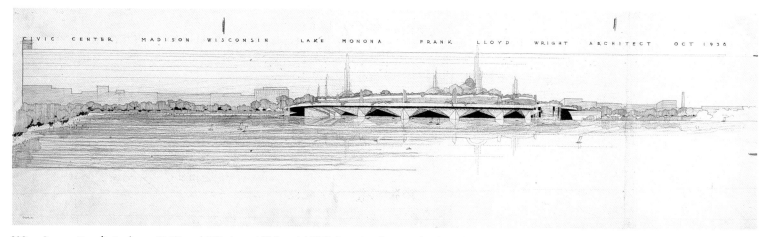

319. Perspective, first scheme (FLLW and JHH; insc. 1938 and 1953). Pencil, color pencil, ink, and gold ink on tracing paper, 11⅝ x 39⅞".
The Frank Lloyd Wright Foundation

MONONA TERRACE CIVIC CENTER Madison, Wisconsin. Project, 1938–53

320. Aerial perspective, first scheme (FLLW and JHH). Pencil, color pencil, and ink on tracing paper, 17¼ x 40". The Frank Lloyd Wright Foundation

Wright's identification with the Southwest confirmed the gradual but steady reorientation of his architectural practice from the city and garden suburb to the less developed regions of the country, which were increasingly accessible owing to the expansion of the country's highway system and the popularity of the automobile in the 1940s and 1950s.

Nevertheless, his reemergence as a leading figure in architecture ensured that he would continue to receive commissions for projects within a traditional urban context, many of them quite large. Among his projects during this period, the Monona Terrace Civic Center (above) displayed the most sympathy for its metropolis: it formed an extension of the existing axis between Madison's domed capitol and Lake Monona.

Later projects, such as Crystal Heights in Washington, D.C. (opposite), and Pittsburgh Point Park Civic Center (plates 322–326), were characterized less by their relationship to the traditional city than by Wright's attempt to integrate his vision of a mobile society into the city's fabric. The open plaza of Crystal Heights hovers above street level, separated from it by a multistory parking garage. In the proposals for the redevelopment of Pittsburgh's Point Park, bridges brought high-speed traffic to the architectural focal point—a monumental, hivelike structure containing a host of civic amenities, including an auditorium, theaters, a plane-

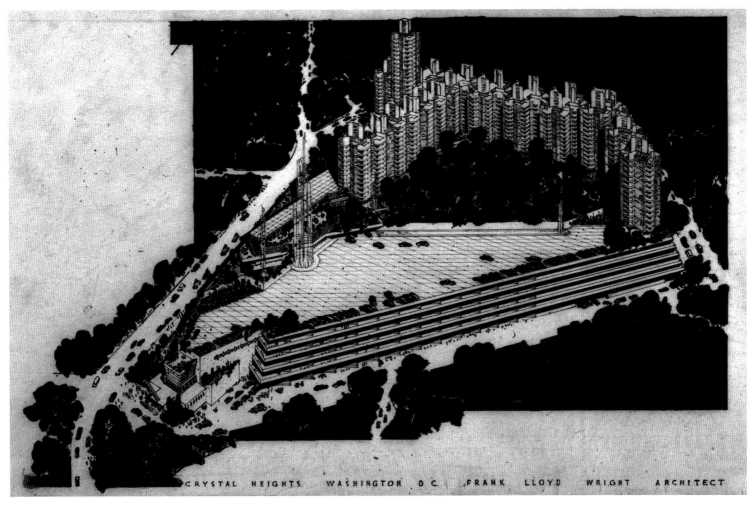

CRYSTAL HEIGHTS Washington, D.C. Project, 1939
321. Aerial perspective (FLLW and JHH). Ink and pencil on tracing paper, 31½ x 34⅞". The Frank Lloyd Wright Foundation

tarium, and an aquarium—which was ringed by parking facilities. The festive atmosphere on the waterfront was an imaginative transformation of a gritty industrial city. When the grandiose designs, financed by Edgar J. Kaufmann, Wright's greatest patron, had little chance of realization, Kaufmann commissioned a Self-Service Garage (plates 327–328) attached to his department store; it was an enormous structure of interlocking, spiral ramps suspended from massive concrete pylons that monumentalized the city's ambivalent relationship with the automobile.

Wright's urban projects of this period also included the further development of his tap-root skyscraper, culminating in the dramatic proposal for The Mile High Illinois (plates 341–342) on Chicago's lakefront, an appropriately hubristic proposition for a city whose maxim "Make no little plans" still rings true. The Mile High far surpassed any of the great towers of the past. Unlike the pattern of high-rise construction Wright had earlier endorsed in his Skyscraper Regulation proposal, his new designs, such as the Rogers Lacy Hotel (plates 331–332), which featured a shimmering tower sheathed in glass rising out of an open atrium, and the H. C. Price Company Tower (plates 333–338), the only one of these projects to have been realized, were designed as isolated, sculptural structures for the relatively open landscapes of Dallas, Texas, and Bartlesville, Oklahoma.

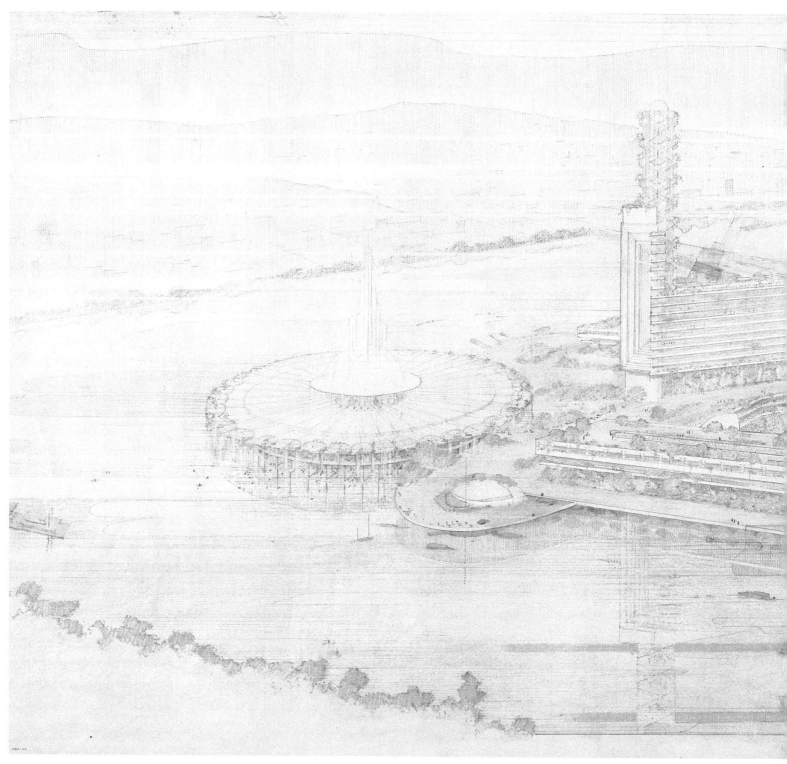

322. Aerial perspective, first scheme (JHH). Ink, pencil, and color pencil on tracing paper, 33½" x 6'1¾". The Frank Lloyd Wright Foundation

PITTSBURGH POINT PARK CIVIC CENTER
Pittsburgh, Pennsylvania. Project, 1947–48

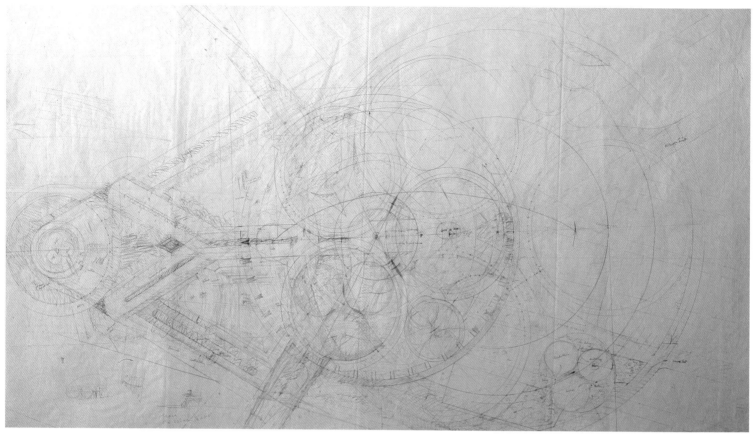

323. Plan, first scheme (FLLW). Pencil and color pencil on tracing paper, 54½" x 8'5". The Frank Lloyd Wright Foundation

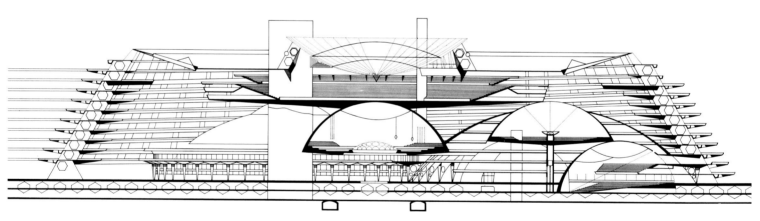

324. Section, first scheme

PITTSBURGH POINT PARK CIVIC CENTER
Pittsburgh, Pennsylvania. Project, 1947–48

Opposite
325. Perspective: bridge, second scheme (AD). Ink, gold ink, pencil, and color pencil on tracing paper, 29 x 44". The Frank Lloyd Wright Foundation

326. Elevation: bridge, second scheme (AD). Color pencil on tracing paper, 28⅛ x 56³⁄₁₆". The Carnegie Museum of Art, Pittsburgh. Museum purchase: Gift of Women's Committee of the Museum of Art, Carnegie Treasures Cookbook Fund

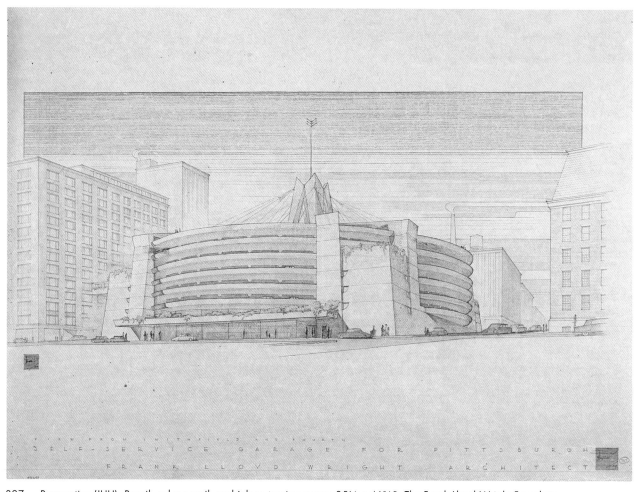

327. Perspective (JHH). Pencil, color pencil, and ink on tracing paper, 35½ x 46¾". The Frank Lloyd Wright Foundation

SELF-SERVICE GARAGE   Pittsburgh, Pennsylvania. Project, 1949

328. Section (JHH). Color pencil and ink on tracing paper, 35⅝ x 46⅝". The Frank Lloyd Wright Foundation

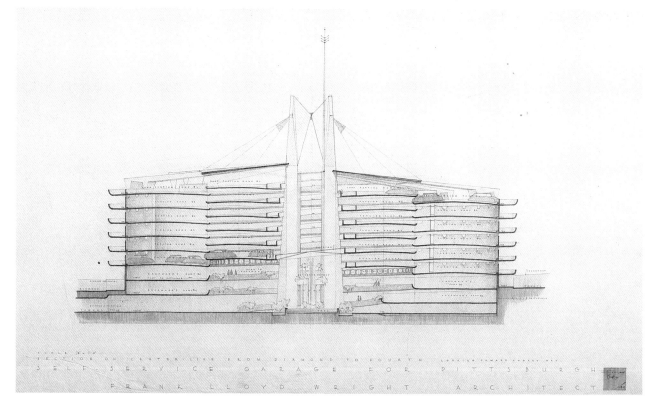

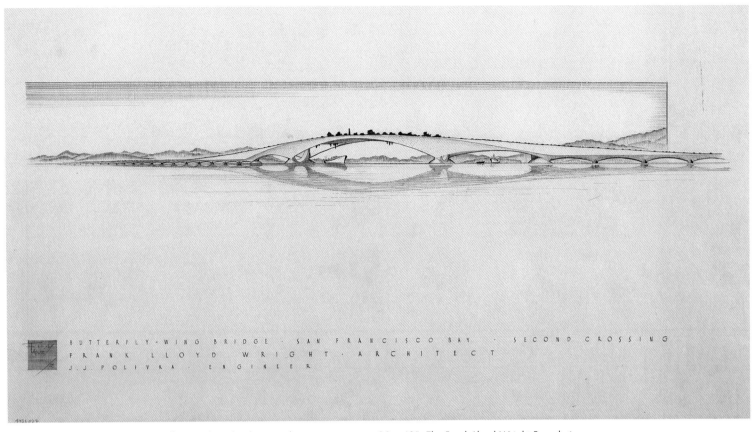

329. Perspective (AGG; 1953). Ink, pencil, and color pencil on tracing paper, 23 x 42". The Frank Lloyd Wright Foundation

Frank Lloyd Wright and J. J. Polivka, Engineer **SAN FRANCISCO BRIDGE** San Francisco, California. Project, 1949–53

330. Aerial perspective (1949). Ink, pencil, and color pencil on tracing paper, 19¾ x 35¼". The Frank Lloyd Wright Foundation

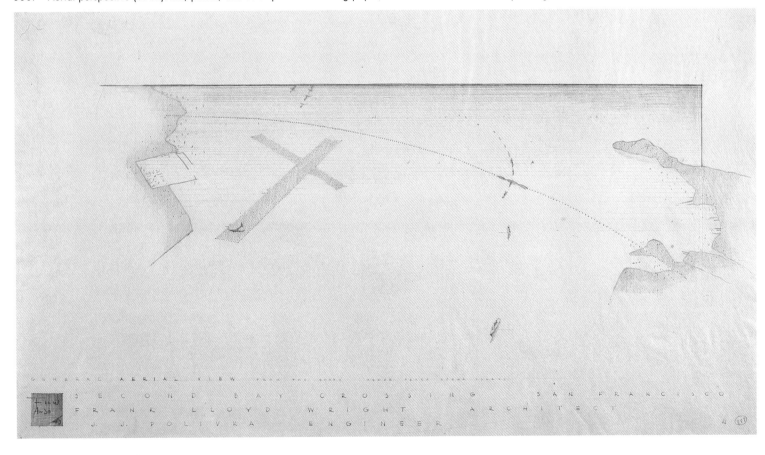

ROGERS LACY HOTEL
Dallas, Texas. Project, 1946–47

331. Perspective (JHH). Pencil, color pencil,
and ink on Japanese paper, 52¾ x 27⅞".
The Frank Lloyd Wright Foundation

332. Section (JHH). Color pencil and ink on Japanese paper, 65¾ x 36¼". The Frank Lloyd Wright Foundation

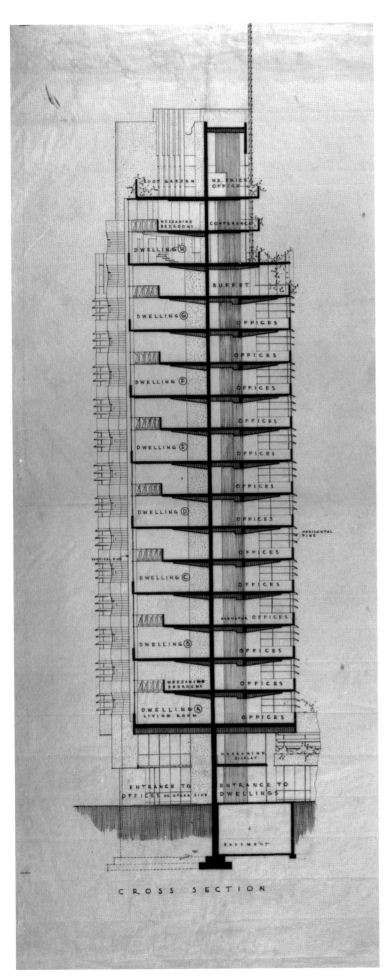

CROSS SECTION

H. C. PRICE COMPANY TOWER

Bartlesville, Oklahoma. 1952–56

333. Perspective (JHH). Color pencil and ink on tracing paper, 47⅞ x 33⅞". Erving and Joyce Wolf Collection

334. Section. Ink on tracing paper, 64¾ x 36". The Frank Lloyd Wright Foundation

335. Interior of typical apartment

336. Typical floor plan (ALW). Ink on tracing paper, 25½ x 36". The Frank Lloyd Wright Foundation

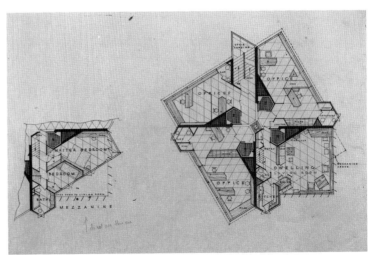

H. C. PRICE COMPANY TOWER
Bartlesville, Oklahoma. 1952–56

337. Exterior detail

338. General view

Opposite
POINT VIEW RESIDENCES
Pittsburgh, Pennsylvania. Project, 1952–53

339. Perspective, second scheme (FLLW and JHH; 1953). Ink, pencil, and color pencil on tracing paper, 34½ x 29". The Frank Lloyd Wright Foundation

VIEW FROM NORTHWEST
POINT VIEW RESIDENCES
FOR THE EDGAR J. KAUFMANN CHARITABLE TRUST
FRANK LLOYD WRIGHT ARCHITECT SHEET

**THE GOLDEN BEACON
APARTMENT BUILDING**
Chicago, Illinois. Project, 1956–57

340. Perspective (FLLW and AD). Pencil, color pencil, and gold ink on tracing paper. 46½ x 22¾". The Frank Lloyd Wright Foundation

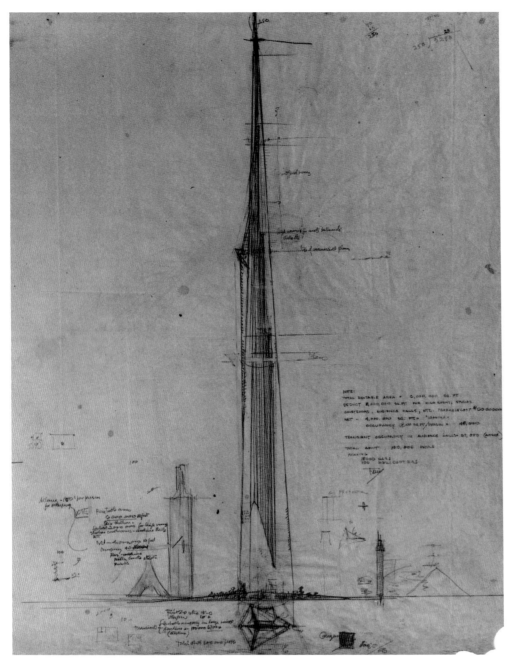

341. Elevation and plan (FLLW). Pencil on tracing paper, 36⅛ x 38¾". The Frank Lloyd Wright Foundation

THE MILE HIGH ILLINOIS
Chicago, Illinois. Project, 1956

342. Perspective (FLLW and AD). Pencil, color pencil, ink, and gold ink on tracing paper, 8' x 23⅜". The Frank Lloyd Wright Foundation

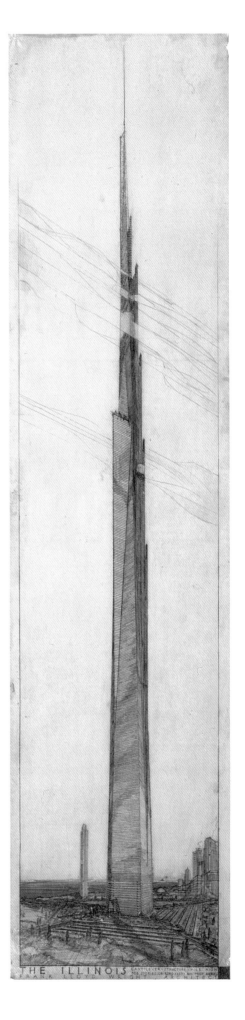

Nearly eighty years old at the end of World War II, Wright was widely hailed as the dean of American architects. While his relationship with the architectural establishment remained controversial, no other architect enjoyed such great popularity and celebrity among the American public. The transformation from a wartime to a consumer economy and the ensuing economic growth of the 1950s gave Wright a continuously expanding practice that, at his death in 1959, was as busy as it had ever been.

Wright's success in the postwar years had as much to do with his acuity in understanding American culture as any economic factors, particularly with regard to the automobile. His roadside projects such as the Lindholm Oil Company Service Station (plate 366) and Daniel Wieland Motor Hotel (plate 367) represent the evolution of a new type of American architecture, related to and dependent on the roadway.

Wright had predicted that the automobile would make home ownership feasible to a broad section of the middle class and greatly expand the scale of private living for his wealthier clients, as seen in the Boulder House for Liliane and Edgar J. Kaufmann in Palm Springs (plate 351), Crownfield, the Robert F. Windfohr House in Fort Worth (above and opposite), and the Grandma House for Harold C. Price in Paradise Valley (plates 360–363), which were characterized by sprawling plans and sensuous profiles. Wright also continued his interest in low-cost construction systems that could keep the single-family home affordable. The Usonian Automatic, such as the W. B. Tracy House (plates 355–356), was a simplified version of the concrete-block system, designed to allow the less wealthy but industrious client to assist in the construction of his or her own home.

The assimilation of modern architecture into the postwar mainstream presented a new challenge for Wright and other avant-garde architects. In the wake of rapid suburban development, new churches and synagogues were needed to serve congregations that had migrated from the inner city, and Wright found himself in his advanced years with numerous projects for religious structures. He also began several government projects, such as the Marin County Civic Center, his first government building (plates 386–392), and a proposal for the Arizona State Capitol (plates 383–385), which like his late churches were designed in a triumphant style that confirmed the buoyant optimism of postwar America.

Wright's last projects serve as a portrait of the architect in his late years: the bold gesture, which had characterized his life's work, remains, though frequently without the intense elaboration and development of his earlier work. The ornamentation, more effusive and sensuous but decidedly less architectonic, conveys a sense of lightness in its diaphanous materials and ethereal forms.

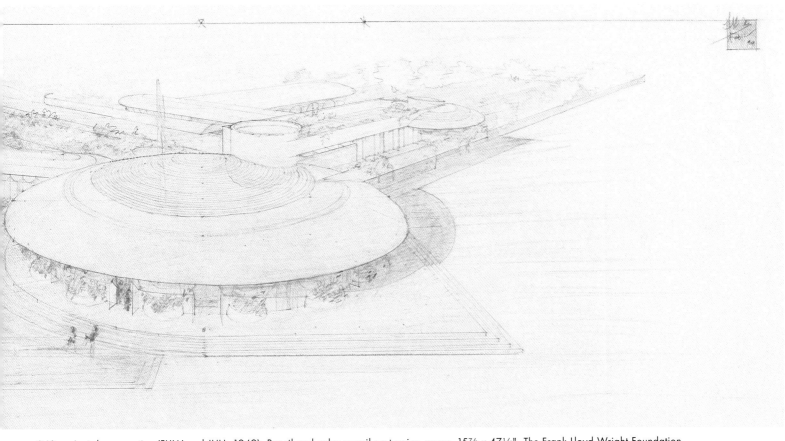

343.   Aerial perspective (FLLW and JHH; 1949). Pencil and color pencil on tracing paper, 15⅞ x 47¼". The Frank Lloyd Wright Foundation

Crownfield   ROBERT F. WINDFOHR HOUSE   Fort Worth, Texas. Project, 1948–50

344.   Interior perspective (1949). Pencil, color pencil, and ink on tracing paper, 23 x 47". The Frank Lloyd Wright Foundation

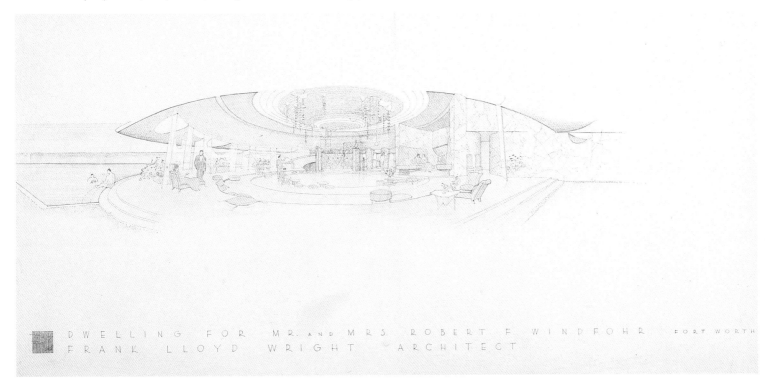

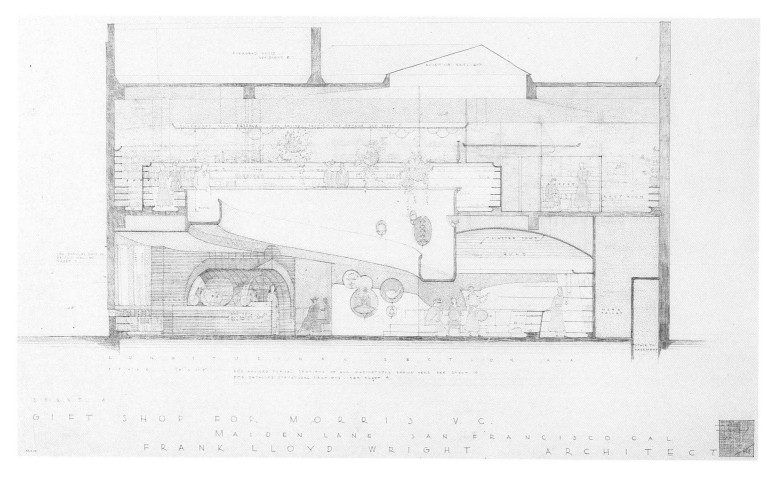

GIFT SHOP FOR MORRIS V.C.
MAIDEN LANE SAN FRANCISCO CAL.
FRANK LLOYD WRIGHT ARCHITECT

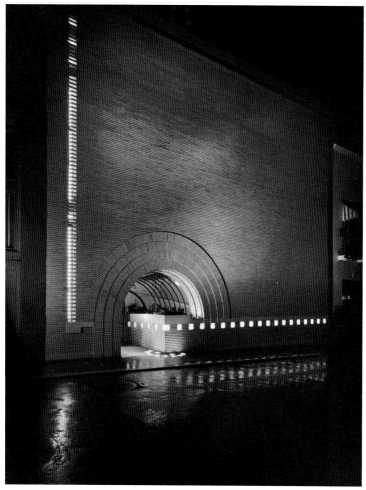

Opposite

V. C. MORRIS GIFT SHOP
San Francisco, California. 1948–49

345. Section (FLLW and JHH). Pencil, color pencil, and ink on tracing paper, 29½ x 36". The Frank Lloyd Wright Foundation

346. Exterior

347. Interior

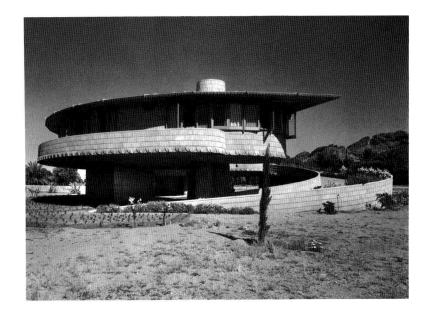

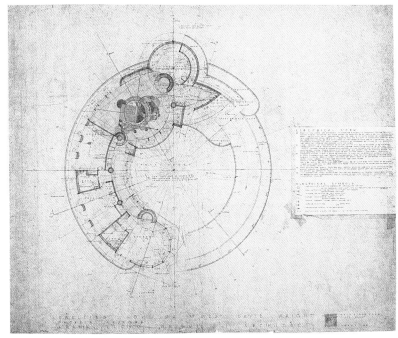

DAVID WRIGHT HOUSE
Phoenix, Arizona. 1950–52

348. Exterior

349. Plan (FLLW and JHH). Pencil and color pencil on print, 29 x 36". The Frank Lloyd Wright Foundation

350. Living room

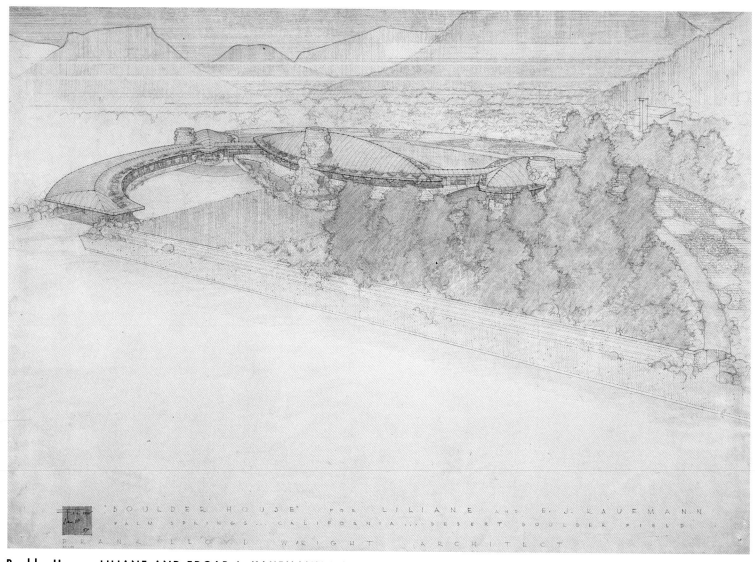

Boulder House LILIANE AND EDGAR J. KAUFMANN HOUSE   Palm Springs, California. Project, 1951

351.   Aerial perspective. Pencil, color pencil, and ink on tracing paper, 25¼ x 35¼". The Frank Lloyd Wright Foundation

352. Exterior

353. Living room

ROBERT LLEWELLYN WRIGHT HOUSE Bethesda, Maryland. 1953–57

354. Plan and elevation (FLLW). Pencil, color pencil, and ink on tracing paper, 18¼ x 25¼". The Frank Lloyd Wright Foundation

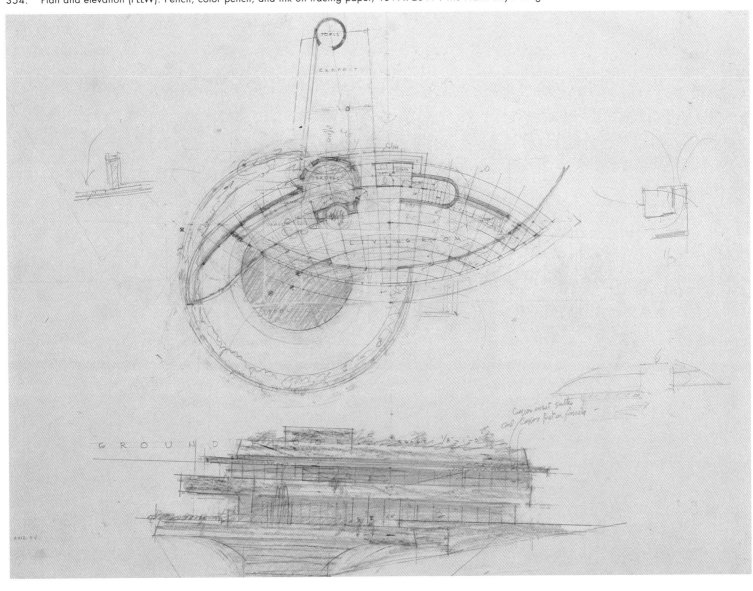

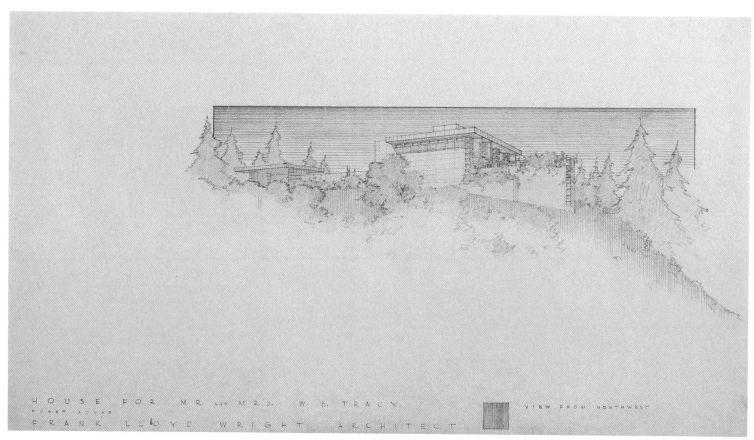

HOUSE FOR MR. AND MRS. W. B. TRACY
PUGET SOUND
FRANK LLOYD WRIGHT ARCHITECT   VIEW FROM NORTHWEST

355.   Perspective. Pencil and color pencil on tracing paper, 19½ x 35¼". The Frank Lloyd Wright Foundation

356.   Exterior

W. B. TRACY HOUSE
Normandy Park, Washington. 1954–56

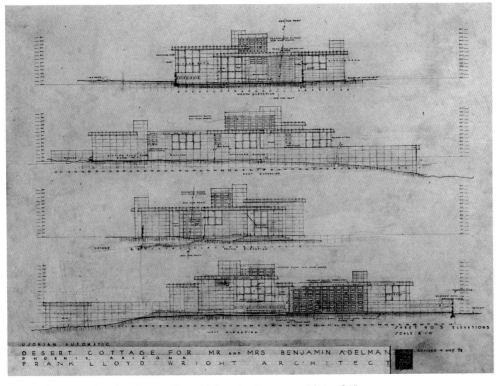

BENJAMIN ADELMAN HOUSE
Phoenix, Arizona. 1951–53

357. Elevations. Pencil, color pencil, and ink on tracing paper, 30¼ x 36".
The Frank Lloyd Wright Foundation

358. Exterior

359. Interior detail

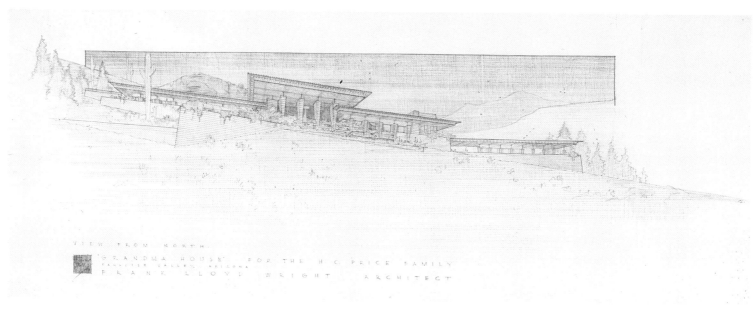

360.   Perspective (JHH). Pencil, color pencil, and ink on tracing paper, 19½ x 50¼". The Frank Lloyd Wright Foundation

Grandma House   HAROLD C. PRICE HOUSE   Paradise Valley, Arizona. 1954–55

361.   Plan and elevation (FLLW). Pencil, color pencil, and ink on tracing paper, 36 x 62⅜". The Frank Lloyd Wright Foundation

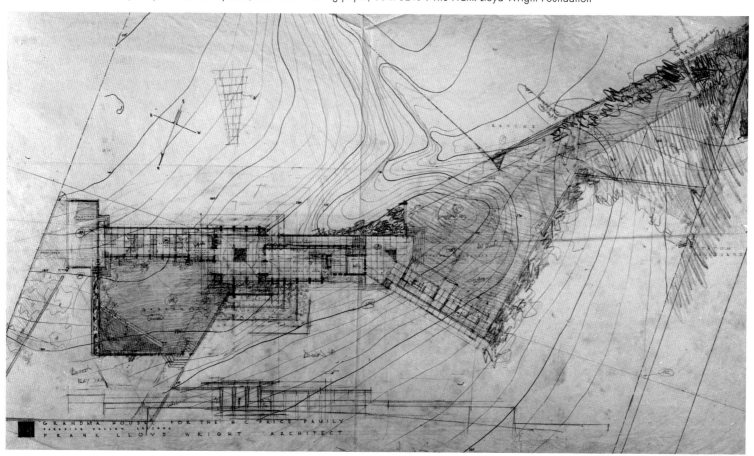

362. Entrance

363. Atrium

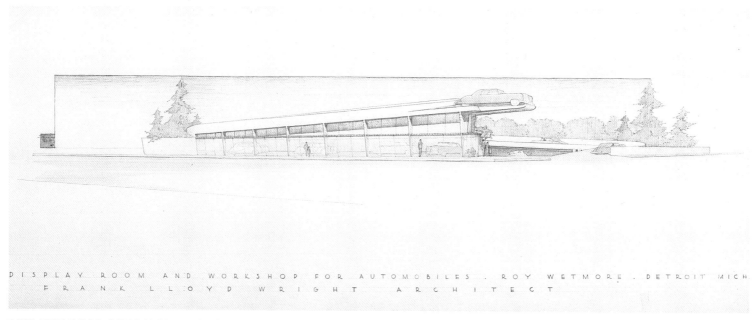

DISPLAY ROOM AND WORKSHOP FOR AUTOMOBILES . ROY WETMORE . DETROIT MICH.
FRANK LLOYD WRIGHT ARCHITECT

ROY WETMORE AUTOMOBILE SHOWROOM   Detroit, Michigan. Project. 1947–48

364.   Perspective (JHH). Color pencil and ink on tracing paper, 18 x 44⅝". The Frank Lloyd Wright Foundation

Below
ADELMAN LAUNDRY   Milwaukee, Wisconsin. Project, 1945

365.   Aerial perspective (JHH). Ink and sepia ink on tracing paper, 23½ x 36½". The Frank Lloyd Wright Foundation

Opposite

LINDHOLM OIL COMPANY SERVICE STATION   Cloquet, Minnesota. 1956–57

366.   Perspective (JHH). Pencil, color pencil, and ink on tracing paper, 17¾ x 22¾". The Frank Lloyd Wright Foundation

DANIEL WIELAND MOTOR HOTEL   Hagerstown, Maryland. Project, 1955–57

367.   Aerial perspective (AD; 1955). Ink, pencil, and color pencil on tracing paper, 17⅜ x 36⅛". The Frank Lloyd Wright Foundation

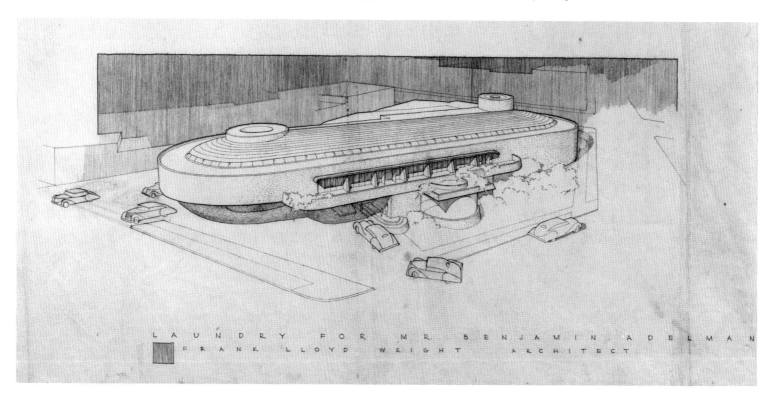

LAUNDRY FOR MR. BENJAMIN ADELMAN
FRANK LLOYD WRIGHT ARCHITECT

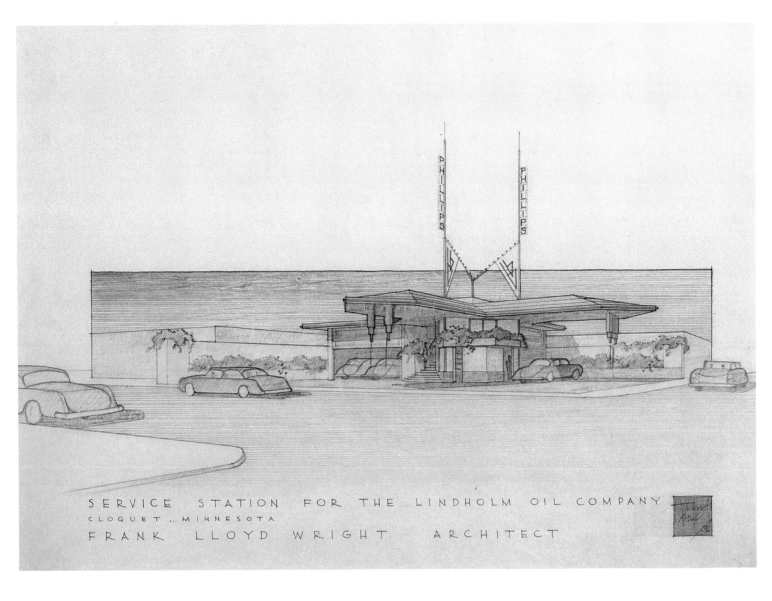

SERVICE STATION FOR THE LINDHOLM OIL COMPANY
CLOQUET , MINNESOTA
FRANK LLOYD WRIGHT ARCHITECT

MOTOR HOTEL FOR MR. DANIEL WIELAND HAGERSTOWN, MD
FRANK LLOYD WRIGHT, ARCHITECT

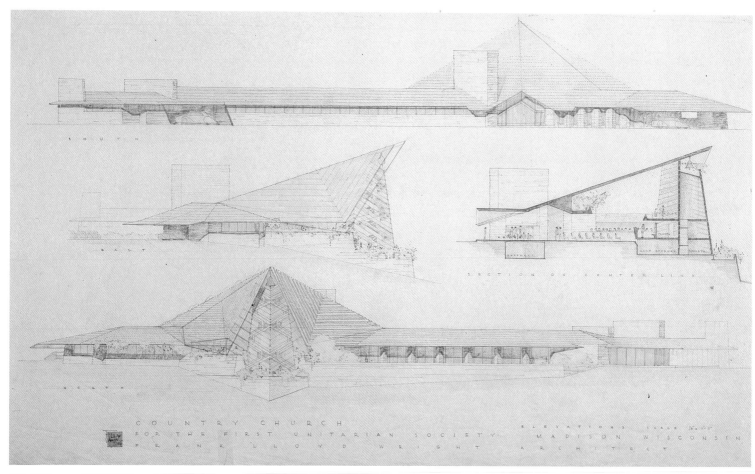

368. Elevations and section (JHH; insc. 1945).
Pencil, color pencil, and ink on tracing paper.
The Frank Lloyd Wright Foundation

UNITARIAN CHURCH
Madison, Wisconsin. 1945–51

369. Exterior

Opposite above
370. Interior

Rhododendron Chapel
EDGAR J. KAUFMANN FAMILY CHAPEL

Mill Run, Pennsylvania. Project, 1951–52

371.   Plan and elevations. Pencil on illustration board, 28 x 35¼". The John H. Howe Collection, The State Historical Society of Wisconsin

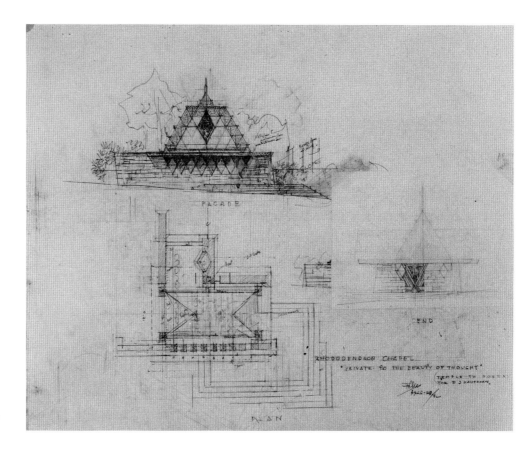

372.   Elevation and section. Pencil, color pencil, and ink on tracing paper, 28¾ x 36⅛". The Frank Lloyd Wright Foundation

BETH SHOLOM SYNAGOGUE
Elkins Park, Pennsylvania. 1953–59

373.   Exterior

374.   Plan: 1 entrance, 2 vestibule, 3 sanctuary, 4 altar

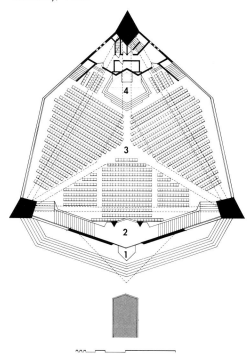

375. Interior

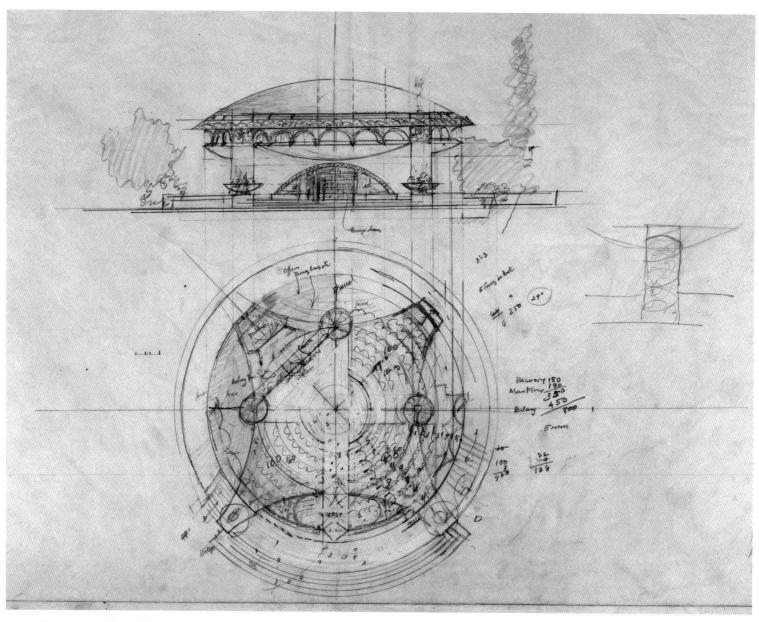

376.   Elevation and plan (FLLW). Pencil and color pencil on tracing paper, 29¾ x 36". The Frank Lloyd Wright Foundation

ANNUNCIATION GREEK ORTHODOX CHURCH
Wauwatosa, Wisconsin. 1955–61

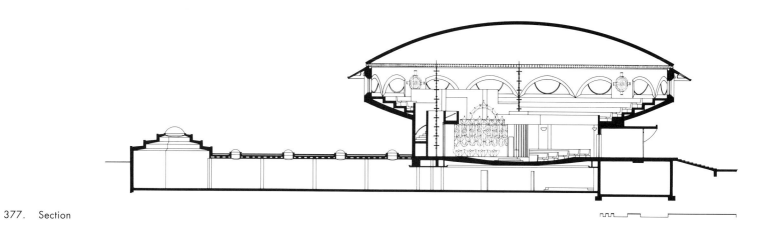

377.   Section

378. Entrance

379. Interior

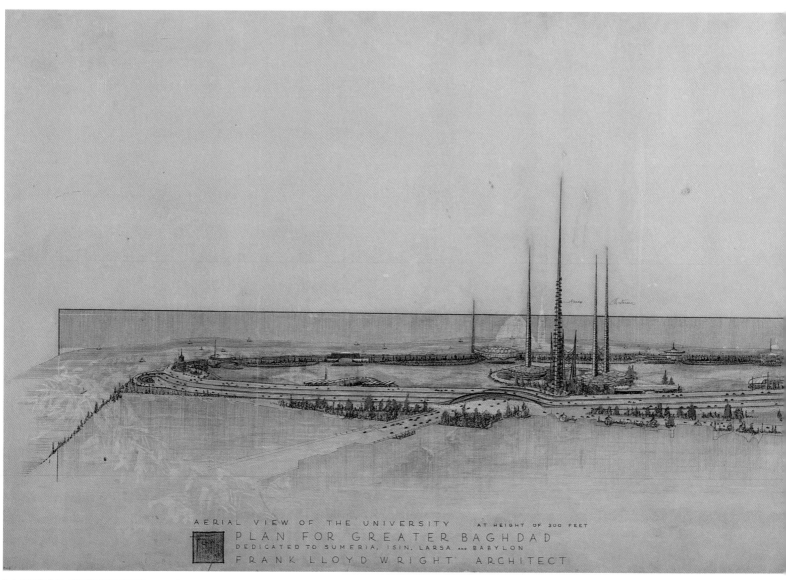

BAGHDAD UNIVERSITY   Baghdad, Iraq. Project, 1957

380.   Aerial perspective (JR). Pencil, color pencil, ink, and tempera on tracing paper, 33¾ x 70¾". The Frank Lloyd Wright Foundation

Opposite

MONUMENT TO HAROUN AL-RASHID, BAGHDAD CULTURAL CENTER
Baghdad, Iraq. Project, 1957

381.   Elevation (FLLW and ALW). Pencil and color pencil on tracing paper, 27 x 34½".
The Frank Lloyd Wright Foundation

OPERA HOUSE, BAGHDAD CULTURAL CENTER
Baghdad, Iraq. Project, 1957

382.   Perspective (AD). Pencil, color pencil, ink, and gold ink on tracing paper, 36 x 59¾".
The Frank Lloyd Wright Foundation

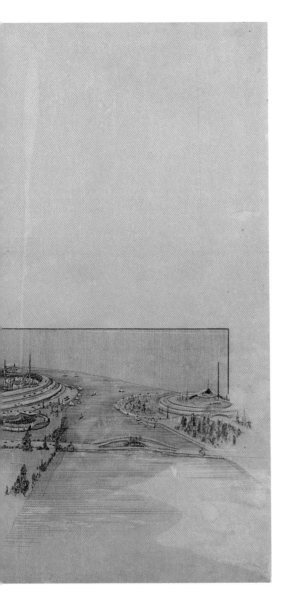

HAROUN AL RASHID

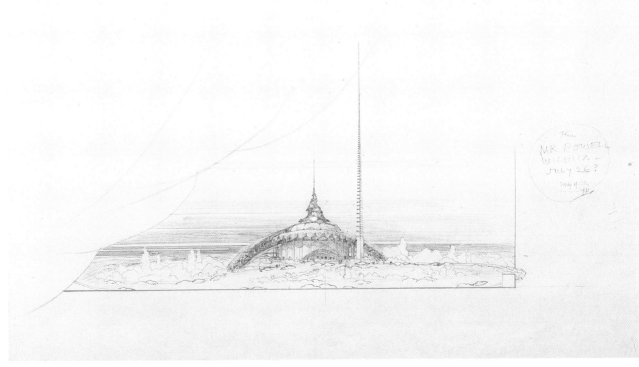

FROM
MR POWELL
WICHITA —
JULY 26?

315

383. Aerial perspective (FLLW and JHH). Pencil, color pencil, and ink on tracing paper, 35⅛ x 45½". The Frank Lloyd Wright Foundation

Oasis
ARIZONA STATE CAPITOL
Phoenix, Arizona. Project, 1957

Opposite
384. Perspective of colonnade (FLLW and JHH). Pencil, color pencil, and ink on tracing paper, 35¼ x 45⅝". The Frank Lloyd Wright Foundation

385. Section. Pencil, color pencil, and ink on tracing paper, 36 x 60". The Frank Lloyd Wright Foundation

PRO BONO PUBLICO ARIZONA
FRANK LLOYD WRIGHT ARCHITECT
LONGITUDINAL SECTION

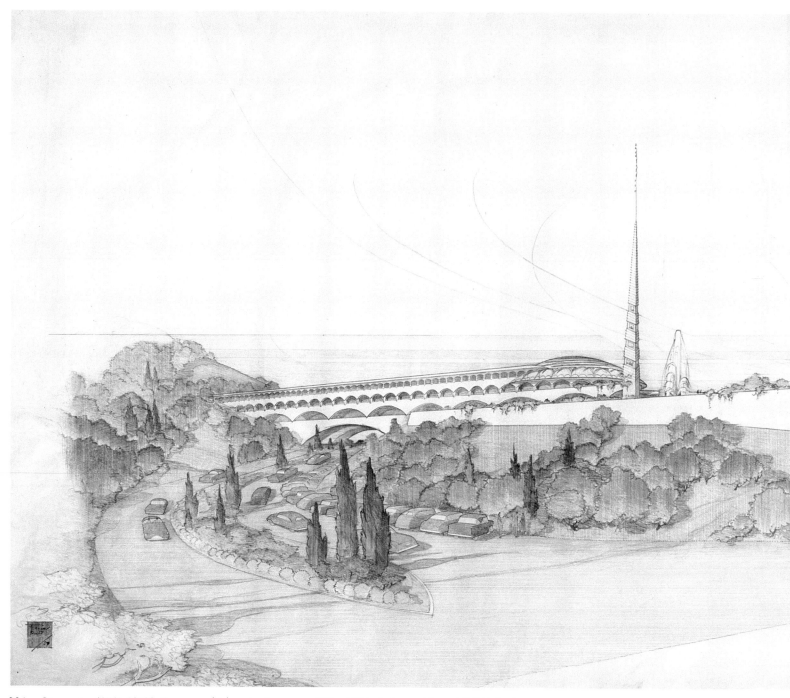

386.   Perspective (ALW; 1957). Crayon and ink on tracing paper, 34" x 6'11". Erving and Joyce Wolf Collection

Frank Lloyd Wright and Aaron G. Green, Associate
MARIN COUNTY CIVIC CENTER
San Rafael, California. 1957–62

MARIN COUNTY GOVERNMENT CENTER
FRANK LLOYD WRIGHT ARCHITECT

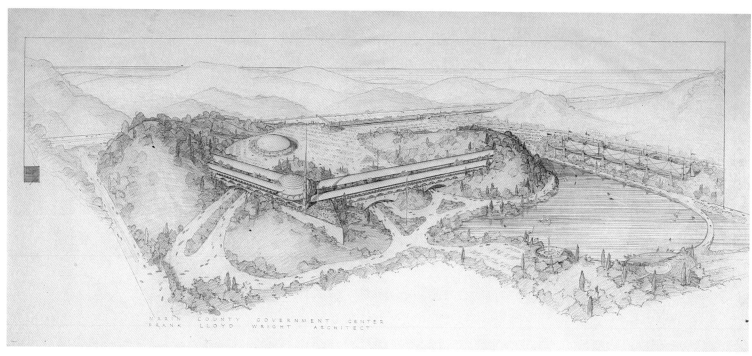

387.   Aerial perspective (JHH and ALW; 1957). Ink, pencil, and color pencil on tracing paper, 34½" x 6'2⅜". The Frank Lloyd Wright Foundation

Frank Lloyd Wright and Aaron G. Green, Associate
MARIN COUNTY CIVIC CENTER
San Rafael, California. 1957–62

388.   Perspective: fair pavilion (AD and JR; 1959). Pencil, color pencil, ink, and gold ink on tracing paper, 34¼ x 53½". The Frank Lloyd Wright Foundation

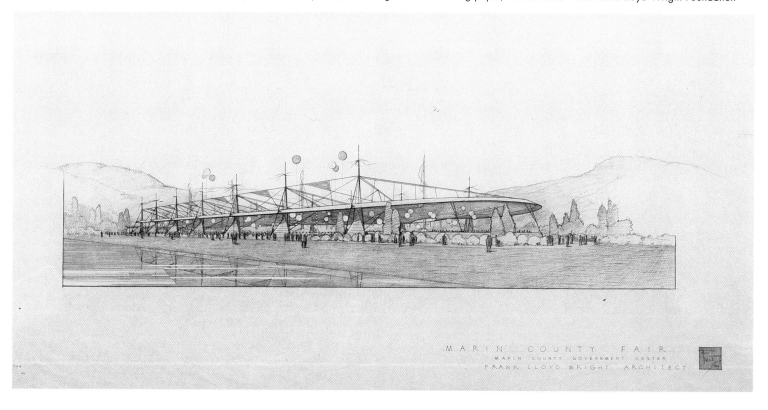

389. General view

390. Mall

391. Entrance

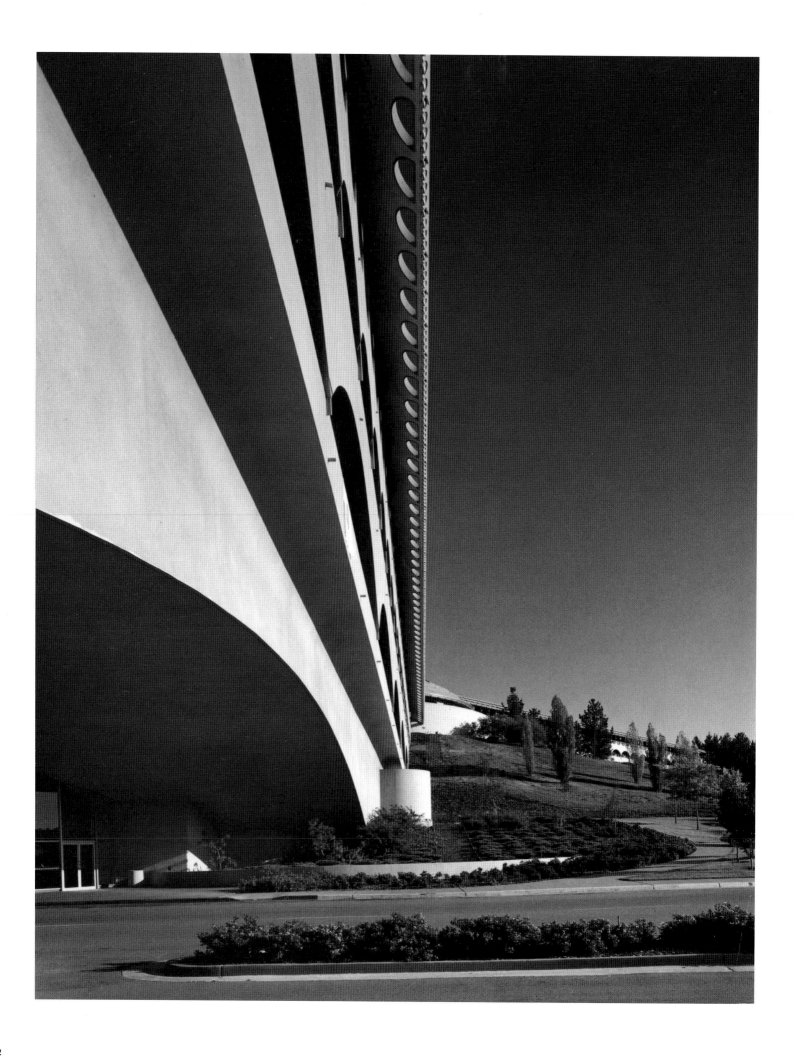

Frank Lloyd Wright and Aaron G. Green, Associate
MARIN COUNTY CIVIC CENTER
San Rafael, California. 1957–62

392.   Exterior detail

FINE ARTS CENTER, ARIZONA STATE UNIVERSITY   Tempe, Arizona. Project, 1959

393.   Plan and sketches (FLLW). Pencil on tracing paper, 30⅛ x 41⅝". The Frank Lloyd Wright Foundation

QUADRUPLE BLOCK PLAN FOR C. E. ROBERTS Oak Park, Illinois. Project, c. 1900–03

394. Plan (insc. 1911). Ink, ink wash, pencil, and color pencil on board, 11⅝ x 15". The Frank Lloyd Wright Foundation

Throughout his career Wright designed community plans that ranged in size from several blocks to a vast, utopian vision for America. As elaborations of the issues addressed in his architecture, these plans also provided a picture of his changing attitudes toward city and landscape, and the relationship between the individual and society in American culture.

His early schemes, such as the Quadruple Block Plan for C. E. Roberts (above and opposite), reflected his experiences as a young architect working in the suburbs. This plan elaborated on his ideal Prairie house, with four identical houses sited in rotated orientations (to allow privacy) on a single plot. The project addressed not only the economics of construction but also the principal concerns of city planners in the early twentieth century: increased light and openness, more green space, and lower density. A later scheme, the Noncompetitive Plan for City Residential Land Development (plate 400), represented these concerns in an entire neighborhood.

In the design of a new Montana town in the Bitter Root Valley, Wright's first scheme (plate 396) seems inspired by the relatively formal, gridded City Beautiful plans of Chicago architects such as Daniel Burnham and Edward Bennett. Despite the informal character of the natural site, Wright designed a grid whose principal axis was a two-level boulevard separating vehicular and pedestrian traffic. In his second scheme this was tempered by a picturesque plan (plates 397–398).

Wright's commissions for resort communities offered opportunities to indulge in

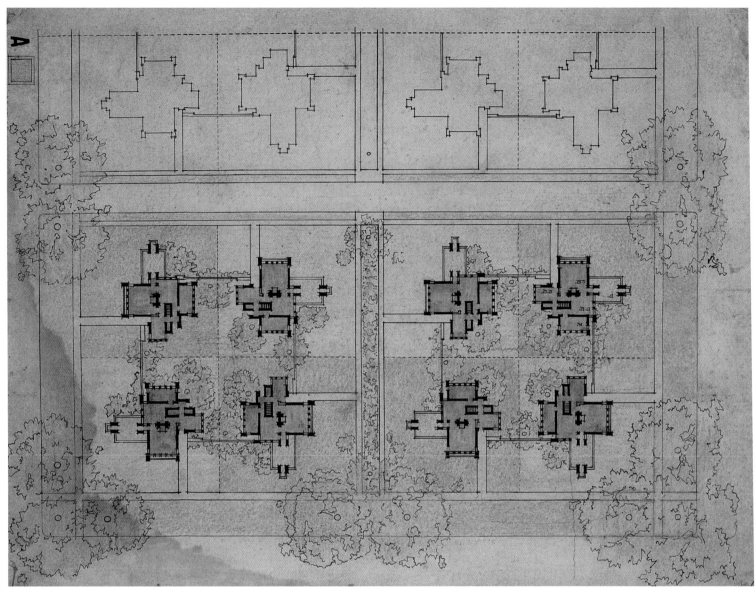

395. Plan. Ink and color pencil on linen, 11⅝ x 15". The Frank Lloyd Wright Foundation

more fanciful and romantic visions. For the Doheny Ranch Resort, on a terraced hillside in southern California, the road and viaduct threading through the hills invited the motorist to escape the city (plate 402).

Broadacre City, conceived during the Depression, was Wright's most comprehensive and polemical plan for a deurbanized America, which stressed individual home ownership and small businesses (plates 403–404). For Wright, only ruralism could foster true democracy. With a minimum density of one person per acre, Broadacre City was dependent on the automobile and electronic technology. A huge model, unveiled in 1935 and modified in later years, showed a four-square-mile settlement with the patchwork imagery of midwestern farmlands and an overall grid of highways.

To the extent that Broadacre City reflected the aspirations of the American middle class, Wright's prediction that it would build itself was nearly accurate. Inspired by his philosophy and architecture, several small cooperatives commissioned Wright to design residential communities, such as Cooperative Homesteads and Galesburg Country Homes (plates 407–408). These were among the few built components of the ideal Broadacre City. As society became increasingly mobile, the patterns of development in America, particularly after World War II, followed inexorably an expanding system of highways—the "horizontal line of Freedom," as Frank Lloyd Wright called it.

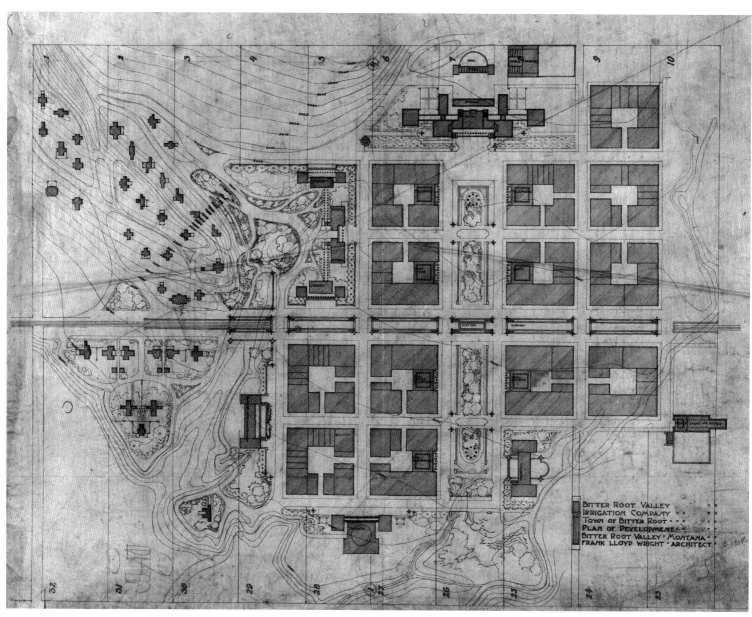

396.   Site plan. Ink and pencil on linen, 34⅝ x 37⅞". The Frank Lloyd Wright Foundation

VILLAGE OF BITTER ROOT
Darby, Montana. Project, 1909

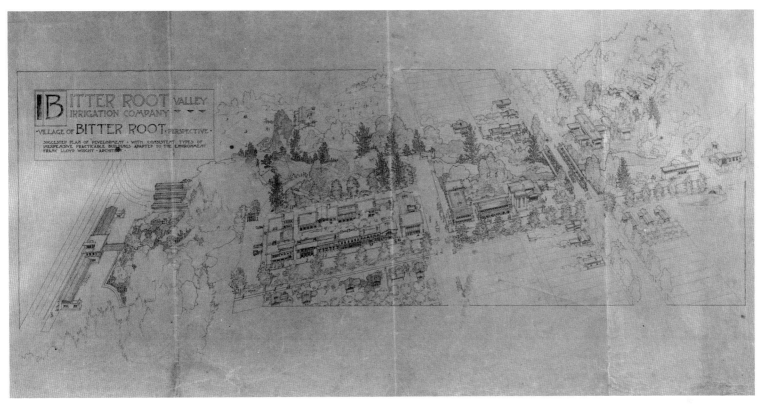

397.   Aerial perspective. Print on paper, 31½ x 63⅛". The Frank Lloyd Wright Foundation

398.   Site plan. Ink and pencil on linen, 39⅛ x 63⅜". The Frank Lloyd Wright Foundation

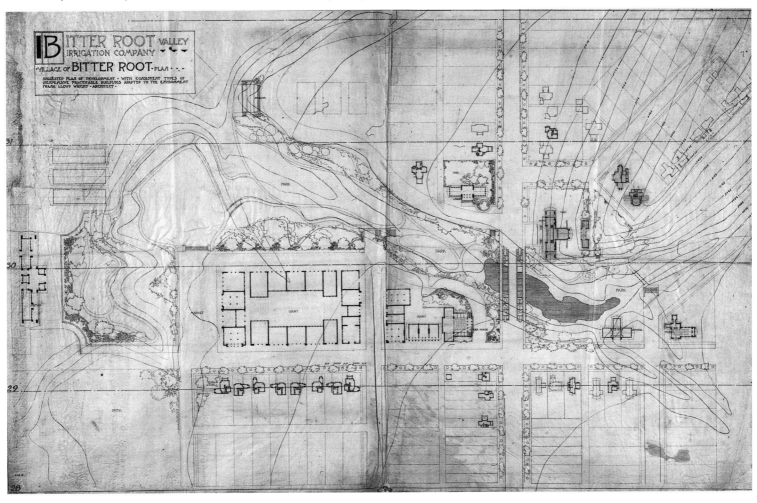

University Heights   COMO ORCHARDS SUMMER COLONY   Darby, Montana. 1909–10 (partially demolished)

399.   Aerial perspective (MM). Print on paper, 26⅝ x 41½". The Frank Lloyd Wright Foundation

NONCOMPETITIVE PLAN FOR CITY RESIDENTIAL LAND DEVELOPMENT   Chicago, Illinois, Project. c. 1913–16

400.   Aerial perspective. Whereabouts unknown

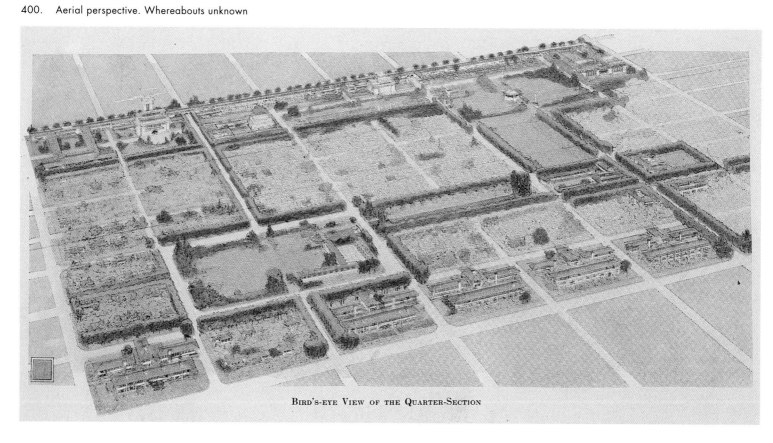

BIRD'S-EYE VIEW OF THE QUARTER-SECTION

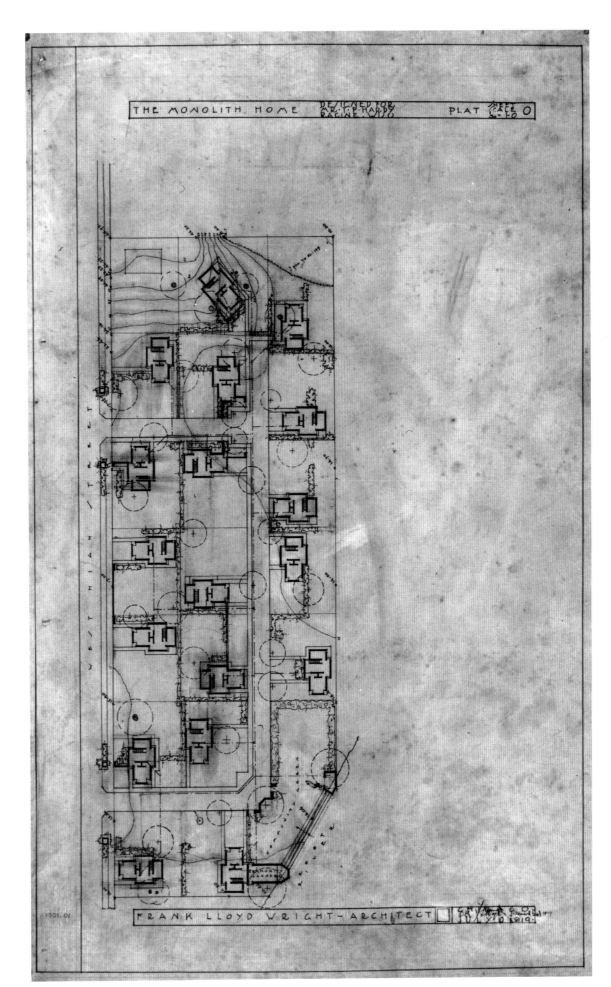

THE MONOLITH HOMES
FOR THOMAS P. HARDY
Racine, Wisconsin.
Project, 1919–20

401.   Site plan (RMS). Ink on
linen, 27¾ x 17¾". The Frank
Lloyd Wright Foundation

402. Perspective (FLLW; insc. 1921). Pencil and color pencil on tracing paper, 12½ x 28⅞". The Frank Lloyd Wright Foundation

DOHENY RANCH RESORT
Los Angeles, California. Project, 1923

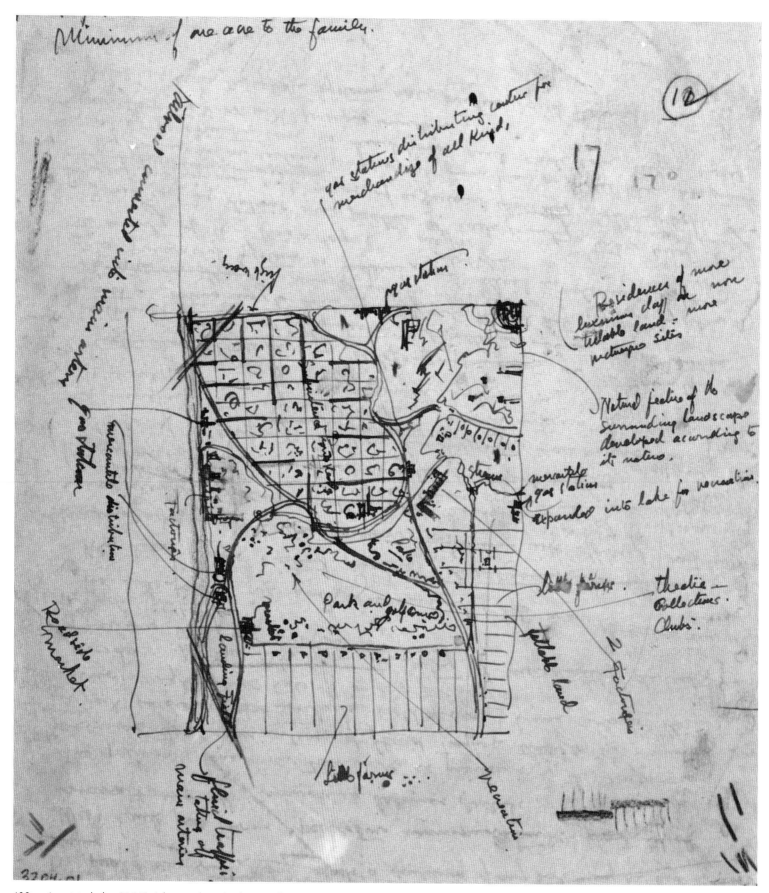

403. Annotated plan (FLLW). Ink, pencil, and color pencil on paper, 9⅜ x 8½". The Frank Lloyd Wright Foundation

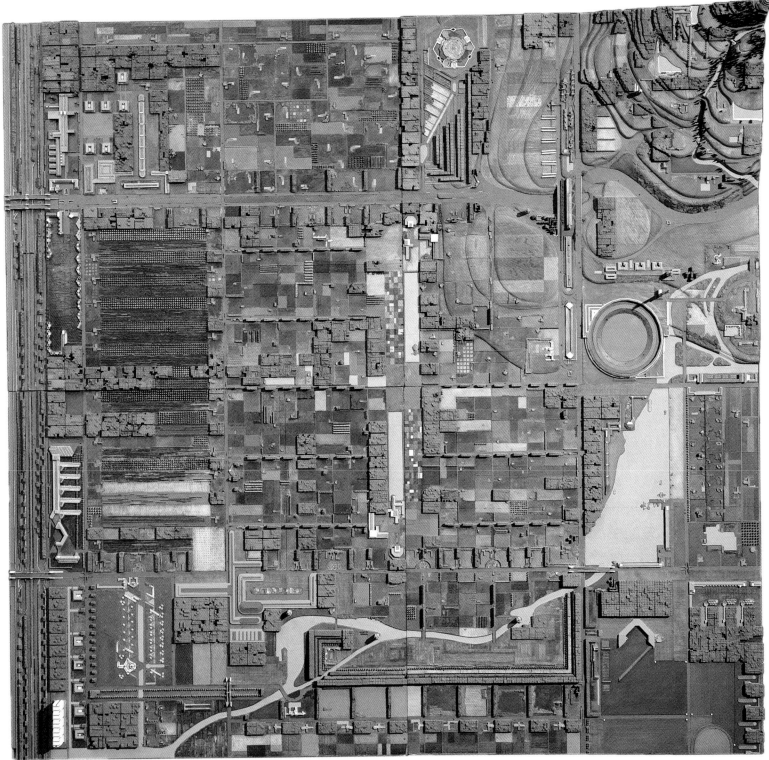

404.   Model (FLLW and the Taliesin Fellowship). Painted wood, cardboard, and paper, 12'8" x 12'8". The Frank Lloyd Wright Foundation

BROADACRE CITY
Project, 1934–35

USONIA I
Lansing, Michigan. Project, 1939

405.   Site plan (FLLW). Pencil and color pencil on tracing paper,
25½ x 24⅜". The Frank Lloyd Wright Foundation

CLOVERLEAF HOUSING PROJECT
Pittsfield, Massachusetts. Project, 1942

406.   Aerial perspective (1942). Pencil, color pencil, and ink on tracing
paper, 29⅞ x 36". The Frank Lloyd Wright Foundation

COOPERATIVE HOMESTEADS   Detroit, Michigan. Project, 1941–45

407.   Aerial perspective (1942). Ink on tracing paper, 27⅜ x 45⅜".
The Frank Lloyd Wright Foundation

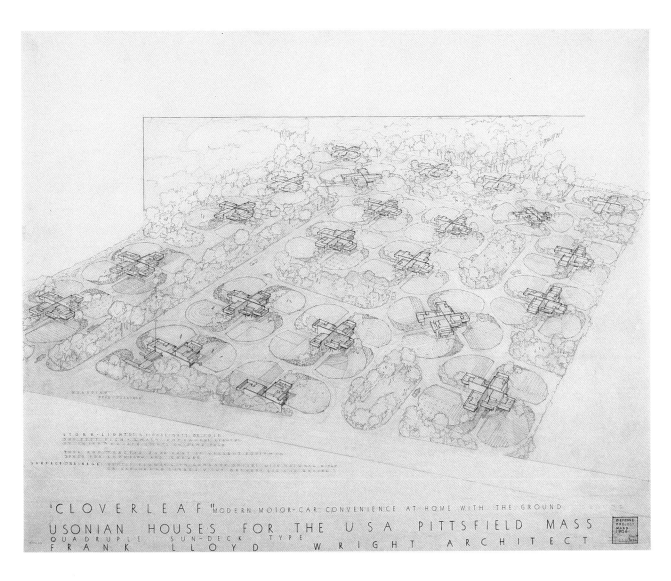

"CLOVERLEAF" MODERN·MOTOR·CAR·CONVENIENCE·AT·HOME·WITH·THE·GROUND

USONIAN HOUSES FOR THE USA PITTSFIELD MASS
QUADRUPLE SUN-DECK TYPE
FRANK LLOYD WRIGHT ARCHITECT

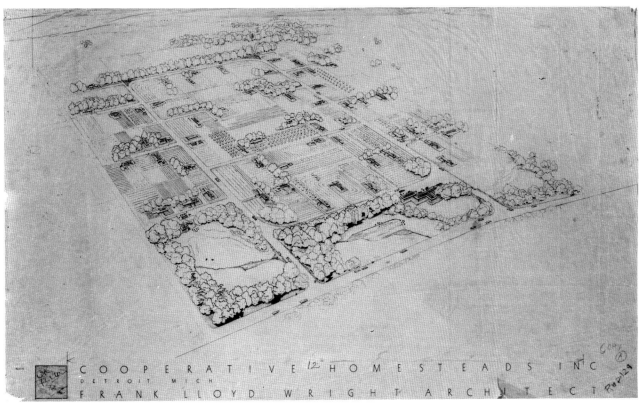

COOPERATIVE HOMESTEADS INC
DETROIT MICH
FRANK LLOYD WRIGHT ARCHITECT

THE GALESBURG COUNTRY HOMES
FRANK LLOYD WRIGHT ARCHITECT

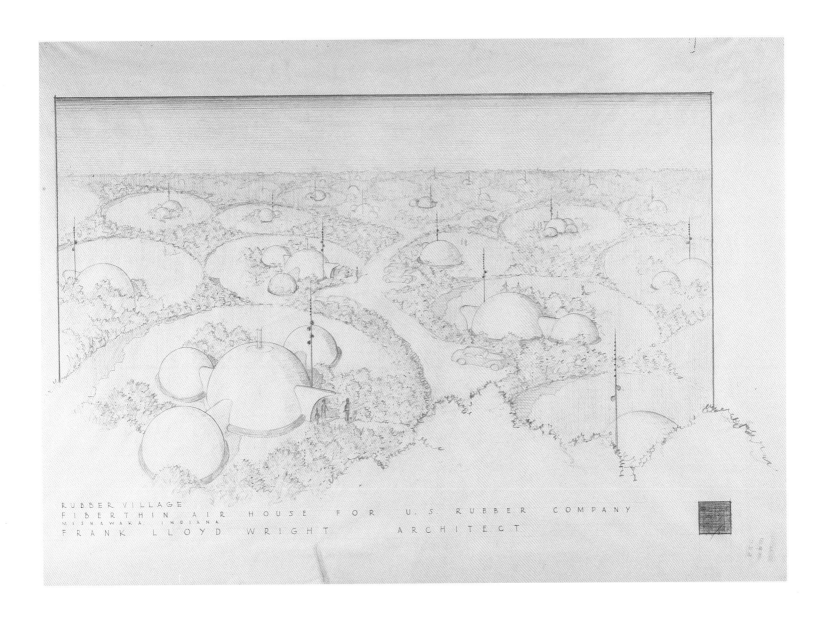

RUBBER VILLAGE
FIBERTHIN AIR HOUSE FOR U. S. RUBBER COMPANY
MISHAWAKA, INDIANA
FRANK LLOYD WRIGHT ARCHITECT

Opposite

GALESBURG COUNTRY HOMES

Galesburg, Michigan. 1946–49 (partially realized)

408.   Site plan (JHH; 1947). Color pencil and ink on tracing paper, 46¾ x 37". The Frank Lloyd Wright Foundation

FIBERTHIN AIR HOUSES FOR U. S. RUBBER COMPANY

Project, 1956–57

409.   Aerial perspective. Pencil and color pencil on tracing paper, 24½ x 36". Private collection

Paradise on Wheels
TRAILER PARK FOR LEE ACKERMAN AND ASSOCIATES

Paradise Valley, Arizona. Project, 1952

410.   Aerial perspective. Photostat of print, 14 x 20⅝". The Frank Lloyd Wright Foundation

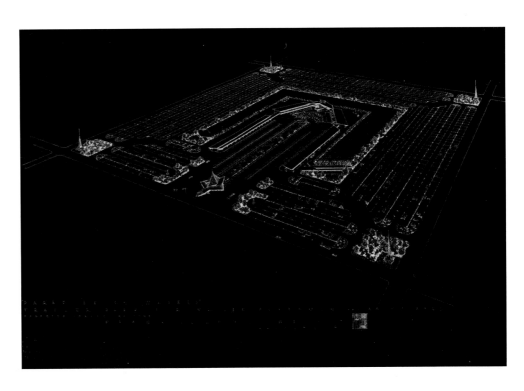

THE LIVING CITY
Project, 1958

411.   Aerial perspective (JR). Pencil on tracing paper, 32¼ x 42".
The Frank Lloyd Wright Foundation

ACKNOWLEDGMENTS

This exhibition would not have been possible without the unqualified support and cooperation of The Frank Lloyd Wright Foundation. The Museum of Modern Art is privileged to have had unparalleled access to the vast holdings of The Frank Lloyd Wright Archives, from which the core of the exhibition is assembled. Richard Carney, Managing Trustee and Chief Executive Officer of the Foundation, and the staff of the Archives have demonstrated unwavering support for all aspects of the exhibition. For his role in establishing the basis for this institutional cooperation and in the early development of the exhibition, credit is owed Stuart Wrede, formerly Director of the Museum's Department of Architecture and Design. From the outset, I have been fortunate to have as curatorial consultants, Bruce Brooks Pfeiffer, Director, The Frank Lloyd Wright Archives, who has spent a lifetime devoted to the care of the architect's drawings and papers, and Anthony Alofsin, Sid W. Richardson Centennial Fellow in Architecture, and Director, Center for American Architecture and Design, University of Texas at Austin, a leader in the new generation of Wright scholars.

Large exhibitions of this kind depend heavily on the generosity of sympathetic, knowledgeable friends, and I would first like to thank those individuals and institutions whose support has been crucial. First, I extend my deep gratitude to Museum Trustees Marshall S. Cogan and Lily Auchincloss for their early and unqualified support of this undertaking. This exhibition would not have been possible without generous grants from Andersen Windows, Inc., the David H. Cogan Foundation, and the National Endowment for the Humanities. Additional support for the exhibition was provided by Lily Auchincloss and the National Endowment for the Arts. The Bertha and Isaac Liberman Foundation, Inc., and Joel Silver made possible a critical aspect of the exhibition—the construction of the full-scale reproductions of Wright's most well-known building innovations; Malcolm Nolen and Mary Ellen Donovan supported related programs. The publication was made possible by The Henry Luce Foundation, Inc.

In addition to The Frank Lloyd Wright Foundation, a number of private and institutional lenders have generously made works available from their collections. It would be hard to imagine this exhibition without selections from the Erving and Joyce Wolf Collection of architectural drawings. Other lenders I would like to thank are Alden Franz Aust, Jon Bell, Michael Fitzsimmons, Seymour H. Persky, Max Protetch, Tim Samuel-son, Der Scutt, Gil and Lila Silverman, Donald and Elaine Singer, Julie L. Sloan, and Kelmscott Gallery. I am also grateful for the participation of many lending institutions and to their staff members who assisted with these loans: Angela Giral, Librarian, and Janet Parks, Curator at the Avery Architectural and Fine Arts Library, Columbia University; Joel Cahan, Chief Curator and Deputy Director, and Virginia Torgovnik, Curator of Collections, at Beth Hatefutsoth—Museum of the Jewish Diaspora; Guy Chase, Curator, Richard W. Bock Sculpture Collection; Nicholas Olsberg, Chief Curator, and Howard Shubert, Assistant Curator of Prints and Drawings at the Canadian Centre for Architecture; Phillip M. Johnston, Director of the Carnegie Museum of Art, and Christopher Monkhouse, Curator of Architecture, Heinz Architectural Center; Russell Panczenko, Director, and Lucille Stiger, Registrar of the Elvehjem Museum of Art; Virginia Kazor, Curator of the Hollyhock House owned by the City of Los Angeles; Pierre Apraxine, Curator of the Gilman Paper Co.; Gregory L. Anderegg and Joedy Simonsen at S. C. Johnson & Son, Inc.; Yasuo Takahashi and Kiyoshi Sey Takeyama of the School of Architecture of Kyoto University; C. Ford Peatross and Tambra Johnson of The Library of Congress; Dr. Elliot Davis, David Kiehl, and Peter M. Kenny of The Metropolitan Museum of Art; Teijiro Muramatsu, Director of the Meiji-Mura Museum; Carol Gibson, Director, and William Jerousek, Historian of the Oak Park Public Library; Christine Schelshorn and Andy Kraushaar of the State Historical Society of Wisconsin; Donald P. Hallmark, Dana-Thomas House Site Manager; George Ranalli, Associate Professor of Architectural Design, Yale University; Bernard Tschumi, Dean, Graduate School of Architecture, Planning and Preservation, and Kenneth Frampton, Ware Professor of Architecture, Columbia University.

Among The Frank Lloyd Wright Archives staff, very special thanks are owed Margo Stipe and Oscar Muñoz. Our daily requests throughout the planning and production of the exhibition and publication were handled with remarkable efficiency and enthusiasm and never seemed to overwhelm this redoubtable duo. I would also like to thank Indira Berndtson, Penny Fowler, David Teague, Anthony Puttnam, Suzette Lucas, and Betty Bergstrom. To the other members of the Taliesin Fellowship I would like to extend my thanks for many hours of enjoyable and informative discussions and their gracious hospitality. I would also like to thank Steve Kroeter, Archetype Associates, an important liaison between the Museum and the Foundation; O. P. Reed, Jr., for appraisals; and David Restad for matting and framing several hundred drawings.

To prepare the many objects in the exhibition for display, painstaking conservation was required. T. K. McClintock and his assistant Lorraine Bigrigg treated drawings for The Frank Lloyd Wright Foundation. Bruce Severson devoted a year to the restoration of existing models for the Foundation. New models were also commissioned for the exhibition. It has been a pleasure to work with such skillful artisans as Daniel X. Wood, Ken van Kestren, and Richard Sturgeon of Mesa Model Makers, and Barbara and Mark Jones of Environ Architectural Modelmakers. New plans and sections were also prepared for the publication and exhibition by a team of young architects: Joseph Bruno devoted an extraordinary amount of time to this effort. Charles Rhyu, Toby O'Rorke, Dragan Mrdja, and Brian Messina made further contributions to this project. The full-scale wall constructions in the exhibition were made possible with the critical assistance of Eric Lloyd Wright; Flex Aimijo; T & L General Contracting; R. Nicholas Loope, AIA, and current and former fellows and apprentices at Taliesin West; Toshihara Nakahama, Meiji-Mura Museum; Yuko Yamazaki, Hakone Open-Air Museum; and Raku Endo.

The architecture of Frank Lloyd Wright is a field that has attracted numerous scholars, former associates of the architect, clients, and enthusiasts. We have benefited from conversations and information gleaned from many sources. In addition to the aforementioned individuals and institutions, I would like to thank for their various contributions: Narciso Menocal, Cathaline Cantalupo, Jeffrey Chusid, Jonathan Lipman, David Larkin, Jack Quinan, Kathryn Smith, Neil Levine, Vincent Scully, Thomas Hines, Mr. and Mrs. John H. Howe, Curtis Besinger, A. Louis Wiehle, and John Szarkowski. I would also like to thank Shonnie Finnegan and Chris Densmore, University Archives, SUNY Buffalo; Terry Marvel, Milwaukee Art Museum; Carol J. Callahan, Curator of the Glessner House Museum; Paul Bonfilio; Harold F. Mailand, Textile Conservation Services; Elaine Harrington and Meg Klinkow, Frank Lloyd Wright Home and Studio; Catherine Voorsanger, The Metropolitan Museum of Art; Lord Peter Palumbo and Nicola Redway; John Zukowsky, The Art Institute of Chicago; Edgar Smith; Wim de Wit, Chicago Historical Society; Christopher Wilk, Curator of the Furniture & Woodwork Collection, Victoria and Albert Museum; Blair Davenport, Death Valley National Monument; Elizabeth Isles, Shadelands Ranch Historical Museum; Dietrich Neumann, Brown University; and Leonard Morse-Fortier, MIT.

First-hand experience of Wright's buildings is not only memorable but essential to understanding his work. While many of the buildings are open to the public, a number of home owners and others were exceptionally gracious in opening doors: James M. Dennis, Mr. and Mrs. Robert Elsner, Meg Klinkow, Joel Silver, Ted Smith and Susan Shipper Smith, Vada Stanley, Mr. and Mrs. William B. Tracy, Augustus Brown, Audrey Laatsch; and the administrators of the Annunciation Greek Orthodox Church and the Jiyu Gakuen School. Also I would like to thank Thomas Schmidt, Director, and Lynda Waggoner, Curator of Fallingwater, and Judith Trent of the Frank Lloyd Wright Building Conservancy.

Nearly every architecture exhibition must rely on the skill of photographers to help convey the spatial and material qualities of buildings. Many photographers and numerous institutional and private collections of archival photographs made their images available to us. In addition to those listed in the Photograph Credits I would like to thank: William Clarkson; Scott Elliott and Charles Wood, III; Suzelle Baudouin, Canadian Centre for Architecture; Darwin Matthews; Mary Woolever, The Art Institute of Chicago; Eileen Flanagan, Chicago Historical Society; Bill Kipp; Carol Kelm, Oak Park and River Forest Historical Society; Suzanne Box, Phillips Petroleum Company; Julius Shulman; Skot Weidemann; Cindy Knight, The State Historical Society of Wisconsin; Gail Kohl, Frank Lloyd Wright Heritage Tour Program; Nancy McClelland, Christie's; Mosette Broderick; Noboyuki Yoshida, The Japan Architect, Co., Ltd.; Yoshio Watanabe and the Pacific Press Service; Karen Banks, Architectural History Foundation; and Jonathan Elderfield, Black Star.

Frank Lloyd Wright: Architect has been complemented by a number of educational programs. Two symposia were sponsored by the Museum and the Temple Hoyne Buell Center for the Study of American Architecture and the Society of Architectural Historians, respectively. My thanks to Dean Bernard Tschumi and Richard Buford for arranging the Buell program. At the Society of Architectural Historians I especially thank Professor Keith Morgan and David Bahlman. For films about Frank Lloyd Wright's architecture I am grateful to Steven Snow and Kenneth Love. The programs were further enriched with lectures by Vincent Scully, Bruce Brooks Pfeiffer, Narciso Menocal, and Thomas Hines.

Last but not least it behooves me to express a great debt of gratitude to many colleagues at The Museum of Modern Art. Foremost among them is Richard E. Oldenburg, Director, to whom I extend my profound thanks for his support and trust. At many critical junctures in the six-year development of this project, his judicious counsel was instrumental in guaranteeing its success. I would also like to thank Agnes Gund, Chairman of the Board of Trustees of the Museum, as well as the full Board for its support of this exhibition. Thanks go to Beverly Wolff, General Counsel, and Charles Danziger, Assistant General Counsel, and to James S. Snyder, Deputy Director for Planning and Program Support, and Richard L. Palmer, Coordinator of Exhibitions, for their advice and comment throughout the project. Eleni Cocordas, Associate Coordinator of Exhibitions, provided excellent administrative skills. The efforts of Sue B. Dorn, Deputy Director for Development and Public Affairs, and Daniel W. Vecchitto, Director of Development, to secure funding for the exhibition at a time of scant resources must be acknowledged; John L. Wielk, Manager, Exhibition and Project Funding, and Rebecca Stokes, Grants Assistant, deserve special commendation for their efforts in making difficult and lengthy grant applications.

With regard to this publication, the authors of the essays, William Cronon, Anthony Alofsin, Kenneth Frampton, and Gwendolyn Wright, are to be thanked for their commitment to the project and for their stimulating conversations on two formal occasions and in numerous other individual instances throughout the project. In the Department of Publications, Osa Brown, Director, was instrumental in forming the initial conception of this volume. The quality and timeliness of its execution are due to the diligent efforts of Harriet S. Bee, Managing Editor, who also deserves special acknowledgment for her role in shaping and refining both essays and illustrations. Thanks go to Vicki Drake, Associate Production Manager, for her supervision of the book's production; to Nancy T. Kranz, Manager, Promotion and Special Services; and to Christine Liotta, Assistant Editor. The Department of Graphics, under the direction of Michael Hentges, performed in a highly professional manner in developing the design and layout of the catalogue under tight time restraints. Jody Hanson, Assistant Director, and Emily Waters, Senior Graphic Designer, made every effort to insure the design of the book was to the highest standards. Mikki Carpenter, Director, Department of Photographic Services and Permissions, and Kate Keller, Chief Fine Arts Photographer, assisted in providing images of the best quality.

On other aspects of the exhibition, the office of the Museum's Registrar, Diane Farynyk, and particularly Nestor Montilla, has coped admirably with the uniquely challenging tasks of assembling the disparate materials that make up an architectural exhibition. Equally, Jerome Neuner, Director of Exhibition Production and Design, Karen Meyerhoff, Assistant Director, and Douglas Feick, Exhibition Supervisor, have risen to the challenge of installing such a difficult exhibition, again, under tight time and funding restraints. Numerous individuals at the Museum enriched the public's understanding of the exhibition and the work of Frank Lloyd Wright. In the Department of Education: Carol Morgan, Acting Director; Emily Kies Folpe, Museum Educator/Education Publications; Cynthia Nachmani, Associate Museum Educator/Museum Programs; Romi Phillips, Assistant Museum Educator, Public Programs; and Ann Koll, Intern. The Department of Public Information: Jessica Schwartz, Director; Lucy O'Brien, Manager, Periodicals and Special Projects; and Alexandra Partow, Press Representative. Jo Pike, Director of Visitor Services; Joan Howard, Director of Special Events; and Louise Chinn, Director of Sales and Marketing, deserve special mention for their invaluable contributions. Preliminary research for the exhibition and publication was greatly aided by the staff of the Museum's Library and Archives, under the direction of Clive Phillpot and Rona Roob, respectively. Elizabeth Streibert, Associate Director of the International Program, made special efforts to assist with the initial research overseas, as did former Registrar Eloise Ricciardelli.

In addition to their other duties, members of the Department of Architecture and Design have made many contributions to this effort: Jennifer Brody, Assistant to the Chief Curator, and Timothy Rohan, Executive Secretary, for overall support activities; Matilda McQuaid, Assistant Curator, for organizing all the lectures, symposia, and other special events, and Christopher Mount, Curatorial Assistant; Anne Dixon, Study Center Supervisor; and Pierre Adler, Senior Cataloguer, Mies van der Rohe Archive, for assisting with the installation. I also acknowledge Museum interns Edward Eigen, Jason Lundy, Simon O'Driscoll, Brian Dillman, and Massimo Bazzo. And finally, but not last in importance, special note must be made of the efforts of Peter Reed, Assistant Curator in the Department of Architecture and Design. His superb professionalism, scholarly diligence, enormous capacity for detail, and endless patience have contributed greatly to the success of both the exhibition and publication, and I might say, have made the entire project more enjoyable.

Terence Riley

PHOTOGRAPH CREDITS

Photographs of works of art reproduced in this volume have been provided in most cases by the owners or custodians of the works, identified in the captions. Individual works of art appearing herein may be protected by copyright in the United States of America or elsewhere, and may thus not be reproduced in any form without the permission of the copyright owners. The following copyright and/or other photograph credits appear at the request of the artist's heirs and representatives and/or the owners of the individual works. Additional credits for photographers and sources of illustrations are listed alphabetically below, followed by the number of the page on which the illustration appears. The publishers have sought, as far as possible, permission to reproduce each illustration, and gratefully acknowledge the cooperation of all those who have made photographs available. Credits are also given for delineators of certain illustrations. A separate list of Frank Lloyd Wright Foundation archive numbers appears below.

Amerco Real Estate Company: 305 top and bottom. C. D. Arnold, courtesy Chicago Historical Society: 23 right; courtesy Division of Drawings and Archives, Avery Architectural and Fine Arts Library, Columbia University, New York: 23 left. Courtesy The Art Institute of Chicago: 113. Mark Ballogg, © Steinkamp/Ballogg, Chicago: 159 top. From Reyner Banham, *The Architecture of the Well-Tempered Environment* (London: The Architectural Press; Chicago: University of Chicago Press, 1969): 63. © Herbert K. Barnett, all rights reserved: 148 right, 149, 161. From William E. Bell, *Carpentry Made Easy* (Philadelphia, 1858), courtesy Avery Architectural and Fine Arts Library, Columbia University, New York: 59 right. Richard Bowditch: 175 top. Buffalo and Erie County Historical Society: 66 right. © Wayne Cable/Cable Studios: 239 top. Drawn by James Cahill: 66 left. Doug Carr, courtesy Illinois Historic Preservation Agency/The Dana-Thomas House: 126 top and bottom, 127. Centre Canadien d'Architecture/Canadian Centre for Architecture, Montreal: 138, 139 top, bottom left and right. Courtesy Chicago Historical Society: 163. From *Columbian* *Album, World's Columbian Exposition* (Chicago and New York: Rand McNally, 1893), courtesy The Frank Lloyd Wright Foundation: 21. William Cronon: 24. © 1962, Lucile Fessenden Dandelet, Marin County, California: 321 bottom right. Drawing by Robt. Day; © 1952, 1980, The New Yorker Magazine, Inc.: 81 right. Domino's Pizza Collection: 115 bottom, 121 bottom left, 135, 153, 154 bottom, 159 bottom, 160, 165 top and bottom, 171, 181 left and right, 182, 189 center, 192 top and bottom. Raku Endo, The Frank Lloyd Wright Foundation: 189 top, 190. From Edward R. Ford, *The Details of Modern Architecture* (Cambridge, Mass.: MIT Press, 1990): 72 left and right. Reimar F. Frank: 251 bottom. © 1993, Art Grossmann, St. Louis; courtesy Illinois Historic Preservation Agency/The Dana-Thomas House: 128. Pedro E. Guerrero: 104 left, 136 top right, 258, 262 left, 263 left, 265, 299 top, 301 left and right, 310, 311; The Frank Lloyd Wright Foundation: 259; courtesy Frank Lloyd Wright Heritage Tour Program: 313 bottom. Hedrich-Blessing, courtesy Chicago Historical Society: 98 right, 172 bottom, 175 bottom, 240 left and right, 241, 260 top and bottom. Thomas A. Heinz: 16, 115 top and center, 236, 257. Historical Society of Oak Park & River Forest: 137. From Henry-Russell Hitchcock, *In the Nature of Materials: The Buildings of Frank Lloyd Wright, 1887–1941* (New York: Hawthorn Books, 1942): 70 left. HOUSE AND HOME/Hanley-Wood, Inc., courtesy Avery Architectural and Fine Arts Library, Columbia University, New York: 81 left. The John H. Howe Collection, State Historical Society of Wisconsin: 105. Herbert Jacobs, courtesy The Art Institute of Chicago: 184. Peter Johnsen, courtesy Frank Lloyd Wright Home and Studio Foundation: 120. S. C. Johnson & Son, Inc.: 74 right, 75 left and right, 251 top. From William H. Jordy, *American Buildings and Their Architects. The Impact of European Modernism in the Mid-Twentieth Century* (Garden City: Anchor Press/Doubleday, 1976): 76. From Kurt Junghanns, *Bruno Taut 1880–1938* (Berlin: Henschelverlag, 1970): 54 right. Donald Kalec, courtesy Frank Lloyd Wright Home and Studio Foundation: 121 top. © Balthazar Korab: 196 top, 205 right, 208, 246 left, 308, 309, 313 top. Torkel Korling, courtesy David R. Phillips: 46. From Spiro Kostof, *A History of Architecture: Settings and Rituals* (New York: Oxford University Press, 1985): 60. J. Spencer Lake: 292 top, 299 bottom. Robert E. Mates, © The Solomon R. Guggenheim Foundation, New York: 274. Mies van der Rohe Archive, The Museum of Modern Art, New York: 41 right. Jon Miller, © Hedrich-Blessing: 112 bottom, 121 bottom right. The Museum of Modern Art, New York: 45 left and right, 47, 112 top; courtesy H. C. Price Co.: 292 bottom; drawn by Joseph Bruno, Charles Rhyu, Toby O'Rorke, Dragan Mrdja, and Brian Messina: 112 bottom right, 114 bottom, 120 bottom left, 123 bottom, 133 bottom, 134 top, 136 bottom, 140 bottom, 142 bottom, 146 bottom left and right, 153 bottom, 156 top right, 158 bottom, 168 bottom, 170 bottom, 178 bottom, 204 bottom, 206 bottom, 229 bottom, 234 bottom, 235 bottom, 238 bottom, 245 bottom, 250 bottom, 254 bottom, 272 bottom, 284 bottom, 310 bottom right, 312 bottom. From *Joseph Maria Olbrich—Architecture* (Tübingen: Wasmuth, 1988): 38 right. Maynard L. Parker, The Museum of Modern Art, New York: 298 left and right. Anthony Peres, © 1992, all rights reserved: 203 right, 209; © 1993, all rights reserved: 204, 205 left. R. Peterson, The Museum of Modern Art, New York: 239 center. From Julius Posener, *Hans Poelzig: Reflections on His Life and Work,* (New York: The Architectural History Foundation; Cambridge, Mass.: MIT Press, 1992): 40 right. Anthony Puttnam, The Frank Lloyd Wright Foundation: 261. John Reed, The Frank Lloyd Wright Foundation: 154 top. © Cervin Robinson: 42. Paul Rocheleau: 148 left, 185, 234, 239 bottom, 267 top, center, and bottom. Julius Shulman: 53. G. E. Kidder Smith, From *The Architecture of the United States* (Garden City: Anchor Press/Doubleday, 1981): 322. Ezra Stoller, © Esto: 99, 101, 193, 235, 237, 247, 249, 255 bottom, 262 right, 263 right, 273, 275, 276, 277. Tim Street-Porter: 196 bottom left and right, 203 left, 207 top and bottom. Copyright 1938, Time Inc., reprinted by permission: 86. © 1980, John Troha, Black Star: 97 left. Raymond Trowbridge, courtesy Chicago Historical Society: 19. Lynda S. Waggoner, Fallingwater: 73. State Historical Society of Wisconsin: 59 left. From *Frank Lloyd Wright: Ausgeführte Bauten* (Berlin: Wasmuth, 1911), courtesy The Frank Lloyd Wright Foundation: 68. The Frank Lloyd Wright Foundation: 12, 15, 22, 41 left, 44, 71, 82, 83, 84, 92, 93, 102 right, 116, 136 left and bottom right, 143, 144, 145, 172 top, 179, 189 bottom, 227 left and right, 246 left, 248, 255 top and center, 291, 303 left and right, 328 bottom. Frank Lloyd Wright Home and Studio Foundation: 11. Scot Zimmerman: 302, 321 top and bottom left.

THE FRANK LLOYD WRIGHT FOUNDATION ARCHIVE NUMBERS

Plates							*Text Figures*
1: 8501.001	74: 0611.003	134: 1401.091	208. 2602.002	255: 3601.019	325: 4836.004	381: 5751.001	(Alofsin)
4: 8801.001	77: 0611.008	137: 1401.081	209: 2505.023	260: 3601.029	327: 4923.053	382: 5733.023	1: 0403.162
15: 9304.001	80: 0611.016	138: 1401.080	210: 2505.057	262: 4401.070	328: 4923.047	383: 5732.001	2: 1207.005
16: 9406.001	83: 0211.006	141: 1401.011	211: 2905.006	264: 4401.003	329: 4921.027	384: 5732.002	4: 2704.199
17: 9501.001	84: 0612.001	143: 1401.015	212: 2905.038	268: 3710.001	330: 4921.003	385: 5732.006	9: 0403.002
18: 9501.002	85: 0706.001	144: 1401.120	213: 2905.028	269: 3807.002	331: 4606.001	387: 5746.001	15: 4303.004
20: 9510.017	86: 0905.001	145: 1205.008	214: 2905.031	270: 3701.001	332: 4606.002	388: 5754.005	17: 5313.001
21: 9506.002	87: 0803.019	150: 1602.011	215: 3001.001	275: 3703.001	334: 5215.018	393: 5911.002	(Frampton)
27: 9509.001	90: 0803.042	152: 1509.640	216: 3001.003	276: 3703.013	336: 5215.016	394: 0309.010	4: 1509.016
28: 9408.001	93: 0803.010	157: 1509.650	217: 3103.001	278: 3803.003	339: 5310.001	395: 0309.008	9: 2111.004
30: 9606.005	94: 0803.003	159: 1509.674	218: 3103.003	284: 3805.001	340: 5615.004	396: 0918.019	11: 2905.094
31: 9606.002	95: 0803.117	162: 1509.044	219: 2902.002	291: 4011.002	341: 5617.005	397: 0918.017	16: 3601.014
33: 9901.030	96: 0506.003	165: 1705.004	220: 2902.019	293: 4015.005	342: 5617.002	398: 0918.018	21: 5825.003
37: 9905.010	98: 0713.002	170: 2005.003	221: 2902.018	294: 4015.007	343: 4919.008	399: 1002.006	(Riley)
39: 9905.008	99: 0715.001	171: 2301.008	224: 2903.016	298: 4202.001	344: 4919.016	401: 1901.001	3: 0309.006
40: 9905.001	105: 0908.014	172: 2205.001	225: 2903.015	299: 4202.004	345: 4824.009	402: 2104.005	6: 2306.002
42: 0007.002	107: 0902.002	173: 2205.004	226: 2902.015	302: 4305.007	349: 5121.001	403: 3402.001	8: 2702.004
43: 0008.001	108: 0902.001	177: 1901.002	227: 3102.018	303: 4305.0627	351: 5111.001	405: 3912.001	9: 4721.031
44: 0002.006	109: 0910.001	179: 2302.002	229: 3204.002	304: 4305.014	354: 5312.004	406: 4203.007	11: 3301.001
53: 0505.001	111: 1108.004	186: 2304.003	230: 3202.008	305: 4305.017	355: 5512.001	407: 4201.003	
55: 0405.002	115: 1005.003	187: 2402.001	231: 3502.003	308: 4305.735	357: 5101.012	408: 4828.001	
60: 0111.002	116: 1113.007	192: 2401.004	232: 3502.010	311: 4812.002	360: 5419.001	410: 5221.007	
61: 0111.028	117: 1113.004	194: 2401.001	233: 3502.017	313: 4812.001	361: 5419.001	411: 5825.006	
63: 0010.013	118: 1118.004	196: 2306.001	234: 3602.004	315: 4822.002	364: 4726.020		
64: 0010.001	120: 1118.008	200: 2704.047	241: 3702.002–.003	317: 4731.020	365: 4507.002		
65: 0403.004	121: 1118.014	201: 2704.004	246: 4008.002	318: 4731.001	366: 5739.001		
68: 0403.006	122: 1403.013	202: 2706.008	250: 4012.002	319: 3909.001	367: 5521.002		
69: 0403.009	125: 1403.022	203: 2706.004	251: 3705.004	320: 3909.002	368: 5031.014		
70: 0403.079	128: 2501.041	204: 2705.001	252: 3101.001	321: 4016.001	372: 5313.006		
72: 0403.026	129: 2501.011	206: 2603.002	253: 3101.008	322: 4821.003	376: 5611.001		
	130: 2501.060	207: 2602.003	254: 3601.002–.003	323: 4821.001	380: 5759.006		